Christopher Hibbert

Benito Mussolini

The Rise and Fall of Il Duce

With eight plates

Penguin Books

Penguin Books Ltd, Harmondsworth,
Middlesex, England
Penguin Books Inc., 3300 Clipper Mill Road,
Baltimore 11, Md, U.S.A.
Penguin Books Pty Ltd, Ringwood,
Victoria, Australia
First published by Longmans, Green 1962
Revised edition published in Penguin Books 1965

Made and printed in Great Britain by
Cox and Wyman Ltd,
London, Reading, and Fakenham
Set in Monotype Plantin

To Hamish and Helen

You cannot have a king without subjects or a leader without those who are willing to be led . . . . 'victrix causa deis placuit'

IGNAZIO SILONE

Contents

Acknowledgements

We are indebted to the following for permission to reproduce copyright material:

Allen & Unwin Ltd and Frau E. Ludwig for material from *Talks with Mussolini* by Emil Ludwig; Giulio Einaudi for material from *Storia d'Italia Nel Periodo Fascista* by Luigi Salvatorelli and Giovanni Mira; Elek Books Ltd and Messrs Rizzoli, Milan, for material from *Due Dittatori Di Fronte* by Dino Alfieri; Robert Hale Ltd for material from *My Life with Benito* by Rachele Mussolini; William Heinemann Ltd and Messrs Rizzoli, Milan, for material from *Diaries* (1939-43) by Galeazzo Ciano; Methuen & Co. Ltd and Cappelli, Bologna, for material from *Diaries* (1937-9) by Galeazzo Ciano; Messrs Mondadori, Milan, for material from *Dux* by Margherita Sarfatti.

Associated Press Ltd for plates 1a, 2b, 4b, and 5a; E.N.A. for plates 1b and 3; Radio Times/Hulton Picture Library for plates 2a, 7a, and 7b; Mirrorpic for plate 4a; Fox Photos Ltd for plate 5b; London Express News and Features Service for plate 6a; Imperial War Museum for plate 6b; Keystone Press Agency Ltd for plate 8.

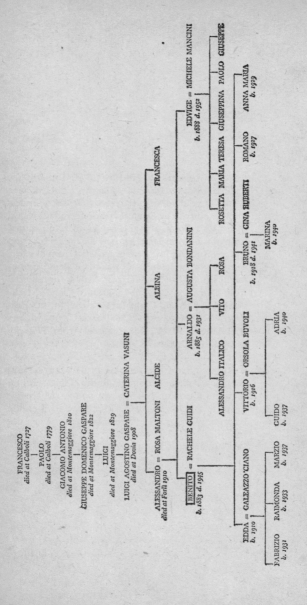

FRANCESCO
died at Calboli 1727

PAOLO
died at Calboli 1779

GIACOMO ANTONIO
died at Montemaggiore 1810

GIUSEPPE DOMENICO GASPARE
died at Montemaggiore 1822

LUIGI
died at Montemaggiore 1839

LUIGI AGOSTINO GASPARE = CATERINA VASUNI
died at Dovia 1908

ALESSANDRO = ROSA MALTONI   ALCIDE   ALBINA   FRANCESCA
died at Forlì 1910

BENITO = RACHELE GUIDI   ARNALDO = AUGUSTA BONDANINI   EDVIGE = MICHELE MANCINI
b. 1883 d. 1945   *b. 1885 d. 1931*   *b. 1888 d. 1952*

ALESSANDRO ITALICO   VITO   ROSA   BRUNO = GINA RUBERTI   ROSETTA MARIA TERESA GIUSEPPINA PAOLO GIUSEPPE
                                              b. 1918 d. 1941

VITTORIO = ORSOLA BUVOLI   MARINA   ROMANO   ANNA MARIA
b. 1916   *b. 1940*   *b. 1927*   *b. 1929*

EDDA = GALEAZZO CIANO   GUIDO   ADRIA
b. 1910   *b. 1937* *b. 1940*

FABRIZIO   RAIMONDA   MARZIO
b. 1931   *b. 1933*   *b. 1937*

MUSSOLINI'S ANCESTRY AND DESCENDANTS

Preface

'No one understands him,' wrote Fernando Mezzasoma of Mussolini during the last week of both their lives. 'By turns shrewd and innocent, brutal and gentle, vindictive and forgiving, great and petty, he is the most complicated and contradictory man I have ever known. He cannot be explained.'

During the eighteen years between the March on Rome in 1922 and the outbreak of war in 1940, numerous books were written in an attempt to explain this extraordinary man; most of them were by Fascists or by expatriate Italians who had cause to hate Fascism.

Ever since I came home from Italy after the War I have felt the need of an impartial book which answered at least some of the questions which had puzzled me. I wondered how much Mussolini resembled the monstrous buffoon of war-time propaganda and how much the demi-god of Fascist doctrine; I wondered how it was that some Italians could shoot at his corpse as it swayed upside down in Piazzale Loreto in Milan and yet others, who were, so it seemed to me, just like them, could weep in the streets when told that he was dead; and I wondered whether it could really be true, as Mr Churchill had said, that 'one man and one man alone' had plunged Italy into tragedy. I wondered, too, how Mussolini had retained this power so long and how during the final, twilight phase on the shores of Lake Garda, when defeat was certain and death likely, he had still been able, though physically and morally decayed, to find so many men still willing to follow him.

It was with these questions in mind that I went back to Italy in 1960 to read books and papers about Mussolini and the Fascist dictatorship which are not available in London, to talk to people who knew him, and to discover as much as I could of his last years, about which so little reliable information is available. Not being qualified to pass judgement on him – even if such a judgement were yet possible – I have written the book in the form of a historical narrative, hoping that in telling the story of his life I have given at least the more important of the evidence about him upon which opinions can be based. There are no references to sources in the text, but at the end of the book I have commented on the material that I have used and I think that the authority for any controversial statement and the sources of all direct or indirect quotations will be found there.

For their great help in a variety of ways I want especially to thank – in addition to those who have asked to remain nameless – Professor G. Baldini, Fr J. A. Barrett, S.J., Lord Beaverbrook, Signor Pietro Beneventano, Sir Noel Charles, Brigadier R. C. Edge, Professor Vittorio Gabrieli, Viscountess Hambleden, Sir Ivone Kirkpatrick, the late Sir Percy Loraine, Dr Roger Manvell, Admiral Franco Maugeri, Prof. Dott. Paolo Milano, Signor Paolo Monelli, Conte Umberto Morra di Lavriano, Signor Romano Mussolini, Herr Hans Pächter, Conte Novello Papafava, Sir Charles Petrie, Herr Otto Reitsch, Signor Ernesto Ricci, Signor Dino Rosselli, Miss Frances Ryan, Signor Pietro Sanarelli, Mrs Joan St George Saunders, Mr B. A. C. Sweet-Escott, Colonel Otto Skorzeny, General Kurt Student, Colonel Hedley Vincent, Professor Roberto Weiss, and Miss Elizabeth Wiskemann. I owe a particular debt of gratitude to Signora Linda Bertelli-Attanasio for helping me with my researches when I was in Rome; to Mr Roy MacGregor-Hastie, who has been good enough to provide me with information about Mussolini's family; and to Senatore Generale Raffaele Cadorna, who has kindly helped me with some of my final chapters. I want also to thank the staffs of the London Library, the British Museum, the Istituto Italiano di Cultura, the Italian Embassy in London, the British Institute in Florence, the Biblioteca di Storia Moderna e Contemporanea, the Biblioteca Universitaria Alessandrina, and the Generale Direzione di Accademie e Biblioteche del Ministero della Pubblica Istruzione.

C.H.

Part One

The Fight for Power

The Young Rebel

29 JULY 1883–DECEMBER 1912

*The fact that I was born among the common
people put the trump cards into my hands.*

I

At about half past ten on the night of 9 May 1936 a sudden roar,
which a journalist described as being like the noise of a volcanic
eruption, broke out from a crowd of some 400,000 people standing
shoulder to shoulder around Palazzo Venezia in Rome. Benito
Mussolini, *il Duce del Fascismo*, had stepped out on to the palace
balcony above their heads and gazed silently down at them. His
hands were on his hips, his immense jaw thrust out, his legs
splayed apart in a pose which was familiar to them all. He was
wearing the black shirt, grey uniform, and round black cap of
the Fascist Militia, and for a few moments he stood in front of the
floodlit latticed windows as motionless as the symbol of his régime
– the axe and the lictor's rods – carved in stone on the wall beside
him.

He lifted his hand. The crowd fell into silence. Not only in
Rome but all over Italy millions of people were listening and waiting for the sound of the Duce's voice. In the warm spring evening,
already given a strangely augural air by a moon of unusual clarity,
crowds of excited listeners, summoned out of doors by church
bells and sirens, looked up at the loudspeakers in the squares.

'Officers, non-commissioned officers, and men,' Mussolini announced at last in a deep, sonorous voice which Lady Oxford had
described as one of the most beautiful she had ever heard, 'Blackshirts of the Revolution, Italian men and women at home and
throughout the world, hearken: a great event has been accomplished. The destiny of Abyssinia has been sealed today in the
fourteenth year of the Fascist era. Every knot has been cut by our

shining sword, and the Abyssinian victory will remain in the history of our country, complete and pure like the *legionari* who have fallen. Italy has her Empire. . . .'

His final words were lost in a wild torrent of cheers, in the swelling, repetitive, ululating chant, '*Duce ! Duce ! Duce !*', in the screams of hysterical women, in the shouts of adoration and protestations of loyalty to death. And the Duce stood looking down calmly, not acknowledging the cheers, his hands gripping the stone balustrade, his massive face expressionless in the brilliant light of the flood-lamps.

'He is like a god,' one of his *gerarchi* said as he watched him standing there with such Olympian impassivity. 'No, not *like* a god,' his companion replied, 'he *is* one.'

2

Mussolini was fifty-two then. Twenty-five years before, in October 1911, while serving a sentence in cell 39 at Forlì prison for having 'incited the people to strike and insurrection', he had begun his autobiography.

'I was born on 29 July 1883,' he wrote, 'at Varnano dei Costa, an old hamlet on the top of a hill in the village of Dovia, which is near the village of Predappio. I was born at two in the afternoon on a Sunday. . . . The sun had entered the constellation of Leo eight days before.'

His father was a blacksmith, and the son was always proud of this. 'I am a man of the people,' he was fond of saying. 'I understand the people because I am one of them.' In 1935 a plaque was made and embedded in the wall of a farmhouse near Predappio to inform the passers-by that 'On this farm Mussolini's peasant ancestors lived and worked.' But they were not really peasants; they were members of a class which the Duce was later to despise – the *petite bourgeoisie*. His grandfather had owned the farm on which his father was born, and had been a lieutenant in the National Guard. His mother Rosa was a schoolmistress, a quiet, religious woman, gentle and kind, 'esteemed by everyone', as the Forlì paper, *Il Pensiero Romagnolo*, wrote when she was dead, 'for her virtues and for the love and intelligence with which she fulfilled her noble function'. She was extremely thrifty and she needed to be, for her husband Alessandro, although a skilled blacksmith and the owner of a threshing-machine, was not interested much in his work and spent more of his time in talking politics than in working at his anvil. He had never been to school, but he was not an uneducated man and he was certainly an intelligent one. He contributed articles to various Socialist journals as well as to the local paper, the republican *Il Pensiero Romagnolo*, and his sons afterwards described how he would spend hours reading to them from political works which they did not begin to understand. Like so many men of the Romagna, that lovely yet rugged part of Italy between Tuscany and Emilia, his political views were passionately held and vehemently expressed. He started in Predappio a local branch of the International and had been in prison, like his father before him, for his beliefs. He christened his elder son Benito after the Mexican revolutionary Benito Juarez, the leader of the savage revolt against the Emperor Maximilian, and he gave him two other names – Amilcare after Amilcare Cipriani, the Romagnol anarchist, and Andrea after Andrea Costa, one of the founders of the Italian Socialist Party.

It was a poor house where the Mussolinis lived at Dovia, a small, tumbledown palace, two miles from Predappio, known as Palazzo Varano, where they were crowded together in two rooms on the second floor. To get to these rooms the family had to pass through the room which Rosa Mussolini used as her schoolroom and in which, during the summer holidays, Alessandro stored the wheat that he had threshed with his home-made machine.

Benito and his quiet, fat little brother Arnaldo slept together in the room that was used as a kitchen and wood-store; Edvige, his sister, slept with her parents in the other room, where the family lived by day and where the children played and looked at the pictures in their father's books and newspapers stored in a bookcase by the wall. But when he was old enough to hold his father's bellows Benito was sent to work in the smithy, where he was given a slap on the back of the head if he did not pay sufficient attention to his work or showed fear of the flying sparks.

There was little money for food. Rosa Mussolini earned only fifty lire a month from her work at school, and much of what Alessandro earned was spent on his mistress. Meals would often be little more than vegetable soup and wild radishes and chicory with flat cakes made of flour and water.

Benito was a difficult child. Disobedient, quarrelsome, self-willed, and moody, he lost his temper quickly when provoked and often came home with his clothes torn and his face scratched and bleeding after fighting with other children in the village when he did not get what he considered his fair share of the proceeds of the poaching expeditions which he went on with them. But despite his aggressive ill-temper and surly obstinacy he was capable both of arousing and of feeling deep affection. His brother and his sister both adored him, and even the village children with whom he was so often quarrelling and fighting remembered years later the warmth of his rare smiles and the unshakeable loyalty of his friendship once obtained. They remembered too that he was a dreamer as well as a fighter and that he would sit for hours on end watching the birds and gazing across the beautiful valley of his birth, with his chin in his hands, his enormous dark eyes beneath the bulging forehead wondering yet watchful. 'One day,' he said to his mother, 'I shall astonish the world.'

Each year he became more arrogant, less controllable. At school he crawled under the desks to pinch the bare legs of the other children, and on Sundays when Rosa took her children to Mass down the rough track which led to the church, with their shoes tied round their necks to keep them clean, Benito would lag behind the others, kicking at the stones with his bare feet. He would never stay long in church. The smell of the incense made him feel sick, he said, while the colours of the vestments, the light of the candles, the singing and the noise of the organ, all upset him profoundly. He waited for the others to come out, sitting at the top of a tree and throwing stones at the children on their way to Sunday school.

When he was nine he was sent away to school at Faenza, where it was hoped that the rigid discipline of the Salesian Fathers would achieve what his parents could not. Alessandro, his atheistic and anti-Catholic spirit revolting at the idea of handing his wayward son over to the care of the Church, but admitting that he could not control him himself, took him there in a donkey-cart.

'I don't remember being much upset about leaving my brother and sister,' Benito wrote later. 'Edvige was only three years old,

Arnaldo was seven. But I was miserable at having to leave behind me a little bird which I kept in a cage beneath my window. On the day before we started, I had quarrelled with a companion and had tried to hit him but missed and my fist went smash against a wall and I hurt my knuckles so badly that I had to leave with my hand bandaged up. At the moment of parting I cried.'

He remembered how the donkey stumbled and fell just outside Dovia and how his father grumbled and cursed and muttered that it was an ill omen. It was October and the leaves were falling from the trees and the streams were fast and full and the vines were turning from red to yellow. They arrived at Faenza in the early afternoon, and Alessandro knocked on the heavy door of the school and handed his son over to the headmaster and then bent over him to kiss him good-bye with rough tenderness. As the door closed Benito burst into tears again. The master took him into the yard where the other pupils were playing, and he watched them silently, standing alone in a corner, aloof and hostile.

He hated the school. He hated the Fathers, particularly his form-master, who had a piercing laugh which frightened him, and he hated the other boys, and most of all he hated the rich boys, who sat at a different table and ate better food. He did not even try to work. One day a Father beat him and he hit back and threw an inkwell at him. He had only one friend, a boy with a skull so thick that he let Benito amuse himself by hitting him hard with a brick. In a fight with an older boy he pulled out his penknife and stabbed him, and the headmaster decided that in the interest of his other pupils he must expel the uncontrollable child; but on reflection he decided to keep him until the end of the school year. Frustrated by the strict rules, the interminable sermons, the lectures on sin and corruption, he confessed before his first Communion to a long catalogue of sins both real and imagined. The Fathers were overcome with relief when he left, and one of them afterwards said that he had never had so difficult a pupil. At his next school, the Giosuè Carducci school at Forlimpopoli run by the poet's brother, Valfredo, he was as deeply unhappy and as obstinately intractable. In a fight with a boy who had pushed his arm when he was writing, he lost control of himself and once more pulled out his penknife to stab the boy in the bottom. And again he was expelled.

In spite of his passionate rebelliousness, however, and his refusal to do work that seemed boring and unnecessary, he was recognized as an unusually intelligent boy. He was readmitted to the
Forlimpopoli school as a day pupil and three years later, at the age
of eighteen, he passed his final examinations and obtained a teach-
ing diploma. He had not lost his ferocious temper or his sulky
independence, but he had discovered a hunger for knowledge and
an ability to learn. He had developed too a passion for declama-
tion. He loved to stand on the hills above Predappio reciting in his
already powerful voice the lyrical and patriotic poems of Carducci,
and one of his earliest oratorical triumphs was in the civic theatre
at Forlimpopoli, where, chosen by the masters at his school, he
made a dramatic and emotional speech to commemorate the death
of Giuseppe Verdi.

On 13 February 1902 he applied for an appointment in a school
at Pieve di Saliceto in the commune of Gualtieri, and the town's
Socialist councillors, preferring his politics to those of older and
more experienced teachers, gave it to him. He came into the town
wearing a black hat with an immense brim and a floppy black
cravat. His pale face and his wide, black, piercing eyes gave him
the appearance of a poet or a revolutionary, and he liked to think
of himself as both. 'I was a Bohemian in those days,' he said
proudly. 'I made my own rules and I did not even keep them.'
The mild, respectable Socialists of Gualtieri were 'tagliatelle
Socialists', weak and flabby as spaghetti, and he did not trouble to
disguise his contempt for them. The 'injustices of the world,' he
wrote, 'will never be reformed by such men'. He was restless and
impatient, overwhelmingly anxious to make his mark, to do something to astonish and challenge the world and not to remain the
teacher of forty pupils in a village school.

In the four months that he spent at Gualtieri he found his first
mistress. She was a beautiful girl of twenty, the wife of a soldier,
and he treated her with violent ruthlessness. 'Our love was wild
and jealous,' he admitted with a kind of savage exultation. 'I did
what I liked with her.' They quarrelled and fought and fornicated
with that furious abandon that was to characterize all the love-
affairs of his youth. Once he stabbed her, driving the knife, which
he always carried still, deep into the flesh of her thigh; and always
he abused her and bullied her and made love to her violently and

selfishly. She was not the first woman he had treated so. Already as a student at Forlimpopoli he had visited the local brothel and fallen on a whore whose flaccid body, 'exuding sweat at every pore', is described in the fragment of autobiography he wrote in prison but whose existence – as that of other women of his youth – is not mentioned in the more staid versions of his autobiography published later. Also in this early fragment are descriptions of his raids on dance halls with other hooligans, his fights over girls, and his triumphant, unashamed account of his first assault on a girl who was not a prostitute. Her name was Virginia. She was 'poor', he wrote condescendingly, 'but she had a nice complexion' and 'was reasonably good-looking. . . . One day I took her up the stairs, threw her on to the floor behind the door, and made her mine. She got up, crying, and insulted me between her sobs. She said that I had violated her honour. I probably had. But what sort of honour ?'

Throughout his life he was to remember these wild days of youth with pleasure and pride, to speak and write of his violence and passion, his impatience and hunger and savage discontent. And it is difficult now to disentangle the facts from the legends created by his own imagination and his insatiable appetite for self-dramatization. In June 1902, feeling, as he later put it himself, the urge to escape, he went to Switzerland 'as a worker without any money', and he claimed that while he was there he experienced long days of hunger and despair, illness and imprisonment, his pockets empty save for a nickel medallion of Karl Marx. He slept in a packing-case under a bridge, or in a public lavatory, or with a Polish refugee, a medical student whose love-making was 'unforgettable'. In July he found work as a mason's mate and wrote from Lausanne to a friend to tell him of his experiences.

'Eleven hours' work in the day at 32 centesimi the hour. I made one hundred and twenty-one journeys with a hand-barrow full of stones up to the second floor of a building in process of construction. In the evening the muscles of my arms were swollen. I ate some potatoes roasted on cinders and threw myself in all my clothes on my bed – a pile of straw. At five in the next morning I woke and returned to work. I chafed with the terrible rage of the powerless. The *padrone* made me mad. . . . Saturday evening came. I said to the *padrone* I intended to leave and therefore

wanted to be paid. He went into his office and I remained in the
lobby. Presently he came out. With ill-disguised rage he threw
into my hands twenty lire and some centesimi, saying "Here is
your money and it is stolen." I remained as though made of stone.
What was I to do with him? Kill him? What did I do to him?
Nothing. Why? Because I was hungry and had no shoes. I had
worn a pair of light boots to pieces on the building stones which
had lacerated both my hands and the soles of my feet.'

He worked later, he said, as a navvy and a butcher's boy, as an
errand boy for a wine shop and in a chocolate factory. He was
arrested one day for begging in the streets of Lausanne and another day when he was out of work in Geneva he attacked 'two
English women sitting on a bench with their lunch – bread, cheese,
eggs. I could not restrain myself', he confessed. 'I threw myself
upon one of the old witches and grabbed the food from her hands.
If they had made the slightest resistance I would have strangled
them – strangled them, mind you!'

How much of all this is true it is impossible now to say, but it is
certain that by the end of the summer he had found regular work
and was never hungry. Considered an intellectual by the workers
with whom he had come into contact, he was offered the Secretaryship of the Lausanne Association of Bricklayers and Manual
Labourers and was put in charge of propaganda. He was also
giving Italian lessons and being paid for articles in which he gave
vent to his peculiar form of anarchistic Socialism, his anti-
Clericalism, his erratic sense of social injustice, his angry hostility
towards types and classes of people for whom he felt a personal
antagonism. He began to read a great deal, impatiently and hap-
hazardly, as though he wished to absorb the whole history of
political philosophy within a few months. He rushed through
various works of Lassalle, Kautsky, Kropotkin, Marx and Schopenhauer, Sterner and Neitzsche, Blanqui and Bertoni, picking up
ideas, misinterpreting them, extending them. Later he fell upon
Baboeuf, Proudhon, Kant and Spinoza, Hegel, Fichte, Sorel and
Guyau, and everything he read affected him deeply so that, as a
woman he had met in Geneva said afterwards, 'his philosophical
views were always the reflection of the book he had happened to
read last'. He found the most inspiration not in the turgid pages
of Marx, with which he never got very far, but in the angry

writings and dramatic lives of Louis Auguste Blanqui, the violent French revolutionary, and Prince Peter Alexeivich Kropotkin, the Russian anarchist. And it is significant that the only book mentioned in his autobiography is *The Psychology of the Crowd* by Gustave Lebon.

Fired by visions of violence he wandered through the streets of Lausanne and Berne arguing, quarrelling, and making inflammatory speeches to his trade union. He spent most of his evenings with Russian students, strange, wild, dissolute Bohemians and nihilists, and he drank with them and made love with them and argued with them so intently that he seemed to believe, as one of them said, 'that each day might be his last'. Benitouchka they called him, but he found the endearment objectionable and preferred to refer to himself, in the style of Sorel, as *'un apostolo di violenza'*. 'When will the day of vengeance come?' he asked repeatedly. When would the people free themselves from tyranny and from religion, that 'immoral disease of the mind'? Who was Christ, he asked outrageously, but a 'small mean man who in two years converted a few villages and whose disciples were a dozen ignorant vagabonds, the scum of Palestine'? What was Switzerland but a 'sausage-maker's democracy which had never known how to find the road of protest and pretended to be unaware of its immense shame, believing, perhaps, that William Tell's apple was enough to perpetuate the tradition of liberty'? In the summer of 1903 he went too far for the peaceable Swiss, who had him arrested for making a speech to his union in Berne in which he proposed a general strike and advocated violence as a means of enforcing the workers' demands. After twelve days in prison he was expelled from the canton of Berne and hustled over the frontier to Chiasso. Within a week, however, he was back in Switzerland and became more wild than ever.

He was twenty now, and already he had the appearance of a seasoned revolutionary burned and aged by the agonies of an inner passion. His fine, long black hair was already beginning to grow thin, and his intense, dark eyes were heavily shadowed. The pallor of his skin was emphasized by a black moustache and the stubble of a beard which he rarely shaved more than twice a week. Angelica Balabanoff, a clever, hunchbacked, sensual Russian Socialist he met in Geneva a few months later, said that he rarely washed either.[1] He was also, she thought, neurotic, excitable, self-pitying, excessively blasphemous, vindictively revengeful, aggressively ill-dressed, and a sponger who hated manual work and considered himself an intellectual. He was constantly complaining of his health and boasting of his virility. Angelica Balabanoff was not sure that behind the flashing, positive façade he was not shy and unsure of himself when in the presence of those whom he suspected might be his social or intellectual superiors. When she first spoke to him she thought that she had never seen 'a more wretched human being. In spite of his large jaw, the bitterness and restlessness in his black eyes, he gave the impression of extreme timidity. Even as he listened, his nervous hands clutching at his big black hat, he seemed more concerned with his own inner turmoil than with what I was saying'. But she liked him at the time although she grew to hate him later for his betrayal of Socialism. Indeed, most people liked him then; he was not a man to inspire hatred.

Towards the end of 1903 he returned to Italy as his mother was ill; but as soon as she was better he went back to Switzerland to escape military service, for he was, of course, a violent anti-militarist with a bitter contempt for the 'paid slaves of kings' in their 'gaudy uniforms, their chests covered with crosses, decorations and similar foreign and domestic hardware . . . blinding the public with dust and flaunting in its face their impudent display'. Within a few weeks he was arrested again and spent Easter Day 1904 in Lucerne prison. It was, he said afterwards, 'one of the saddest days of my youth', and as he listened to the church bells ringing he wondered whether the Swiss would send him back to Italy on his release from prison to serve the year's imprisonment to which he had been sentenced as a deserter. But he was, to his profound relief, put off the train before it reached Chiasso, and although expelled from the canton of Geneva he was allowed to return to Lausanne, where thousands of other Italian emigrants lived and tried to find work. Mussolini, however, was more for-

1. Margherita Sarfatti, then a fellow-Socialist and later to become one of Mussolini's earliest biographers and closest friends, who admired Angelica Balabanoff's intelligence but could not disguise her dislike of her as a woman – perhaps her jealousy of her as a woman – said that Balabanoff also did not wash. 'The saving grace of humour failed her completely,' Margherita Sarfatti thought. 'She lacked a sense of beauty even more. This was fortunate for her! Otherwise she would probably have thrown herself down the nearest well. As things were she had the slightest possible acquaintance with water.'

tunate than most. His French was good by now, his German passable; he had also learned a little English and some Spanish. He managed to support himself by giving Italian lessons, by translating philosophical and political works with the help of his Russian and Polish friends, by writing articles, by borrowing money from his mother and from anyone else who would lend it to him, until in November 1904 the King of Italy, in order to celebrate the birth of his son Prince Umberto, granted an amnesty to deserters.

Mussolini had thought of emigrating to America, but he changed his mind and decided to go back to help his mother teach in her school at Dovia. On his way home he met Angelica Balabanoff in Lugano and left for Italy, so she says, having delivered himself of a characteristic outburst against the rich. 'Look!' he said, waving his arm towards the restaurants and hotels along the promenade. 'People eating, drinking, and enjoying themselves. And I will travel third class, eat miserable cheap food. *Porca Madonna*, how I hate the rich! Why must I suffer this injustice? How long must we wait?' Two days later Mussolini arrived back in the Romagna with a reputation for political extremism which was now of more than local interest. On 18 April 1904 the Rome paper *La Tribuna* had published an item from its Geneva correspondent in which Mussolini was referred to as '*il grande duce*' of the local Italian Socialist club. Already the pattern of his life had begun to form.

3

On 19 February 1905 Rosa Mussolini died of meningitis at the age of forty-six, and Benito, so *Il Pensiero Romagnolo* said, was overcome with grief. At her funeral he 'wanted to utter a last farewell, but in the painful effort to do so he burst into tears and he was able only to throw some flowers on to the grave'. After his mother's death he went to teach in a school at Caneva, a small town in the commune of Tolmezzo in the Venetian Alps north of Udine. He was not a good schoolmaster and he knew it. The children liked him well enough, but it seems that he found it difficult to control them and his mind was often far away. Sometimes he would lose his temper and bang his fist on the desk and swear at them. But although they called him '*il tiranno*' they were not frightened of him. Some of them thought he was mad. His collar was usually askew and nearly always dirty, his shoe-laces were often undone and his hair long and untidy. He walked about the town and the two and a half miles from his boarding-house to the school, reading a book or murmuring poetry; he took Latin lessons from the priest, began to study Indian arithmetic, and made notes for a history of philosophy and for a critical study of German literature; but most of the time when he was not giving lessons in the school or private lessons at the boarding-house where he lived, he was drinking or indulging his craving for sexual excitement. He said himself that his year at Tolmezzo was one 'of moral deterioration'. Frequently he was drunk, and frequently after his drinking companions had gone to bed he continued to stumble alone through the dark streets shouting, reciting the poems of Carducci, and making speeches to the fountain in the square. He made love to any girl who would have him and threatened to rape any who would not. He contracted syphilis, and when he discovered the symptoms he loaded a revolver and said he would shoot himself and was with difficulty persuaded to see a doctor instead. He had a passionate affair with his landlord's wife, and when he had left Tolmezzo he travelled 300 miles from Predappio in the middle of a winter night because he wanted her so urgently, and he crept up the stairs and ravished her on the floor while her husband was asleep in another room.

By the middle of the following summer he was in prison again. With his accustomed uncompromising vehemence he had, during one of the recurrent agrarian conflicts which repeatedly disturbed Romagnol life, joined a political argument on the side of the casual labourers of Predappio against their 'oppressors', the tenant farmers, and was sentenced to three months' imprisonment.

He was becoming well known in the Romagna now. He was talked about and he was written about in newspapers. 'Comrade Mussolini', at the age of twenty-five, was already a formidable force. After his release from prison he went north to Trento, at this time part of Austria, to take up an appointment with a trade union and to become a frequent contributor to the weekly paper of the Left, the revolutionary and internationalist *L'Avvenire del Lavoratore*. But he did not like the Socialists of the Trentino and their worship of Mazzini any more than he had liked the '*tagliatelle* Socialists' of Gualtieri. They were 'toadies of bourgeois capitalism', 'slaves of nationalism and patriotism' who must be attacked and attacked again until 'their treachery to the proletariat' was exposed. For the proletariat must consider itself 'anti-patriotic by definition and necessity', and made to realize that nationalism was a mask for 'rapacious militarism', which 'should be left to the masters', and that the national flag was, as Gustave Hervé had said, 'a rag to be planted on a dung-hill'.

Although his distaste for the nationalism of the Trentino Socialists went very deep, he agreed to write for *Il Popolo*, a newspaper edited by Cesare Battisti, a man of irredentist sympathies. In the articles he wrote for *Il Popolo* and for another paper, owned and edited by Battisti, *La Vita Trentina*, he attacked with his by now familiar indiscrimination a complex range of targets, from the anti-proletarian mentality of Freemasonry to the cupidity of landlords, from the evil influence of Neo-Malthusianism[1] to the bourgeois spirit which had led to the degeneration of May Day as a revolutionary holiday. His most savage attacks, however, were made in *L'Avvenire del Lavoratore* against militarism and nationalism and above all against the powerful Catholic influence in Trent supported by the widely read Catholic paper, *Il Trentino*, one of whose leading political writers was Alcide de Gasperi. Indeed, as Gaudens Megaro has shown, it was his violent attacks on the Catholic Church – 'that great corpse' – and on the Vatican – 'that den of intolerance and of a gang of robbers' – and on Christianity itself – 'humanity's immortal stigma of opprobrium' – which led to his arrest and expulsion from Austria, rather than those occasional

1. For the whole of his life Mussolini was obsessed by what he called 'Italy's demographic problem'. When the German writer Emil Ludwig suggested to him in 1932 that 'Malthusianism was more necessary in Italy than anywhere else in the world,' he 'flared up in wrath. Never before or afterwards,' Ludwig said, 'did I see him lose his self-command in this way. Speaking twice as fast as usual, he flung his arguments at me like missiles "Malthus! Malthus is economically a blunder and morally a crime! A reduction in population brings poverty in its train! When the population of Italy was only sixteen millions, the country was poorer than it is today when we have forty-two million inhabitants."'

Every family, he said repeatedly, ought to have five children, like his. The fathers of such large families received higher wages than their less fortunate fellow-workers, and prolific mothers were made honorary members of the Fascist Party.

Once having promoted an officer general in the morning, he cancelled the promotion in the afternoon when he discovered he was a bachelor. 'A general must be the first to realize,' he said, 'that without men you cannot have divisions.' A large population, it could be argued, provided not only cannon-fodder but excellent reasons for wanting colonies and for keeping wages low.

diatribes against Austrian nationalism and articles supporting the rights of Italians working under Austrian domination that Mussolini and his Fascist biographers were later to pick out of his writings as evidence of his irredentist sympathies.

On 10 September 1909 he was arrested yet again and on the 26th expelled from Austria as he had been expelled from the cantons of Berne and Geneva. The following month he went home once again to his father, who had given up the smithy at Dovia and had moved with his tall, thin, *farouche* mistress, Anna Guidi, and her five children to Forlì, where he had become the landlord of the Bersaglieri inn. The younger of the widow Anna's daughters was named Rachele. She was a pretty girl of sixteen with fluffy fair hair and a manner at once provocative and dissuasive; and Mussolini decided that he would like to marry her. He had fallen in love with her elder sister Augusta, but she, thinking him too unstable, had married a man in regular work as a gravedigger, and Mussolini had immediately transferred his attentions to Rachele. In the evenings, when he had emptied the jugs and washed up the glasses he wrote short stories, finished a book about John Huss, the Bohemian reformer, and began a novel which was published as a serial in *Il Popolo*, the editor of which had suggested the plot. *Claudia Particella*, translated into English in 1928 as *The Cardinal's Mistress*, is not a very interesting book and certainly not a very lively one. Margherita Sarfatti described it, as all Mussolini's trivial but nevertheless revealing fiction might be described, as 'a clumsy hash without head or tail, a flashy film of long footage'. But Rachele liked it, for one of its most sympathetic characters is the heroine's maid who gives her life for her mistress, and Benito had called her Rachele.

Rachele has described the night when Benito took her to the theatre for the first time. He brought her back to the Bersaglieri and demanded to be allowed to live with her. Both his father and her mother refused to consider it. He took out a pistol and said that he would shoot himself and her if he could not have his way. They gave in and a few days later Mussolini rented two rooms in a damp and crumbling *palazzo* in Via Merenda. 'We moved into the place one night,' Rachele wrote afterwards. 'I remember how tired and happy he was – perhaps a little uncertain of my reaction because the marriage papers were not yet ready. But I understood

I saw a man of my heart there before me, eagerly awaiting the only gift life could give him – my love. His young face was already lined by his daily struggle. There was no hesitation. I went with him.'

They lived together in the squalid rooms in Palazzo Merenda for three years. Towards the end of the first year, on 1 September 1910, their first child, Edda, was born, and Mussolini went out to buy a cradle and brought it home on his shoulders. It had cost fifteen lire – half a week's wages – and for the rest of that week he and his wife lived on cabbages. He had a job as Secretary of the Forlì Socialist Federation, but it was poorly paid and much of his money was spent on the weekly newspaper that he had founded, *La Lotta di Classe* – *The Class Struggle* – all four pages of which he wrote himself. He was a dedicated Socialist now. He drank wine with his friends, but he never got drunk; occasionally he kissed a pretty girl or pinched her bottom, but he remained faithful to Rachele. All his energy and all the drive of his growing ambition were thrown into politics and into *La Lotta di Classe*, which soon became a much more influential paper than most of the many Italian Socialist weeklies of its sort and which was often quoted in *Avanti!* the official Socialist newspaper. He was rarely at home, often to be seen strolling through the town on his way to a meeting, looking at the ground, his hands deep in his pockets, pale and unshaven, poorly and untidily dressed, murmuring to himself. When he was at home, he was usually working, writing or reading, translating Kropotkin, preparing his speeches. Sometimes he would break off suddenly and pick up his violin, which he had first been taught to play by a fair-ground fiddler when he was a little boy. He was not a graceful musician but a loud and powerful one, and it eased his nerves, he said, to play as the words of his articles and speeches went through and through his mind. Occasionally he went to the theatre with Rachele and her curious, witch-like mother, but even there, so he later confessed, his mind was full of his speeches and he was anxious to get home and write down the thoughts that had come to him. If the play did not start on time, he would take off his shoe and threaten to throw it at the stage.

He was becoming a good speaker, forceful and authoritative. His attacks were outlandish, his facts often wrong, his opinions usually contradictory and aggressively didactic, his attitudes theatrical; but there was no denying the compelling fascination of his voice and of his provocative, repetitive, vigorous gestures, his gift for the dramatic phrase, for the enigmatic allusion, the improbable but apt and striking metaphor. He had developed a skilful ability for arousing emotion by building up a series of apparently disconnected sentences, delivered in staccato bursts but in varying tones of voice and emphasized by a calculated contrast of gestures into a climactic whole. He had developed, too, that ability which was later to become a genius for imposing a mood upon an audience and then abandoning himself to it until his speech became not a speech at all, but a dialogue, a kind of unrehearsed litany in which the congregation chanted their responses to the preacher's urgent questions and he would re-phrase them and throw them back to receive a louder answer, a more passionate encouragement, a stronger affirmation of their unity. He had already learned as well the advantages of having a reliable *claque* whose infectious applause and shouts of agreement could be evoked by a nod of the head or an agreed gesture. And he had realized, above all, the necessity for a band of faithful admirers around whom could be built a powerful following of men ready to regard him as their leader.

For he had by now recognized himself as the leader in chrysalis. Prompted by ideas, still largely uncorrelated and not always understood, picked out of Nietzsche and Schopenhauer, Blanqui, Hegel and Sorel, and borrowed from the Russian Bolsheviks, he was coming to the belief which was soon to dominate his life – that the existing order must be overthrown by an *élite* of revolutionaries acting in the name of the people, and that this *élite* must be led by himself.

But only the most violent of his fellow-Socialists were prepared to follow him by endorsing his extreme and violent views, by supporting him in his indiscriminate attacks on Turati, Bissolati, and Treves, the moderates within the Party, and indeed on any group, inside or outside the Party, which disagreed with him. He was an outstanding man all right, the most conventional Socialists had to agree, but a dangerous one, already as dangerous as Constantino Lazzari. They heard with alarm his speeches advocating the efficacy of violence – 'the iron necessity of violence', as he later termed it – the compelling need to 'use force surgically'. They read with nervous disapproval accounts of his methods in Forlì and in particular of one occasion when he marched to the town hall, followed by a large crowd, and threatened to throw the Mayor out of the window if he did not obtain a reduction in the price of milk.

When in the summer of 1911 the Government of Giovanni Giolitti sent troops to Tripolitania and Cyrenaica with the declared object of protecting the property of Italian subjects, but with the real intention of replacing Turkey as the dominant power in these areas, Mussolini demonstrated just how dangerous he could be. To his fury the Socialist National Congress in Milan, to which he had been sent as Forlì's representative, had refused to discuss anti-militarism; and there were even some 'bourgeois lickspittles' who were prepared to support the Government's aggression. 'Marx,' Giolitti commented with satisfaction, 'has been relegated to the attic.' Mussolini made it acutely clear in his articles in *La Lotta di Classe* and in his speeches that he was not, under any circumstances, prepared to support the war. 'International militarism continues to celebrate its orgies of destruction and death,' he shouted angrily. 'Every day that passes, the huge pyramid of lives that have been sacrificed rears its bloody summit upon which Mars stands waiting with his unsated and contorted mouth in an infernal grin. . . . So long as there are Fatherlands, there will be militarism. The Fatherland is a spook . . . like God, and like God it is vindictive, cruel, and tyrannical. . . . Let us show that the Fatherland does not exist just as God does not exist.'

As a protest against this disastrous war, the committee of the General Confederation of Labour called a general strike and drafted a protest. But this was not enough for Mussolini. Shouting to the workers of Forlì to come to political meetings not with their arms hanging loosely by their sides but with weapons, he joined forces with the young republican Pietro Nenni in inciting them not merely to strike but to revolution; and he himself led a gang of men who, during two days of rioting in Forlì, occupied itself by tearing up the town's tramlines with pickaxes. A few weeks later, after a trial in which he defended himself with a remarkable display of skilful double-talk, he was in prison for the fifth time.

Released after five months, he returned to his rooms in Via Merenda more determined than ever to become the leader of the Socialists and to mould them into a revolutionary and republican party. After the Socialist National Congress of Milan, which he had been unable to dominate, he had demanded that the Forlì Socialist Confederation should declare itself outside the Party; now that opinion within the Party appeared to be swinging to his side, he demanded that it should return to it. Obediently it did so, and at the next National Congress at Reggio Emilia the fiery delegate from Forlì, of whom many delegates had not even heard and others remembered as an incoherent speaker at the last congress at Milan, initiated his campaign against his opponents in the parliamentary group by a spirited, eloquent, and malicious attack on Leonida Bissolati, Ivanoe Bonomi, and Angiolo Cabrini, the middle-class Socialist Deputies who had laid themselves open to 'serious accusations from the Party' by publicly congratulating the King after the anarchist bricklayer had attempted to assassinate him. The Party, Mussolini declared, must be purged of such dross. It must learn never to compromise with anti-proletarian institutions. It was a triumphantly forceful speech. Even the supporters of Bissolati and Turati were impressed. One of these, Margherita Sarfatti's husband, wrote to his wife to tell her of the emergence of 'a wonderful young man' who was 'destined to dominate the Party'. 'Spare of figure, hard, fiery, most original with occasional bursts of eloquence,' he was a man with a great future before him.[1]

Six months after this National Congress, in December 1912, the Executive Committee of the Party, now dominated by left-wing members, also recognized the startling talents of the young journalist and announced that it had 'unanimously decided to nominate Professor Benito Mussolini of Forlì as editor of *Avanti!*' 'I have decided,' Mussolini told his staff as soon as he arrived at the offices in Milan, 'to write all the political articles myself.' Within a few months his great gifts as an editor and his boldly original typographical ideas had doubled the circulation of the paper. By the

---

1 Another delegate, the Russian nihilist Anna Kulishov, who had been imprisoned at the same time as Filippo Turati in 1898 for her part in the revolutionary meetings held that year in Milan, gave a different and more perceptive opinion of the fiery young man. 'He is nothing of a Marxist,' she said. 'In fact he is not really a Socialist at all. . . . Nor is he really a politician. He is a sentimental poetaster who has read Nietzsche.' Another less enthusiastic opinion of his performance at the Congress was given in *Il Resto del Carlino*, which described his 'abundant gestures and expressions that make him resemble a Chinaman'. The *Corriere della Sera*, however, endorsed the view of Margherita's husband: 'Mussolini spoke with candour and sincere agitation . . . lean, bitter, speaking with explosive sincerity, he is liked by the Congress which feels it has in him an interpreter of its feelings.'

end of his editorship the circulation had increased from 28,000 to nearly 100,000 copies.

'I don't know what to make of this queer fellow Mussolini,' one of the young reporters said. 'But I know one thing – he's going to get somewhere.'

The Interventionist

Nobody loves a neutral.

In October 1913, Mussolini stood as Socialist candidate for Forlì and made a series of election speeches in condemnation of militarism, nationalism, and imperialism. He was heavily defeated. Although he was soon afterwards elected a councillor in Milan, he ascribed his defeat and the defeat of extremists like himself to the 'bourgeois spirit of the people', who did not have the courage or the energy to fight for their demands and who needed to be aroused by some cataclysmic event to an awareness of their destiny. At Forlì, after leading his assault on the tramway lines, he had addressed a meeting of over ten thousand workers in the municipal park, but when some boys had climbed on to the bandstand the knocking of their wooden clogs on the boards had seemed like the clattering of horses' hooves. The shouts of 'Up with the revolution!' changed to alarmed cries of 'The cavalry are coming!' and the crowds ran out of the park. 'This is a nation of cowards,' Mussolini had said angrily to one of his companions. 'They won't fight.' Now they disappointed him again. At the beginning of 1914 a general strike was called in Emilia and the Marche. Soon the whole area was in uproar. There were savage anti-clerical and anti-military demonstrations, while self-declared republics grew up overnight. Ancona announced that it was an independent commune, and the red flag flew over the town hall at Bologna. In Milan, where the Socialists and Syndicalists had united to form an action committee, Mussolini rushed once more into the streets, commanding the workers to occupy the squares, but in Piazza del Duomo he watched them retreat headlong before a cavalry charge. In his own offices, when a column of nationalists threatened to storm the building, his shouts of 'To arms!' were met without enthusiasm. Margherita Sarfatti, at this time the art editor of the paper, encouraged him in his advocacy of violent resistance and suggested that they should use the editorial scissors as daggers; but the others were less resolute and seemed relieved when the nationalists called off their assault.

A few weeks later, Austria declared war on Serbia and the Great War had begun. 'Down with the war!' Mussolini thundered from the offices of *Avanti!*, repeating the slogans he had used when attacking the nationalists of Trento. 'Down with arms, and up with humanity!' If the Government intervened in favour of Austria and Germany, its partners in the virtually defunct Triple Alliance, the workers' revolution would surely begin. Intervention on behalf of France would be equally disastrous. It was the duty of the Socialists, in fact, to fight to ensure that Italy maintained a policy of 'rigid neutrality'. He sent a referendum to his fellow-Socialists asking them to confirm their agreement with this uncompromising stand, and his admiring followers immediately replied with their support. When the Government declared that Italy would, in fact, remain neutral and the Syndicalists declared that the decision was wrong and that the country should enter the war, Mussolini attacked them furiously as subversive traitors to the working-class.

Behind the outspoken condemnation of the interventionists, however, different ideas were taking shape in Mussolini's mind. On the day of the Sarajevo murder, he was on holiday at Cattolica with a fellow-journalist, Michele Campana; and as they travelled back to Milan together, Mussolini confessed his growing disillusion with his Socialist colleagues. 'I want to guide the Party intelligently,' he told Campana, 'steering it as it should be steered through the great events that lie ahead,' but he doubted that it would follow him intelligently.

'Let's understand this clearly,' he went on. 'The Central Powers are attacking England and France through Serbia. A general conflict is inevitable, and France will be its first victim if the civilized countries do not unite to save her. The defeat of France would be a death-blow to liberty in Europe. The Socialist Party should not turn its back on the possibility of intervention in favour of France if she is dragged into the war. But will the Party leaders understand these truths?'

Michele Campana reminded him of his speech at the last

Socialist Congress at Reggio Emilia, when he had spoken with such force against nationalism and against those Syndicalists who were supporting the war against Turkey in Libya.

'That was different,' Mussolini said quickly. That was a war of aggression. This war could be Italy's salvation. It could settle the problem of Trentino and Trieste and deliver them from the grasp of Austria, a country which the irredentist Cesare Rossi had taught him to consider the enemy of liberty; and it could bring forward the day of revolution. Apart from the belief that the Socialists should take advantage of the war in order to provoke unrest and eventually destroy the bourgeois system, there was another belief helping to alter Mussolini's mind. The Syndicalists, led by Alceste De Ambris and the violently nationalist Filippo Corridoni, who were advocating war, were obviously being listened to with a respect and sympathy which led Mussolini to fear that he might lose control of the Socialist conscience to them. Some of them were quoting Karl Marx's aphorism that a social revolution usually follows war and, there can be little doubt, this exercised a profound influence on Mussolini's mind.

Karl Marx's aphorism was certainly mentioned during an important conversation Mussolini had in Milan with Filippo Naldi, owner of the Bologna newspaper *Il Resto de Carlino*, which had previously advocated a neutral attitude favourable to Austria and Germany but was now advocating intervention on the side of France. Mussolini repeated to Naldi what he had already said to Campana, that his Socialist colleagues would not agree to support an interventionist policy and, in any case, he could not actively support such a policy himself as editor of *Avanti !* Well, then, Naldi advised him, why should he not resign and start a new paper of his own ? Naldi would finance it.

And so on 26 October Mussolini resigned his editorship of *Avanti !* and on 14 November the first number of *Il Popolo d'Italia* appeared. On either side of the title were two maxims which might well have been interpreted as the birth cries of Fascism – *Chi ha il ferro ha anche il pane* ('who has iron has bread'), from Blanqui, and *La rivoluzione è un' idea che ha trovato delle baionette* ('Revolution is an idea which has found bayonets'), from Napoleon. And on its front page was an article signed by its editor Benito Mussolini and headed '*Audacia*'.

'I address my first word to you,' he had written, 'the young men of Italy, the young men of the factories and of the universities, those who are young in years and young in spirit, the young men belonging to a generation to whom fate has given the task of making history. It is a word which in normal times I would never have used, but which today I am forced to utter loudly and clearly in sincere good faith, the fearful and fascinating word – *War*.'

Ten days later, at a meeting of the Socialist Party in Milan, amidst shouts of '*Traditore! Venduto! Sicario!*' Mussolini's expulsion from the Party was proposed. Pale and visibly trembling, he approached the platform to answer his critics. He was wearing the shabby black suit which he always wore, and a delegate noticed that his trousers were so short that they scarcely reached to his ankle-bones. He had not shaved that day nor, so it seemed, the day before. He stepped on to the platform, and the shouting and jeering grew louder. He began to speak, but no one could hear what he said. Coins and balls of paper, even chairs, were thrown on to the stage as he shouted back at the angry delegates, not excusing himself but accusing them of harbouring a petit bourgeois spirit, which was always for him the final insult. 'I tell you you are wasting your breath,' he yelled at them. 'You will all be forced into the war. . . . You cannot get rid of me, because I am, and will always be, a Socialist. . . . Your votes against me mean nothing at all.' The words were shouted at the delegates in a voice which sounded close to hysteria, and some of those present afterwards said that his eyes were full of tears. 'You hate me,' he told them desperately, throwing out one of those apparently paradoxical but at least partly justifiable assertions which he was later never to tire of making. 'You hate me because you still love me!'

But it was no good. As he said himself, his fate was already decided, and there was no point in trying to make himself heard by people who were determined to reject everything he said. With a small group of his supporters he left the People's Theatre and returned to the offices of *Il Popolo d'Italia*.

The resentment of the Socialists was bitter and implacable. Former friends and admirers felt a disillusion which went as deep as hatred. With one of them, Ciccotti, who had previously referred to him as having 'the brains of a direct descendant of

Socrates', he fought a duel; by many others, including Angelica Balabanoff, he was considered to be Socialism's most dangerous traitor. They accused him not only of betraying Socialism but of accepting money through the French Institute in Milan for having done so.[1] By the beginning of 1915, however, he had gained more supporters by his *volte-face* than he had lost. He had swung to his side most of those who agreed with his declarations that, in the last analysis, one's country must come first, that the German Socialists having supported the Kaiser had secured the collapse of the International, and that freedom was in danger. He had gained the support also of Corridoni's Syndicalists, of Libero Tancredi's anarchists, of the irredentist Cesare Battisti, even of the right-wing Socialist Bissolati whose expulsion from the Party he had helped to secure after the attack on Tripoli. His opinions were endorsed by patriotic workers, by nationalists, by thousands of young people for whom war was still a dramatic adventure, by many intellectuals and by writers such as Gabriele D'Annunzio who believed that participation in the war would help Italy on her way towards complete unity, towards the realization of her rightful sovereignty in the Adriatic and her place of influence in Europe.

Encouraged by this growing success, by the resignation of Giolitti and the appointment to the premiership of the opportunist Antonio Salandra, which made intervention more likely, Mussolini became more and more clamorous for war, increasingly intemperate. He fought a duel with the reformist Socialist Claudio Treves, a former editor of *Avanti !*; he was arrested after a wild meeting of interventionists in Rome; he fought with police officers who broke up one of his meetings in Milan. And then, at last, on 24 May 1915, to the satisfaction of the King, the irredentists, the futurists and the Freemasons as well as of Mussolini, Italy declared war. The interventionists who greeted the declaration with such noisy enthusiasm were not, however, representative of the country as a whole; and Mussolini was later to record with pleasure that they had demonstrated unmistakably how a forceful minority could always impose its views on the masses. It was a lesson which he did not forget.

1. Although the money supplied by Filippo Naldi for starting *Il Popolo d'Italia* does not seem to have come from French sources, there is good evidence to suggest that when the paper ran into financial difficulties in 1915 Mussolini received contributions from 'French comrades to help the interventionist campaign'.

'From today onwards,' he wrote triumphantly in *Il Popolo d'Italia*. 'we are all Italians and nothing but Italians. Now that steel has to meet steel, one single cry comes from our hearts – *Viva l'Italia!*'

Already the seed of Fascism was sown.

3   The Fascist in the Making

*For my part I prefer fifty thousand rifles
to five million votes.*

I

Mussolini was a good soldier. He did not volunteer like most of
his supporters, waiting until August to be called to the 11th
Regiment of Bersaglieri, but he refused his colonel's suggestion
that he should work at regimental headquarters on a war diary;
and within a few weeks he was in the front line. He had already
done nineteen months' military service on his return from Switzerland in 1905 and 1906, and during that time had shown that,
despite his reputation for rebelliousness, he could be a disciplined
soldier. He had shown then, as he showed now, an anxiety to
please and to demonstrate his capacity for hard work and enthusiasm. Determined never to appear at a disadvantage he performed his duties uncomplainingly, without undue heroism but
with sufficient zeal to be described in an official report as a soldier
whose behaviour was exemplary and whose spirit was truly that
of a Bersagliere. He was promoted corporal. In letters home he
made the most of the dangers and hardships of an infantryman's
life in the trenches and he spoke of being under fire for weeks on
end, of the times his life had been endangered. He came home on
leave from his trench beside the Isonzo river looking impressively
tired and ragged, his coat done up with bits of wire instead of
buttons.[1]

One day in February 1917 while watching the demonstration of

1. Angelica Balabanoff – not an impartial critic – says that Mussolini was not only
a *poseur* but a hysterical and hypochondriacal coward. It is a judgement which is not
supported by her contemporaries, even by those anti-Fascist writers like herself who
knew him at this time and had good cause to attack him as a traitor to their ideals. A
man I met in Milan in 1945, who claimed to have been a fellow-corporal with
Mussolini in the Bersaglieri, said that he was 'always showing off and he talked too
much; but he was a nice chap. We all liked him. He wasn't much under fire so far as
I know but when he was they say he behaved all right'.

a new mortar, there was a thunderous explosion and five men standing near him were killed as pieces of jagged metal from the bomb and the burst barrel flew into the air. He was thrown violently to the ground himself and carried back to the dressing-station scarcely conscious and with more than forty pieces of the mortar embedded in his flesh. The hospital to which he was taken at Ronchi was so badly damaged in a bombardment that most of the wounded had to be evacuated, but he was too ill to be moved.

Some weeks later, when he was well enough to return to Milan, Margherita Sarfatti went to visit him. 'I shall never forget going to see him,' she wrote. 'He was so exhausted he could scarcely speak. He smiled out at us from his pale face, his eyes sunken in great hollows. His lips scarcely moved; one could see how horribly he had suffered. Someone asked if he would like a book to read. He refused. "I read only this, because it is familiar. I cannot read anything new" and he indicated a volume of Carducci's poems.'

Mussolini, of course, was not a man to let the advantages of being a wounded soldier pass by without using them. 'I am proud,' he wrote with characteristic self-dramatization as soon as he was sufficiently recovered to hold a pen, 'to have reddened the road to Trieste with my own blood in the fulfilment of my dangerous duty.' 'I faced atrocious pain,' he wrote in his autobiography in no less dramatic a strain. 'My suffering was indescribable. I underwent practically all my operations without the aid of an anaesthetic. I had twenty-seven operations in one month; all except two were without anaesthetics.'

Recognizing the value of a wound at such a time, he went back to the offices of *Il Popolo d'Italia* leaning on crutches, which he continued to use long after the need for them had gone. As a veteran of the war he felt able to attack the Socialists, the clerical pacifists, and the neutralists, whom he took to be responsible for the disaster at Caporetto, with more licence than he could have allowed himself as a civilian journalist; and as one of those to whom he repeatedly referred as 'the survivors', he began to urge the participation of the returned soldier in the Government of the new Italy, a Government which must be strong and uncompromising. As early as February 1918 he was advocating the emergence of a dictator, 'a man who is ruthless and energetic enough to make a clean sweep'. Three months later, in a widely reported speech at Bologna, he hinted that he himself might prove such a man.

It was to those who had fought in the war that these aspirations were principally addressed, and it was amongst them that they found their most enthusiastic support. Mussolini's urgent claims on behalf of Italy to Fiume and Dalmatia in addition to those areas – the Trentino and Venezia Giulia – which the Treaty of St Germain was eventually to grant her, were enthusiastically endorsed by those who had fought on the Carso; while his attacks on the Russian Revolution and Lenin's totalitarianism made a wide appeal to all those who associated the October Revolution and the Bolsheviks with the discredited Italian Socialist Party. He no longer considered himself a Socialist even in name. The Party had not only opposed the war, he said, they had opposed the victory and were prepared to forgo the fruits of it; and in their advocacy of the principles of international Bolshevism had forfeited the right even to be considered as champions of the Italian working class. Realizing that his own views would not prevail unless he could weaken the links which traditionally bound the workers to the Socialist Party, he was careful to demonstrate by his articles and speeches that he himself was still their friend and advocate. He was, he assured them, although no longer a Socialist, still unremittingly anti-bourgeois and anti-capitalist.

But although there could be no doubt now what Mussolini was against, there was still in 1919 considerable doubt what he was for. And on 23 March, when at his instigation a group of men met in a room at the Milan Association of Merchants and Shopkeepers in Piazza San Sepolcro in Milan to found a new force in national politics, there was still doubt as to what his policy was. His supporters were a curious rag-bag of discontented Socialists and Syndicalists, republicans, anarchists, unclassifiable revolutionaries, and restless soldiers many of whom had been *Arditi* (the impetuous Commandos of the Italian Army), and some of them were wanted by the police.[1] They formed themselves into what

1. The number of men who attended this meeting is not known. There were, perhaps, less than 200. Mussolini, who wanted to emphasize the importance of a dedicated minority, subsequently put the number of men who signed the programme at forty-five. After the triumph of Facsism, however, hundreds of men who called themselves *Sansepolcristi*, after the place where the meeting had been held, claimed to have been there. They were recognized as the *élite* of Fascism.

Mussolini called a *Fascio di Combattimento*, a fighting group, bound by ties as close as those that secured the *fascinae* of the lictors, the symbols of Roman authority. But apart from forthright declarations in favour of nationalist sentiments, the Milan *Fascio* had little to offer a largely unimpressed and vaguely suspicious public which doubted the honesty, let alone the political possibility, of a programme which included an 80 per cent tax on war profits, a heavy capital levy, the confiscation of property belonging to the Church, the annexation of Dalmatia, the abolition of the Stock Exchange, and the handing over of industrial management to the workers. Throughout 1919 the new movement gained little support. It was joined by other ex-soldiers, by a few more disillusioned Socialists and angry young Syndicalists, by conservative monarchists and former Army officers such as Cesare Maria de Vecchi and General Emilio De Bono. But the hybrid nature of the movement, the contradictions between Mussolini who still, as Mr Denis Mack Smith has said, 'fancied himself the Lenin of Italy', and the conservative elements who considered his ideas on the occupation of the factories more Bolshevik than the Bolsheviks, were its ruin. When the Fascists put themselves forward as candidates for the Chamber of Deputies in October 1919 they received only 4,000 votes. Their Socialist opponents received more than forty times as many, and 100 Christian Democrats were elected to the Chamber of Deputies. Mussolini, *Avanti !* declared in triumph, was a political corpse. His coffin was paraded up and down the streets of Milan surrounded by candles and accompanied by dirge-chanting demonstrators. His effigy was burned in Piazza del Duomo. A few days after his heavy defeat the offices of his paper were entered by the police. Concerned by his unequivocal support of D'Annunzio's dramatic and flamboyant action in occupying Fiume in the name of Italy, Francesco Nitti, the Premier, had ordered Mussolini's arrest on a charge of 'armed plotting against the State'. The charge seemed justified. The comfortless offices of *Il Popolo d'Italia* were like an arsenal.[1] The cupboards and filing-cabinets were filled with bombs and explosives. There were even bombs in the stove in

1. He never overcame this taste for the flamboyant display of weapons. For many years after he had come to power he exhibited on a table in the ante-room outside his office at Palazzo Venezia a case of duelling-pistols and a pair of sabres.

Mussolini's room, behind the opaque glass walls of his bookcase and in the drawers of his desk; and on top of the desk were his revolver and a stiletto and behind it the skull-embroidered flag of the *Arditi*. Despite these symbols of violence, however, Mussolini was soon released. Nitti was advised that Fascism was a still-born movement and that there was no point in making a martyr of its leader – 'a relic, a defeated man'.

By the beginning of the following June, however, the description applied more truly to Nitti himself. His failure either to meet the challenge of revolutionary strikes and riots or to solve the Adriatic problem, and his weakness in resisting the demands of the Socialists contributed much to the growing influence and strength of Fascism. On 6 June 1920 Nitti retired for the third time in three months and was succeeded by Giovanni Giolitti. But even the skilful and calculating Giolitti was no more able than Nitti had been to control what was widely interpreted as a mounting Bolshevik menace to the security of the state. His efforts to satisfy both Right and Left satisfied neither, and when in September he allowed the Socialists to take over the organization of the workers' occupation of the factories, although he demonstrated the ineffectiveness of the strikers, he lost most of the support of the middle class, who saw in his refusal to intervene the continued toleration of lawlessness. The fact was that the national situation could no longer be controlled by a Government which could not rely upon a working majority in an already discredited Parliament. Inflation was aggravated by subsidies which did not relieve the distress of a painfully impoverished country left milliards of lire in debt by the sudden end of economic help from its Allies; while the problem of unemployment was aggravated by the demobilization of thousands of soldiers and the problem of crime by the existence of no less than 150,000 former deserters who had grown accustomed to living by their wits.

Mussolini and the Fascists were quick to realize the full measure of their opportunity, and it was to be one of Fascism's proudest boasts that power had been achieved after a fierce struggle with Communism, a denial of the true fact that Fascism had drawn its strength from Socialism's weakness. Accepting his defeat in the 1919 elections as evidence that the Fascists could not wrest the working-class from their traditional support of the

Socialists, Mussolini, with characteristic opportunism, dropped his Leninist notions and adopted the language and attitudes which then became essential to the Fascist ethos.

While the strikes and riots against the cost of living grew in frequency and intensity, while all over Italy trains and barracks, banks and public buildings were attacked by mobs, while local Soviets were proclaimed and many areas passed wholly into the hands of the Bolsheviks, while neither the ill-led Socialists nor the Christian Democrats could decide on a common policy which would offer a firm alternative to Fascism, the Fascists put themselves forward as saviours of the country, the only force by which Bolshevism could be checked and strangled. Protesting that violence could only be met by greater violence, squads of Fascists armed with knives and cudgels or with revolvers and rifles brought back from the war attacked Bolsheviks and Bolshevik sympathizers with a ferocity and regularity which soon resulted in a situation almost comparable to civil war. Three thousand anti-Fascists and three hundred Fascists, it was afterwards computed, lost their lives between October 1920 and the March on Rome. Fascist statistics virtually reversed these proportions, but the total numbers are probably correct.

Wearing the black shirts which the labourers of the Marche and Emilia had adopted as the uniform of the anarchists, and carrying the flag of the *Arditi*, the Fascist *squadristi* marched to the attack singing patriotic songs and shouting *legionari* slogans. Composed for the most part of men who had fought in the war and of youths who wished that they had been old enough to fight, of older men fired with that mystical patriotism that had brought volunteers from all over Italy to serve D'Annunzio in Fiume in defiance of the Governments of Europe, and of the criminal adventurers which D'Annunzio had also attracted, these *squadre* obtained the support and admiration of thousands of Italians who were prepared to condone their methods in the belief that only by terrorizing their opponents, by making them salute the Fascist flag as Italo Balbo did in Ferrara, by filling them with castor oil, even killing them, could the disease of international Bolshevism be wiped out. For the Socialists, many of whom were indistinguishable from Bolsheviks, were terrorists and murderers too, and it was folly to show mercy to the merciless. When, for instance, riots

were provoked in Bologna in November 1920 against the Bol-
shevik-dominated town council, it was the Fascists who directed
the demonstrations, organized the resistance, and made the most
of the opportunity of presenting themselves as being on the side of
freedom against tyranny. They were undoubtedly helped in
Bologna as in other towns by the Government's complicity. Neither the Army, nor the *carabinieri,* nor the *guardie regie* were
called out against them by Giolitti or by the other liberal Governments which succeeded him. And so the virus of Fascism was
allowed to spread. Even some trade unions, disillusioned by
Bolshevik interference and broken promises, became converted to
Fascism; and several others, and many town councils, were
forcibly taken over. Despite all this, many liberals and Catholics,
as well as a majority of the most influential of the country's newspapers, took the view that, despicable as the Fascist *squadristi*
might appear to all opponents of violence, they were unquestionably more effective than either Nitti or Giolitti or any of their
supporters had been in saving the country from chaos. There was,
too, running through the hooliganism, the degrading savagery,
the bombast and rather absurd devotion to the less admirable
military virtues, an unmistakable thread of patriotic zeal and
idealism. There were those, of course, who supported the Fascists
for selfish reasons – industrialists and war profiteers who saw
their factories and capital threatened and who hoped, as Giolitti
himself did, that they could use Fascism to crush Socialism, landlords who looked to the *squadristi* to protect their property,
peasants who hoped to wrest land from Socialist farmers, angry
soldiers impatient to satisfy grievances against those who had
stayed at home and anxious to enjoy the fruits of the social revolution which the war had brought about, opportunists who saw in a
possible Fascist State careers and money and power which would
otherwise have been denied them. But there were also many
idealists in the movement. Puccini, for instance, supported it and
Toscanini was actually a Fascist candidate in 1919. Benedetto
Croce thought Fascism in power would be better than the existing
anarchy and believed, like Giolitti, that the Party might be converted to constitutionalism. Many Catholics supported the movement too, as they saw in it the only firm defence against the athe-
ism of the Bolsheviks. And so by the end of 1920, from bad sources

and from good, Fascism had built for itself a large body of political support. In the elections of May 1921 in an anti-Socialist alliance with Giolitti, for which the liberals never forgave the ageing Premier, thirty-five Fascists were elected to the Chamber of Deputies, and one of these was Mussolini. He fully realized now the opportunities which were being presented to him. In the uncertainty and chaos of Italian life he was beginning to gather round him, as Lenin and the Russian Bolsheviks had done, a group of dedicated revolutionaries prepared to seize power in the name of the workers whether or not the workers supported them. And it was he who would lead them. He had seen the Socialists losing influence before Italy's entry into the war and he had abandoned a Party which he saw that he could no longer lead to power; but Fascism he could lead to power, and power excited him and never failed to excite him. 'I am obsessed by this wild desire,' he confessed without shame years later. 'It consumes my whole being. I want to make a mark on my era with my will, like a lion with its claw. A mark like this!' And savagely he scratched the covering of a chair-back from end to end. He would do anything to fulfil his ambitions, he admitted. The end was always the justification of the means. The Fascist policy of *squadrismo*, for instance, had been a calculated effort to stir up unrest and disillusion. Presenting themselves as patriotic anti-Bolsheviks, the *squadristi* had been able to provoke and intensify an anarchic situation which would make the people willing to accept the authoritarian régime that was to be imposed upon them.

After the elections of May 1921, two years after having been a somewhat discredited and friendless revolutionist, the editor of a Milan newspaper, Mussolini had become a national figure, the leader at thirty-seven of a political party which was growing every month in size and influence. His maintained leadership was the most remarkable tribute to his political gifts, for the Fascists, despite their militaristic techniques and proclaimed ethos of unity, were still, in fact, a widely disunited group. And Mussolini was constantly obliged to qualify a previous declaration, change a course formerly pronounced unalterable, even to contradict himself in his efforts to control the more impetuous *squadristi*, while in his speeches and in the columns of his paper appearing as the fiery Romagnol revolutionary. To widen the basis of Fascist support he referred, for example, to the great role which the House of Savoy had played and could play in the nation's history, although not long before he had spoken often of the 'republican tendencies of Fascism'. Anxious to obtain Giolitti's support for the inclusion of Fascist candidates in his lists, he had been prepared to support the Treaty of Rapallo, by which Italian claims to Dalmatia were renounced. Concerned to keep the support of the industrialists and manufacturers, upon whose financial support he had come to rely, he declared in one of those rare speeches in the Chamber of Deputies that there must be 'no further attempt to occupy the factories', an attempt he had supported eighteen months before. And yet in August 1921 he went so far in the opposite direction as to sign a pact of pacification with the Socialists, declaring that it was 'ridiculous to talk as though the Italian working-class were heading for Bolshevism' and that he would defend the pact with all his strength. 'If Fascism does not follow me in collaboration with the Socialists,' he added, 'at least no one can force me to follow Fascism.' Three months later, however, after it had become clear that Fascism was not prepared to follow him and that the Fascist federations were not willing to accept Mussolini's warning that public opinion was slipping away from them and it was necessary to consolidate Fascist successes by a parliamentary compromise, the pact was abandoned. And all the time while repeatedly insisting at Fascist meetings that a *coup d'état* to overthrow Parliament and the liberal State was necessary and imminent, he was as constantly restraining his more impatient colleagues Italo Balbo, Dino Grandi, and Roberto Farinacci from putting any plans for a *coup* into effect. He was, indeed, not as confident as they were that Fascism was sufficiently powerful yet to be sure of success, and he was also more anxious than they that the Fascists should assume power with an approval which was at least general if not universal. Many Fascist Deputies had been helped on their way to the Chamber by the bludgeons of their supporters, and the number of deaths on polling day had disturbed him. 'The trouble with Mussolini,' one of his more arrogantly ruthless henchmen said, 'is that he wants everybody's blessing and changes his coat ten times a day to get it.'

In August 1922, after months of vacillation and uncertainty, Mussolini saw his chance clearly. In that month, to the fury of an exasperated public, a general strike was called. Mussolini declared that unless the Government prevented the strike, the Fascists would. The opportunity of violence in the name of law and order was again presented to him. At Ancona, Leghorn, and Genoa, the *squadristi* attacked Socialist buildings and burned them to the ground; and in Milan they broke up the printing presses of *Avanti !*

Two months later, at a Party congress held in Naples, Mussolini was so impressed by the obvious determination of 40,000 Fascists that he said more and threatened more than he had ever done before. 'What we have in view,' he declared, 'is the introduction into the liberal State, which has fulfilled its functions . . . of all the forces of the new generation which has emerged from the war and the victory. . . . Either the Government will be given to us or we shall seize it by marching on Rome.'

'*Roma ! Roma !*' repeated the *claque*. '*Roma ! Roma !*' thousands of other voices shouted, taking up the cry.

2

The March on Rome had already been discussed by Mussolini and four leading Fascists who were later to be known as the *Quadrumviri* – Italo Balbo, the strikingly handsome twenty-six-year-old leader of the *squadristi*; General Emilio De Bono, a former commander of the Italian Army's IX Corps; Cesare Maria De Vecchi, a Fascist Deputy; and Michele Bianchi, General Secretary of the Party. Balbo later suggested that it was himself and Bianchi who advocated the March on Rome and that Mussolini was so cautious that it was considered necessary to tell him that the Fascists would march on Rome whether Mussolini agreed or not. This was not Mussolini's own version, and there is no doubt that, whether his apparent hesitation was contrived or not, it did enable him to maintain contacts with all his opponents, none of whom was certain until the last moment whether he might even then choose collaboration with them instead of leading a purely Fascist revolution. It is at least certain that when he returned from the Naples Congress in October, he was convinced that the time for action had come and that Luigi Facta's Government, which had succeeded Ivanoe Bonomi's, which in turn had succeeded

Giolitti's, was unable and unprepared to resist determined action. On 27 October Fascist riots broke out in several Italian towns, and the *Quadrumviri* called on Facta to resign. The following morning, in four converging columns, the March on Rome began. The Government, stung at last into action, proclaimed its intention to declare martial law, but the King, fearing that this would mean civil war and already, in any event, prepared to countenance a Fascist Government, refused to sign the decree and so left the Government powerless. In desperation, as the Fascist columns closed on the capital, various leaders of the Party were offered seats in a new coalition Government of the Right under Antonio Salandra. Grandi and De Vecchi advised Mussolini to accept. But he refused. He saw full power in sight now and he was not prepared to compromise, although the fear that he might have gone too far obsessed him.

He was still in Milan. His offices were surrounded by units of the Army and the police, and he kept looking out of the window and telephoning constantly for news. He was making a strenuous effort to appear calm and controlled, but his excitement was close to hysteria. When a squadron of tanks rolled through the streets towards *Il Popolo d'Italia* he ran out of the building with a rifle in his hands shouting incoherently and was nearly shot by a sup- porter even more excited than he was. In fact there was practi- cally no opposition to the march of Fascism. Both the Army and the police were prepared to stand aside and let it take its course.

At last a telephone message came from Rome calling him there for a consultation with the King. 'I shall want it in writing,' he said curtly, his confidence returning. A telegram arrived shortly afterwards: 'Very urgent. Top Priority. Mussolini – Milan. H.M. the King asks you to proceed immediately to Rome as he wishes to offer you the responsibility of forming a Ministry. With respect – Cittadini, General.'

He left by train that evening. As if to make his black shirt more respectable he was wearing, in addition, a journalist delightedly noticed, a bowler-hat and spats. When he presented himself to the King he apologized for this unconventional attire. 'Please excuse my appearance,' he said, and then added a dramatic comment both predictable and unashamedly vainglorious: 'I come from the battlefield.'

> *The crowd loves strong men. The crowd is like
> a woman. . . . Everything turns upon one's
> ability to control it like an artist.*

'I could have transformed this grey hall,' Mussolini reminded
the Chamber of Deputies in the first speech he made there after his
acceptance of the King's request that he should form a Government, 'into an armed camp of Blackshirts, a bivouac for corpses. I
could have nailed up the doors of Parliament.'

Although his Fascist supporters, most of whom did not get
within forty miles of Rome, could easily have been overpowered
by the troops in the capital if the King had agreed to use them, it
was not in effect an unfounded boast; but having achieved power
by the threat of force he began to exercise it with restraint. The
day following his meeting with King Victor Emmanuel he gave
orders for the 25,000 *squadristi* who were still camped outside
Rome to be brought into the capital by special trains and after
marching past the Quirinale to go peaceably home again. He
punished severely those who had been guilty of violence and
seemed anxious to demonstrate that he was now not only the
leader of Fascism but the Head of the Government of Italy. His
Cabinet, which he had formed within seven hours, included men
from all the main political groups except the anti-nationalists,
portfolios being given to Social Democrats, Catholics, and liberals.
Only four Fascists were included.

There could be no doubt, however, that he had come to Rome
not to preside over a coalition but to govern authoritatively and
personally through his own Party. He appointed himself Minister
of Foreign Affairs as well as Minister of the Interior and demanded from the Chamber of Deputies full powers for a year to
carry out what he considered to be essential reforms. These

powers were voted to him by a majority of 275 votes to 90.

He set to work with an energy and determination which even his severest critics could not but admire. He got up early, performed a variety of violent exercises until his hairy, barrel-shaped chest was glistening with sweat, and then after a breakfast of fruit and milk rushed to his office, where he was at work by eight o'clock having already read with astonishing speed several of the Italian and foreign newspapers with which his rooms were always cluttered. His meals were sparse, for the ulcer which was to trouble him increasingly for the rest of his life had already formed in his stomach; and often he would have nothing at either lunch or dinner but spaghetti with a little wholemeal bread, fresh vegetables, and fruit, preferably spinach and black grapes. He drank quantities of milk and fruit juice, but, because of the ulcer, very little wine, and he had not smoked since the war. He had once been fond of his food, but now he ate hurriedly and without interest, proud of his Spartan table and his rigorous abstinence at State banquets, attacking the *buongustai* and the *bevitori* for indulging in such decadent pleasures. He had no pleasures himself, he insisted, he only had his work. It was at this time largely true. He took fencing lessons and boxing lessons, he swam and took up tennis, but those who taught him or played with him believed he took this exercise not so much because he enjoyed it as because he had a passion for physical fitness and for the possession of a hard, strong body.[1] He was, in fact, becoming rather fat. His fingers were chubby and soft, and the flesh of his massive jaw sagged when he did not remember to keep it well thrust out. He looked older than thirty-nine, for his dark and flashing eyes were heavily shadowed and the front part of his head was quite bald and the hairs at the back were greying. But his energy was indefatigable. Restless, impatient, vibrant, nervous, he seemed never tired and never relaxed. Still compulsively sexual he assaulted the various women who came to the room he took in a hotel, and afterwards to his flat in an upper floor of a *palazzo* in Via Rasella with a phrenetic passion which was always exciting and often frightening. As impatient with them as with his less effective Ministers, he

1. He had a horror of physical deformity and could summon no sympathy for sickness, which embarrassed him. One day he met Prince Torlonia, who complained of a boil. 'I once had a friend with the same trouble,' Mussolini told him shortly; 'he died almost at once.'

ravished them as a conquering war-lord might ravish his captured slaves, and seems to have enjoyed the process whoever his companion might be. For his taste was wonderfully catholic. As a young man he had preferred intellectual women and had had a particular interest in schoolteachers. But now he liked all women indiscriminately, provided they were not too thin; and his only requirement was that they should smell strongly, either of scent if their bodies had little natural smell or preferably of sweat. He did not mind if they were not clean and often dabbed his own body with *eau-de-Cologne* instead of washing. Totally uninhibited and wholly egocentric, he gave little thought to his lovers' comfort or their pleasure, often choosing the floor in preference to the bed, removing neither his trousers nor his shoes. The whole uncontrolled process was usually over in a minute or two. The women – unmarried journalists and the wives of Fascists, countesses and maids, actresses and foreign visitors – who then and later were ravished by Mussolini in this way spoke of their experiences afterwards without regret and frequently with pride. One of them, who had at first been disgusted by his habit of experimentally squeezing her breasts before thrusting himself upon her, went back to him again because she found herself unable to 'refuse a man of such importance'. Others less conscious of his importance were enraptured by the unfettered sensuality of his love-making, particularly when his brutality and savage curses in the moments of climax were followed by words of tenderness, however brief and however commonplace, when he was satisfied. For Mussolini was capable, so most of these women have said, of affection as well as of ferocity, of caresses, even of sentiment. One of them has spoken of his habit of taking up his violin to play some appropriate piece to her as soon as he lifted himself from her body. And all of them were agreed that despite his selfish roughness, broken only occasionally by flashes of affection, there was something appealing in Mussolini's completely unselfconscious clumsiness, his refusal to conform to any accepted patterns of behaviour.

He carried this unconventionality into public life. He had not shaved every day in Milan; he did not do so during these first few months in Rome and went so far as to attend unshaven a reception held at the Constanzi in honour of the King and Queen of Spain. The clothes he wore on these occasions were often startling. His shirts were not always clean and his shoes were rarely polished. The shoes, however, were not often seen, as he had developed a taste for spats which he wore buttoned high up his ankles in a fashion long outmoded. He had no interest in, nor indeed any conception of, fashion and did not see why he should not wear spats with evening dress if they kept his feet warm. Nor did he see why he should not wear a black tie with tails, and he did so. He could not be bothered to tie up shoelaces, so he had elastic laces with made-up bows. He bought a morning suit for wearing at the office as the striped trousers and cut-away black coat appealed to him, but he did not look well in it and was constantly wriggling his neck in the butterfly collar and shaking back the cuffs of his starched shirt. When Rachele came to Rome he looked a little better starched than he had done before; but at the beginning she stayed behind in Milan with Edda and their two boys – Vittorio, born in 1916 soon after they were married, and Bruno, born in 1918. Rachele did not want to come to Rome. She was conscious of the fact that she looked and talked like a Romagnol peasant and would feel out of place and unhappy. She did not want to share Benito's public life but just to remain a wife and a mother to his children, and she knew that was all he expected or wanted from her. When friends had called to see him in Via Merenda before the war, they had often found Rachele doing the family's washing in the courtyard.

'Is he in?' one of them called to her one day.

He was out, Rachele said, referring to him as 'the master' as wives do in the Romagna.

'Where's he gone?'

'I don't know. He never tells me what he's doing.'

He never did. There was no resentment. Men were like this. It was a happy marriage. She realized her husband was a *donnaiuolo* and she was later to admit that she knew he had about twenty mistresses – 'and what of it?' she wanted to know; he loved his family as well. *Donnaiuoli* usually do. She did not blame him. She was a hard-working, capable housewife, loyal, humourless, sometimes ill-tempered, often sulky. She was simple, but she had a peasant's shrewdness. She understood little about her husband and less about his work and always irritated him when she attempted to advise or warn him, and so rarely did. Later when she moved to

Rome she was constantly receiving anonymous letters and telephone calls and messages from her friends, but when she spoke to her husband he would say sharply, 'You know nothing about it.' And it was true, and she did not mind him telling her so. 'He was always the best of fathers and a good husband,' she said when he was dead, and that was true as well.

'What a character!' she is reported to have exclaimed, amused and proud and puzzled, when told that Benito had been made Head of the Government.

The men who had to work for him expressed their opinion of him in similar terms. To some he was a genius, to others merely *louche*, but to all remarkable. He was, of course, a brilliant propagandist and he did not hesitate to use his genius for publicity not merely in order to project his own personality but to create an image, part fact and part fantasy, of a man of destiny natively cunning and widely learned. Often, it must be said, his anxiety to demonstrate his cleverness was manifest and therefore absurd. The German writer Emil Ludwig, to whom he granted a series of interviews in 1932, while presenting in his *Mussolinis Gespräche mit Emil Ludwig* the picture of an experienced and deeply read man, gave at the same time the impression of one who could never let pass an opportunity of showing off. Being an egotist he could not, of course, bear to be laughed at – and it is interesting to reflect how many actions of his life were prompted by a desire to have his revenge on those whom he took to be guilty of this offence and offences like it – but being also an unsophisticated man he constantly gave cause for men to laugh at him. 'He never attempted to correct my faulty Italian,' Ludwig said, 'but when, on one occasion, I mispronounced a French name, the sometime schoolmaster peeped out amusingly, and in a low tone he uttered it as it should have been spoken. When, in his turn, he wanted to speak of the *Umwertung aller Werte* and, despite his intimate knowledge of our language, made a slip, he corrected himself by adding "*genitivus pluralis*".' 'Forgive my learned references', was a phrase which he often used when talking to members of his Government and the *gerarchi*. Ulrich von Hassell, later to become German Ambassador in Rome, and Filippo Anfuso, the Italian diplomat, both noted this anxiety of the Duce's to appear more learned that he was. Anfuso tells the story of a conversation he once had with Mussolini and his family during which the Duce commented on Nietzsche's excellent knowledge of Greek. 'But, Papa, you don't know Greek!' one of his children interrupted him in a piping voice, and when his father affected not to have heard him he said it again. Mussolini felt obliged to lead his guest from the room. Hassell recorded with contempt an occasion upon which Mussolini was photographed winning at chess, a game which he did not even play. Hassell also suspected, as many others did, that Mussolini's celebrated memory was little more than a trick, and that in order to impress his listeners he committed various figures and statistics to memory shortly before he intended bringing them out as if from a great store of remembered knowledge. Ludwig, however, was taken in by this and so were most of Mussolini's Ministers, to whom he behaved in a way calculated to inspire their fear and admiration. By turns he was outlandishly rude and graciously charming, impetuous and wary, ferocious and forgiving; they never knew how he would react to them or when they might be, as they often were, replaced without warning for no reason which they could understand, but which, often enough, was because the Duce had felt their influence a threat to his position on the pinnacle of power, where he was frankly determined to remain. In the morning he would telephone a Minister and without any greeting shout at him a string of peremptory instructions and then, a few hours later, he would telephone again and speak to him perhaps as if he were his closest friend. Unpredictable, excitable, and glowing with vitality and the proud knowledge of his power, he was as capable of arousing craven fear by his anger as devotion by the benedictory peace of his forgiveness.

Within a few months of his rise to power, his success seemed assured. The tumult of Italy had subsided into a mood of guarded but admiring watchfulness. The workers went back to the factories, production increased, the streets were quiet, the students took up their books again. On assuming office he had no political programme and contented himself with undertaking to balance the budget, ensure a fair deal for the workers, and conduct the country's foreign policy with determination and dignity. 'We shall succeed,' he said, 'because we shall work.' And with the skill of the great propagandist that he was, he succeeded in impressing upon the people how hard he worked himself, not only at his desk but in the factories and fields encouraging the workers. Pictures of him laying bricks, hammering with fierce concentration in smithies, cutting corn with his great chest photographed as he liked to have it photographed, naked and glistening in the sun, appeared daily in the Press.

The Italians followed his lead. He was the youngest Prime Minister they had ever had, and most of them were proud of him. They accepted with pleasure the restoration of the eight-hour day, enormous cuts in Government expenditure (which had grown so large under previous administrations that the estimated deficit for 1922–3 was 6,500 million lire), the transference to the retired list or to other work of thousands of officials. Within two years a deficit in the postal services of 500 million lire was converted, according to Fascist calculations which have not been shown to be false, to a surplus of 43 million lire and a deficit on the railways of 1,400 million lire was converted to a surplus of 176 million lire. And what was more, Italians were proud to tell you, the trains ran on time.

The Italians, indeed, began to feel pride in many things. Fascism seemed to work. Mussolini had the backing of the people and he was careful to nourish the impression that he had saved them from chaos and Bolshevism. The disillusion of the workers with their Socialist leaders, their reaction against social-reformism, and the inability of the Italian Bolsheviks to agree on a common policy had, in fact, done more to save them, and Mussolini himself realized this; and, because he realized it, he was infuriated by those who discovered and propagated the truth that Fascism was a counter-revolution against a revolution which never took place. 'Bolshevism in Italy,' he declared without undue exaggeration long before the March on Rome, 'is dead.' But that it had come to power to save the country from Bolshevism was one of Fascism's most assiduously fostered myths. A second, which grew from it and became in the end the principal tenet of faith, was the myth of the leader as Superman and not only as the all-powerful, all-wise *Duce del Fascismo* who was never wrong, but who was also, like God himself, just and merciful and benevolent. For Fascism, although its prophets had at first proclaimed that it was a movement and not a doctrine – 'our programme',

Mussolini had said, 'is deeds. We have no ready-made doctrine' – now presented itself as a moral force as much as a political one. Authoritative, virile, austere, and nationalist, the true Fascist must, as the Duce explained, 'consider himself the devotee of a faith of corporate discipline . . . the rightful descendant of Caesar'. Fascism, in fact, as Professor Alfredo Rocco, one of its early intellectuals, said, explaining the Duce's more abstruse and often derivative philosophizing, 'rejects democratic theories of the State and proposes that society does not exist for the individual but the individual for society. Fascism does not abolish the individual as individuals have abolished society in other more primitive doctrines, but subordinates him to society leaving him free to develop his personality on lines which will benefit his fellow-men'.

Attempts were made by Rocco and Gentile and other Fascist apologists to show that the theory of Fascism was in no sense contradictory to the 'fundamental trends of Italian history'. Garibaldi and Mazzini were shown to be Fascists at heart. But attempts like these to explain Fascism intellectually or historically made little impact upon the Italian people, and Mussolini himself once said that they should only be made with a view to the effect that they might have on the foreigner. The Italians, he thought, should not try to understand Fascism, but experience it. They should not think, they should feel. And it was in order to impress them with its emotional nature that Fascism was presented as a 'mystical vision' with symbols and fetishes, liturgical formulas, and choreographic techniques; with atavistic incantations, medieval trappings, and suggested affinities to the 'classic spirit of Rome'. Fascism, its critics said, was a fraudulent substitute, a kind of mental and political margarine, as Ignazio Silone called it, but Mussolini saw virtue in this. Fascism could replace truth, liberty, art, and thought, as well as Socialism and democracy, and it could above all, supremely above all for him, provide the need for a leader and a prophet.

And in himself Fascism had such a man. In speeches all over the country, painstakingly prepared but delivered as if spontaneously, full of easily remembered catchwords and phrases, he developed that eloquence and wonderful power of communication that he had practised long ago in the Romagna. The dialogue with the crowd, which had delighted the audiences of his home-land and which D'Annunzio had found so inspiring in Fiume, thrilled a whole country that felt itself awakened to a new and brilliant future under the guidance of a man who could achieve anything. The repetitive and meaningless cries, such as the '*eia! eia! alalà!*' invented by D'Annunzio during the war, that became an essential part of the ritual hysteria of Fascist demonstrations, increased the illusion of unity and power, and heightened the fever of adulation.

And yet, the people were told, in spite of his consummate genius the Duce was a simple man and a good one. When he had spoken to the hungry peasants of the South and seen their dry and withered skins the tears had poured from his eyes. 'I will care for you,' he said. 'I too have known hunger.' They believed him and they trusted him.[1]

They were told too that he was modest. 'I do not feel myself worthy of this honour,' he said when created an honorary citizen of Florence. He would only accept an honorary degree in law from the University of Rome on condition that he wrote a thesis to justify it, and when it was first offered to him he refused the collar of the Order of the Annunziata, Italy's most coveted decoration. The refusal was not, as even his enemies admitted, entirely calculated. He had an apparently genuine lack of interest in such things. Years later his Foreign Secretary described an occasion on which he asked the Duce if he might award Baldur von Schirach the Grand Cordon of San Maurizio. 'Certainly,' Mussolini replied impatiently. 'And you can give him my decorations too if you like.' Ciano also described another occasion when the Ministry of Fine Arts were having difficulty in finding a work of art which would be suitable as a present for Reichsmarshal Goering on his fiftieth birthday. 'At home the Duce only owns one good piece,' the Minister wrote, 'a self-portrait by Mancini. . . . Well, when he heard that a gift had to be made to Goering . . . he immediately

1. Two stories illustrate the idolatry with which hundreds of thousands – if not millions – of ill-educated Italians regarded their Duce. When Etna exploded and he visited the endangered areas it was widely believed in the South that he had succeeded where Canute had failed and checked the forces of nature; and at least one newspaper reported it as a fact. When a visitor to the Etruscan tombs of Orvieto was told that the inscriptions had not yet been deciphered, for they were written in an unknown language, she replied confidently, 'Oh, that's because Mussolini hasn't been here yet. When he comes he'll find out.' This trusting confidence was not in the least exceptional.

thought of giving his Mancini. I had to argue a great deal to make him change his mind. . . . The Duce's indifference to personal possessions is moving.'

Soon after coming to Rome he decided not to accept any salary as either Premier or Minister or Deputy, living on the money he received for the articles he still wrote, mainly for American papers and from *Il Popolo d'Italia*.[1] He had a profound contempt for those whose overriding ambition was to be rich. It was a mania, he thought, 'a kind of disease', and he comforted himself with the reflection that the rich were rarely happy, and he would refer with satisfaction to Rockefeller, who had lived 'on milk and oranges for the last sixteen years of his life'. But although he had no private wealth, nor ever wanted it, Mussolini did not live austerely. He was not a gourmet, his mistresses rarely received as presents so much as a pair of stockings or a bottle of scent, his children went to State schools, his wife lived simply, he wore the same suit day in and day out for weeks on end, but he never, on the grounds of economy, refrained from indulging a whim. He had taken flying lessons in Milan, and now that he was qualified as a pilot he had his own aeroplane and took it up whenever he felt inclined; he enjoyed driving, and so ordered an expensive red sports car; he enjoyed riding, and soon had a string of horses in his stables; he liked reviewing the Fleet and the Army and later on he took immense pleasure in air displays, and his opponents frequently accused him of ordering these expensive demonstrations because of the personal satisfaction they gave him; he was fond of animals, so when he had grounds in which to keep them he had what amounted almost to a zoo – not only horses and dogs, but gazelles, a monkey, an eagle, a deer, a tiger cub, several cats which were his favourite animals, even a puma which he kept on a leash in his room until it broke loose one night and roamed through the house to the terror of the staff; he liked films – particularly newsreels that showed him impressing a crowd and the comedies of Laurel and Hardy – so he had his own cinema built. In addition to a sea-side villa he had two large houses – Villa Torlonia in Rome and in

---

1. He remained uninterested in money to the end. It was with the greatest difficulty he was persuaded to accept a salary as President of the Social Republic in 1943. 'What do I want with all that money?' he asked when a secretary brought him a decree prepared by one of his Ministers which allowed him 125,000 lire a month; and he refused to sign it.

the Romagna, Rocca delle Caminate, which was presented to him by the province of Forlì.

Villa Torlonia, a large, cool, graceful house of classical symmetry, stands behind high walls in a lovely garden in Via Nomentana beyond Piazzi di Porta Pia. It belonged to Prince Giovanni Torlonia of the Rome banking house, who offered to place it at the Duce's disposal for as long as he wanted it. Mussolini, who admired its dignity and those deep ochre walls which give to buildings of Rome their incomparable loveliness, accepted the offer gratefully and enjoyed living in the house well enough; but he liked to get away whenever he could to Rocca delle Caminate, a feudal, battlemented castle perched on a high hilltop from which he could look across the countryside of his youth to the Apennines in the south and in the distance, eastwards, to the shores of the Adriatic. This castle was a ruin when he was presented with it, but over the years large sums were spent on its renovation, and it became filled with the gifts which came to the Duce from all over the world, so that outside his tastelessly furnished study, the walls of which were lined with photographs, many of them depicting himself in his various activities as sportsman, pilot, father, and ruler, Rocca delle Caminate was more like a museum than a house. Indeed, towards the end of his life he told the German doctor, Professor Zachariae, that that is what he hoped it would become. He also told him that one item there, a painting on silk given to him by the Emperor of Japan, was the finest of its sort in the world and that an American millionaire had shocked him by offering him several million dollars for it. But it was not his to sell, Mussolini reminded the American curtly, it was not a personal possession, it belonged to Italy.

This identification of himself with his country, later to become so obsessive that any attack on Italy was resented as a personal insult, was part of the secret of the Duce's firm hold on the loyalty and imagination of his people. For the young, patriotic Italians of the early nineteen-twenties, at least, the Duce's arrogant nationalism was his finest contribution to the new *risorgimento*. But it was not only to these young men but to a large majority of the Italian people as a whole that Mussolini seemed, in these early years of power, an impeccable paragon. He could do little wrong. He was careful enough to move so slowly and to act so unobtrusively that the construction of a new, illiberal State was scarcely noticed at first; he had no settled policy, adopting ideas and methods as they came to hand, solving problems fortuitously as they arose, now giving his régime what he called a 'progressively Fascist' look by Gentile's Education Act of 1923, now making it appear sound and respectable by a respectful attitude towards the susceptibilities of Catholic voters and the Church. The growing suppression of liberty, which he felt able to refer to publicly as a 'more or less putrid goddess', over which Fascism had stepped and 'would if need be quietly turn round to step over again', was accepted as a necessity if Italy was to become strong and throw off the atrophy of dissension which had been crippling her for years. The reduction of Parliament to an assembly of ineffectuals was not regretted by those millions of Italians who had agreed with Mussolini's youthful description of it as 'a gathering of old fossils'. The gradual denial of freedom to the Press, the establishment of a regular Fascist Militia of nearly 200,000 men to take the place of the ill-organized *squadristi*, many of whom were incorporated in it, the enforced but weakly resisted dissolution of the *guardie regie*, the spreading of Fascist ethics into every aspect of Italian life which could be infected, even the violent punishments dealt out to outspoken critics of the régime, were accepted by the great majority of the people as essential prerequisites to the establishment of the sort of Italy which was promised them. 'The people,' Mussolini declared in July 1924, 'on the innumerable occasions when I have been face to face with them and have spoken with them close at hand . . . have never asked me to free them from a tyranny which they do not feel because it does not exist. They have asked me for railways, houses, drains, bridges, water, light, and roads.' It was largely true. The benefits of Fascism were felt to outweigh its disadvantages and faults.

Mussolini, himself, was exempted from most of the blame attending the savage and squalid beatings-up of his opponents; and indeed he did not, so far as can be known, specifically order them and certainly took care not to appear the instigator. Only occasionally was his complicity made known, as when a French newspaper discovered and published the facsimile of a message from Mussolini to the Prefect of Turin in which orders were given for life to be 'made impossible' for the dangerous anti-Fascist Piero

Gobetti, who was beaten up so badly in Turin that his broken ribs punctured a lung. Similarly in July 1923, according to Cesare Rossi, at that time head of the Fascist Press Office, the Fascist headquarters in Florence, Pisa, Milan, and Monza and other smaller towns received instructions from Mussolini to wreck the premises of the local Catholic associations. At the same time the prefects of each town where an anti-Catholic demonstration had been held received a telegram from Mussolini which said: 'In view unfavourable repercussions Vatican latest anti-Catholic incidents it would be well if local leaders provincial Fascist Federation officially approached the archiepiscopal see to present regrets renewing assurances of high respect of Fascism for Catholicism.'

The attempt of Fascist biographers to absolve Mussolini altogether from the charges of connivance at crimes like these or to ignore their existence is, to say the least, disingenuous. Once the Press was brought largely under Fascist control the incidents were only briefly reported and sometimes not at all; but it is certain that they continued for some time and that the Duce made it known within the Party that it was his conviction that, for Fascism to survive, its enemies must be made to 'live in fear'.

In the summer of 1924, however, millions of non-Fascists who were prepared to overlook even the worst excesses of the régime in the hope that they were the price which had to be paid for an honourable future, were suddenly and deeply shocked by an outrage which it was difficult to forgive and impossible to ameliorate. Mussolini did not give orders for the outrage to be committed, nor did he know that it was being contemplated, but his responsibility for it is at least as great as Henry II's for the murder of Thomas Becket. Unlike Henry, however, Mussolini did not do public penance at the victim's tomb.

13 JUNE 1924–10 JUNE 1940

Liberty is not an end. It is a means.
As a means it must be controlled and dominated.

I

In the summer of 1923 Mussolini had drafted a Bill, afterwards known as the Acerbo Electoral Law, by which Italy was to be divided into fifteen constituencies, each elector being asked to vote for the party of his choice. The party which secured relatively the largest number of votes, provided it was at least a quarter of the total of votes cast, was to be granted two-thirds of the seats in the Chamber, the remaining third being given to the other parties on a proportional basis. Although the Bill met with opposition from Socialists, Liberals, and Catholics alike, most deputies had not lost their confidence in Mussolini's Government and were prepared to support it or at least to abstain from voting against it. In July, watched by armed Blackshirts in the public gallery, they passed it by a large majority; and in November it was given an even larger majority in the Senate. In April the following year the elections were held, and the voters went to the polling-booths past the watchful eyes of the Fascist Militia. Helped by the failure of his opponents to agree on a common policy of opposition, and by the intimidation of opposition newspapers, his appeal to the country for support in continuing the work which had so far been accomplished was triumphant – 65·25 per cent of the votes, excluding those given for minority candidates prepared to support the Government, were cast in his favour. It was an overwhelming victory, the largest majority given to a Government since the time of Cavour, and it had been achieved, so the Fascists afterwards boasted, without physical bullying except in some isolated instances. But while it was true that violence was not widespread as has sometimes been maintained its incidence was nevertheless much greater than Fascist boasts would suggest, and the intimidation of voters was commonplace. It is also undeniable that Fascism's triumph was largely attributable to fraud. Votes were planted, ballots and totals tampered with in almost every constituency.

But superficially, Fascism having achieved power by the threat of force was confirmed in power by the apparent will of the people. Mussolini, immensely encouraged by his success, considered a return to normal political conditions and even some form of collaboration with the Socialists. On 7 June, after the newly elected Chamber had given the Government a vote of confidence of 361 to 107, Mussolini indicated that he was prepared to include two Socialists in his Cabinet.

Three days later a Socialist deputy, Giacomo Matteotti, a rich – Mussolini called him 'a millionaire' – landowner from Rovigo, disappeared from Rome. He was one of Fascism's most outspoken critics and was believed to be about to publish documents exposing the activities of its most irresponsible and ruthless henchmen. On 13 June his body was discovered buried in a shallow grave twenty kilometres outside the city.

The murder of the brave and respected man reached the headlines of newspapers all round the world. While Fascist apologists referred to him as an insignificant and malicious agitator whose death was a 'regrettable incident', liberals everywhere spoke of him as one of the great heroes and martyrs of Socialism whose name would be remembered for ever. And so it is; and Mussolini is remembered as his murderer; and so in a sense he was, but not in the sense that his enemies have insisted. Carlo Silvestri, an anti-Fascist journalist, who saw much of Mussolini during the last few months of his life, was convinced that he knew nothing of the plot and had no responsibility for it. Signora Matteotti was also convinced that Mussolini had nothing to do with her husband's death and that he was deeply upset by it. At an anti-Fascist court set up in 1947 to re-try the survivors of the episode these views were generally confirmed, and it was suggested that the murderers – extremist Fascists disturbed by Mussolini's apparent drift towards parliamentarianism – had not intended to kill Matteotti but only to beat him up in the way that they had beaten up his supporters and that his death was actually due to a heart attack. Certainly Mussolini's behaviour after the murder is scarcely consistent with that of an assassin or an accomplice. 'I did not have a moment of doubt or discouragement,' he boasted in his autobiography; but in fact, for several weeks, he was in a state of anxiety verging on hysteria. 'His life,' Margherita Sarfatti says, 'seemed completely wrecked.' He maintained a brave front in public, but in private his distress was pitiable, and he told Silvestri that he considered handing in his resignation. When a woman friend offered him sympathy he broke down. 'My worst enemies,' he said, 'could not have done me as much harm as my friends.'

Two days after the discovery of the body the Socialist Deputies and their allies, led by Giovanni Amendola, whose brave and final condemnatory speech was interrupted by a savagely angry Mussolini twenty-seven times, withdrew from the Chamber and formed an opposition group, which received a degree of support which would have been unthinkable a week before. Known as *I deputati dell'Aventino*, in memory of the Roman plebs who had withdrawn to the Aventine Hill in protest against the aristocracy, they reminded the country of Mussolini's recent attacks on Matteotti and *Il Popolo d'Italia*'s declaration that 'if Matteotti gets his head broken, he will only have himself and his obstinacy to thank'. Hoping that their action would persuade the hesitant King to use his influence in support of parliamentary Government, they demanded the repression of all acts of violence by Fascists and the disbandment of the Fascist Militia. Each evening when Mussolini left his office at Palazzo Chigi to go home, a crowd of people stood in silence to watch him reproachfully; and in the streets of Rome anti-Fascist slogans appeared in hundreds on the walls.

Giovanni Marinelli, the administrative secretary of the Party, Filippo Filippelli, editor of the *Corriere Italiano*, Cesare Rossi, head of the Fascist Press Office, and Filippo Naldo were all arrested as accomplices. But the clamour did not die down. Towards the end of the month those opposition newspapers which had not already come under Fascist influence became more outspoken than ever before, and on 8 July Mussolini brought into force a decree which provided for the suspension of publication of newspapers that continued to print what was interpreted as being seditious matter or incitements to violence. In this way one of Italy's most influential papers, the *Corriere della Sera* of Milan, was later taken out of the hands of the anti-Fascist Senator Albertini and passed into the hands of an editor who was prepared to support Mussolini. Several other liberal and democratic newspapers, including *La Stampa*, were similarly forced into Fascist hands. One of those that for the time being escaped, however, Amendola's paper *Il Mondo*, published at the end of December a document which ended Italy's six months of uneasy opposition to the Fascists. It was a statement by Cesare Rossi, the former head of the Fascist Press Office who had been arrested after the murder, accusing Mussolini of being implicated in the plot. The Duce gave up all hope of reconciliation with the liberals. Accepting the advice of Roberto Farinacci, a former railway clerk who had become a lawyer and one of Fascism's most intransigent leaders, and of various former *squadristi* who had come from all over Italy to bolster up his apparently flagging confidence, he announced in the Chamber, five days after Rossi's allegations had been published, that he had stayed his hand against his perfidious opponents only to calm his more impetuous followers. But now the time for action had come. 'I declare here in front of this assembly,' he said, 'and in front of the Italian people that I and I alone assume the political, moral, and historic responsibility for everything that has happened. If misquoted words are enough to hang a man, then out with the noose and the gallows! If Fascism has been castor oil and club and not a proud passion of the best Italian youth, the blame is on me. If Fascism has been a criminal plot, if violence has resulted from a certain historic, political, and moral atmosphere, the responsibility is mine, because I have deliberately created this atmosphere. . . . Italy wants peace and quiet, work and calm. I will give these things with love if possible and *with force if necessary*.'

The date was 3 January 1925. It was one of the fundamental dates in the history of Fascism.

Thereafter there was no further thought of compromise, no turning back. Although the Matteotti murder had provoked a widespread reaction against Fascism in a suddenly disillusioned country, it had also shown how weak and disorganized were its opponents and how few of them were prepared actively to resist it. Within five years Mussolini was able, with the help of Roberto

Farinacci, the newly appointed Secretary of the Party, to achieve his declared object – the 'complete Fascistization' of Italy. Most of the remaining free newspapers were either suppressed or came under Fascist control. A few self-styled independent papers remained, but were so colourless as to be treated with contempt by the State and with indifference by its opponents. Opposition parties were dissolved, and free elections came to an end. The Chamber of Deputies became little more than a means of clothing Fascist decrees with an aura of national approval; the Senate was filled with *senatori* prepared to wear black shirts when required and to chant Fascist slogans; the Grand Council of Fascism, formed by Mussolini who became its president with full powers to decide its agenda and its membership, was grafted on to the Constitution as a check on any independence which might be displayed by individual members of the Cabinet. Nominated *podestà* took the place of elected mayors in an increasingly centralized autarchy. The Fascist Party song, *Giovinezza*, was sung at all the flamboyant, choreographic displays which the Duce loved, and often instead of the *Marcia Reale*, for the Party was now taken to be synonymous with the State. Strikes and lock-outs were declared to be incompatible with the new, elaborately involved and characteristically corrupt Corporative System, which, Mussolini said, was 'destined to become the civilization of the twentieth century'. In this Corporativism, a less complicated form of which had been evolved in D'Annunzio's Fiume, all labour conflicts were to be referred to labour tribunals, which were attached to the courts of appeal and purported to represent both employers and employed. As all union officials in the twenty-two different categories of trades and professions were eventually appointed by the Party, the Corporative System became in time a convenient mask for dictatorship. More obviously illiberal were the laws which were directed against Freemasonry and against anti-Fascist Italians living abroad and those which extended the authority of the Head of the Government.

As in all totalitarian régimes, particular attention was paid to the young; and children from the age of four were dragooned into Fascist youth organizations, which supplied them with toy machine-guns and black shirts. These measures, each one taken with the intention of imposing an essentially and indisputably

Fascist character on the State and all its institutions and citizens, and of securing – on the Russian Bolshevik model – the hold of the State on all the country's media of information, aroused little opposition amongst the mass of the Italian people, who did not quarrel with the Government's repeatedly voiced contention that whereas a responsible opposition would have been tolerated and even welcomed, a mischievous, anti-national, scandalmongering, hypocritical, and factious opposition could not be. Totalitarian as they were, the laws were accepted – as the more moderate early Fascist laws had been accepted – as a fair price to pay for the new Italy which was already astonishing the world.

For, after years of recurrent economic crises, Italy's exchange seemed steady at last, and the country was enjoying a prosperity general to the whole of Europe but ascribed to the advent of Fascism and its determination to achieve self-sufficiency through a planned economy. Although, in fact, he never comprehended the problems of economics and commerce, Mussolini was quick to accept the credit for a period of recovery which had already begun before he came to power, just as he was quick later on to accept the credit for the country's recovery after a slump which was at least partly caused by his own policies. On the surface the credit did not seem misplaced. In his determination to settle the country's crippling war debt to the United States, he sent his Finance Minister to Washington with his Under-Secretary for Foreign Affairs, Dino Grandi, who concluded an agreement whereby a large reduction was secured. In his determination to win what he called the 'battle for wheat', he toured the country making speeches to the 'brave farmers, fighting in the front line'; and each year the crops grew bigger. Already by 1925 there was a crop of 64 million quintals in comparison with a pre-war average of 49 million. In his determination to make Italy the powerful, modern state of his imagination he instituted a programme of public works hitherto unrivalled in modern Europe. Bridges, canals, and roads were built, hospitals and schools, railway stations and orphanages; swamps were drained and land reclaimed and irrigated, forests were planted and universities endowed. By the end of the nineteen thirties immense schemes had been completed not only on the Italian mainland but in Sicily and Sardinia, Albania and Africa, and even more grandiose schemes were promised, planned and contemplated. In these years, Fascist statisticians boasted, never less than 100,000 labourers were engaged on public works, and by the summer of 1939 170,000 men were working on roads and irrigation schemes in Albania alone. Between 1922 and 1942 the Ministry of Public Works spent 33,634 million lire on such enterprises. Archaeological works were financed in an effort to awaken the people to the memories of their glorious past. 'In five years,' Mussolini told Rome's City Council, 'this city must appear wonderful to the whole world, immense, orderly, and powerful, as she was in the days of the first empire of Augustus. The approaches to the theatre of Marcellus, the Campidoglio, and the Pantheon must be cleared of everything that has grown up round them during the centuries of decadence. Within five years the hill of the Pantheon must be visible through an avenue leading from Piazza Colonna. . . . The third Rome will extend over other hills, along the banks of the sacred river, as far as the shores of the Tyrrhenian Sea.'

But although much that was undeniably imposing and impressive was done, performance in the field of public works, as in the field of economic development and industrialization and indeed in most fields of Fascist enterprise, fell far below both intention and claims. Work was begun but often left unfinished, and immense sums of money disappeared on impossibly grandiose plans or drifted into the pockets of corrupt officials and high-ranking Fascists anxious to make their fortunes while the going was good. Meanwhile, behind the façade of well-advertised schemes of modernization and welfare services, half a million people were still existing in conditions of pitiable squalor. For the sake of the tourists, beggars were kept off the streets by the police; but poverty was not lessened by being kept out of sight. For the sake of victory in the *battaglia del grano*, farmers were given medals and subsidies for helping to cut wheat imports; but the farming industry was seriously affected by this concentration on cereals, which were not, and never had been, an economical agricultural product for Italy. Thousands of small farmers and discontented peasants left the land, while nothing was done to break up the vast landed estates which were one of the main causes of their discontent. As year followed year wages and conditions of work in the towns as well as in the country failed to improve at the rate they did in most other countries in Western Europe.

And yet few blamed the Duce. Fascism was seen to be imperfect; but its founder was still the man of destiny. There might be anti-Fascists, but there were few anti-Mussolinians. Hardly anyone questioned him. He was not only a dictator. He was an idol. Photographs of him were cut out of newspapers and stuck on the walls of thousands of homes, slogans in praise of him were splashed in white paint everywhere, glasses that he had drunk from and pick-axes that he had used during his extensive tours were prized as holy relics. In 1929 when he settled a problem which had been dividing Italy since 1870 and signed with the Vatican the agreement known as the Lateran Pacts, his popularity reached new heights. Every former anti-clerical statement and blasphemous attack on 'the small and insignificant Christ' was forgiven or forgotten by his former Catholic critics, who recognized in the Lateran Pacts the beginning of a new and satisfactory relationship between Church and State. His equivocal attitude to Catholicism and Christianity, which led him at one moment to speak of himself as 'profoundly religious. . . . A Catholic and therefore a Christian' and at another moment to profess himself an unbeliever, was overshadowed by the new official Fascist presentation of the Duce as a practising Catholic.

He was, in fact, never more than an intermittent Catholic. He was, on the contrary, and always had been, extremely superstitious and was quite unashamed of being so. He was seen frequently in public to put his hand in his pocket to touch his testicles to guard himself from the gaze of someone whom he suspected of having the evil eye. He had strange beliefs also, Margherita Sarfatti says, 'about the moon, the influence of its cold light upon men and affairs and the danger of letting its rays shine on your face when you are sleeping'.[1] He was proud of his skill in interpreting dreams and omens and in telling fortunes by cards, and he always enjoyed having his own fortune told and his palm read; and one clairvoyante who had, to his own satisfaction at least, forecast the Matteotti murder so impressed him that he even sent his Chief of Police to consult her when faced with an apparently insoluble problem. One evening, after reading in *The Times* of the treasures

1. The belief in the malign influence of moonlight was perhaps inherited from his father, who blamed its rays for an attack of scurvy he once suffered when he was in prison in 1902.

discovered in the tomb of Tutankhamen and of the maledictions invoked by the Egyptians upon those who disturbed their remains, he rushed to the telephone to give orders that a mummy which had been given to him and which had been placed in a salon at Palazzo Chigi must be removed immediately. The drawers of his desk were full of charms and religious objects which admirers had given to him and which he never dared to throw away; and to the end of his life he wore round his neck a scapular which his mother had bequeathed to him and an ancient medal which the King's mother, Queen Margherita, one of his most devoted admirers, had asked him to keep in memory of her. These charms protected him, he said, from death at the hands of his enemies.

The first of four attempts on his life was made on 4 November 1925, when the Socialist ex-Deputy Tito Zaniboni – according to Mussolini 'a drug-addict in the pay of Czechoslovakia' – was arrested near Palazzo Chigi in a hotel room from which he had intended shooting the Duce as he came out to take the salute at a military review. Five months later an Irishwoman, the Hon Violet Gibson, shot at him as he was on his way to visit Tripoli. But only after a fourth attempt was made at Bologna on 31 October 1926, and a boy whom Mussolini did not think was the culprit was lynched by the mob, did the Duce take reprisals. His previous tolerance was highly praised; his action now against the Freemasons and Socialists was considered no more than just; his bravery and coolness on each occasion was admired. 'Fancy!' he said without apparent concern after Miss Gibson's bullet had grazed the bridge of his nose, 'Fancy! A woman!' 'If I go forward,' he shouted to a group of officials after his face had been bandaged, 'follow me! If I go back, kill me! If I die, avenge me!' Immediately after one of the other attempts he received a visit from the British Ambassador, who did not realize that it had been made until he heard the shouts of thanksgiving in the streets below the window.[1]

'God', the Secretary of the Party declared to wildly cheering crowds, 'has put his finger on the Duce. He is Italy's greatest son, the rightful heir of Caesar.'

1. King Victor Emmanuel, also physically courageous, behaved in a similarly admirable way when a youth tried to assassinate him in Tirana in 1941. 'That boy,' he said calmly to the Albanian Prime Minister, who was sitting opposite him in the carriage, 'is a poor shot, isn't he?'

'*Duce ! Duce ! Duce !*' the crowds responded. 'We are yours to the end.'

As the months went by and the triumphs were multiplied, the set-backs discounted or denied, the legends created and sustained, the truth distorted or suppressed, the image of the Duce as benevolent Superman loomed ever more pervasive in the public mind. His inconsistency, his superficialities, his vanity in public, his dangerous belief that he could always master and solve a problem with speed, decision, and correctness, his constant dismissals of Ministers, Party Secretaries, and officials in case anyone should build himself up as a rival, as Balbo had once tried to do, the pettiness which made him order Italian journalists to hiss Haile Selassie when he came to speak on behalf of Abyssinia before the League of Nations, the concentration of power in his own hands so that at one time he was not only Prime Minister, Foreign Minister, Minister of the Interior, and President of the Grand Council, but Minister for Corporations, Commander-in-Chief of the Militia, and Minister of the Navy, Army, and Air Force as well – all these things were forgiven or ignored, suppressed or unknown.

There were, of course, the dissident ones, the isolated voices crying for freedom and for deliverance from the bad taste, the intellectual vulgarity, and shallow materialism of the Fascists, but they were generally disregarded, even despised. Success and esteem seemed better than political freedom; guaranteed wages better than the right to strike in an impoverished industry. Brilliant and courageous anti-Fascists, such as Ignazio Silone, working against the State either from abroad or in Italy were few, and for the most part made little impression on a people not so much bullied as coerced and deluded into conformity. Liberty, it was suggested by the Fascists, was not of much importance to a peasant who fears the return of hunger. Those writers and intellectuals and the kind of political and social agitator that the Duce himself had once been, who protested and reminded the people of the dangers of submission, were removed, or more often constrained or bribed into obedience and sometimes even into open support by a policy which Mussolini referred to with frank cynicism as one of 'the olive and the club'. And those other writers, artists, and scientists, who found good reasons to remain silent, could pretend to hope that authoritarianism would come to an end when the emergency was over or that Fascism could be reformed from within; and, in the meantime, they could at least point with satisfaction to the lenience with which the non-conformists were treated. Exile abroad, to the Mediterranean islands or the villages of Calabria, and imprisonment in the few and rarely vicious *confini* were compared with the death in the torture-chamber, the life-long incarceration in the concentration-camp, or the years in the forced-labour mines which awaited the outcasts in more intolerant dictatorships. The punitive expeditions of local Fascist gangs, which, uncontrolled by the police, degraded their opponents by forcing them to swallow castor oil or to eat live toads in public, were disgusting; but they could be compared with the relative freedom granted to such opponents of the new Fascism as Benedetto Croce. The OVRA[1] seemed an almost harmless institution when compared with the OGPU or the Gestapo; and its chief, Arturo Bocchini, was sardonic but not, despite his subsequent reputation, malevolent. By 1927 the Duce, assured of his success, and conscious of the fact that Matteotti was all but forgotten, felt able to tell his prefects that *squadrismo* was no longer necessary and that 'the period of reprisals, devastation, and violence is over'.

Mussolini had never for a moment considered himself unjust. Emil Ludwig once asked about his own prison experiences. '"I have tasted prison in various countries," Mussolini said, leaning forward into the light of the tall standard lamp, laying both his arms on the table as is his way when he wants to explain something clearly or to relate an anecdote. At such times,' Ludwig went on, 'he is especially genial, thrusting his chin forward, pouting his lips a little, while fruitlessly endeavouring to mask his good humour by knitting his eyebrows. "I have tasted prison in various countries, eleven times in all. . . . It always gave me a rest which otherwise I should not have been able to get. That is why I do not bear my jailers a grudge. During one of my terms of imprisonment I read *Don Quixote* and found it extraordinarily amusing."'

'I suppose that is why you clap your political opponents in jail?' Ludwig asked ironically, and he smiled. 'But does not the memory

1. Opera Vigilanza Repressione Antifascismo.

of your own prison experiences sometimes give you pause?'

'"By no means! It seems to me that I am perfectly consistent. They began by locking me up. Now I pay them back in their own coin."'

It was, indeed, difficult to believe that this man – disingenuous as his arguments were – was capable of the excesses usually expected of a dictator. He was – and in this the public estimate was just – not a cruel man. He was stern, he could be unforgiving, he was often cynical and disconcertingly remote; but he was, behind the blusterings of the tyrant and the marble-like impassivity which he delighted to impose upon his massive face, both emotional and compassionate. Margherita Sarfatti tells the story of his decorating 'a number of men well on in years' with the Star of Labour. He began with a formal embrace for the old man at the head of the line, but by the time he had reached the far end he was hugging the others and chatting to them with an excitement which was so infectious that they 'might have found in him a long-lost brother.' M. H. H. Macartney, the Rome correspondent of *The Times* during the nineteen-thirties, describes two other occasions when the Duce was overcome by his emotions. The first was on hearing of the death of his brother, the news of which had been brought to him by Admiral Count Costanzo Ciano, the Foreign Secretary's father. Mussolini broke down completely and wept on the old admiral's shoulder without reserve. He broke down too, Macartney says, when he was presented with a doll at a reception given by the President of the Foreign Press Association for the foreign correspondents in Rome. It was a gift for his youngest daughter Anna Maria, who was recovering from meningitis, the disease from which his mother had died. . . . 'The tears rushed to his eyes,' said the *Daily Mail*'s correspondent, who was also there. 'He took the doll and stood up for a moment, clearing his throat as if about to speak. Then in a strained whisper he said to Signor Alfieri, the Press Minister, "I can't reply. You must say something." The Duce walked away and stood with his back turned, looking out of the window.' He wept again in a paroxysm of sorrow when his second son, Bruno, was killed in the war; and when the widow came to receive her husband's gold medal at a public investiture, carrying Mussolini's grand-daughter Marina, who held out her arms to him, Ciano saw in his eye 'a light that betrayed everything his iron will had sought to hide' and felt himself very close to his father-in-law's 'heart and to his sorrow'.

He was passionately fond of his five children. He loved to play with them and to teach them games. Photographs of him with them appeared regularly in the national Press, where he was presented not only as a great sportsman, a brilliant horseman, and a fine aircraft pilot, but as a devoted *uomo casalingo* – Italy's most perfect example of a family man. The fact that he was also a *donnaiulo* was, however, little known. Occasionally a scandalous story was printed in a foreign newspaper, but the Italian public remained strangely ignorant of their Duce's proclivities, which he himself took pains to conceal. One of his earlier mistresses, for instance, a strange, neurotic woman, Ida Dalser, by whom he had had a mentally retarded and physically deformed child, was for years a constant source of anxiety to him. In the end she proved so savage in her resentment when he finally broke off his relationship with her that she had to be confined to a mental hospital. Ever since 1913 she had been insisting that Mussolini had promised to marry her, or had in fact done so, and that she could not be bought off with a maintenance allowance. She came often, Cesare Rossi said, to the offices of *Il Popolo d'Italia* in Milan, and once when she came with her son on her hip she shouted to Mussolini to come down if he dared, and he went to the window to threaten her with a pistol. On another occasion she was arrested for causing a breach of the peace in Trento, where she had set fire to the furniture in a bedroom of the Hotel Bristol, screaming hysterically that she was the Duce's wife. She died in a mental hospital at Venice in 1935, and her son, Benito, died in another one near Milan in 1942. But of all this the Italian people, with few exceptions, knew nothing. Shortly after Ida Dalser's death, however, Mussolini became involved in a scandal which it was impossible to conceal. A French actress, Magda Corabœuf, whose stage name was Fontanges, came to Rome in 1937 to interview the Duce for *La Liberté*. She would not return to Paris, she declared openly, until he had made love to her. 'I stayed in Rome two months,' she boasted later, 'and the Duce had me twenty times.' Revelations such as these, framed in more prosaic but no less revealing language, appeared in the Press, and Mussolini made it known to the police and the French Embassy that Mlle Fontanges was no longer welcome in Rome. She reacted violently, first by trying to poison herself and then by shooting and wounding the French Ambassador, the Comte de Chambrun, who, she said, had made her 'lose the love of the world's most wonderful man'. When she was arrested over three hundred photographs of Mussolini were found in her flat.[1] During the time that Mussolini was having his brief affair with her, he had already begun a much more deeply emotional affair with another young woman, for whose body he was later to develop an insatiable appetite.

She was Claretta Petacci, the daughter of a doctor and the wife of a lieutenant in the Italian Air Force from whom she later obtained a divorce in Hungary. Mussolini met her, it seems, on the road to Ostia in 1932. He was sitting in the back seat of his Alfa Romeo and turned round to look at Claretta as he was driven past her. She was waving and shouting '*Duce! Duce!*' and she looked so excited and pretty that he told the driver to stop. He got out of his car and walked back towards her, and she trembled with excitement, she said afterwards, when he spoke to her.

She was a pretty girl with green eyes and long, straight legs and those large and heavy breasts which he liked his women to have, and her voice was delightfully husky. Her clothes were tastelessly fussy, and her black hair was tightly curled in the same frippery style. Her upper lip was short and her teeth were small, so that when she smiled she showed her gums until she learned to smile with her lips only slightly parted. She was generous, hysterical, vain, obsessively sentimental, and fundamentally stupid. Her devotion to Mussolini was complete and touching. She was often ill with real and imagined ailments, and once when she had a miscarriage she nearly died of peritonitis and Mussolini visited her regularly, impressing her parents with the obvious sincerity of his concern and even insisting on being present at her operation. Usually she went to him at Palazzo Venezia, entering by a side door and going up by the lift to a flat on an upper floor where the Duce visited her, sometimes going up for a few minutes only, to fornicate urgently between one interview and the next.

---

1. She was sentenced to a year's imprisonment for malicious wounding and served a second sentence after the war for having been an Axis agent. She poisoned herself in Geneva in 1960.

Like most compulsive *donnaiuoli* Mussolini was a lonely man. He had few friends and no intimate ones, and even seemed proud of this fact. 'If the Eternal Father were to say to me, "I am your friend,"' he often boasted, 'I would put up my fists to him'; and 'If my own father were to come back to the world, I would not place my trust in him.' 'I have not known the warmth of real friendship,' he said in a gentler mood at the end of his life, 'although I have loved many women. But I don't mean that. I mean a strong and unbreakable bond of intimate affection between two men. I have not known that since my brother Arnaldo died.'

Arnaldo died in December 1931, and to commemorate his love for him Benito wrote a book in which his affection not only for him, but for his parents too, is sincerely and movingly evoked. Unlike the writing of his autobiography and the self-consciously emotional passages in *Parlo con Bruno* which he wrote during the war after the death of his second son in an aeroplane accident, *Vita di Sandro e di Arnaldo* contains many passages of great beauty. After reading those which describe the author's family and the lovely countryside in which he was born, Giovanni Gentile said that no man who was a tyrant could have written them. It was an extravagant claim, but an understandable one. And it was probably true that they were written from the heart, for Mussolini did not have the ability to recognize beauty in a work of art.

Margherita Sarfatti describes an occasion when they were looking at the tapestries of the Vatican museum together. He could not find much beauty in them. 'What are they when all's said and done?' he said. 'Just bits of material.' Even the Vatican itself did not greatly impress him – only its size. 'What a lot of rooms,' he said like a little boy in a palace, 'and how big they are. They knew how to build then.'

Hitler also noticed Mussolini's lack of appreciation of any of the visual arts, and on a visit to the Pitti and Uffizi galleries in Florence in 1938 he was shocked by the Duce's obvious boredom. Later, at Naples, Mussolini's indifference to the pictures he had taken Hitler to see shocked the Führer again. When he 'had looked at three pictures,' Hitler said, 'he could not bear any more. Consequently I saw nothing of them myself.' Mussolini was never able to sympathize with the Italians' pride in their great artistic heritage and could not understand the dismay caused by the

Fascist Government's gift of Myron's *Discobolus* to Hitler, who had expressed admiration for it on his visit to Rome. He also refused to sympathize with their fear that their works of art might be destroyed by British or American bombs during the war.

But although painting and sculpture and all objects of art and virtu left him puzzled and unmoved, and although a visit to the opera drove him to boredom and, so his son Vittorio says, eventually to sleep, literature continued throughout his life to exercise upon him a compelling fascination which was none the less sincere because while flaunting his literary taste he had a secret passion for cheap and erotic novels.[1] It was one of his great sorrows, so he later complained, that Fascism had not produced a single great poet, or even a worthwhile writer.

'I wouldn't complain,' he said, 'if there was even just one good Fascist book. But what have we had? Ill-written claptrap! I'd rather have well-written abuse than that.' Despite the absurdities of Fascist censorship, which banned the books of Robert Graves and Axel Munthe (among many others) from the public libraries, he may even have meant it.

In a recent interview Alberto Moravia spoke of his satirical anti-Fascist book *La Mascherata*, which he wrote on Capri in 1940.

'We were in the full-flood of war, Fascism, censorship, etc. The manuscript, once ready, like all manuscripts had to be submitted to the Ministry of Popular Culture for approval. This Ministry, let me explain, was overrun with grammar-school teachers who received three hundred lire for each book they read. And, of course, to preserve the sinecures, whenever possible they turned in negative judgements. Well, I submitted the manuscript. But whoever read it, not wishing to take any position on the book, passed it to the Under-Secretary; the Under-Secretary, with similar qualms, passed it to the Secretary; the Secretary to the Minister; and the Minister finally to Mussolini.'

1. Ignazio Silone, of course, disagrees with this view. In his brilliant anti-Fascist book *The School for Dictators* he makes one of his characters say when commenting on Mussolini's account of his father reading Machiavelli's *The Prince* to him every Saturday night: 'Our knowledge of Mussolini's father makes it certain that the last thing he was capable of on Saturday nights was reading anything to anybody. Mussolini's only object in encouraging such legends is to create an impression. He uses medieval uniforms and rides on horseback for the same purpose. It is Mussolini's great good fortune that throughout his life he has read and still reads nothing but newspapers. However, as a talented journalist, he is able to talk and write arrogantly about all the things that he knows nothing whatever about.'

'I suppose, then,' the interviewer said, 'you were called on the carpet?'

'Not at all. Mussolini ordered the book to be published.'

'Oh!'

'He was not a bad man.'

'This interview, you realize, is being published abroad. Abroad, Mussolini is seen in quite a different light.'

'But we understand what Mussolini was. I hope that doesn't make us Fascists. His worst fault was his abysmal ignorance of foreign affairs. If he had had a foreign policy as clever as his domestic one perhaps he'd be Duce today.'

2

Although too casual and too tolerant of the nonconformist ever to be guilty of the excesses of the National Socialist régime in Germany, the Fascist State in Italy was nevertheless by the end of 1936 one in which the doctrine of *Gleichschaltung* was a dominating influence. In order to force the Italians to live up to the Fascist ideals of discipline and duty, determined, strenuous, and often absurd attempts were made to impose upon them a rigidity and uniformity of behaviour wholly alien to their character and alien also to the early and irresponsible Fascist motto '*Me ne frego*' ('I don't care a damn'). It was now, as the Duce himself never tired of saying, 'the classic and historical responsibility' of Fascism to insist on the '*severa osservanza dello stile fascista*'; just as it was the duty of the Fascist to set an example of efficiency, decisiveness, *dinamismo*, in contrast to the laxness of pre-Fascist Italian life and to the way of life in the Western Democracies, which was characterized as sedentary, traditionalist, bourgeois, and *pantofolaie* – as decadent as carpet-slippers. 'Live dangerously', 'Life must not be taken easily', were not merely slogans; they were fundamental tenets of Fascist faith. 'In other countries,' Mussolini was fond of pointing out, 'revolutionists have by degrees become more complaisant; but here in Italy, year by year, we have grown more radical, more stubborn.'

The Fascist must be ever on guard against a relapse into the lazy habits, both mental and moral, of the past. He must be '*l'uomo nuovo del tempo di Mussolini*', ardent, determined, dedicated, ready to renounce pleasure and even personality in the service of the strict ideals of Fascist morality. 'We are advocates,' Mussolini said, 'of the collective significance of life, and we wish to develop this at the cost of individualism.' In pursuit of this aim, the registered Party members, who in March 1937 numbered more than two million, were to set a rigid standard of behaviour to which the whole race would eventually conform.

The five years preceding the outbreak of war became known as *l'era Starace*, because of the repeated efforts made by the Secretary of the Party, Achille Starace, to mould the Italians into the obedient conformists and Spartan disciples of Mussolini's ideal. Starace was a blindly devoted follower of the Duce, unimaginative and unintelligent, hated particularly in the north because he was an ignorant and vulgar southerner, the kind of official, indeed, that Mussolini liked to place in positions of responsibility in the Fascist hierarchy. By the later nineteen-thirties there was, Ciano noted in his diary, 'a veritable popular uprising against the pettifogging restrictions of the Party Secretary. He had made,' the Foreign Minister went on perceptively, 'the two most serious mistakes which you can make when you have to deal with the Italian people. He has created an atmosphere of persecution and he has caused annoyance by a thousand little things of a personal nature. Now the Italians like their rulers to rule with heart. They may forgive you if you do them harm, but not if you pester them.'

Starace's passion for uniforms and medals, his insistence that the Roman salute should take the place of the handshake, his devotion to slogans, and his eager and sycophantic adoption of all the Duce's ideas, earned him not only the dislike but also the contempt of his fellow-countrymen. When in 1938 Mussolini endorsed the views of Bruno Cicognani, who had written an article in the *Corriere della Sera* attacking the 'ridiculous' use of *lei* in polite conversation as being a form of address not in keeping with the best Italian literary tradition or with personal dignity, Starace took up the campaign against *lei* with zealous fury and issued circulars demanding the immediate and compulsory use of *voi* in its place. His extravagant attacks on *lei* deepened the derision with which the Italian people regarded him and provoked the opponents of the régime to use this form of address as often as possible. Benedetto Croce, now a strong and outspoken anti-Fascist who had always used *voi* with his family and friends,

abandoned the custom and in defiance of Starace addressed them
all with *lei*. On occasions Starace went beyond even the wide
limits of Mussolini's approval, as, for instance, when he attempted
to make it a rule that all official letters should end with the words
'*Viva il Duce*'. Mussolini first heard of this new rule when he saw
it announced in the newspapers and called the Secretary to his
angry presence. 'Dear Madam,' he dictated furiously as soon as
Starace entered the room. 'This is to inform you that your son, a
corporal in this regiment, has fallen off his horse and cut his head
open. *Viva il Duce*. . . . Dear Sir, This is to inform you that
reduction of personnel next month will mean your dismissal from
this office. *Viva il Duce*.' Mussolini dictated several more imagin-
ary letters before turning on Starace and sending him away with
the enraged charge that he had succeeded in making him 'look
ridiculous to the whole of Italy'.

As Party Secretary, Starace was also responsible for the increased intrusion of Fascist ideals into sport, which ultimately
became a virtual State monopoly over which the propaganda departments of the State exercised a typically absurd control,
decreeing, for instance, that the national tennis team should wear
black shirts and refuse to shake hands, and that photographs
showing Primo Carnera knocked out in the ring should never be
published. While the organization known as *Dopolavoro* did much
good in providing cheap games and even cheap holidays for
workers, the insistence on the *stile fascista* in sport and recreation
was resented as both meddlesome and pretentious. The institution of what became known as the 'Fascist Saturday', a weekly
holiday which was, as a replacement of '*il weekend*' and all that
that term implied, to be 'imbued with the spirit of the Revolution' was a typical example of this. Workers and clerks, whether
in the Government service or not, were required to spend the
afternoon playing games or taking part in military exercises and
parades or attending some sort of political discussion group.

'The natural inclinations and passive resistance of the people,
however,' as the historians of the Fascist era, Luigi Salvatorelli
and Giovanni Mira, have written in their *Storia d'Italia nel
periodo fascista*,

reduced this programme to a minimum: and the Fascist Saturday in
the end became no more than an afternoon of rest and amusement,

that is to say an English Saturday. And it was not only in this particular case that resistance to Staracian discipline manifested itself. ... The accepted difference between what was required and what was performed, between theory and practice, appearance and reality in the whole field of Fascist discipline contributed on the one hand to preserve the Italians from complete servility and degradation of the spirit, but on the other hand it engendered that scant respect for the law, that insufference of regulations, that lack of a social conscience which were and remain grave defects of the national character. This is by no means the least important of the charges which can be brought against the Fascist régime.

Italo Balbo, the most intelligent of the *Quadrumviri*, whom Mussolini, jealous of his popularity and angered by his outspoken criticisms, had sent away to be Governor of Libya, was well aware of this. 'In Italy,' he said sadly in the summer of 1938, 'there is no longer a taste for sincerity.'

Part Two

Empire and Axis

The Diplomat

28 OCTOBER 1922–10 JUNE 1940

The Germans should allow themselves to be
guided by me if they wish to avoid unpardonable
blunders. In politics it is undeniable
that I am more intelligent than Hitler.

I

'I have always held that having broken the pride of Bolshevism,'
Mussolini declared before the March on Rome, 'Fascism should
become the watchful guardian of our foreign policy.' It was, indeed, because of this constantly reiterated promise that he would
lead Italy towards a more respected position in Europe that he
gained such powerful support from the young. In his first speech
in the Chamber he gave voice to their urgent aspirations, and
within less than a year had been encouraged to behave with a
defiance which brought the country to the verge of war.

On 27 August 1923 the Italian General Enrico Tellini, president of the international commission for the demarcation of the
Graeco–Albanian frontier, was murdered with three other Italian
soldiers by some Greeks who accused him of being prejudiced in
favour of Albanian claims. Two days later Mussolini presented
Greece with an ultimatum and a demand for 50 million lire compensation. When the Greeks denied responsibility, he despatched the Italian fleet to Corfu and occupied the Island. On 1
September Greece appealed to the League of Nations, and Italy
responded by insisting that the League was not competent to deal
with the dispute. Eventually the Greek Government were pre-
vailed upon to agree to Italy's demands to make full compensation
and to pay the indemnity. The Italians evacuated Corfu.

The nearness of war alarmed Mussolini, although it was not
until years later that he admitted it, and he trod with more caution

after this first foray into the treacherous field of power politics. Indeed, for the first ten years of his régime it seemed that he had no ambitions in Europe or in Africa and was content to spend all his energies in promoting the welfare of his Fascist State. On the occasional appearance he made abroad – in Lausanne and in London for the Conference of 1922 and at Locarno to put Italy's signature to the famous treaty of December 1925 – he seemed, in his butterfly collar and spats, his top hat, white gloves, and badly pressed trousers, a person very different from the ferocious revolutionary the foreign journalists had been led to expect. They were above all surprised by his smallness – he was only 5 ft 6 in. – and by the warmth of an unexpected, almost diffident, smile. There seemed no cause for alarm. 'He is really quite absurd!' Curzon commented with dismissive, patrician scorn.[1]

His views seemed reasonable, a great deal more reasonable, in fact, than those held by many other European statesmen of his time, and the speeches in which he expressed them, compared with his later outbursts, were positively conciliatory. He gave an example of his apparent generosity by concluding with Yugoslavia a series of agreements which were a good deal less to Italy's advantage than many Italian nationalists had expected; and seeing in 'revisionism' a chance to exploit the prejudices of Europe in Italy's favour, he constantly urged the need for modifications of the Treaty of Versailles. 'This absurdity,' he said in 1926, 'will one day soon bring about not only revolution in Germany but war in Europe.' It was a warning which he was constantly to repeat. Although he remained faithful to Italy's allies of the war and generally supported their endeavours to find a peaceful solution to the problems of Europe, he could not always agree that they were dealing with these problems in a realistic way and frequently pursued an independent and contradictory policy of his own, following what Lord Halifax later called 'the classic Italian role of balancing between Germany and the Western Powers'. Taking the side of those countries which he felt had been unfairly and dangerously treated by the Peace Treaties, he pressed for a more sympathetic and practical approach towards the problems of his

---

1. Mussolini returned the insult. He hated Curzon and disliked London, which seemed full of men like him. After his brief visit to London he decided it was 'a nightmare to anyone from Italy', and hoped he would 'never have to go back'.

former enemies and demanded, in particular, a more realistic attitude from France, whose resistance to his demands for naval equality with her at the London Conference of 1930 he was never to forgive. In 1933 he proposed a Four Power Pact, between France, Great Britain, Italy, and Germany, in the hope that 'peaceful revision' might be carried out by Italy and Britain acting as mediators between France and Germany and, no doubt, also in the hope that he could take advantage of Germany's revival to extract concessions from France; but the French, suspicious of his motives, treated his proposal with reserve, and in the following year events in Austria persuaded him that the chance of improving Italy's standing in Europe by a sympathetic appreciation of Germany's legitimate complaints was gone. What was now wanted, he believed, was a firm stand against the growing ambitions of a country which was learning that it could take anything that its hostile neighbours denied it.

Mussolini's advocacy of a strong anti-German front and his consequent closer ties with France and Britain were, however, soon to be radically modified. During the last days of 1934 there was a clash between Abyssinian and Italian soldiers on the borders of Abyssinia and Italian Somaliland; and in October 1935, after ten months of preparations, rumours, threats, warnings, and hesitations, Italy invaded Abyssinia. The clash by the wells of Wal Wal was, of course, no more than a pretext. Mussolini had had his eye on this only remaining potential colony in Africa long before and, according to General De Bono, had decided on invading it as early as 1932. Although he had been afraid at first that the British might intervene to stop him, Dino Grandi, now his Ambassador in London, assured him that he knew from Eden's opponents in the Cabinet that the British would not fight and an intercepted message proved it. Hitler, hoping that Italy's involvement in Africa would distract her from his own ambitions in Austria, actually encouraged him.

People all over the world listened to the accounts of defenceless natives being mown down by machine-guns and choking on poison gas, and they were outraged. The Italians, however, had these matters interpreted for them in a different light; and when the short campaign was over Mussolini was at the height of his power and his popularity.

He had defied the world, and he had triumphed; and to most Italians his triumph was a just reward and his defiance a proud and honourable attitude; for they did not recognize in his determination to build an empire in Africa either cruelty or rapacity. The British and French had built their empires by the same means but under the protection of international agreements, and had, therefore, no right to condemn with such hypocrisy the legitimate claims of another European nation dying for want of space for a rapidly increasing population. They protested in the name of humanity, but their real enmity was caused by a wish to keep Italy out of Africa and a determination to deny her both an economic outlet and the possibility of territorial expansion. It was absurd to talk about Abyssinia as a sovereign State when it was nothing but a collection of heterogeneous tribes dominated by various primitive chieftains most of whom, including Haile Selassie, were revered by Italy's critics for little other reason than that they had been converted to some sort of Christianity. It was absurd, too, to deny that Italy's influence in Abyssinia would be a good one. Britain herself had objected to the admission of 'this barbarous country' into the League of Nations when Italy had proposed her membership in order to check British encroachments. Tribal wars and slavery would be abolished, and the people would be provided with great social benefits. The charge, widely spread in both Britain and France, that the Italian Army had killed thousands of innocent Africans by poison gas had been no more than malicious propaganda. The only gases used had been tear-gas and a mild kind of mustard-gas which was never fatal nor even permanently disabling. Had not Bernard Shaw himself found reasons for condoning their use? 'If you want to talk about atrocities,' the Duce himself had said to an English journalist, 'I will show you pictures of what Abyssinians have done to our men which are too horrible for any newspaper to print. We have never used gas clouds like those of the Great War, and to drop mustard-gas bombs into ravines down which Abyssinians might have crept to attack an isolated column was really a measure of humanity, for it had the effect of saving lives.'

The Italians had a clear conscience. They had not felt the need for an Empire as strongly as the Duce had done, and no enthusiasm for its conquest by force. Several leading Fascists, indeed, told Prince Starhemberg, the Austrian Vice-Chancellor and head of the Heimwehr, who was a personal friend of Mussolini, that they were against the Abyssinian adventure. They did not share the Duce's belief that Fascism would be strengthened both at home and internationally by a show of power, which, he insisted, was always more respected than any amount of political manoeuvring, however successful. Nor did they endorse the Duce's emotional assumption that the authority of Italy in Europe and the 'future progress of the Fascist ethos demanded the avenging of Adowa', where, forty years before, the Italians had been humiliatingly defeated by the Abyssinians to the undisguised pleasure of a mocking world.

But now the reservations were invalidated and the voices of caution and restraint were silenced. 'My objective is simple,' Mussolini had declared some years before. 'I want to make Italy great, respected, and feared.' And few Italians now denied that he had done so. There were still those, of course, who doubted that Italy's action was compatible with twentieth-century morality and who feared that Mussolini was prompted by his envy of Hitler's growing success in Europe and his desire to demonstrate that Italy too was strong; but even they felt compelled to admire the speed with which, contrary to the forecasts of military experts in both London and Rome, the Abyssinian campaign had been completed, a speed for which the Duce took the credit, remarking – as if it were a subject for boasting – that he had given the commander in the field constant instructions, amounting on some days to more than 100 top-priority telegrams which dealt with every conceivable aspect of the Army's business. The military success, however, was but a small part of the Duce's triumph. The more important effect of the war was the lasting spirit of national unity which it had engendered. Anthony Eden, British Minister for League of Nations Affairs, after an acrimonious meeting with Mussolini in Rome which settled the opinions they held about each other for ever, had successfully rallied support for a policy of 'sanctions', and on 10 October 1935, by a vote of fifty to one, the Assembly of the League had resolved to take collective measures against Italy. The result of the resolution could not have favoured Italy more. Stanley Baldwin, the British Prime Minister, following the now accepted rule of British diplomacy by simultaneously refusing either to sustain the League of Nations at the risk of war or to abandon it by condoning Mussolini's action, declared that sanctions meant war; 'secondly,' as Sir Winston Churchill afterwards said, 'he was resolved that there must be no war; and, thirdly, he decided upon sanctions. It was evidently impossible to reconcile these three conditions.' Pierre Laval, the clever and cynical French Foreign Minister, had realized their irreconcilability from the beginning, advocating a deal with Mussolini. And once sanctions had been decided upon he encouraged Britain's efforts to ensure that the list of prohibited exports would not include any, such as oil, that might provoke a European war.

Mussolini was, therefore, not prevented from attacking and defeating Abyssinia, but on the contrary was given an opportunity of uniting his country under the protection of Fascism against the actions and slanders of a hostile world. 'Italy will meet sanctions,' he declared, 'with discipline, with frugality, and with sacrifice.' And she did. As the outraged members of the League of Nations rallied round Anthony Eden, so the isolated Italian people, most of whom had been trained to share Mussolini's dislike of Eden, rallied round the Duce. Old ladies sent him their jewellery to help him pay for his war, and young men said they would gladly die in it by suicidal air-raids on the British Fleet. Many former liberals supported the war, and the Church did not oppose it. Several former anti-Fascists living in voluntary exile returned to support their country in her hour of need. 'The Italian people,' Mussolini announced in one of those speeches which delighted Italians whether Fascists or not, 'are worthy of their great destiny.' The shocked reaction of the British people when they were told about the Hoare–Laval Pact of 1935, which planned the partition of Abyssinia between Italy and the Emperor, had been interpreted as anti-Italian; and when, in the uproar after its publication, Sir Samuel Hoare was obliged to give up the Foreign Office to the detestable Anthony Eden, who could be relied upon to pursue a more rigid and unsympathetic policy towards Italy, Mussolini's popularity rose to new heights.

There was yet another and more fateful consequence of Mussolini's victory. Watching the success of his Italian friend in his quarrel with the League of Nations, from which he himself had flamboyantly withdrawn in October 1933, Adolf Hitler drew his own conclusions. It was not merely a vindication of the philosophy of force, it was not only another demonstration of the decadence of democracy; the League's *débâcle* marked the end of the so-called Stresa Front and the beginning of the Italo-German alliance.

2

There had been a time when such an alliance had seemed impossible. Only two years before, relations between the two countries had been not merely strained but on the point of disruption. Mussolini, anxious to protect Italian interests in Central and South-eastern Europe, was determined to prevent Hitler realizing his known ambitions in Austria. On 17 February 1934 he made a declaration, in which the British and French Governments joined, upon the necessity for the maintenance of Austrian independence; a month later he emphasized Italy's resolve to prevent German expansion across her northern and eastern borders by signing with Austria and Hungary the Rome Protocols, which provided for mutual consultation in the event of a threat to any one of the three countries; and when in July the Nazis so far overplayed their hand as to attempt a *coup d'état* by murdering the Austrian Chancellor, Engelbert Dollfuss, while his wife and children were guests of Mussolini in Italy, the Duce's reaction was immediate and forceful. He telegraphed Prince Starhemberg, the acting Chancellor, promising Italian support and despatched three Italian divisions to the frontier as a guarantee that the promise was not an idle one. Hitler, realizing that his supporters had gone too far, was obliged to give way; and Mussolini's carefully disguised envy of the man, whom after his first meeting with him he had referred to contemptuously as 'that mad little clown', came close to hatred. Hitler, he told Prince Starhemberg, was the murderer of Dollfuss and responsible for all that had happened. He was 'a horrible sexually degenerate creature', a 'dangerous fool'. He was the natural leader of National Socialism, which was a travestied and brutalized imitation of Fascism and a 'barbarous and savage system, capable only of slaughter, plunder, and black-mail'. The ferocious purge of June 1934 had been 'an inevitable crisis of so despicable a political system'. 'I should be pleased, I suppose,' he said to another friend of his, the journalist Michele Campana, 'that Hitler has carried out a revolution on our lines, but they are Germans so they end by ruining our idea. They are still the barbarians of Tacitus and the Reformation in eternal conflict with Rome.'

Mussolini's anger was understandable. With the independence of Austria threatened, Italy was in danger of losing her principal guarantee of security and in danger too of losing her 300,000 formerly Austrian subjects in Alto Adige to the subversions of German nationalism. He felt obliged to abandon his policy of 'revisionism' in favour of a more friendly attitude towards France whose backing he now needed. It was with these thoughts in mind that he joined the anti-German front created at Stresa on 11 April 1935, when he combined with the British and French Governments in condemning any attempt to change the treaty settlements by force.

Mussolini had attended the conference himself with Fulvio Suvich, his Under-Secretary of State and principal adviser on Foreign Affairs, and revealed that his determination to curb Germany's ambitions was not the only reason for his presence. An understanding with France and England would certainly help preserve Italy's position in Europe, but it would also help her to extend her influence in the Mediterranean and Africa.

In his speech he had made reference to the final declaration of the conference, which condemned 'any unilateral repudiation of treaties which may endanger the peace of Europe'. The Duce spoke the word 'Europe' with so obvious an emphasis and paused for so long before continuing that the British Foreign Office representatives realized at once what was in his mind and conferred together that night to decide whether or not to warn him against an attack on Abyssinia. They decided his support in their stand against Germany was too important to risk, and did not do so. Mussolini had left Stresa believing that he had gained his point. And when in June the Anglo-German naval treaty was signed, his belief that Britain did not really care what happened in the world so long as her own interests were not threatened was again understandably reinforced.

Four months later the invasion of Abyssinia had begun. And

that autumn, as Western Europe turned so ineffectually against him, the idea of an alliance with the one powerful country which had not openly done so came to the forefront of Mussolini's mind.

3

The first overtures had come from Hitler, who had admired the Duce for the whole of his political life and had been deeply influenced by many of Fascism's ideological conceptions and choreographic techniques. In 1926 he had written to Rome asking for a signed photograph. 'Please thank the above-named Gentleman,' the Italian Foreign Office had coldly replied to the Embassy in Berlin, 'for his sentiment and tell him in whatever form you consider best that the Duce does not think fit to accede to the request.'

Although there is some evidence to suggest that the Nazis were being subsidized from Italy as early as 1932, the Duce himself had no wish to sully his remarkable reputation by open contact with the 'unsavoury adventurer' who was their leader. Even after Hitler's rise to power in 1933, which took him by surprise, Mussolini's suspicion and wary disdain did not relax. He had made Fascism, he believed, both respected and admired and had no wish to taint it by association with National Socialism, which he described at this time as being the 'revolt of the old German tribes of the primeval forests'. There was certainly no doubt that Mussolini was held in a higher regard both in Europe and in America than Hitler ever was or could be. The accolades which had been so enthusiastically and gratuitously cast upon him by conservative writers and public figures in the nineteen-twenties and early thirties had been so frequent and so unequivocally phrased that he had no trouble in believing that he was indeed the greatest statesman of his time.

In December 1924 Sir Austen Chamberlain, then Foreign Secretary, referred to him when on a visit to Rome as 'a wonderful man . . . working for the greatness of his country'. In later years Lady Chamberlain was often to be seen wearing the Fascist badge. In 1927 Winston Churchill visited Rome and was widely reported as having said, 'If I were an Italian I would don the Fascist Black Shirt.' 'I could not help being charmed,' he said at a Press conference reported by *The Times*, 'like so many other people have been, by Signor Mussolini's gentle and simple bearing and by his calm and detached pose in spite of so many burdens and dangers. Anyone could see that he thought of nothing but the lasting good, as he understood it, of the Italian people, and that no lesser interest was of the slightest consequence to him. . . . If I had been an Italian I should have been wholeheartedly with you from start to finish in your triumphant struggle against the bestial appetites and passions of Leninism.' The following day *The Times* congratulated Mr Churchill 'on having understood the real spirit of the Fascist movement'. Lloyd George publicly agreed with him that the Corporative System was a 'very promising development'. In 1928 the *Daily Mail* gave expression to a more emphatic enthusiasm when Lord Rothermere declared in its columns that Mussolini was 'the greatest figure of our age'. An English biographer in an extremely laudatory book published in 1932 agreed that he was 'the greatest statesman of our time' – a view which, as late as January 1939, the *Manchester Guardian* confessed itself as sharing. These were not exceptional verdicts. Foreign diplomats and visitors, both official and unofficial, who were granted interviews by Mussolini in his palatial office in Palazzo Venezia were similarly impressed and did not hesitate to say so. Mr Richard Washburn Child, the American Ambassador in Rome between 1921 and 1924, felt for the Duce a respect which was close to idolatry. 'He has not only been able to secure and hold an almost universal following,' he wrote in the preface to Mussolini's *My Autobiography*. 'He has built a new state upon a new concept of a state. He has not only been able to change the lives of human beings, but he has changed their minds, their hearts, their spirits.' He spoke of the Duce's humanity and his wisdom, his strength and dynamic energy. He was 'the greatest figure of this sphere and time'. 'One closes the door when one leaves him,' he decided, 'feeling that one could squeeze something of him out of one's clothes.'

Stories were told of his vanity and histrionics, his pretentious behaviour and absurd gestures; but most visitors discovered that he was a sensible, charming, even (surprisingly) a diffident man with an uncertain, sometimes self-conscious manner. They were told that he would sit at his immense desk in the vast and ornate Sala del Mappamondo and balefully watch them approach across

the sixty feet of coldly echoing mosaic floor or ignore them altogether as he continued writing. They were told even that they
would have to pass rows of daggers held at arms' length by grim-
faced Blackshirts; and sometimes, indeed, they did. But these
occasions were rare. More often the scene was as Duff Cooper
found it on a visit to Rome in 1934. 'There were no histrionics,'
Duff Cooper wrote, 'nor was I obliged, as I had been told would
happen, to walk the length of a long room from the door to his
desk. He met me at the door and accompanied me to it when I
left. We agreed on the importance of rearmament and he laughed
when I said that the idea that armaments produced war was as
foolish as to think that umbrellas produced rain. Because he
laughed at my joke I thought he had a sense of humour and was
quite prepared to imagine he had other good qualities. . . . I was
favourably impressed.'

It was a common reaction. Few men, indeed, were not favourably impressed. As he came towards them, walking with a springy,
rather cat-like step, friendly and courteous, they were immediately disarmed. Even when he gave the impression, as he did to
Lord Vansittart, of a man who 'took such obvious pleasure in his
own company' that he was reminiscent of 'a boxer in a flashy
dressing-gown shaking hands with himself', he managed to give
pleasure to his visitor as well as to himself. 'He was no joke,' Vansittart thought, 'nothing like the pantaloon depicted by envy.' He
spoke in a low voice, and his conversational gifts seemed of a high
order. Always fluent, often striking, sometimes witty, his comments were enlivened by unusual but rarely inapt allusions and
remarkable capacity for neologism. 'When the Duce starts to
talk,' his Foreign Secretary once said of him, 'he is delightful. I
know nobody who uses such rich and original metaphors.' Like
most good talkers he was not a patient listener, sometimes even
getting up abruptly from his chair to carry on the conversation,
distractingly striding up and down the room; but with foreign
visitors he made an effort to overcome this habit, and although –
perhaps because of his ulcer – he found it difficult to keep still
in his chair he gave the impression of attentiveness as he sat at his
desk, stiffly upright, his finger-tips pressed together. He rarely
laughed, and when he did it often sounded more like a laugh of
scorn or the hearty, shoulder-heaving laugh of a man who feels

T — D

he ought to be amused but is not. But a smile, flatteringly appreciative, often flashed across his usually grave face. 'He is not only a great man,' Aristide Briand said. 'He is a good one.' Franz von Papen, in Rome for the signing of the Concordat with the Vatican in the summer of 1933, 'found the Italian dictator a man of very different calibre from Hitler. Short in stature, but with an air of great authority, his massive head conveyed an impression of great strength of character. He handled people like a man accustomed to having his orders obeyed, but displayed immense charm. . . . Hitler always had a slight air of uncertainty, as though feeling his way, whereas Mussolini was calm, dignified, and appeared the complete master of whatever subject was being discussed. . . . He spoke excellent French and German.'

In America the praise was as emphatic as it was in Europe. As Lord Rothermere had compared him to Napoleon, so the President of Columbia University compared him to Cromwell.'Fascism,' he went on to say, 'is a form of government of the very first order of excellence.' Otto Kahn, the famous banker, agreed with him and in a speech which he gave to the students of Wesleyan University referred to the Duce as a 'genius'. It was an estimate which Cardinal O'Connell of Boston endorsed. 'Mussolini,' the Cardinal said, 'is a genius in the field of government given to Italy by God to help the nation continue her rapid ascent towards the most glorious destiny.' The Archbishop of Chicago after a visit to Rome gave it as his opinion that 'Mussolini is the man of our time.' Fiorello La Guardia, Mayor of New York, said that he wished the Duce every success and that there was no resemblance between Hitler and Mussolini.

Suggestions that there might be a resemblance between the two dictators were certainly and angrily rejected by Mussolini himself. He was forced to agree that National Socialism, like Fascism, was authoritarian, collectivist, anti-parliamentary, anti-democratic, and anti-liberal, but further than that he would not go. As for the transcendental theme in Nazi philosophy – the idea of a master race – he dismissed it as 'arrant nonsense, stupid and idiotic'. If Hitler's theories of racial superiority were correct, he thought, 'the Lapps must be considered the highest type of humanity'. 'Thirty centuries of history,' he said in a speech at Bari in September 1934, 'enable us to look with majestic pity at certain doctrines taught on the other side of the Alps by the descendants of people who were wholly illiterate in the days when Rome boasted a Caesar, a Virgil, and an Augustus.' Anti-Semitism he described in a conversation with Emil Ludwig in 1932 as 'the German vice'. There was 'no Jewish question in Italy and could not be one in a country with a healthy system of government.'

It was not until 14 June 1934 that he met Hitler for the first time. He disliked him as much as he had expected. The meeting, arranged by German diplomats who hoped that Mussolini might have more success than they in moderating Hitler's attitude towards Austria, took place in the Royal Villa at Stra on the River Brenta near Padua. Hitler, accompanied by numerous S S men including Sepp Dietrich, looked nervous and insignificant. Mussolini, noticing in particular his lank ill-brushed hair and his watery eyes, murmured, 'I don't like the look of him.' He was wearing a yellow mackintosh and striped trousers with patent leather shoes and held against his stomach a grey felt hat which he twisted convulsively in his hands as if, a French journalist commented, he were a 'little plumber holding an embarrassing instrument'. Mussolini, who had also arrived in civilian clothes, changed on arrival into a splendid uniform with a dagger and black boots with silver spurs.

Before their first conversation was over, Mussolini had already made up his mind about Hitler. Leaving the conference table during a pause in the discussion to walk over to the window, he murmured with a kind of amused contempt, 'He's quite mad.' By early evening both of them were seen to be not merely losing patience but on the verge of a quarrel. They agreed that they both disliked France and Russia, but they could not agree about much else, least of all about Austria, where, Mussolini said, the Nazis ought to drop their terrorist campaign. All that night the mosquitoes buzzed incessantly, and Mussolini spent a sleepless night disturbed not only by the insects and the memory of the pretentious talk of the 'silly little clown', but also, so it was suggested, by the ghost of Napoleon, who had once himself passed an uncomfortable night at Stra. In the morning it was suggested that the conference should be moved to Venice.

Here the atmosphere was even more strained. The Duce was

cheered wildly by the Venetians, who greeted his guest in silence. Later, during a conversation on the Alberoni golf course when the two men were left alone, their anxious staffs, who were following at a distance, heard shouts which Constantin von Neurath, the German Foreign Minister, later compared to 'the barking of two mastiffs'. What they were arguing about no one knew or could afterwards discover. They spoke in German, which perhaps left Mussolini at a disadvantage as although he had loftily declined the services of Paul Schmidt, the German Foreign Office interpreter, his proficiency in the language was not as great as he liked to suppose. He enjoyed speaking German, Kurt von Schuschnigg, Dollfuss's successor as Austrian Chancellor, thought, but the effort was an obvious one and he was slow and carefully articulate. He may well have had difficulty in understanding Hitler's still strong Austrian accent with its Bavarianized overtones.

Although the subject of this particular disputation was never mentioned by Mussolini, he later referred to other occasions on which they were left alone together during the conference when 'instead of discussing concrete problems, Hitler merely recited *Mein Kampf* from memory – that boring book which I have never been able to read'. And towards the end of the visit, when Mussolini took him out in a motor-boat on the Laguna Veneta, instead of sitting back and enjoying the trip he made a long speech about his racial theories. 'He spent the whole time declaiming about the superiority of the Nordic races,' Suvich told Starhemberg, 'and condemning all the Mediterranean people, particularly the Italians, as having Negro blood in their veins.' Mussolini, who had given up arguing with the man and sat listening in silence, 'was much amused', Suvich thought. The next day, after Hitler had left Venice on his way back to Germany, Mussolini was asked what he had thought of him. He replied, with a gesture of dismissal, 'He's just a garrulous monk.'

Soon, however, despise Hitler as he might, Mussolini felt the need of his friendship and persuaded himself that Italy would do better out of an alliance with Germany than she could do out of an alliance with the Western Democracies. The hostility of France and England towards Italy during the Abyssinian war had destroyed any chance of an anti-German agreement between those three countries, but it had not yet brought Italy very much closer to Hitler, who had been careful to derive any advantage he could from the conflict and had been disturbed at the thought that it might be ended by a compromise such as the Hoare–Laval Pact. In Mussolini's mind the Anglo-German Treaty of 1935 also still rankled and, more persistently, the question of Austrian independence and the threatened *Anschluss*. So long as this particular problem remained at issue between Mussolini and Hitler, an alliance was impossible. But Hitler felt the need of the outward appearance of Mussolini's friendship more strongly than Mussolini felt the need of his; and it was partly with a view to the gaining of that friendship that the Austro-German Agreement was, with the Duce's approval, signed in July 1936. The Agreement, although apparently settling Austro-German differences to the mutual satisfaction of both countries, gave Hitler the opportunity to gnaw slowly away at Austrian independence; but it also gave him the first real opportunity he had had to bring about a *rapprochement* with Italy. For Mussolini, now estranged from the Western Powers, could no longer successfully defend the independence of Austria and could not fail to be grateful that her independence was still to be nominally preserved. The opportunity for closer ties between Germany and Italy was made ideal a month later when civil war broke out in Spain, and Mussolini, by rushing to the help of Franco not only in the hope that a third Fascist state might be created in Europe, but also in the hope that he might obtain naval bases in Spain from which to threaten France, drew further apart from Germany's enemies. Ulrich von Hassell, the German Ambassador in Rome, realized at once the significance of the 'Spanish conflict as regards Italy's relations with France and England'. In a despatch to the German Foreign Office he suggested that its role could be 'similar to that of the Abyssinian conflict, bringing out clearly the opposing interest of the Powers and thus preventing Italy from being drawn into the net of the Western Powers'. The war could also serve another purpose. By allowing Italy to bear by far the greater burden of Nazi-Fascist help to Franco, under the pretext that Spain was a Mediterranean country and therefore in the Duce's province rather than his own, Hitler was able to ensure that Germany had a substitute for the Abyssinian war as a drain on Italian strength and a consequent security against an inflexible stand by the Duce on the Austrian issue, which he was determined that Germany should settle in her own way.[1]

Hitler made his preliminary overtures to Mussolini by offering to recognize the Italian Empire. This was a matter on which the Duce was violently susceptible, for the recognition was an acknowledgement of Italy's new status which most countries had so far withheld; and Mussolini, as Hassell predicted, was immensely gratified. In September Hitler sent to Rome his Italian-speaking Minister of Justice, Hans Frank, with a pressing invitation for the Duce to visit Germany. Mussolini listened with practised reserve to Frank's insistent compliments and to his protestations of the Führer's belief in the need for close collaboration between their two countries. Despite his granitic pose Mussolini was, however, flattered; and soon after this meeting with Hitler's envoy he made a speech in Piazza del Duomo at Milan in which for the first time he used a term which was for ever afterwards to hold a special connotation of ruin for his country. Referring to the better understanding between Italy and Germany, he borrowed a dramatic metaphor used two years before by the Hungarian Premier Combos in describing this understanding. There had been created, the Duce said, 'a Rome–Berlin axis around which all European states that desire peace can revolve.' Delighted by this public announcement of friendship, the Germans read much more into the speech than had been intended and were given the impression by their Press that a common policy had already been established.

Meanwhile in Germany, Mussolini's new Foreign Minister, Count Galeazzo Ciano, was paving the way for the State visit to Germany which the Duce was shortly to make. The son of Admiral Count Constanzo Ciano, a hero of the First World War, Galeazzo had entered the Diplomatic Service at the age of twenty-two after working as a journalist in Rome. Three years later, on 24 April 1930, he had married Edda Mussolini, the Duce's eldest daughter and, so it was believed, his favourite child. Thereafter Ciano's rise to power was meteoric. Within two months he was Consul-General in Shanghai and soon became Minister Pleni-

---

1. This, of course, explains what seemed inexplicable to many Republicans at the time – the fact that they, as well as the Nationalists, were receiving arms from Germany.

potentiary in China. By 1933 he was back in Rome as head of the Press Office, and after service as a pilot during the Abyssinian war he was appointed Foreign Minister. He behaved in those early years as a devoted disciple of the man who had made him and who now treated him not only as a well-liked son-in-law but as an intimate confidant. Vain, self-indulgent and indulged, ambitious, pretentious, and evasive, Ciano attempted to conceal by a superficial cynicism what was undoubtedly a deep admiration for the Duce. Even in the diary which he began to keep with assiduity after he became Foreign Minister he often made transparent efforts to disguise the idolatry which in conversation with his friends he took pains to hide altogether. Only occasionally did he allow himself to lapse into emotional eulogy. 'The Duce praised me several times today,' he wrote in one such moment of frank avowal. 'This so overwhelmed me that I am incapable even of thanking him. The truth is that one works for only one reason – to please him. To be successful in this is my greatest satisfaction.' After an illness in 1938 he confessed that when he heard the Duce's voice on the wireless he 'started to cry like a small child.'

His infrequently admitted but heartfelt admiration was apparent in other ways which made him appear almost ridiculous. He was unconsciously imitative. He copied the Duce's attitudes and mannerisms both in public and in private; he copied his rapid, jerky, emphatic way of talking; he even copied his pose of stone-like impassivity when on the point of hearing some anxiously awaited news. But he was not a ridiculous man. He had a quick eye for an opportunity, an undoubted gift for assimilation, and a sincere patriotism. He was often indiscreet and sometimes ruthless, and on more than one occasion he was to push his country into adventures which were both immoral and inept. He was so lazy that he refused to read a memorandum if it were more than a page long, and he spent as much time on the golf course and at parties given by his rich acquaintances in Roman society as he did in his office at Palazzo Chigi. He was so irresponsible that, according to Raffaele Guariglia, who was Ambassador in Paris from 1938 to 1940, the only instructions the Embassy ever received from him were to find a French governess for his children. But he was nevertheless a man of many qualities rarely found in Fascism's *gerarchi*. He was intelligent, alert, brave, not insensitive and, in spite of his postures and pretensions, charming. He was a devoted son and brother; he loved his children; and, although he had his own friends, both men and women, he did not lose the affection of his wife. 'He was a bounder,' wrote Lord Vansittart, who met him for the first time in 1934. 'But bounding is no sin in the sun. He liked women and advancement; others have had the same tastes with less fulfilment. He enjoyed good looks with some good nature and an occasional sense of humour. . . . He was having too good a time to want trouble; and a *jouisseur's* repugnance to war is more reliable than a pacifist's because it is more practical.'

Dino Alfieri, who as Italian Ambassador to Germany was later to know Ciano well, painted a similar, if more flattering portrait of his fellow-*jouisseur*.

In spite of his fickleness and his inconsistency, which sometimes left one with a feeling of genuine perplexity, Ciano was a good-natured, generous man. He was always glad to be of service to his friends, and it gave him a particular pleasure to be able to pass on a welcome piece of news. . . . He had a slightly Tuscan turn of phrase, and his conversation was animated, his language graphic and concise. By turns serious, paradoxically witty, mocking, sometimes even a little cynical . . . he was by nature extremely vivacious, whimsical, inquisitive, ironical, and sentimental. He always had a ready retort and his wit was facile and spontaneous.

Not everyone found him so quick-witted and attractive as Alfieri, but few people disliked him and none found him insignificant. With the Germans, however, he created a less favourable impression. He was always careful to suggest in his official memoranda that he got on well with them. But in fact he did not, and they found him superficial, vain, and so anxious to assert himself that his behaviour was often merely absurd. On one occasion during a visit to Berlin, William Shirer, the American foreign correspondent, described him as 'the clown of the evening. Without the slightest pretext he would hop to his heels and expand in a salute. Could not help noticing how high-strung Ciano is. He kept working his jaws and he was not chewing gum.'

His first official visit, which took place in October 1936, a month after Hans Frank's visit to Rome, was, however, successful enough. Ribbentrop, who grew to hate Ciano, had not yet replaced Neurath at the Foreign Ministry, and Hitler, who also grew to

hate him, treated him at Berchtesgaden with a flattering deference. He was obviously pleased with the friendly messages which
Ciano had brought with him. 'Mussolini,' the Führer said in a
sentence which delighted the son-in-law, 'is the leading statesman
in the world, to whom no other may even remotely compare
himself.' Talking rapidly he went on to survey the international
situation, the growing danger of Bolshevism and the comforting
speed of German rearmament. 'Every subject,' Ciano wrote
afterwards, 'brought forth a long exposition by Hitler and every
conclusion was repeated several times in different words.' From
the tangle of verbosity Ciano was, nevertheless, able to gather
that, so far as Britain was concerned, Hitler had not yet made up
his mind and he did not even now preclude the possibility of some
sort of agreement with her. Mussolini, more furious than ever
with the British since Haile Selassie had been invited to the
coronation of King George VI, was afraid of this and anxious that
at all costs an Anglo-German *rapprochement* should be avoided.
He was glad to hear from Ciano that, despite the Führer's
moderate attitude, this seemed unlikely and that Hitler thought
that if England continued to work against them, Germany and
Italy would have the combined power to defeat her. 'In three
years,' the Führer had said, 'Germany will be ready, in four years
more than ready; if five years are given, better still. . . . According
to the English there are two countries in the world today which
are led by Adventurers, Germany and Italy. But England, too,
was led by adventurers when she built her Empire. Today she is
governed by mere incompetents.' Some months later, on 10
September 1937, at a conference at Nyon, Britain gave further
offence to Mussolini by signing an agreement with France to
protect merchant ships in the Mediterranean, where supposedly
Spanish, but in reality Italian, submarines had been 'committing
acts of piracy' on Franco's behalf. Again Hitler, disapproving
this belated but perhaps infectious attempt of the democracies to
unite effectively against the developing Axis, gave Mussolini his
sympathy.

For, anxious as Mussolini was that Germany should not achieve
the agreement with Britain that was never in these years far from
Hitler's mind, the Führer, himself, was also anxious that Italy and
Britaih should not renew friendly relations at his expense. With a

view to preventing this and to emphasizing the solidarity of the Axis he had sent several representatives to Rome in 1937 on visits which superficially seemed friendly enough. None of the visits, however, was notably successful. When Goering arrived and had two discussions with Mussolini at the beginning of the year, the atmosphere was even strained. Mussolini had already decided that he did not like Goering. He thought him 'flashy and pretentious' and did not approve of his admiration for Balbo. On this occasion when Goering spoke of Austria as if the *Anschluss* were inevitable, the interpreter Paul Schmidt said that Mussolini shook his head violently.

Austria, however, was only one of Mussolini's problems, and his unfulfilled ambitions in Europe and the Mediterranean and his rancour against the Western Powers brought him to the view that he should no longer resist Hitler's blandishments. In September it was announced that he would visit Germany. He had agreed to accept the invitation, he said, on two conditions; that he would not have to bring any formal evening clothes with him and that he would be allowed to meet not only the leaders of the country but also the common people. These conditions were not prompted by modesty. He wanted to show that even in a foreign language he could excite a Berlin crowd to the same pitch of enthusiasm as he excited the people of Rome; and he wanted also to ensure that he would not have to wear civilian clothes in which he did not appear to his best advantage.

Wearing a splendid uniform specially designed for the occasion, he left for Germany on 23 September 1937 with a large staff almost as beautifully caparisoned as himself. Hitler, not to be outdone, ordered the reception committee which was to meet him at the frontier to wear uniform too, while he himself put on the brown shirt and tunic and the black trousers of the Nazi uniform and waited in Munich, whose streets were lined with troops and whose buildings were emblazoned with flags, for the Duce to arrive.

For weeks Germany had been preparing not only a welcome and a tribute but a carefully calculated display of power, regimentation, and organization which Mussolini should never forget. He never did forget. For the rest of his life, disillusioned with the Germans as he was to profess himself, he never lost his admiration for their efficiency, their dedication, their violently militaristic industry. From the beginning of his visit he was seen to be impressed; and he had cause to be. In spite of the rain, the cheers of the crowds were deafening, the countless lines of steel-helmeted soldiers motionless and seemingly unending. There were banquets in Munich, manoeuvres at Mecklenburg, visits to the factories of the Ruhr and parades of goose-stepping troops everywhere. In Berlin, towards the end of his tour, over 900,000 people gathered on the Maifeld to hear him speak, and even there, although Goering had previously put him in a bad mood by allowing his pet lioness to jump on him and by keeping him playing with his electric trains until the last minute, and although a thunderstorm of savage force interrupted his speech, soaked his notes, and played havoc with the loudspeaker system, he was deeply impressed. The crowds had waited in the pouring rain, as if on parade, to cheer the end of a speech which they could no longer hear and, from its beginning, had had difficulty in understanding. The Duce arrived back in his car soaked to the skin and obviously worn out, but he was undeterred. He had seen 'the most powerful nation in modern Europe rising magnificently to greatness.' His own progress through the country had been triumphal. 'His magnetism, his voice, his impetuous youthfulness,' Ciano wrote proudly, 'completely captivated the German crowds.' He had hardly had time to see Hitler alone for more than a few moments, so nothing of importance had been discussed, and Austria, as he later told Schuschnigg, had not even been mentioned. But he had made up his mind about Germany. 'When Fascism has a friend,' he had shouted into the crackling loudspeakers above the roar of the downpour on the Maifeld, 'it will march with that friend to the last.'

This categoric promise of loyalty marked the beginning of a fall into disaster. For many Italians it also marked the beginning of disillusion. They had until now been able to see the Fascist revolution as something clean and beneficial and, although authoritarian and anti-liberal, unadulterated by the grosser barbarisms of National Socialism. They had been content to see Germans described as uncouth and Hitler as a political criminal, paranoic, imitative, even grotesque. But now they had to read a different story. The Duce himself had referred to the Germans as 'a great people with proud traditions and a noble future', while Hitler was no longer the 'clown' but publicly eulogized in a widely reported speech as 'a genius, one of those few geniuses who make history and are not made by it'. A month after the Duce's visit, on 6 November 1937, Italy signed the Anti-Comintern Pact. Italy and Germany were to 'stand side by side against the threat of Bolshevism'.

The German influence on Fascism was soon apparent. So overwhelmed with admiration had Mussolini been at the sight of those thousands of rigidly drilled troops goose-stepping past him, their heavy boots falling with so rhythmic and intimidating a crash on the rainswept streets, that he decided to introduce this magnificent evidence of virility into the Italian Army and the Fascist Militia. Unconscious or disdainful of the antagonism and ridicule which such degrading plagiarism would arouse, he ordered the goose-step to be the new march of the Italian soldier. He called it the *passo romano*, 'the firm, inexorable step of the legions for whom every march was a march of conquest'. Ten years before, the Nazis had adopted the Roman salute as their own; but now, although he vehemently denied it, maintaining that the goose was a Roman animal because it had saved the Capitol, it was Mussolini who was the imitator, taking the goose-step without acknowledgement from Hitler as he had taken the Roman salute from D'Annunzio. The step was a difficult, tiring one to perform, and unless done well looks absurd. This criticism as much as the charge that it was a mere copy of *il passo dell'oca* infuriated Mussolini. When the King made it, he commented contemptuously to Ciano, 'It isn't my fault if the King is physically no more than a half-cartridge. It's natural that he can't perform the step without appearing ridiculous. He doesn't like it for the same reason that he doesn't like riding a horse – because he has to use a ladder to mount.' 'Clearly,' he said, on another occasion after practising the step himself, 'that wretched little thing could never do this on parade; but it's of no consequence. I shall get rid of him. The course of history can be changed in a night.' Mussolini's increased resentment against the King rose from the fact that Victor Emmanuel did not like the Germans and did not hesitate to say so or to express his concern about the growth of friendship between Italy and the Reich. 'The monarchy,' Mussolini angrily decided, has become 'a useless super-structure.' When told that the King also objected to the introduction of the Roman salute into the Army, Mussolini exploded with indignation. 'It has needed all my patience,' he said, 'to tow this tiresome monarchy along. It has never done anything which would commit it to the régime. I am still biding my time, because the King is seventy and I hope that nature will come to my help.'

A more alarming result of Mussolini's friendship with Germany, and one infinitely more despised than the introduction of the goose-step and the Roman salute into the Army, was the introduction of anti-Semitism into national life. The evil never went very deep. A declaration by some well-known university professors printed in the Fascist Press in July 1938 that the Italians were Nordic Aryans whose blood had not been mixed since the Lombard invasions was greeted with the ridicule which it deserved. But three months later the Fascist Grand Council decided upon a programme of racial legislation. Marriages with those of non-Aryan race – a term never precisely defined – were to be forbidden unless permission was obtained from the Ministry of the Interior; foreign Jews and those who had come to Italy after 1 January 1919 were to be expelled; no Jew was to be allowed to be a teacher, lawyer, journalist, banker, or a member of the Fascist Party; special elementary schools were to be established for Jewish children; marriage, or even fornication, with African natives was to be punished by imprisonment. 'All this,' the Duce said, would 'increase the hatred of foreigners for Italy. Good!'

It also increased the opposition to Fascism, and this drove Mussolini to frequent and extravagant outbursts against 'spineless people in Italy who were moved by the fate of the Jews'. The King was one of them, and his expression of 'infinite pity for the Jews' made Mussolini remark that the little milksop ought to be treated as one of them himself. Even before his visit to Germany, Mussolini had, in Ciano's phrase, let fly at America as 'the country of niggers and Jews – the forces which disintegrate civilization'. In the year 2000, he prophesied, the races playing an important role in Europe would be the Italians, the Germans, the Russians, and the Japanese. 'Other countries will be destroyed by the acid of Jewish corrosion. The Jews even refuse to breed because it costs pain. They don't realize that pain is the only

creative factor in the life of a nation.' He approved unconditionally, he said later, the reprisals carried out by the Nazis when they
used the murder of the Third Secretary of the German Embassy
in Paris by a Polish Jew as the pretext for an increase in their anti-
Semitic activities.

And yet the Duce himself viewed with apparent unconcern the
haphazard and uncertain way in which his own racial legislation,
as indeed so much other Fascist legislation, was enforced. 'It's
typical of him,' a German Embassy official said to a friend. 'He
barks like mad, but he doesn't bite.' He changed his dentist and
told a leading Fascist to change his secretary, but these gestures
did not impress the Germans with the seriousness of his attitude
to the Jewish question. The OVRA was never instructed to ensure
that the racial legislation was enforced, and Bocchini himself was
known not to take it seriously. As an anti-Semite Mussolini was,
and remained, a disappointment to Hitler. When a Fascist scholar
went to him to protest against the treatment of some Jewish
friends, he was reported as replying, 'I agree with you entirely.
I don't believe a bit in the stupid anti-Semitic theory. I am carrying out my policy entirely for political reasons.' But the impression
that he was carrying it out in deference to German wishes was
nevertheless inescapable.

By the beginning of 1938 Mussolini's enthusiasm for Germany
had somewhat cooled. Throughout the winter he had been aware
of the imminence of a new German assault on Austrian independence, but Hitler had not troubled to inform him of his plans. On
12 February Schuschnigg, the Austrian Chancellor, who ever
since the signing of the Austro-German Agreement of July 1936
had been playing for time and making concessions in order to
avoid a Nazi *Putsch*, paid a visit to Berchtesgaden for a conversation with Hitler. The Führer was abusive and threatening, and
Schuschnigg was presented with far-reaching demands of which
the Italians had been given no previous notice. Ciano was instructed to make it known that the Duce was annoyed, but that
was as far as the protest went. He knew he would have to suc-
cumb if Hitler's threats provoked war, and the following month,
when Schuschnigg had taken the dangerous but courageous step of
announcing that he would hold a plebiscite in Austria in which
the people would be asked to declare their views on the *Anschluss*,

Mussolini said that the decision was a mistake. For Hitler it was a great deal more serious than a mistake. It was, as A. J. P. Taylor has written in an apt phrase, 'as though someone had trodden on a painful corn'. He fixed Saturday 12 March as the day for marching across the frontier, and on the previous Thursday sent a letter which was to be delivered personally in Rome to the Duce by Prince Philip of Hesse, a Nazi sympathizer who was married to the King of Italy's daughter, Princess Mafalda.

'I am now determined to restore law and order in my homeland,' Hitler wrote. 'I wish now solemnly to assure your Excellency, as the Duce of Fascist Italy: (1) I consider this step only as one of national self-defence. . . . (2) In a critical hour for Italy I proved to you the steadfastness of my sympathy. Do not doubt that in the future there will be no change in this respect. (3) Whatever the consequences of the coming events may be, I have drawn a definite boundary between Germany and France and now draw one just as definite between Italy and us. It is the Brenner. This decision will never be questioned or changed.'

Although extremely anxious to obtain Mussolini's agreement not to intervene as he had done in 1934, Hitler had decided in any event to attack, and while Hesse was still on his way to Rome instructions for Operation Otto had already been issued. By the time he received Hitler's letter Mussolini was aware of this. He knew that it would be pointless to resist and had in fact, since Schuschnigg's visit to Berchtesgaden, decided that it would not be politic to do so. All he could hope for now was that some advantage might be gained by a ready acknowledgement of Hitler's provocation. Just before half past ten on the Friday night Prince Philip telephoned Hitler to give him the Duce's reply to his letter.

'I have just come back from Palazzo Venezia,' Prince Philip said. 'The Duce accepted the whole thing in a very friendly manner. He sends you his regards. . . .'

Hitler's relief was overwhelming. He knew that Mussolini had once passionately declared that Italy 'could never permit Austria – the bastion of Mediterranean civilization – to be the victim of Pan-Germanism.' But now the Duce's support, of which he had not till now felt completely assured, was granted him.

'Please tell Mussolini that I shall never forget him for this.'

'Yes.'

'Never, never, never, whatever happens. . . . As soon as the Austrian affair is settled, I shall be ready to go with him, through thick and thin, no matter what happens.'

'Yes, my Führer.'

'Listen, I shall make any agreement. . . . You may tell him that I thank him so very much; never, never, shall I forget.'

'Yes, my Führer.'

'I will never forget, whatever may happen. If he should ever need any help or be in any danger, he must be assured that I shall stick to him, whatever may happen, even if the whole world were against him.'

'Yes, my Führer.'

Two days later Hitler repeated his assurances of lifelong gratitude. 'I shall never forget this,' he said in a cable sent from Austria, which was already officially described as 'a province of the German Reich'.

'My attitude,' Mussolini replied, 'is determined by the friendship between our two countries, which is consecrated in the Axis.'

His attitude, however, had still to be explained to an indignant Italian public which not many months before had listened to the Duce's determined declaration that 'the independence of Austria, for which Dollfuss died, is a principle for which the Italians have fought and will continue to fight.' It certainly could not be explained by dismissing Austria, as he did in conversation with Ciano, as 'an ambiguity which has been removed from the map of Europe'. In the Chamber, Mussolini disingenuously attempted to silence opposition by affirming in a particularly bombastic speech that Italy had 'never given any pledge, either directly or indirectly, either verbally or in writing, to intervene to save the independence of Austria.' This was demonstrably false, and the Italian people knew that it was. For the first time since the murder of Matteotti a general and deep sense of disenchantment swept over them; and although the Axis survived the *Anschluss*, the Duce's hitherto unquestionable popularity did not. Apart from the sudden and seemingly abject change of policy to please an unwanted ally, no intelligent observer could fail to realize the dangers for Italy in allowing a strong and militant Germany to extend its frontiers to the Alps. The whole traditional theme of Italian foreign policy had been contradicted.

For Hitler the annexation of Austria was a triumph, the realization of his most compelling ambition. But it was also a stepping-stone towards an even larger empire in the East. As early as November 1937 he had spoken at a secret meeting at the Reich Chancellery of his intention to annex Czechoslovakia. Now he was ready to do so. The reaffirmation by the French Government of its guarantees to Czechoslovakia he did not take seriously. He felt, with that instinct which he was beginning to consider infallible, that France, like England, was so anxious not to go to war that her protestations could be discounted; but, to make sure that France was driven by fear to atrophy, he decided before taking any irrevocable step that he would strengthen the Axis.

Mussolini had invited him to visit Italy the previous September. On 2 May 1938 the Führer left for Rome with the expressed intention, so a secretary at the Italian Embassy in Berlin reported, of flattering the Italians' pride and of demonstrating that the Axis was a living reality. He had much lost ground to regain. The *Anschluss* was not forgiven and had revived fears about German intentions in Alto Adige. Also the British Government, taking advantage of what it hoped was Italy's disillusion with Germany over Austria, and in an attempt to prevent Hitler from further aggression, had come to a settlement with Mussolini.

This settlement, suggested by Ciano, was welcomed by Chamberlain but strongly resisted by Eden – 'that sworn enemy of Italy', as Mussolini had called him – and a heated argument between the two Englishmen, which resulted in Eden's resignation two days later, was carried on in the presence of Count Dino Grandi, the Italian Ambassador. Gratified by Eden's resignation, which was celebrated in the Italian Press as a triumph for Italy (editors were instructed to tone down their pleasure in case the hated English politician might be turned into a martyr), Mussolini accepted the settlement with a sulky pleasure. He knew that Hitler's actions had put him in a good bargaining position, and for indeterminate promises of support in Central Europe he had been able to obtain acceptance of his conquest of Abyssinia and of his intervention in Spain in addition to satisfactory guarantees in the Mediterranean. 'The Italian pact,' Churchill wrote in disgust to Eden, 'is of course a complete triumph for Mussolini.' Ciano thought so too, and could not conceal a mild contempt for the English for having given so much ground. 'How romantic!' he commented when it was suggested that the Agreement should be signed on Easter Day because it was also Halifax's birthday. 'The scope of the agreement is vast,' he wrote excitedly in his diary. 'It is the beginning of a new era in our relationship with Great Britain. Friendship on a footing of equality – the only kind of friendship we can accept with London or with anyone else.' Italian public opinion would welcome it, he said, 'with immense enthusiasm partly because it will be seen as a possible way of disengaging ourselves from Berlin'. Certainly when Lord Perth, the British Ambassador, left Palazzo Chigi after signing the Agreement on 1 April 1938 he was loudly cheered; and on his way to report to the Duce at Palazzo Venezia, Ciano was given an even more enthusiastic ovation. By eight o'clock the crowds had become so large that Mussolini himself went on to the balcony to acknowledge their cheers.

It was, as Churchill said, a 'triumph'. But so far as the British were concerned the Agreement was worthless. Not for a moment did Mussolini envisage it as the first step in a policy of disengagement from Germany; it was, for him, merely yet another acknowledgement of Italy's influence and growing power. He was more gratified, in fact, by Germany's recognition of how one-sided the Agreement was than with the benefit which Italy would derive from it; and seems not to have realized now or later what great opportunities were open to him in steering the traditional middle course between Germany and the Western Democracies, or that his Axis partner would have treated him with a greater respect if he had felt less able to rely upon him. But Mussolini was so anxious to impress the Germans with his ruthlessness that he threw away the chance of pursuing a skilful diplomacy.

Ever since his last visit to Germany this wish to impress the Germans had been a growingly persuasive influence on his policies. In the early stages of his negotiations over the Anglo-Italian Agreement Lord Perth had remonstrated with Ciano about the Italian air raids on Spanish towns. The Duce, though, 'wasn't at all worried' about the Ambassador's comments. 'In fact,' Ciano wrote, 'he said he was delighted that the Italians should be horrifying the world by their aggressiveness for a change instead of charming it by their skill at playing the guitar. In his opinion this will send up our stock in Germany, where they love total and ruthless war.'

Mussolini was determined that Hitler's visit to Italy should be as impressive as his own to Germany. The planning had begun six months before, and Ciano, anxious that nothing should be done in a 'commonplace, countrified, Humbertine sort of way', had paid particular attention to the decoration of the streets and, although many shopkeepers refused to display portraits of Hitler, they were made to look splendidly welcoming. The Duce spent hours supervising the arrangement of military parades and checking the detail of every march-past; and he was rewarded. Achille Starace, for all his faults, was a brilliant stage manager. 'The military parades,' as Ciano said, 'were magnificent. The Germans, who may have been a little sceptical on this point, will leave with a very different impression.'

Hitler certainly was impressed. He had seen more expert displays in Germany and knew that Italy could not be considered a strong military Power, but she was obviously an ally he could not afford to lose; and Mussolini himself lived up to the Führer's estimate of him as the only leader in the world worth comparison with himself. Hitler, for his own part, behaved admirably. He was far from being the 'silly little clown' he had seemed at Venice; and the only fault that the Duce could now find in him was that he appeared to wear rouge on his cheeks to hide his pallor. He was acclaimed in Rome, cheered enthusiastically in Florence and Naples; and he spoke to the crowds well and with dignity. Disclaiming any intention of demanding the return of the South Tyrol, he said, 'It is my unalterable will and my bequest to the German people that it shall regard the frontier of the Alps, raised by nature between us, as for ever inviolable.' 'The Führer has had a great personal success,' Ciano thought. 'He has succeeded quite successfully in melting the ice around him. . . . His personal contacts too have won sympathy, particularly among women.' Not even the photographs of him leaving the San Carlo Opera House, looking absurd in evening dress and a top-hat, destroyed the favourable impression that he had created.

But if the *gerarchi* were satisfied, King Victor Emmanuel was not. He disliked and distrusted him on sight, and accepted him as his guest at the Quirinale with obvious reluctance. He told Mussolini that on his first night there Hitler had asked for a woman. This request caused a convulsive tumult in the Royal Household until it was explained that the Führer could not get to sleep until he had seen a woman remake his bed. Was the story really true, Ciano wondered ? Or was it rather malice on the part of the King, who also insinuated that 'Hitler injects himself with stimulants and narcotics' ? The whole atmosphere of the Palace, Ciano decided, was 'moth-eaten – a dynasty a thousand years old does not like the manner of self-expression of a revolutionary régime. To a Hitler, who is nothing but a *parvenu*, they prefer any paltry little King.'

Hitler disliked King Victor Emmanuel as much as the King disliked him, and for the rest of his life he nursed a resentment against the House of Savoy. In their last public appearance together their mutual antipathy was apparent. But no less apparent was the cordiality that existed between the Duce and the Führer. At the station when they said good-bye, both of them were moved and Hitler was seen to stare at Mussolini with an almost dog-like devotion. 'From now on,' the Duce told him, 'no force on earth will be able to separate us.' The Führer's eyes filled with tears.

He returned from Italy satisfied that the Duce would not interfere with his designs on Czechoslovakia. Only the vaguest reference to the problem had been made during the visit, but Mussolini was known to dislike the Czechs and had already referred to their country – as he had referred to Austria – as 'an ambiguity on the map of Europe'. As if to prepare his country for Italian acceptance of a German solution, the Duce referred in his speeches to the necessity of facing the Czechoslovak problem and of 'settling it in a general manner'. 'If Czechoslovakia finds herself today in what might be called a delicate situation,' he said in one such speech, 'it is because she was – one may already say was – not just Czechoslovak but Czecho-Germano-Polono-Magyar-Rutheno-Roumano-Slovakia.'

The Duce's main concern, indeed, was not that the Germans would, if necessary, settle the problem by force but that he would not be informed beforehand of the date of their intended action. On more than one occasion Bernardo Attolico, the Italian Ambassador in Berlin, was instructed to ask Ribbentrop, Neurath's successor as Foreign Minister, to 'communicate in good time the probable date of action against Czechoslovakia'. When it seemed probable, however, that Hitler's diplomacy would provoke a general war, Mussolini, as always at the thought that German threats were about to cause a crisis, became less sure that he should continue to give Hitler his unqualified support. Chamberlain, as Ciano said, was more interested than the Duce in reaching a peaceful agreement; but Mussolini himself was increasingly aware of how close to the brink of war Hitler was moving and of how dangerous it would be to allow his own unprepared country to be forced into the conflict or for his own insistently gascon-ading bluff to be called. 'If war breaks out in Germany, Prague, Paris, and Moscow,' he confided to Ciano, 'I shall remain neutral.'

By 28 September war seemed inevitable. Hitler's ultimatum to the Czechs, delivered at Godesberg four days before, was due to expire that afternoon at two o'clock. During the morning an urgent telephone call was made to Palazzo Chigi. The British had again looked to Mussolini as a moderating influence on Hitler. Could Lord Perth see Count Ciano immediately? 'I receive him at once,' Ciano recorded. 'He says, with much emotion, that Chamberlain appeals to the Duce for his friendly intervention in these hours, which he considers the last in which something can be done to save peace and civilization.'

Mussolini was delighted. It was far better, he admitted, to pose as a peace-maker than risk being dragged into a war he was not ready to fight; besides, the eyes of the world were upon him. He told Ciano to telephone Berlin, and as soon as Attolico's voice came on the line he snatched the receiver to tell the Ambassador to go to Hitler to assure him that Italy was at Germany's side but to suggest a delay in mobilization for twenty-four hours. 'Get a reply by noon,' Mussolini added.

It was already after eleven. Attolico ran downstairs and jumped breathless and without his hat into a taxi. When he arrived at the Chancellery, Hitler was talking to the French Ambassador, André François-Poncet, who had brought a last-minute offer from his Government. An SS officer went into the room to announce that Attolico had arrived with a message from the Duce, and the Führer left François-Poncet immediately. Hitler read the Duce's message, which Attolico had had translated into German. He hesitated for a moment, but then he agreed. He confessed later to Goering that he was left wondering whether if he did not agree Mussolini would leave him to pursue his course alone. 'The Communists have lost their chance,' Attolico said to the British Ambassador, Nevile Henderson, a few hours later. 'If they had cut the telephone wires today between Rome and Berlin there would have been war.'

At three o'clock Hitler's agreement was made known in the House of Commons by the Prime Minister. 'That is not all,' Mr Chamberlain went on with rising emotion as a further message was handed to him, 'I have something further to say to the House yet. I have now been informed by Herr Hitler that he invites me to meet him at Munich tomorrow morning. He has also invited Signor Mussolini and M. Daladier. Signor Mussolini has accepted, and I have no doubt M. Daladier will also accept. I need not say what my answer will be.'

Mussolini, for his part, considered that Chamberlain's obvious pleasure and pride were misplaced. When Ciano telephoned to give him the news of Hitler's decision he commented with satisfaction 'There will not be a war, but this is the annihilation of English prestige.'

On his way to Germany that night he elaborated on the point. 'In a country where animals are adored to the point of making cemeteries and hospitals and houses for them,' he said in high good-humour, 'and legacies are bequeathed to parrots, you can be certain that decadence has set in. Besides, other reasons apart, it is also a consequence of the composition of the English people. Four million surplus women! Four million sexually unsatisfied women artificially creating a host of problems in order to excite or sublimate their desires! Not being able to embrace one man, they embrace humanity.'

He went on talking till late at night. He was in excellent spirits. He knew that without his influence the conference would not be taking place. Only he could reason with Hitler; it was only his sponsorship of the talks that had provided the Führer with a face-saving reason for agreeing to them; and it was only on condition that the Duce attended in person that the Führer had agreed to them at all. Mussolini had even been asked to choose the meeting-place; Hitler had suggested Frankfort or Munich and the Duce had chosen Munich.

About seventy miles south of the town the train stopped at Kufstein on the Inn, where Hitler, anxious to talk to Mussolini before the conference begun, boarded it with Prince Philip of Hesse. He invited the Duce to come across to his carriage, where he showed him some large-scale maps of the country which he intended to liquidate. If the conference was not successful, he insisted, a solution would be imposed on Czechoslovakia by force. It was with difficulty that Mussolini persuaded him not to condemn the conference to failure before it had even begun, and only when the Duce promised that Italy would support Germany in the event of failure did Hitler seem satisfied. 'The time will come,' the Führer added, 'when we shall have to fight side by side against England.' Mussolini did not answer him, and Hitler still did not know how far he could rely on Italy's support.

The Führer's display of intractability was repeated when, a few hours later, the conference began at the *Führerhaus* in the Königsplatz. He came down the stairs to meet his guests looking white and obdurate. He greeted the Italian delegation with calculated warmth, but shook hands briefly and coldly with Chamberlain and Daladier. He had already announced, he said, talking fast and excitedly, that he would act against Czechoslovakia, but had been told that his action would have the character of violence. Hence the conference's task was 'to absolve the action from such a character. Action, however, must be taken at once.'

Despite his categoric words he seemed nervous and curiously unsure of himself. When he had finished speaking he walked away from the others and stood restlessly by the wall watching Mussolini, who, by contrast, appeared not merely self-assured but patronizing, as he walked around the room with his hands in his pockets talking easily in French to Daladier, to Ribbentrop in his careful German, to Chamberlain in his less certain but adequate English. He produced a Memorandum which closely followed, with slight modifications, the German proposals that had been telephoned to him in Rome by Attolico. Accepting the Memorandum as Mussolini's own draft and one which the Germans would consider a satisfactory basis for discussion, the other delegates were prepared to examine it carefully. Other drafts were written and discussed, but it was this one which formed the basis of the Agreement which was signed at two o'clock in the morning of 30 September. Hours before, Mussolini had decided that Hitler had already gained every material point, and the continued discussions clearly seemed pointless to him. He did not enter into them and succeeded in giving Chamberlain the impression of being 'extremely quiet and reserved', even 'cowed by Hitler'. Ivone Kirkpatrick, too, thought that Mussolini, despite his apparent self-confidence, was afraid of Hitler and that he now seemed to be 'a man who was deeply relieved at the outcome'.

Ciano, deeply relieved as well, watched the Duce standing aloof from the others and could not conceal his admiration. 'His great spirit,' he wrote afterwards, 'always ahead of events and men, has already absorbed the idea of agreement and while the others are still wasting their breath over more or less formal problems he has almost ceased to take an interest. He has already passed on and is meditating on other things.'

Although he was later constantly to express his dissatisfaction with the Munich agreement, Hitler himself appeared to share Ciano's admiration for the Duce. He watched him constantly, François-Poncet said. 'He seemed fascinated. If the Duce laughed, he laughed; if the Duce frowned, he frowned.'

The Duce's performance was greeted in Italy as a triumph. The King came to Florence from his country estate at San Rossore to congratulate him, and when his train reached Rome enormous crowds came to cheer him with an enthusiasm which, according to himself, they had not shown since the proclamation of the Empire. But the excitement did not please him, for the title 'Angel of peace' which he heard shouted through the more familiar chant of '*Duce! Duce!*' was not one which in the least appealed to him. At the sight of an arch of laurel leaves which had been built across Via Nazionale he exploded with anger. 'Who's responsible,' he asked furiously, 'for this carnival?' The Italian people must not be allowed to hope for peace, their 'character must be moulded by fighting'. Determined not to let them suppose that he should be compared with Chamberlain as a peace-maker – a term which for him could be nothing but pejorative – Mussolini celebrated his return to Italy by making a series of speeches intended to dragoon them – and in particular the *bour-*

geoisie, who needed a 'good punch in the stomach' – into accepting an aggressive Germany as their friend and ally and France as their enemy. 'Italy cannot be sufficiently Prussianized,' he thought. 'I will not leave the Italians in peace till I have six feet of earth over my head.' 'I am preparing a great surprise for them,' he had told Ciano the year before. 'As soon as Spain is finished I shall issue an announcement which will become historic.' His Ministers had learned to accept these enigmatic threats with reserve, but they could not help feeling now that the Duce was in earnest. On 26 September he told Ciano that he had definitely decided to mobilize the next day and to send troops to Libya, and Ciano confessed later that he believed he was really going to do so. Ciano, indeed, afterwards told a friend he had feared the Duce would go to war purely to spite the hated *bourgeosie*, who were showing alarm at the fearful cost of Fascist policy and of the vast bureaucracy which Fascism had developed. The published figures of State expenditure showed a rapidly increasing deficit, which from just over two thousand million lire in 1934–5 was over 11,000 million by 1937–8 and by 1939–40 was to be more than twenty-eight thousand million. Characteristically, Mussolini attributed the growing restlessness of the middle classes to their selfish concern for their own welfare, their refusal to recognize the national interest or, as he put it in a familiar but fustian phrase, 'the historical and classic direction of Fascist dynamics'. The rich, too, were wavering in their support of the régime and were becoming infected with bourgeois ideas. They must all be bludgeoned into selflessness and discipline, he said, and Starace was to consider the possibility of an anti-bourgeois exhibition.[1] The Party leaders must set an example of the true, anti-bourgeois Fascist spirit by not wearing starch in the black collars of their shirts or attending night-clubs or drinking coffee. Later on he considered closing the Stock Exchange, abolishing first-class travel on the railways, outlawing golf and the importation of French magazines, French clothes, and French books.

The campaign against France had been started months before.

1. It is an illuminating reflection that men tend to condemn most virulently what they most fear and dislike in themselves. Despite his extravagant Bohemianism, the young Mussolini always took care to be photographed wearing presentable clothes and he had visiting-cards printed with the style 'Professor', to which, by virtue of his qualifications as a teacher, he was entitled.

Ciano's diary for May 1938 is full of references to it. On 13 May the Duce is described as being 'more and more anti-French. He said they are a nation ruined by alcohol, syphilis, and journalism.' The following day he made a speech in Genoa. 'It is a very strong anti-French speech. The crowd hissed France, laughed ironically at the agreement with London.' On May 17 he was still 'very worked up against France'. Two days later he was 'more exasperated than ever'. An intercepted report, containing some disparaging remarks made about him by the French Ambassador, had the predictable effect of driving him to still greater indignation.

After the Munich conference the attacks were sustained until by the beginning of December anti-French demonstrations in Italy were becoming commonplace. On 9 December Mussolini confessed to Ciano that he thought matters had gone far enough for the moment; a little sand would have to be put into the wheels of the anti-French campaign. 'If it continues at this rate,' he thought, 'we shall have to make the cannon speak, and the time has not come for that yet.' It had, after all, been initiated not as a prelude to war but to serve the less drastic purpose of acclimatizing public opinion to a written military alliance with Germany.

The first suggestion of such an alliance had been made by Ribbentrop during Hitler's visit to Rome in May, but Mussolini, although he had at one time seemed favourable towards the idea, eventually instructed Ciano to be evasive. Ribbentrop had broached the subject again at Munich. 'He says it is the biggest thing in the world,' Ciano wrote disdainfully. 'He always exaggerates, Ribbentrop. No doubt we will study it quite calmly and perhaps put it aside for a time.' And this is exactly what Mussolini told him to do.

In October, when he visited Rome, the German Foreign Minister was no more successful. Ciano, after an early flush of enthusiasm, had now decided that he cordially disliked the man and listened impatiently when Ribbentrop, referring to England as a woman might have referred to a 'faithless lover', told the Duce didactically that war was inevitable and that the Anti-Comintern Pact should be made into a military alliance in which Japan should be included. Mussolini was polite but refused to commit himself. He said that Italian public opinion was not yet mature. The generals and the middle-classes would strongly disapprove of it; so would the Church, which was on increasingly bad terms with the German Government; and so would the King, who, although he disliked the French and had his eye on Corsica, disliked the Germans even more.

The quarrel with France, however, was forcing Mussolini, as he had been forced during the Abyssinian war, into reliance on German support. He was concerned to hear that while he was laying public claim to Corsica, Nice, and Tunis, Ribbentrop had been to Paris, and to cause trouble between England and France had signed a Declaration guaranteeing the existing Franco-German frontier. He was also concerned by rumours of a military agreement between Britain and France and of American intentions to supply military material to the Democracies in case of necessity. He was, perhaps, in addition, hoping that if he signed a military pact with Germany he would be able to exercise more influence on German policies. Certainly by the end of 1938 he had come to the conclusion that he could no longer procrastinate. On 3 January Ciano told Attolico to let the Germans know that the Duce would shortly be ready to sign a treaty of alliance. 'In the past,' Ciano wrote in his diary, 'Attolico had been rather hostile to the idea of an alliance with Germany,' but now 'he showed himself openly favourable to it. He said that during this particular leave in Italy, he has been convinced that nothing would be more popular amongst us than a war against France.' Two days later, Achille Starace was given his instructions. Propaganda against France must be steadily increased so that the alliance could be announced when anti-French feeling was at its height; and as soon as the news was made public, 'demonstrations with a sharply Francophobe flavour' were to be organized. Nothing, however, was to be done for the moment as the British Prime Minister was due in Rome in a few days' time and it would be better to wait until he had left.

Chamberlain had himself proposed the visit. He believed that he had come to a satisfactory understanding with Hitler and should now make sure of Italy's friendship also. He was prepared, as many other more percipient Englishmen were prepared, to forgive the Abyssinian adventure and, in Duff Cooper's phrase, to let Italian bygones be bygones. Many members of his Party, indeed, had not condemned the attack even at the time and were, as Mr Michael Foot has shown in a clever and ironic book, willing to condone it. Chamberlain went to Italy hoping to exploit this fact; if he could create a split between Rome and Berlin, so much the better. With the reluctant agreement of the French Government, he wrote suggesting that he and Lord Halifax should visit Mussolini in January.

Despite Chamberlain's efforts to be pleasant the visit was a failure and an embarrassment. The English, Mussolini had already decided, had 'their minds in the seat of their trousers'. 'Chamberlain and his umbrella are coming,' he had told his wife, and although he admitted later that the Prime Minister's conversation was 'very sprightly for an Englishman,' he was even less impressed with him than he had been at Munich. Starace had been instructed to see that Chamberlain and Halifax received a 'not too enthusiastic welcome'. These instructions were carried out exactly. The Englishmen were greeted with restrained courtesy; Mussolini himself was gracious and accepted with apparent pleasure a signed photograph of the British Prime Minister, but out of their hearing he spoke of them with a disdain which was close to contempt. 'How far apart we are from these people,' Ciano wrote when his guests had gone and he had seen Chamberlain's eyes fill with tears as the train moved out of the station to the strains of 'For he's a jolly good fellow', sung by a group of English residents. 'They live in a different world. We were talking about it after dinner with the Duce, gathered together in a corner of the room. "These men are not made of the same stuff," he was saying, "as the Francis Drakes and the other magnificent adventurers who created the British Empire. They are the tired sons of a long line of rich forefathers and they will lose their Empire."' He gave similar expression to his disdain a few weeks later when Lord Perth submitted for his approval a speech he intended to make in the House of Commons. 'I believe this is the first time,' he said, 'that the Head of the British Government has submitted to a foreign Government the outline of one of his speeches. It's a bad sign for them.' It was perhaps natural, he said on another occasion, that the English should be terrified of war. It was only to be expected of a people who lived a comfortable life and 'made a religion of eating and games.' The whole Fascist ethic was opposed to this idea. In a celebrated article signed with his name in the *Enciclopedia Italiana*, Fascism had been officially described as believing 'neither in the possibility nor in the utility of perpetual peace. . . . War alone brings up to its highest tension all human energy and puts the stamp of nobility upon the people who have the courage to meet it.' This was a philosophy which the English 'could not begin to understand.' But what, after all, could you expect of a people, he asked in a subsequent speech in which his misconceptions of English life were so grotesque as to be appealing, who changed into dinner-jackets for their five o'clock tea ?

After Chamberlain's departure Ciano telephoned Ribbentrop to assure him that the meeting with Mussolini accomplished nothing. 'It was a fiasco, absolutely worthless.' The preparation of the text of the military alliance was to go ahead. Before it was signed, however, the Axis was given a jolt which brought it close to dissolution.

On 14 March 1939, without consulting Mussolini, German troops crossed the Czechoslovak frontier; the following day Hitler was in Prague. When he was given the news Mussolini was furious. 'Every time Hitler occupies a country,' he said angrily, after the Führer's envoy Prince Philip of Hesse had called as usual to thank the Duce for his support, 'he sends a message.' The German alliance was an absurdity, he said later, against which the 'very stones would revolt'. His anger, however, soon changed to gloom. When Ciano commented sourly that the 'Axis functions only in favour of one of its parts' and that the reaction of the people would be very hostile, Mussolini replied with a quotation from Dante: 'We must avoid "displeasing God and also God's enemies".' 'The German trick' would have to be accepted with a good grace. Already he had come to the conclusion that Hitler was too strong now to be stopped and that Italy must stay on his side, however insolently he treated her. He was desperately concerned by the inevitable spread of German influence across the Balkans, which he liked to consider as his own diplomatic territory, and he accepted with obvious caution Hitler's reassurances that Germany would leave the Mediterranean and the Adriatic to Italy; but he refused to break the Axis. 'We cannot change our policy now,' he insisted. 'We are not, after all, political prostitutes.'

On the evening of 21 March he made his decision known to a

meeting of the Fascist Grand Council in a speech which Ciano described as 'marvellous, argumentative, logical, cold, and heroic'. He spoke of 'uncompromising loyalty to the Axis' as being a necessity of Italian foreign policy and of the Fascist conception of true friendship. The Council, accustomed to unquestioning obedience, accepted the Duce's decision without complaint. Only Grandi, De Bono, and Balbo appeared dissatisfied, but when Mussolini was told of their criticisms he dismissed them as 'stupidities'. Balbo, who said that to remain a part of the Axis was tantamount to 'licking Germany's boots', was nothing but 'a democratic swine' whose future Mussolini had already decided he 'would not like to guarantee'. De Bono was 'an idiotic old dotard'. He had always been an idiot and now he was old as well. The Duce had made up his mind, Starace told the officials at Party Headquarters, 'and that was that'.

Not only Mussolini's policies but even his character seemed to have been affected by his association with Hitler, by his unwilling but growing dependence upon him, his reluctant admiration, his patent jealousy. Whereas in the past he had been willing to listen to advice and even occasionally to criticism, now he attacked with an alarming venom those who presumed to advise him or to question his political sense. Deciding that the Italians needed hardening and infusing with that spirit which characterized Germany's military success, he forced his Ministers and the leaders of the Fascist Party to set an example by performing hard and even dangerous exercises and by taking part in strenuous sports. With the same end in view he extended the categories of officials who were expected to wear uniforms; he issued decrees intended stringently to enforce the regulations abolishing the handshake and the polite form of address; he obliged the generals and their staffs to run and not to walk during military exercises. 'The Italians must learn,' he was fond of saying, 'to grow less likeable and to become hard, implacable, and hateful.' He himself, he was proud to admit, would rather be feared than loved. He was certainly doing his best to become so. Towards the end of the war in Spain, Franco's forces captured several Italian Communists who had been fighting in Catalonia. He was asked what should be done with them. 'Shoot them,' he ordered, according to Ciano. 'Dead men tell no tales.'

For the Jews he planned a less conventional fate. When considering the advantages of turning part of Italian Somaliland into a concession for international Jewry, he decided that Migiurtinia was the most suitable district. It had many natural resources which the Jews could exploit, including a shark fishery which would have the 'great advantage,' he observed with ghoulish humour, 'that, to begin with, many of the Jews would get eaten.'

Anti-Semitism was now declared to be an essential part of Fascist policy. Although the decrees by which this policy was brought into effect were never strictly applied, by the end of 1938 many distinguished Jews had been dismissed from senior posts in the public service and many had felt obliged to leave the country. By the spring of 1939 confiscation of Jewish property was widespread. It was suggested that the anti-Semitic campaign had been initiated by Mussolini to force upon the *bourgeoisie* – 'sedentary, pessimist, and xenophile', as the Duce described them – a more satisfactorily imperialistic frame of mind; it was also suggested that it was an economic measure prompted by the sad state of Italian finances; it was even suggested that Mussolini wished to ingratiate himself with the Arabs. But no one seriously doubted that the main influence was Hitler.

Nor could it be doubted that the timing of Italy's first major aggressive action since the invasion of Abyssinia was directly influenced by Hitler's occupation of Czechoslovakia. Although an attack on Albania had been discussed months previously, and Easter Week had been set as a possible date as early as the beginning of February, it was not until the middle of March that the Duce made up his mind. For weeks he had been indecisive, promising instructions which never came, threatening blows which were never made. As always when he was uncertain about what he should do, he alternated between moods of almost hysterical excitement and silent depression. One day he would speak of the necessary growth of Italy's Empire with passionate emphasis, the next he would refuse to discuss anything important at all. When he was in one of his exalted moods, his elation was frequently close to ecstasy. Bocchini told Ciano 'that the Duce should take an intensive anti-syphilitic cure'. His constant restlessness was 'obvious now to all his colleagues'.

In one of his moments of exaltation he announced at a meeting of the Grand Council 'the immediate goals of Fascist dynamics'. Albania was to become Italian; the Mediterranean was to be rendered secure for Italy by the acquisition of Tunisia and Corsica; the Alpine frontier was to be moved to the Var. 'I also have my eye on the Ticino,' he went on, 'as Switzerland has lost her cohesive force and is destined, like many little countries, to be disrupted. All this is a programme. I cannot lay down fixed times. I merely indicate the lines on which we shall march. Anyone revealing what I have said, in whole or in part, will have to answer to a charge of treason.' Next day these extravagant claims were extended to include Jibuti and a share of the Suez Canal. Two days later, however, he seemed to have lost all interest in the subject. On 3 March Ciano found him wanting to 'let matters slide' on the Albanian question. But by 23 March he had decided 'to move more rapidly'.[1]

Hitler's occupation of Czechoslovakia ended his doubts. As soon as the news of the German invasion reached him, his mind flew to 'the possibility of a blow in Albania', but immediately afterwards he expressed doubts that the occupation of that poor country, which in any case was already almost a vassal state, would 'counterbalance in world opinion the incorporation into the Reich of Bohemia, one of the richest territories in the world.' And to the chagrin of Ciano, who had long advocated the Albanian venture as a dramatic move which could be set off against 'the undesirable increase in the prestige of the Reich' and so 'raise the morale of Italy', Mussolini gave no definite instructions then and there. But when he heard that the King had repeated a conviction that there was no point in risking war in order 'to grab four rocks', he made up his mind to act 'as soon as Spain is over'.

On 28 March he was overjoyed at the news of the fall of Madrid. He had at one time doubted that Franco's 'flabby conduct' of the war would ever end in victory and had told Ciano during the previous summer to put on record in his book that he prophesied

---

1. Mussolini's sudden changes of mind and of mood, although doubtless accentuated by his declining health, were not, as has often been suggested, a phenomenon of this phase of his life. He had always been subject to them. Margherita Sarfatti speaks of a day on the eve of the 1919 election when Mussolini told her 'in a decided tone' that he had made up his mind not to let his name appear in the list of candidates. The next day he announced, quite as decidedly, that his name must certainly head the list in Milan.

his defeat. But now at last the exhausting war was over, and the world was given evidence of a 'new and formidable triumph for Fascism'. The Duce came in from the balcony overlooking Piazza Venezia, where crowds were cheering the end of the war, and pointed to an atlas open at the map of Spain. 'It has been open in this way for almost three years,' he said with solemn emphasis. 'And that is enough. But I know already that I must open it at another page.' At dawn ten days later Italian troops landed in Albania. There was little fighting, and although the Italian Press, reflecting the inherent difficulties in interpreting and propagating 'Fascist dynamics', did not agree whether this was because the Italian troops had fought so brilliantly or because the Albanians had welcomed them as deliverers from a hated King, it was, nevertheless, a victory of a sort; and by nightfall Italy had gained what Hitler described as 'a stronghold which will inexorably dominate the Balkans'.

A few days before the attack the Duce's indecision had given way to a mood of conviction and determination. 'He is calm,' Ciano reported on 5 April, 'frightfully calm.' By 15 April, when the operation had been successfully concluded and Albanian delegates had arrived in Rome for the ceremony of offering the crown to Victor Emmanuel, he was sublimely confident. Foreign reaction was already negligible and it was 'clear above all,' as Ciano said, 'that the British protests were more for domestic consumption than anything else.' When a message arrived from President Roosevelt proposing a ten years' truce, Mussolini refused at first to read it. When he had done so he threw it to one side with the contemptuous comment, 'A result of infantile paralysis!'

4

Goering was in Rome that day. He had been sent by Hitler to give an account to Mussolini of the state of German preparations for war and the confidence with which the German Government faced 'the solution of the Polish problem'; for the solution of this problem, which was to lead inevitably to war, was now imminent, and the Führer was anxious to be able to declare to the world that Germany and Italy stood together by a military alliance before taking any irrevocable step. He knew that Italy was still not a strong

T — E

military power – although if General von Rintelen, Military Attaché at the Embassy in Rome, is to be credited the Duce's boasts
had deceived him into believing she was much stronger than she
was – but he needed her support politically, and, hoping that the
announcement of an alliance would deter the democracies from
fulfilling their obligations to Poland, he instructed Ribbentrop to
renew his effort to get the Italians to sign. Ciano was reluctant to
do so. He was afraid that the Germans would 'overdo things' in
Poland and would make some move which would have disastrous
repercussions. Five days after Goering's conversation with Mussolini, a report came in from Attolico in Berlin warning that
Germany's action against Poland was 'now close at hand'. Ciano,
who had himself noticed that Goering had spoken of Poland 'in
the same tone used at other times for Austria and Czechoslovakia',
was deeply concerned and took the report to show to the Duce at
Palazzo Venezia. But Mussolini was not in a receptive mood.
Victory in Spain and in Albania had renewed his taste for conquest. He was delighted when Ciano told him of a visit the Nether-
lands Ambassador had made to Palazzo Chigi to express Dutch
concern at reports that Germany and Italy were to divide up
Europe between them. 'I am,' he said, as if in confirmation of the
Ambassador's fears, 'training Italy for war.' And yet despite his
belligerent attitude he realized in his more reflective moments
that Italy was not yet ready for war. He asked Ciano to arrange a
meeting with Ribbentrop to find out how far the Germans intended to go and how soon they intended to act; at the same time
Ciano was to impress on Ribbentrop the necessity of peace for
Italy for at least three years.

'Germany too,' Ribbentrop reassured Ciano when they met in
Milan on 6 May, 'is convinced of the necessity for a period of
peace which should not be less than four or five years.'

Ribbentrop was in an unusually accommodating mood. Ciano,
who had described him in October as 'vain, frivolous, loquacious,
and tactless' and had noted with satisfaction that Mussolini had
said you only had to look at his head to see what a little brain he
had, on this occasion got on quite well with him. After dinner at
the Continental Hotel he telephoned the Duce to say that although Hitler was apparently determined to recover Danzig, the
talks in general were going well and the Germans were agreed that

peace should be preserved for the next few years. Gratified and reassured by this and infuriated by the news that Ribbentrop had not been well received by the people of Milan, Mussolini told him to announce the news that a German–Italian alliance was in existence.

On 21 May Ciano arrived in Berlin for the ceremony of signing the alliance, which Mussolini at first suggested should be known as the Pact of Blood but which afterwards became known to the world as the Pact of Steel. That evening, at a banquet at the Italian Embassy, Ciano bestowed on Ribbentrop the Order of the Annunziata. Goering, who had gone into the dining-room to change the cards on the table so that he rather than Ribbentrop should sit on Ciano's right, came back into the drawing-room to see the Foreign Minister, surrounded by guests, admiring the Collar of the Order which gave him the right to consider himself a cousin of the King of Italy. Feeling that if anyone was to be honoured it should have been himself, Goering, with tears of disappointment in his eyes, made an embarrassing scene, said the collar was really his and was with difficulty dissuaded from walking out of the Embassy. The following day when the Pact was signed at an impressive ceremony at the Chancellery, Goering had not recovered from his ill-temper and was seen to look the other way whenever Ribbentrop passed near him. Hitler, on the other hand, had rarely been seen in so gracious and happy a mood. He was as talkative and boring as ever, Ciano discovered, and looked older and tired, for he slept very badly. There were rumours too of his intimate and time-absorbing affection for a beautiful twenty-year-old girl with a 'magnificent body' whose name was Sigrid von Lappus, but although his eyes were 'much more deeply wrinkled' he was 'very well, quite serene, in fact'. He had good cause to be content. The Pact was far from being the purely defensive alliance which Mussolini had suggested the previous winter. Its character is epitomized in Article III: 'If, contrary to the wishes and hopes of the contracting parties, it should happen that one of them is involved in hostilities with another Power or Powers, the other contracting party will come immediately to its side as ally and support it with all its military forces on land, sea, and in the air.' There was no suggestion in the Article, or anywhere else in the Pact, that the military support should not apply to aggressive hostilities. Clearly for Hitler the Pact of Steel was the prelude to war.

The very day after it was signed, he called a secret meeting of his senior military commanders to tell them this in his study at the Reich Chancellery.

'Danzig is not the object of our activities,' he said bluntly. 'It is a question of expanding our living space in the East. . . . There is no question of sparing Poland, and we are left with the decision: To attack Poland at the first suitable opportunity. We cannot accept a repetition of the Czech affair. There will be war. . . . We must burn our boats. It is no longer a question of right or wrong.'

But Mussolini, becoming increasingly alarmed by what he could deduce rather than by what he was told, continued to advocate a less reckless approach. Before General Cavallero left for Germany to represent Italy on the Military Commission established by the Pact of Steel, he handed him a secret memorandum which repeated the warnings that Ciano had given in Milan. Hitler was recommended to spend the next two or three years wearing down the Democracies by fear and not by force, and he was again informed that in any case Italy needed peace at least until the end of 1942. A war of nerves, Mussolini suggested, should be the immediate policy of the Axis.

Mussolini, himself, was already prosecuting such a war. He encouraged the belief that the Pact of Steel was anti-French and anti-British; he spoke threateningly of Yugoslavia and of Greece; he excluded foreign diplomats from Tirana; he increased the numbers of alarming anonymous letters which he delighted in sending to unfriendly embassies in Rome; and he referred repeatedly to the 'Fascist conception of loyalty'. When Sir Percy Loraine, Lord Perth's successor as British Ambassador in Rome, was formally presented to him on 27 May he was, according to Ciano, aggressively rude to him. In view of the manifest British policy of encirclement, he said, it was necessary to ask whether the Anglo-Italian Agreement had any tangible value left. Loraine, shocked by this sudden attack, blushed deeply and hesitated before he could find words to reply. 'The Duce, who is usually courteous and engaging,' Ciano said, 'was very stern. His face became absolutely impenetrable. It looked like the face of an oriental god sculptured in stone.' On his next visit Loraine was peremptorily told to 'inform Chamberlain that if England is ready to fight in defence of Poland, Italy will take up arms in defence of her ally Germany'. And Mussolini repeated the sentence twice[1].

But although the Duce was anxious to leave no room for doubt that he was now unmistakably on Germany's side, the Germans did not treat him as the trusted and unshakable ally he professed himself to be. Article II of the Pact of Steel provided for prior discussions on matters of common interest, but in his study the day after it was signed Hitler had said, 'our aim must remain hidden from Italy'.[2] Despite Attolico's persistent warnings, however, Mussolini had refused to believe that Hitler would act without consulting him. Even Ciano doubted that he would do so 'after so many protestations of the need for peace'. Nothing had changed in regard to what was said and decided in Milan, Ribbentrop continued to assure him, stressing Germany's intention to ensure for herself a long period of peace – at least three years. But the warnings from Attolico continued to arrive at Palazzo Chigi and on 20 July there were also reports of 'troop movements on a vast scale' in Czechoslovakia. By 2 August Ciano confessed in his diary, 'Attolico's insistence keeps me wondering. Either the Ambassador has lost his head or he sees and knows something which has completely escaped us.'

That week Ciano decided that he would have to go to Germany to find out for himself what was happening there. An international conference which the Duce had advocated and Attolico had keenly supported was refused by Ribbentrop; and a suggested meeting between Hitler and Mussolini at the Brenner had been postponed. But on 9 August Ribbentrop agreed to meet Ciano at Salzburg two days later.

There is no doubt that Mussolini was by this time seriously concerned to save Italy from war. Time was needed to stabilize the situation in Albania, North Africa, and Ethiopia; to relieve the congestion of industrial centres in the Po valley by moving

1. Sir Percy Loraine, however, told me that Ciano's account of Mussolini's attitude was 'somewhat highly coloured'. Mussolini was cold, but not unduly intimidating.

2. Hitler's constant refusal to reveal his plans in advance to the Italians, which so irritated and distressed Mussolini, seems not to have been so much arrogance as a fear that they would no longer remain secret. 'All Italians,' Goebbels once told him, 'chatter like gypsies.' In January 1943 Hitler asked Admiral Raeder to take great care to ensure that German operational plans should be concealed from the Italians. 'There is great danger,' he thought, 'that the Royal Family is transmitting intelligence to Britain.'

factories, plant, and machinery further south; to bring the Navy, Air Force, artillery, and motorized divisions up to strength; to repatriate the million-odd Italians in France; to improve the holdings of foreign currency by an immensely impressive international exhibition planned to be held in Rome in 1942 to commemorate the twentieth anniversary of the March on Rome. For all these reasons, and particularly, so it seemed, on account of the international exhibition the plans for which excited him beyond measure, Mussolini was anxious to preserve peace at least for the moment; and protest as he would that 'whenever Germany finds it necessary to mobilize at midnight, we shall mobilize at five to twelve,' his instructions to Ciano were emphatic.

Ciano was told before leaving for his meeting with Ribbentrop at Salzburg 'to prove to the Germans, by documentary evidence, that the outbreak of war at this time would be foolhardy. Our preparations are not such as to allow us to believe that victory will be certain. Now there are no more than even chances. . . . On the other hand, within three years the chance will be four to one.' 'Before letting me go,' Ciano recorded in his diary on 10 August, 'the Duce recommended that I should frankly inform the Germans that we must avoid a conflict with Poland, since it will be impossible to localize it and a general war would be disastrous for everybody. Never has the Duce spoken of the need for peace so unreservedly and with so much warmth.'

Ciano repeated Mussolini's views with equal warmth in Salzburg, but Ribbentrop was in no mind to listen to them. He was, in fact, as Ciano was shocked to discover, bent on war and obstinately determined to bring it about. 'It was while we were waiting to be seated at the dinner-table,' Ciano wrote long afterwards, 'that Ribbentrop told me of the German design to set a match to the European powder-keg. This he told me in much the same tone that he would have used for an inconsequential administrative detail.

'"Well, Ribbentrop," I asked, as we were walking together in the garden. "What do you want? The corridor or Danzig?"

'"Neither. Not now," he said, gazing at me with his cold metallic eyes. "We want war!"'

Ribbentrop refused, however, to give the Italians any idea how he intended to provoke it. All decisions, he said loftily, using with infuriating self-complacency one of those archaic metaphors which made his conversation so tiresome, 'were still locked in the Führer's impenetrable bosom.' 'He rejects any solution which might give satisfaction to Germany and avoid the struggle,' Ciano said. 'I am certain that even if the Germans were given more than they ask for they would attack just the same because they are possessed by the demon of destruction. At times our conversation becomes very tense. I do not hesitate to express my thoughts with brutal frankness. But he is not moved. The atmosphere is icy and the coldness between us extends even to our secretaries. During dinner not a word is exchanged. . . . I am becoming aware of how little we are worth in the opinion of the Germans.'

The next day, when he went to see Hitler at the Berghof, Ciano was given further evidence of this. The Führer was extremely polite and friendly, but he did not trouble to disguise that, whatever the Duce suggested, his mind was made up. His table was covered with maps, and he was already occupied with military plans. He told Ciano, as Ribbentrop had done the day before, that France and England would not fight and added that even if they did, 'after the conquest of Poland (which could be expected in a short time) Germany would be in a position to assemble for a general conflict a hundred divisions on the West Wall.' So far as Italy was concerned he would 'not have to ask for help according to the existing obligations.'

Ciano was made to realize that 'for the Germans an alliance with Italy means only that the enemy will be obliged to keep a certain number of divisions facing us, thus easing the situation on the German war fronts. . . . The fate that might befall us does not interest them in the least.'

It was a prophetic observation.

As soon as he returned to his hotel that evening, Ciano gave orders for his aeroplane to be kept under special guard in case a German agent should try to arrange for him to have an accident; and when Attolico came to discuss the situation with him, he took him into the bathroom, where he hoped the Gestapo's microphones would not be able to pick up their conversation. It was as if he and the Germans were already enemies.

During the conversation at the Berghof a telegram had been ostentatiously handed to Hitler. Ciano was allowed to know that it had come from Moscow and that it gave the Soviet Government's agreement to Germany's sending a delegation there to negotiate a Pact which would secure Poland's defeat and, by ensuring the neutrality of Russia, kill the hopes that France and England had of enlisting Soviet help in checking the expansion of Germany. The significance of this Pact and the importance which Hitler attached to it were not lost upon Ciano. The following day he did not even trouble to argue any more. He merely asked when Hitler would attack. The whole matter would be over, Hitler told him, by the middle of October. Ciano returned to Rome on 13 August 'completely disgusted with the Germans, with their Führer, with their way of doing things. They have betrayed us and lied to us,' he wrote with unaccustomed passion. 'Now they are dragging us into an adventure which we do not want and which may compromise the régime and the country as a whole. The Italian people will recoil with horror when they learn about the aggression against Poland and will most probably want to fight the Germans.' The Pact of Steel had never been popular in Italy, but this would make it hated.

His own misgivings were at an end. No longer did he have moments when he believed that the Duce might be right in insisting that Italy must remain loyal to the Axis. In the bathroom of his Salzburg hotel Attolico had pleaded with him to tell the Duce that he could consider himself released from the obligation of the Steel Pact by Hitler's arrogant and one-sided interpretation of it. Ciano was not yet certain that Italy should go as far as this. But then as he was flying back to Rome a communiqué, proclaiming that the Salzburg meeting had ended in Italy's complete agreement with Germany's views and aspirations, was published by the *Deutsches Nachrichten Büro*. Ciano's final request had been that no communiqué should be issued for the moment. Both Ribbentrop and Hitler had agreed. For Ciano this was the final insult. He went to the Duce and told him bluntly that the 'Germans are traitors and we must not have any scruples in ditching them.' 'I do not hesitate to arouse in him,' he wrote, 'every possible anti-German feeling by every means in my power. I speak to him of his diminished prestige and of his playing the none-too-brilliant role of second fiddle. And finally, I turn over to him documents which prove the bad faith of the Germans on the

Polish question. The Alliance was based on promises which they now deny.'

Mussolini's immediate reaction was characteristic of the doubts and uncertainties, the sudden tergiversations, which were in the next ten months to drive his Ministers close to distraction. 'At first he agreed with me,' Ciano remembered. 'Then he said that honour compelled him to march with Germany. Finally he said that he wanted his part of the booty.'

The first of these three reactions – that of agreement with Ciano's anti-German arguments – was neither an unexpected nor an unusual one. Even at those times when he was prepared to back his allies unreservedly, he was capable of criticizing them in as harsh a way as he criticized the English or, for that matter, the Italians themselves. 'The Germans are merely soldiers not real warriors,' he said one day with profound contempt. 'Give them enough sausage, butter, beer, and a little car and they won't worry about sticking their bayonets into people.' In the presence of Germans, however, he seemed to lose every reservation. He would thrust out his jaw, carefully compose his features in a pose of rock-like sternness, and for hours after they had left him he would speak with admiration of their 'fine martial spirit', 'their heroic philosophy'. And then a reaction would set in and he would have doubts again.

During this month of August 1939 the entries in Ciano's diary provide eloquent testimony of Mussolini's equivocal, floundering state of mind. On 14 August he was refusing to act independently; the next day he was convinced that Italy 'must not march blindly with Germany', on 16 August he was 'really beginning to resent German behaviour towards him'; three days later he was in his 'usual shifting mood' and obsessed by fears that 'Germany might do good business cheaply' from which he would be excluded. On 20 August Ciano was recalled by telegram from a visit to Durazzo by his Principal Private Secretary Filippo Anfuso, because the Duce had suddenly decided 'to support Germany at any cost in the conflict which is now close at hand.' Ciano flew back to Rome, where he found Mussolini holding 'very stubbornly to his ideas'. Attolico, who had on his own initiative come back from Berlin to support Ciano, was also present at the interview and left it 'discouraged and overwhelmed with grief'. But Ciano, who knew the

Duce better, still had hopes and by the next day he had, in fact, succeeded in persuading him to change his mind once more. He agreed that Ciano should ask Ribbentrop to meet him at the Brenner, where he was to reaffirm Italy's rights as Axis partner.

Ribbentrop, however, had more important matters on his mind. He was due in Moscow the following morning to sign the German–Soviet Non-Aggression Pact; he could not come to the Brenner, but he could spare Ciano an hour or so in Innsbruck. Mussolini's mind quavered again. Ciano must not agree to go to Innsbruck; anti-German feeling was strong enough in Italy already, and while he could not himself fail to admire Hitler's diplomatic *coup* the Italian people were not likely to see it in the same light. Starace had been quite right when he had warned that public demonstrations would break out if the régime supported Hitler's attack on Poland. Besides, the officers of the Army were not qualified for their job and its equipment was old and obsolete. Italy must 'wait events and do nothing'.

A few hours after coming to this decision Mussolini received Giuseppe Bastianini, a former Ambassador to Poland, who described him as being 'furiously warlike'. He was still in this mood when Ciano called at Palazzo Venezia that morning and he was with difficulty persuaded to postpone intervention until preparations for mobilization were more complete. Relieved to have got at least this much from him, Ciano returned to Palazzo Chigi; but the Duce called him back.

'He has changed his mind,' Ciano wrote with sad and painful resignation. 'He fears the bitter judgement of the Germans and wants to intervene at once. It is useless to quarrel. I submit.'

During the afternoon, however, Mussolini received a message from Hitler suggesting that action against Poland would begin in a short time and assuring him that if the Duce were to be in a situation similar to his own he 'would have complete understanding for Italy.' Seeing in this message a chance of playing on the Duce's apprehensions, Ciano returned to Palazzo Venezia, where the Duce was persuaded to write to Hitler informing him that Italy's support, unless immediate supplies of equipment and raw materials were to be made available by Germany, would have to be restricted to 'political and economic assistance'. 'At our meetings,' the Duce added, as both an apology and an implied rebuke, 'the war was envisaged for after 1942 and then I would have been ready on land, sea, and in the air according to our agreed plans.'

This reply temporarily unnerved Hitler. He had counted on more definite support than this. Already upset by news received that afternoon that a Pact of Mutual Assistance had been signed in London between Britain and Poland, he decided to postpone the invasion set for dawn the following morning. When he saw the list of supplies the Italians requested, it was obvious that they could not be met. Mackensen, the German Ambassador, who did not want war, had recommended that the Italians should make a formidable list, and it was, in fact, as Ciano observed, 'enough to kill a bull'. It included seven million tons of oil, six million tons of coal, two million tons of steel, a million tons of timber, 17,000 military vehicles, and no less than 150 anti-aircraft batteries. Attolico, on presenting the list to the Germans, was brusquely asked by Ribbentrop when the items were required. At once, said Attolico, adding on his own initiative, 'before hostilities begin'. It was Attolico's final effort to preserve peace, but it was useless. Hitler had recovered his nerve and was as ready as, according to Gisevius, he had been ready in August to 'throw any swine of a mediator downstairs, even if he had to kick him in the stomach in front of the photographers'. He immediately accepted the impossibility of complying with the Italian demands and asked only that the Duce should give him his political support; that the decision to remain neutral should not be made known until absolutely necessary; that military preparations should be continued in order to impress the French and the British; and that agricultural and industrial workers should be sent to Germany. 'I respect the motives and influences determining your resolution, Duce,' he assured him. 'Perhaps it will nevertheless be for the best.'

But although the Duce was momentarily calmer after he had finally made up his mind, he did not long remain so. Haunted by the idea that he had not only been disloyal to his ally but had also suffered a blow to his prestige, he pressed for another Munich conference as the only way by which war might still be averted, by which he might regain his status as Hitler's superior and by which he might avoid his magniloquent bluff of '*otto milioni di baionette*' being called. He did not press his views, however, with much force and conviction. Painfully aware that Italy was of little use to Germany as a fighting ally, he was not fully aware of the value which Hitler placed upon him as a political one.

'I allow myself to insist afresh,' he wrote mildly on 26 August, when at the same time agreeing to Hitler's request of the day before, 'upon the possibility of a political solution which I still think can be attained – and I do so certainly not on account of considerations of a pacifist character alien to my spirit, but in the interests of our two peoples and our two régimes.'

As late as 31 August he was still diffidently pressing for acceptance of his idea for a conference. On the evening of that day Attolico called at the Chancellery with Mussolini's offer of himself as mediator. But the Duce had left it too late. Hitler had already gone too far.

'I am not in the mood to be slapped in the face time and again by Poland,' Hitler told Attolico sharply. 'And I do not want to bring the Duce into an uncomfortable position.'

Attolico asked him if that meant that everything was at an end and Hitler said, 'Yes.' Two days later Mussolini made yet another and a final appeal, but by then the invasion of Poland had begun.

'Although our paths are now diverging,' Hitler replied in a letter which foreshadowed Italy's catastrophe, 'I have always been convinced personally of the indivisible future of our two régimes and I know that you, Duce, feel the same thing.'

5

The brilliant successes of the German armies in Poland unsettled Mussolini again. Although he announced at a meeting of the Fascist Grand Council on 1 September that Italy would 'not for the time being initiate military operations', he was careful to add, for the benefit of those members of the Council who appeared to take his decision with relief, that this did not constitute a declaration of neutrality. Italy, it was later announced, was assuming 'an attitude of her own, a position of her own in which there are implicit judgements and lines of action. That is the reason why we do not speak of neutrality. A neutral is a person who is a mere onlooker, because his own interests are not at stake and because the struggle does not concern him. On the contrary this struggle concerns us closely. It is not the case that there is nothing to be said by us. We reserve the right to say our word at the right moment, in our own language and in our own style. We watch with cold calm and mature our determination.'

But Mussolini could not watch with cold calm. Each time he read a confidential report or one of those telegrams which were regularly lifted from the files of the foreign embassies in Rome, and saw in it an unwelcome comment on his neutrality, and each time a foreign newspaper, and particularly an English newspaper, commented adversely or even favourably on his decision, he spoke of going to war. 'Whenever he reads an article that compares his policy with that of 1914,' Ciano wrote in his diary, 'he reacts violently in favour of Germany. He was quite pleased with an English article which suggested that the Italian people might fight at the side of Germany for reasons of honour. This is also his own point of view and even when there are a thousand voices to the contrary, a single anonymous voice saying that he is right is sufficient, and he will cling to it and overlook, indeed deny, the others.' Although the economic advantages of neutrality – or 'non-belligerence', as he insisted on calling it – were soon apparent, with stock-market quotations soaring, foreign markets – particularly in the Balkans – captured from Germany, and merchant vessels loaded with exports sailing from every port, Mussolini did not seem to take 'a great deal of interest'. It was the news of German victories that held and fired his imagination. 'It's impossible to keep out of this war,' he told his wife impatiently, 'and even more impossible and dangerous not to enter it on Germany's side. The Russo-German Pact makes Germany unbeatable by any other Power or coalition.' 'Nobody,' he kept murmuring, repeating what he had said so often since 1915, 'nobody loves a neutral.'

But the dangers of entering what might yet prove a long war held him back. He accepted the fact, in his less impatient moments, that Italy must enter the war only when victory seemed certain and imminent. And then after the capture of Warsaw when Ribbentrop met Stalin at the Kremlin and agreed to divide Poland with him and virtually to allow Russia a free hand in the Baltic states of Estonia, Latvia, and Lithuania, Mussolini saw an opportunity to escape his dilemma. He decided to make a fresh attempt to persuade Hitler to agree to mediation. A negotiated settlement would not only allow Italy gracefully to avoid a war which she was not equipped to fight, but it would also rescue the Axis from the position of secondary importance to which Hitler's preoccupation with the Nazi-Soviet alliance had relegated it; and it would in addition do something to appease the Italian people, who were outraged by the spectacle of the Fascist Government standing silently and, so it seemed, approvingly by, while Catholic Poland was brutally cut in half by two heathen butchers. When, therefore, the Führer suggested that Ciano should visit him in Germany, Mussolini eagerly accepted the invitation on his behalf.

Hitler, Ciano discovered, was 'absolutely sure of himself'. Although the German Press approvingly endorsed the joint communiqué issued by Molotov and Ribbentrop to the effect that 'now that the Polish problem had been definitely settled, it would serve the true interests of all people to put an end to the state of war existing between Germany on the one side and England and France on the other', Hitler himself did not appear to Ciano to have much faith in a peaceful solution -- nor, indeed, did he appear to want one. He was at his most charming and persuasive as he told Ciano that he was to make a speech in the Reichstag which would contain his last attempt at peace with the West, and that 'if Italy were disposed to march with me at once I would not even make this speech but would at once have recourse to force in the certainty that Italy and Germany together can smash France and England in no time and settle their accounts with those countries once and for all.' The Duce need feel no concern that he had so few anti-aircraft batteries, Ciano was assured, for the enemy was much too frightened of German reprisals to bomb Italy.

Mussolini, however, was not impressed. He did not disguise the fact that Hitler's attitude irritated him, and the jibes and advice in the foreign Press no longer made him want to join the war on Germany's side but to demonstrate to the world that it was not he who had let Germany down but Germany who had abandoned him. He even began to hope for a German defeat and told Ciano to let it leak out to the Dutch and Belgian Embassies that a German invasion of their countries was only a matter of time. And on 16 December he allowed Ciano to make a speech in the Chamber of Deputies which astonished the world.

The speech contained strong denunciations of Great Britain and France for destroying the Duce's attempt at mediation, but its main thesis was German treachery. Germany, Ciano said, had gone back on her anti-Comintern policy, had rejected Italy's advice that France and England would fight for Poland, and had jumped into war ignoring the undertaking that had been given not to do so for three years. Having let down the Duce, Italy's declaration of non-belligerence was more than Hitler had any juridical right to expect. The speech was acclaimed all over Italy as 'the funeral march of the Axis'; and the people were delighted. Three days after having been instructed to give the speech front-page treatment, the Italian Press was ordered to report war news with complete impartiality; and on 3 January 1940 Mussolini wrote to Hitler to inform him that everything that Ciano had said expressed his own views precisely. It was one of the most forceful letters he had ever written to the Führer:

No one knows better than I, with forty years' political experience, that any policy – particularly a revolutionary policy – has its tactical requirements. I recognized the Soviets in 1924. In 1934 I signed with them a treaty of commerce and friendship. I therefore understand, especially as Ribbentrop's forecast about the non-intervention of Britain and France has not been fulfilled, that you feel obliged to avoid a second front. But you have had to pay for this in allowing Russia, without striking a blow, to become the great profiteer in Poland and in the Baltic.

But I who was born a revolutionary and have not modified my revolutionary mentality tell you that you cannot permanently sacrifice the principles of *your* revolution to the tactical requirements of a given moment. ... I must also add that any further step in your relations with Moscow would have catastrophic repercussions in Italy, where the unanimity of anti-Bolshevist feeling is absolute, granite-hard, and unbreakable. ...[1] Permit me to think that this will not happen.

Attolico handed this sharp rebuke to Hitler, who read it 'almost with avidity' and when the Ambassador had left he called for Goering and Ribbentrop, who discussed it angrily with him for more than five hours. Later Hitler pettishly concluded that Italy would enter the war only in the event of 'great German successes and preferably only against France' and that, in any case, there

---

1. Thousands of Italians had volunteered to fight in defence of Finland.

would not be much advantage in Italy's participation because of the subsequent strain on German supplies.

While impatiently waiting for Hitler's long-delayed reply to his letter, Mussolini's mood began to change again. At the beginning of February, on the anniversary of the founding of the Militia, he made a widely reported speech in which he said the Italians were yearning to fight 'the fight which is bound to come'. In the middle of the month, when still there was no response from Hitler, he said that no one should suppose that Italy's deficiencies in military supplies could constitute an alibi. 'The Duce,' Ciano wrote in his diary on 21 February, 'intends to satisfy the Germans.' The anti-German attitude of the King also had the predictable effect of making Mussolini more anxious to fight on their behalf. 'How dare that little midget presume to tell me what to do!' he exclaimed angrily one day when he heard that the King had deprecated the German alliance and had again compared the straightforwardness of the British with the untrustworthiness of his nominal allies. 'Why doesn't the stupid little sardine stick to his numismatology? That's the only thing he understands.' When the war was over he would 'tell Hitler to do away with all these absurd anachronisms in the form of monarchies'. 'The King would like us to enter the war,' he told Ciano, 'when it's a case of gathering up the broken dishes. I hope they won't all be broken over our heads before that. It's humiliating to remain with folded arms while others make history. It doesn't matter much who wins. To make a people great it is necessary to send them into battle, even if you have to kick them in the pants.'

The Papacy, in the Duce's view, was behaving in quite as infuriating a way as the King. At least the new Pope was not so unreasonable as that 'impossible old autocrat' Pius XI, who had made no bones about speaking against exaggerated nationalism and racial ideology at the time of the Pact of Steel and had driven Mussolini to remark that he was quite ready to 'break a few bludgeons on the backsides of the priests'. It would not be difficult, he thought; the Italians were not religious, merely superstitious; they could soon be familiarized with the idea that they could do without the Vatican. But although Cardinal Pacelli, who succeeded Pius XI at the beginning of 1939, had not at first seemed so obdurate and meddlesome as his predecessor, he too was now proving an annoyance. He had been Apostolic Nuncio in Germany and liked the Germans, but he felt it his duty to do all that he could to prevent Italy fighting on their side. Through the Jesuit Father Pietro Tacchi-Venturi, the Pope's link with Palazzo Venezia since the conclusion of the Lateran Treaty, Pius XII repeatedly advised Mussolini of the necessity for Italian neutrality and of his desire for peace. The Vatican newspaper, *L'Osservatore Romano*, published this advice together with much political comment which was subtly but unmistakably anti-Fascist. In May 1940 it printed the Pope's message of sympathy to the King of the Belgians, the Queen of Holland, and the Grand Duchess of Luxemburg. The circulation of the paper rose sharply, despite the activities of Fascist gangs who intimidated intending purchasers by tearing up and burning copies of it in the streets and by beating up the owners of kiosks who offered it for sale. Eventually the Papal Nuncio was told on Mussolini's orders that the paper must either stop printing political comment which could be interpreted as anti-Fascist or it would be banned altogether. *L'Osservatore Romano* felt compelled to surrender.

One of its sins which Mussolini found it impossible to forgive was its contradiction of the official Fascist policy, strenuously supported in Roberto Farinacci's *Regime Fascista*, that there could be no forgiving those countries which had supported sanctions against Italy during the Abyssinian war. This was a constantly rankling theme in Mussolini's thoughts. In February 1940 Sumner Welles noticed how obsessed by it he appeared to be.

Sumner Welles had been sent to Europe by President Roosevelt to see if there was anything that Mussolini could be persuaded to do to bring Britain and France to terms with Germany. Welles arrived in Rome on 25 February with a long personal letter from the President to the Duce. Mussolini received him with an alarming frigidity which disappeared when the American raised his dormant hopes for a negotiated settlement by suggesting that Roosevelt might be willing to fly half-way across the Atlantic to meet him for a conference which could not fail to have world-wide repercussions. Welles left Rome in a fairly hopeful mood on 29 February. But by 10 March Mussolini was once more securely back in the German camp. On that day Ribbentrop, anxious to counteract any reservations about the German alliance which the

American envoy might have aroused in Mussolini's mind, and accompanied by an immense staff including not only secretaries, interpreters, and Foreign Office officials, but a barber, a masseur, a gymnastics instructor, and a doctor, arrived in Rome with Hitler's reply to the Duce's letter of 3 January. To Ribbentrop's confident assertions that Germany was about to win a great and decisive victory Mussolini replied that Italy's intervention was now a certainty as she was being imprisoned by the British blockade in what he referred to, in his subsequent declaration of war, as 'her own sea'. When three months later Hitler decided to occupy Denmark and Norway and, in accordance with his usual practice, sent Mackensen, the Ambassador, to Mussolini with a letter telling him that the decision had already been acted on, the Duce showed no annoyance, but said on the contrary that he 'approved the action wholeheartedly'. It seemed to Mackensen that he could not wait to join in the conflict himself, and his impatience was increased when long letters arrived from the Führer describing the triumphant successes of the German armies. The idea that the Germans might win the war single-handed was, as Ciano had already commented, unbearable for him. By 21 April he had become 'more warlike and more pro-German than ever'.

The British, however, still shared the American hope that Italy could be kept out of the war. Anxious to offset the effects of the British blockade upon the supply of German coal to Italy, the Government offered Italy eight million tons a year of their own coal as a substitute; and anxious to show that Britain had no fundamental quarrel with Fascism, Lord Lloyd as head of the British Council was authorized to write a pamphlet which carried a commendatory preface by Lord Halifax and which contained these observations:

The Italian genius has developed, in the characteristic Fascist institutions, a highly authoritarian régime which, however, threatens neither religious nor economic freedom nor the security of other European nations. It is worth while to note that quite fundamental differences exist between the structure and principles of the Fascist State and those of the Nazi and Soviet States. The Italian system is founded on two rocks: first, the separation of Church and State and the supremacy of the Church in matters not only of faith, but of morals; second the rights of labour. The political machinery of

Fascism is, indeed, built up on Trade Unionism, while that of the German State is built up on the ruins of the German labour movement.

On 16 May 1940, six days after becoming Prime Minister, Winston Churchill, aware that he must do his 'utmost to keep Italy out of the conflict', wrote to Mussolini, who, as he had told President Roosevelt the previous day, would probably soon 'hurry in to share the loot of civilization'. 'Is it too late,' he asked him in that splendidly grandiloquent phraseology so dear to both their hearts, 'to stop a river of blood from flowing between the British and Italian peoples? We can no doubt inflict grievous injuries upon one another and maul each other cruelly, and darken the Mediterranean with our strife. If you so decree, it must be so; but I declare I have never been the enemy of Italian greatness, nor even at heart the foe of the Italian lawgiver. . . . I beg you to believe that it is in no spirit of weakness or of fear that I make this solemn appeal, which will remain on record. Down the ages above all other calls comes the cry that the joint heirs of Latin and Christian civilization must not be ranged against one another in mortal strife. Hearken to it, I beseech you in all honour and respect, before the dread signal is given. It will never be given by us.'

Mussolini's reply was hard, but, as Sir Winston afterwards admitted, 'It had at least the merit of candour.'

'I reply to the message which you have sent me,' the Duce wrote, 'in order to tell you that you are certainly aware of grave reasons of a historical and contingent character which have ranged our two countries in opposite camps. Without going back very far in time I remind you of the initiative taken at Geneva in 1935 by your Government to organize sanctions against Italy, engaged in securing for herself a small space in the African sun without causing the slightest injury to your interests and territories or to those of others. I remind you also of the real and actual state of servitude in which Italy finds herself in her own sea. If it was to honour its signature that your Government declared war on Germany, you will understand that the same sense of honour and of respect for engagements assured in the Italo-German Treaty guides Italian policy today and tomorrow in the face of any event whatsoever.'

'It was certainly only common prudence,' Sir Winston thinks, 'for Mussolini to see how the war would go before committing himself and his country irrevocably.' And after receiving this reply he no longer had any doubt that the Duce had decided to enter the war on Germany's side. The French too had now come to the same conclusion. Their Ambassador in Rome, François-Poncet, refused to believe that Mussolini would not want 'to rob Stalin of the glory of striking at a fallen man'.

That the man had fallen was now certain. Encouraged by his triumphs in Norway, Hitler had launched his attack on France and the Low Countries early in May. By the end of the month the Allies had been driven back to Dunkirk. On 3 June, in a final and frantic attempt to prevent Italy from attacking in the south, the French Government ordered François-Poncet to buy Mussolini off with territorial concessions, which were immediately rejected out of hand. He was not interested in peaceful negotiation, Ciano told the Ambassador bluntly; he had decided to make war.

'Any further delay is inconceivable,' he had already told Ciano. 'We've no more time to lose. . . . Some months ago I said that the Allies had lost the victory. Now I tell you that they have lost the war.' The Italian people, 'already sufficiently dishonoured', were ready and anxious to fight, he insisted, and were deeply concerned that they were about to miss an opportunity that might never come again. He quoted a tapped telephone conversation between two journalists one of whom had protested that the Germans were 'pinching everything'. Even Nice would fall into their hands now. 'Don't worry,' the other journalist had said. 'He has thought of everything. This isn't a question of war, it's a question of not being absent at the division of the cake.' In fact, as most Fascist leaders realized but few dared say, the Italian people were far from ready and anxious to fight. Bocchini spoke gloomily to his friends, who doubted that he repeated to the Duce, his pessimistic views about the internal situation, the poverty of the country, the decline in the prestige of the régime and, above all, the anxiety of the people not to go to war. There was, indeed, no mistaking the pleasure which the dismissal of certain pro-war Fascists in October had given to a desperately worried country; and in particular the pleasure caused by the replacement of Starace, that 'sinister buffoon' as De Bono called him, by an agreeable and less bellicose friend of Ciano's, Ettore Muti, as Secretary of the Party. From the

King (who had conferred the Collar of the Annunciata on Ciano as much to hold him firm to his neutralist policy as to gain his support against Mussolini's growing anti-monarchism) to the poor peasants and industrial workers, the Italians were overwhelmingly against fighting on Germany's side. The Pact of Steel had never become popular in Italy, and Germany's invasion of Poland had made it positively detested. The thought that the country would be dragged into the war saddened the Catholics, who dreaded the idea of having to fight in support of a régime which was more or less openly anti-Catholic; it saddened the liberal-minded, who feared that a war would end their hopes for a resurrection of liberty; it saddened the patriots, who feared that a German victory would be the end of Italian independence; and it saddened even the more enlightened and better informed Fascists, who realized that despite the Party declarations, the public expenditure, and the Duce's boast of '*otto milioni di baionette*' the country was hopelessly ill-prepared for war. The reputation of Fascism had never been so low. It was losing the support of even those rich financiers who, like Count Volpi, had done so much in the past to support it in times of stress. It was in this atmosphere of depression and disgust that the announcement of Italy's non-belligerence had been made. The country had felt a deep sense of relief. 'It is not easy,' the historian Luigi Salvatorelli says, 'to give an adequate idea of the general and profound satisfaction, of the sense of relief produced by the declaration of non-belligerence in virtually the entire population, including the Fascists.'

But the sad fact was that when it became clear that non-belligerence was a passing phase in Italian policy, the people accepted the approach of war with a kind of numbed, apathetic resignation, so torpid had they grown after seventeen years of Fascist indoctrination. Three years before, a reader had been issued for compulsory use by children in State schools. 'A child who, even though he does not refuse to obey, asks why,' one of its sophisms read, 'is like a bayonet made of milk. . . . "You must obey because you must," said Mussolini when explaining the reasons for obedience.'

It was an explanation which not only children had grown accustomed to accept, for, as Mussolini had learned years before, everything that he said had to be presented as an incontrovertible truth. Never must an appeal be made to the critical faculties of his people. The most effective formulas for a dictator were often the most vague, sometimes even the most meaningless.

6

At the end of May 1940 Hitler had suggested that Italy should launch her attack 'after the liquidation of the Anglo-French-Belgian strongholds', when the Germans could throw the whole weight of their power on Paris. Mussolini had agreed and at that time was considering intervention at the end of June. When the Belgian Army appeared to be about to surrender, however, he decided he could not wait so long. He was greatly encouraged by what he took to be a sudden enthusiasm in the people who 'like whores' always wanted to be on the side of the winner. Even Ciano felt that the mood of the country had changed, and he was surprised to be heartily welcomed at every railway station when making a journey in May up the east coast, where he heard 'many voices calling for war'. In the same month Edda came to see her father at Palazzo Venezia and told him that the country wanted war now and that to pursue a policy of neutrality would be 'dishonourable for Italy'. Marshal Rodolfo Graziani, the influential and pro-German subjugator of Italy's African territories, also supported this view.

After receiving news of the surrender of the Belgian Army on 29 May, Mussolini called for the Air Force Marshal, Italo Balbo, and for the Army Chief-of-Staff, Marshal Pietro Badoglio, to tell them that he would declare war on 5 June. Badoglio, according to his own account, protested that it was suicide. 'You, Marshal,' Mussolini replied imperiously, 'are not calm enough to judge the situation. I can tell you that everything will be over by September and that I only need a few thousand dead so that I can sit at the peace conference as a man who has fought.'

He was standing up behind his desk with his hands on his hips, staring fixedly at the two worried Marshals, and it was in moments like these that men were prepared to suppose that all his sudden changes of opinion and contradictory decisions were cunningly calculated, even inspired; that they were, as he himself had always insisted, clever strokes of intuitive deceit, a demonstration of his instinctive mastery of the techniques of Machiavelli. Certainly the following day Badoglio, so Ciano said, was preparing for war with a good grace.

At the request of Hitler the date of Italy's intervention was postponed for a few days. And then at last on 10 June Mussolini, having already arranged – to the King's sulky annoyance, but without recorded protest from anyone else – for himself to be appointed Supreme Commander of the Forces in the Field, strode on to the balcony overlooking Piazza Venezia to the loud but mechanical-sounding cheers of an enormous crowd.

'Fighting men of the land, the sea, and the air,' he called out in a strangely high-pitched voice. 'Blackshirts of the Revolution and of the Legions, men and women of Italy, of the Empire, and of the Kingdom of Albania, hearken! An hour marked by destiny is striking in the sky of our country; the hour of irrevocable decisions. We are entering the lists against the plutocratic and reactionary democracies of the West, who have always hindered the advance and often plotted against the very existence of the Italian people. . . . At a memorable meeting in Berlin I said that, according to the laws of Fascist morality, when one has a friend one goes with him to the very end. We have done this and will do this with Germany, with her people, with her victorious armed forces.

'Proletarian and Fascist Italy is for the third time on her feet, strong, proud, and united as never before. The single and categoric watchword is binding on us all. Already it is flying through the air and kindling hearts from the Alps to the Indian Ocean – to conquer. And we will conquer. And we will give finally a long period of peace with justice to Italy, to Europe, and to the world. People of Italy, to arms! Show your courage, your tenacity, and your worth.'

A few hours previously Mussolini's intentions had been conveyed to the British and French Ambassadors in a less dramatic manner.

Sir Percy Loraine received them, so Ciano said, 'without batting an eyelid or changing colour. He confined himself to writing down the exact formula used by me and asked me if he was to consider it as advance information or as a general declaration of war. Learning that it was the latter, he withdrew with dignity and courtesy. At the door we exchanged a long and cordial handshake'.

The interview with François-Poncet was no less friendly.

'I expect you understood the reason for your being called,' Ciano told him almost apologetically.

'I am not too bright,' François-Poncet replied with the hint of a smile, 'but this time I have not misunderstood the situation.' Like Sir Percy Loraine he had been aware for some time that war was coming and that Mussolini had already decided his country's fate.

Ciano read out the declaration of war.

'It is a dagger blow at a man who has already fallen,' François-Poncet commented sadly. 'Thank you all the same for using a velvet glove.'

Before leaving he added a warning which Ciano had good cause to remember: 'The Germans are hard masters. You too will learn this.'

7

That night in Rome an atmosphere of gloom hung over the dreadfully quiet city. Going dejectedly home to his flat to do his packing, the correspondent of *The Times* passed down Corso Umberto and across Piazza di Spagna and saw not a single flag hung out. Italian friends came to wish him good-bye, walking past the policeman on watch near his front door and the people muttering anxiously in the doorways, and they shook hands with him with a kind of sad apology.

'The shouts in the piazza,' as Cavour had said, 'cannot be taken as manifestations of public opinion.'

The Commander-in-Chief

> *Cromwell had a splendid idea – supreme*
> *power in the State and no war.*

From the first the war went badly for Italy. It was painfully and immediately apparent that the country – although for eighty years more than half the State expenditure had been applied to military purposes – was shamefully ill-equipped to conduct a major war. The long-continued fighting in Spain had reduced absurdly inadequate military reserves, already weakened by the Abyssinian campaign, to dangerously low levels; and yet the uncoordinated and often contradictory policies of the various departments of the Government allowed valuable stocks to be exported to England as late as the beginning of 1940 and to Finland (whose supplies included aircraft) later even than that.[1] Most of the Army's equipment was obsolete or obsolescent. The artillery was using guns that had been in service in 1918; the so-called armoured divisions were so short of vehicles that, according to Carmine Senise, the Chief of Police, they were obliged to borrow some from him for military parades; the Air Force was also pitiably equipped; the Navy had neither aircraft carriers nor a fleet air arm. At the time of the Albanian invasion in April 1939 mobilization revealed that many units listed as divisions on paper were, in fact, no more than a few battalions strong, and by the end of the summer of that year Mussolini, himself, had to admit that, of the seventy divisions he had claimed the Army possessed, only ten were fit for action. At the beginning of 1938 the Army Chief-of-Staff had said that by the end of the following spring stocks and production of munitions and equipment would be adequate for a

---

1. Another interesting example of the muddles and contradictions of Fascist policies is provided by the fact that when the Anti-Comintern Pact was signed with Japan a ship was on its way with supplies to China and in order to avoid embarrassment her master was ordered to wreck her off the Chinese coast.

full-scale war; in fact, six months before war was declared General Carlo Favagrossa, Under-Secretary for War Production, reported that if he could have all the material already asked for (which would necessitate the factories working double shifts) the earliest date the country would be ready for war was October 1942. General Valle, Under-Secretary of the Air Force, had said that he had over 3,000 effective aircraft; in fact, there were less than one thousand. General Pariani, Under-Secretary of the Army, had persuaded Mussolini that eight million men could be mobilized in a matter of hours; in fact, not half that number of ill-equipped and unenthusiastic men could be mobilized in a matter of weeks, and only then at a disastrous cost to industry and agriculture. Admiral Cavagnari, Under-Secretary of the Navy, tried to show how woefully not only his own department but also every other department of the Government was prepared for war; but the Duce, he complained, was completely unimpressed and unimpressionable. Once De Bono ventured to give a similar warning against the 'Buffoon' Valle and the 'traitor' Pariani, but Mussolini would not listen, he said. 'He believes what he wants to believe.' Occasionally Raffaello Riccardi, the Minister of Commerce, warned him about the economic difficulties of the country, but he blithely observed that Governments did not fall because of economic difficulties and preferred to listen to Thaon di Revel, the Minister of Finance, who implied that everything was all right and that Italy would become rich through the sale of works of art. 'What is the Duce doing?' Ciano asked, exasperated by his attitude. 'His attention seems to be mainly devoted to matters of drill.'

And yet although his capacity for self-deception was apparently limitless there can be no doubt that Mussolini was well aware how unprepared his country was for war. After the final collapse he admitted it in a conversation with Admiral Maugeri, saying that Italy had been better equipped before the First World War than before the Second. With a short break between 1929 and 1933 he had been head of all three Service Ministries since 1925, and despite his willingness to believe what he wanted to believe and to ignore what offended him, to push work on to incompetent subordinates, to concern himself more with the *passo romano* or the date for changing into summer uniforms than with the really urgent problems, to sacrifice truth to propaganda and reality to hope, he was nevertheless forced frequently to realize that the estimates and reports he was given were not merely inaccurate but wilfully misleading. 'He believes,' Ciano wrote in April 1939, 'that beyond appearances more or less carefully kept up, there is little underneath.' Five months later, on 18 September 1939, he was handed a report by Graziani which showed that, instead of the great numbers he had boasted of, the first-line forces of the Army amounted to only ten divisions. The thirty-five other divisions were patched up, under strength, and ill-equipped. 'The Duce admitted this was so,' Ciano said, 'and uttered bitter words about the real condition of the Army, which is, at this time, so lamentable.' On the very day before war was declared General Favagrossa sent to Mussolini an exceptionally gloomy report on Italy's unpreparedness emphasizing particularly the lack of anti-aircraft defences.

Mussolini had, however, been determined to go to war not only 'because Fascist ethics demanded it', but also because he felt convinced that peace would come before the futility of Fascist pretensions was known. So confident, indeed, was he that the war would soon be over that no instructions were given to stop building on the site, extending to several hundred acres, which was to impress the whole world during the forthcoming exhibition in 1942; and demobilization was actually in progress by the autumn of 1940 after the collapse of France and when it seemed that the German invasion of England was imminent. Desperately concerned that his army should at least make a token advance beyond the Alps before the Germans ended the campaign, he ordered an attack within three days although his staff advised him that three weeks would not be enough in which adequately to prepare one. France's request for an armistice, less than a week after his declaration of war and before he had achieved even a token victory, dismayed him, and he left for a meeting with Hitler to discuss the terms which would be imposed upon France, sadly aware, as Ciano put it, that his opinion had 'only a consultative value'. 'The campaign,' Ciano went on, 'has been won by Hitler without any active military participation on the part of Italy, and it is Hitler who will have the last word. This naturally disturbs and saddens him. His reflections on the Italian people and, above all, on our armed forces are extremely bitter. . . . In truth the Duce fears that the hour of peace is growing near and sees that unattainable dream of his life – glory on the field of battle – fading once more.'

As reports of the unenthusiastic way in which the war was being waged were received at Palazzo Venezia, Mussolini's complaints against the Italian people grew more and more bitter. Their reluctance to enter the war at all – and it is certain that despite public statements he was well aware of this reluctance – had already driven him to fury. The cold winter of 1939–40 had pleased him. He watched the snow falling in December and said, 'This snow and cold are very good. In this way our good-for-nothing Italians, this mediocre race, will be improved. One of the principal reasons I wanted the Apennines to be reforested was because it would make Italy colder and snowier.' In January when there was a serious coal shortage he was gratified again, because it was good for the people to be put to tests which would make them shake off their 'centuries old mental laziness'. 'We must keep them disciplined,' he said, 'and in uniform from morning to night. Beat them and beat them and beat them.'

'It is the material that I lack,' he complained. 'Even Michelangelo had need of marble to make statues. If he had only had clay he would have been nothing more than a potter. A people who for sixteen centuries have been an anvil cannot become a hammer within a few years.' The Italians were 'a race of sheep'. Eighteen years had not been enough to change them. Throughout the war he spoke like this. Every setback, every defeat, was angrily blamed on a 'soft and unworthy people', a people 'made flabby by art'; just as every German success aroused in him an agonized longing for the means and the opportunity of emulation. Each hint of an Italian victory was exaggerated both in his mind and in the Press until fantasies became accepted as facts and minor advances became major victories. A month after the war had begun he was blindly insisting that glowing reports received from the Italian Air Force were all justified and that the Italian Navy had 'annihilated fifty per cent of the British naval potential in the Mediterranean'. So gratified was he by favourable news from the war front and so furious when disillusioned or dismayed that many of his Service chiefs concealed from him news which would enrage him, giving him only reports which would please him and magnifying even those. The fact that in the year 1940–1 there was a budget deficit of the enormous sum of 28,000 million lire seems to have been carefully concealed from him.

Having failed to strike a *coup de grâce* in France, he impatiently looked for another target. He considered a heavy attack on Egypt from Libya where the Italian Army had been heavily reinforced; he considered, too, an attack on Yugoslavia. 'We must bring Yugoslavia to her knees,' he had told Marshal Graziani in a directive given before war was declared. 'We need raw materials and we must take them from Yugoslav mines.' But the Germans advised against the attack on Yugoslavia for fear of raising too many hares in Eastern Europe, and Graziani advised against the attack on Egypt, 'a very serious undertaking' for which preparations were 'far from perfect'. Mussolini, however, was insistent and announced at a Council of Ministers on 7 September that unless an attack was launched on the following Monday, Graziani would be replaced. Although all Graziani's generals, so he said, were against the offensive, he gave in and issued his orders. Never had a military operation, Ciano commented, 'been undertaken so much against the will of the commander'. But, in fact, neither Graziani nor Badoglio had pressed their views strongly when in the Duce's presence.

The attack began on 13 September. Within four days, six infantry divisions and eight tank battalions had advanced sixty miles to Sidi Barrani, and Mussolini was, in Ciano's words, 'radiant with joy'. On 4 October he had rarely been seen 'in such good humour and good shape'. But at Sidi Barrani the Italian Army halted; and for three months, while the Duce pressed for a lightning attack on the British position at Mersah Matruh, Graziani held back.

Almost, so it seemed to one of them, as if it were to spite the generals and to show himself independent of Hitler, Mussolini chose a new victim. As early as the beginning of July, General De Vecchi, Governor of the Dodecanese, telegraphed to say that British ships and perhaps British planes were being given supplies and refuge in Greece. Ever since then he had been projecting an attack; and on 12 October he announced that he had come to his final decision. Admitting without compunction that it was Hitler's unexpected occupation of Romania that prompted him to act, he set the date for the attack at the end of the month. Hitler's action in

Romania was reminiscent of his secrecy about his attacks in the West. 'Hitler always presents me with a *fait accompli*,' he said. 'This time I am going to pay him back in his own coin. He will find out from the papers that I have occupied Greece. In this way the equilibrium will be re-established.' He had not yet come to an agreement with Marshal Badoglio, he confessed; but if anyone objected to the attack he would hand in his 'resignation as an Italian'. He wrote to Hitler on 22 October informing him of his plans. The Führer was on his way to Hendaye in what was to prove an unsuccessful attempt to bring Franco into the war, and Mussolini, antedating the letter 19 October, took care to ensure that it was not received until it was too late for any objections to be raised.

This time Ciano, who saw the attack on Greece as a check upon German influence in the Balkans, supported the Duce; but again the generals did not. The three heads of the General Staff were unanimously against it, hesitantly pointing out the difficulties of mountain warfare so late in the season. They were overruled. Military intelligence gave a disturbing and, as it happened, fairly accurate estimate of the likely strength of Greek resistance. Mussolini condemned it as absurdly pessimistic. On 28 October, the anniversary of the March on Rome – after the Duce, so General Armellini says, had changed his mind about the timing almost every hour and once five times in a quarter of an hour – the Italians invaded Greece across the Albanian frontier. Six weeks later, after accepting the retirement of an exasperated Badoglio as Chief-of-Staff, Mussolini was forced to conclude at a meeting of the Council of Ministers that the situation was serious and 'might even become tragic'. It was further evidence, Mussolini decided, that the Army, and in particular its senior officers, were a disgrace to Italy. Once again they had failed completely. 'The human material I have to work with,' he complained savagely, 'is useless, worthless.' In support of this view, Starace, on his arrival back from the front, passed 'severe judgement on the behaviour of our troops', who had fought 'but little and badly'. On 4 December General Ubaldo Soddu, Under-Secretary of State for War, who had been sent to Albania by Mussolini to see for himself exactly what was happening, reported that the military situation was now beyond redemption and the situation would have to be settled 'through political intervention'. Mussolini called Ciano to Palazzo Venezia. 'There is nothing else to do,' he said when Ciano arrived. 'This is grotesque and absurd, but it is a fact. We shall have to ask for a truce through Hitler.' Ciano had never seen him so discouraged.

He had reason to be. Hitler had strongly advised him not to invade Greece, an action which would set the Balkans in uproar, and had gone straight to Italy from a meeting with Marshal Pétain at Montoire, following his meeting with Franco at Hendaye, in an attempt to dissuade Mussolini from making his disastrous attack. Two hours before the Führer's train reached Florence, where his meeting with the Duce was to take place, he was told that he was too late and that Italian troops were already across the frontier. Although Hitler behaved with remarkable restraint and went so far as to promise Italy his full support in the Greek campaign, Mussolini returned to Rome well aware that he was deeply concerned by Italy's action, which might jeopardize all his future plans. Three weeks after the meeting, when the campaign appeared already doomed to ignominious failure, he received a letter from Germany confirming this impression. Not only, Hitler reminded him, would Yugoslavia, Bulgaria, Vichy France, and Turkey become increasingly reluctant to commit themselves, but Russia's concern for the Balkans might lead to a new threat from the east, while Britain had now been able to obtain bases in Greece to bomb Rumania and the south of Italy. The consequences of the Greek adventure were that operations in the desert against Egypt would have to be abandoned for the moment and that the Germans would ultimately be obliged to send troops against the British in Thrace although nothing could be done in this direction until the following year. 'This time,' Mussolini commented sadly when he read the Führer's letter, 'he really has slapped my fingers.'[1]

And now his Under-Secretary of State for War was telling him that he would have to ask the Greeks for an armistice. Eventually he allowed Ciano to persuade him that the situation was not yet as

---

1. According to the Hitler–Bormann documents published in 1961, Hitler considered Mussolini's mistake to be the greatest contribution to his failure. In fact the whole Italian alliance was seen by Hitler at the end of his life as the main obstruction to his success. It even prevented him from making an anti-colonial appeal to the Arabs and Africans, for Italy was committed to colonialism.

bad as that and that it might even now be stabilized by immediate German help. Dino Alfieri, the Italian Ambassador to Germany, was in Rome at the time convalescing after an illness, and Ciano took him to Palazzo Venezia to discuss the matter with the Duce.

I found the Duce plunged in the depths of depression [Alfieri wrote afterwards]. I had never before seen him looking so dispirited. His face was pale and drawn, his expression sad and preoccupied. His dejected look was increased by his wearing a shirt with a grotesquely big turn-down collar and by his not having shaved for at least two days. With unaccustomed courtesy and solicitude – showing in itself how distraught he was because only in a distracted mood would the mask of impassivity he usually assumed in the presence of sub-ordinates desert him – he asked me how I was and whether I was quite recovered from my illness.

He paced slowly round his big desk, taking short steps and, as if developing an idea which dominated his mind, talked of Soddu's telegram and tried to fathom the reasons that had prompted the General to exaggerate the gravity of the situation. He kept passing his right hand nervously across his chin and face, turning now to Ciano, now to me, as though seeking approval or support for his theories and justification for his hopes.

But all his hopes were illusory. He did not have to make peace with the Greeks, but he was forced to rely on German help to ex-tricate himself from his predicament, and that was almost as unpalatable an indignity. While Soddu's telegrams maintained their gloomy note, prompting Mussolini to observe that he would in future form an army from the inhabitants of the Po valley and central Italy, leaving the rest of the nation to make arms for the 'warrior aristocracy', Hitler wrote with a calm and unreproachful reassurance, which Mussolini took as patronizing, to say that arrangements were being made for German intervention. Before these arrangements were complete, a group of Yugoslav officers carried out a *coup d'état* against their Government, which had recently signed a pact binding the country to the Axis. Hitler's reaction was violent. He insisted that Yugoslavia should be crushed with 'merciless harshness' at the same time that Opera-tion Marita was launched against the Greeks. On 5 April, only ten days after the *coup d'état* in Belgrade, having already asked Mus-solini to stop operations in Albania for a few days so that the

Yugoslav–Albanian frontier could be covered by Italian troops, he wrote to him again to tell him that the German attack on Yugoslavia and the invasion of Greece would begin the following day. All Italian forces, he suggested, should be subject to the strategic orders of the German command. Without consulting his generals, Mussolini agreed.

The German attacks, begun on 6 April, were ruthless and completely successful. By 17 April the Yugoslavs had surrendered; ten days later Athens was occupied. The surrender of Greece was accepted and the new frontiers of Yugoslavia were drawn, both without reference to the Italians. Although in his speech to the Reichstag Hitler tried to soften the blow to Mussolini's pride by describing the German intervention as a 'precautionary measure against the British attempt to entrench themselves in the Balkans' and denying that it 'was made for the purpose of assisting the Italians against Greece', no one, and least of all Mussolini, could have any more illusions about the position to which Italy had fallen in the eyes of Germany and of the world. In Berlin, Alfieri was forced to listen to Hitler's criticisms of the Italian action and of the behaviour of the Italian troops. The Führer spoke in 'vehement and aggressive tones,' Alfieri said, and 'contrary to his custom he did not ask me for news of Mussolini'.

The subordinate position of Italy was demonstrated not only by events in Greece and Yugoslavia. On 10 December news had been received in Rome of the assault on the Italian position at Sidi Barrani. Mussolini surprised Ciano by maintaining an appearance of utter calm and impersonal objectivity, hoping that Marshal Graziani would be able to hold the enemy attack. But this hope, like all others that winter, was soon dispelled. By nightfall on the 10th the British had taken so many prisoners it was impossible to count them. There were 'about five acres of officers', the battalion headquarters of the Coldstream Guards reported, 'and two hundred acres of other ranks'.

'Four divisions,' Ciano wrote in his diary, 'can be considered destroyed.' The following day Mussolini admitted that Italy had suffered an unmistakable defeat. By the beginning of January, Bardia had fallen, and the tattered Italian Army, many units of which had fought with pitiable bravery against a far better led and infinitely better equipped enemy, was driven back to Tobruk.

T – F

Mussolini remained calm – 'superhumanly calm', Ciano described his behaviour at a meeting of the Council of Ministers on 7 January – as he maintained that every army had its day of defeat. But it was not so easy for him to disguise the feelings of dismay that Hitler's prescription for the Italians caused him. Rommel he recognized, except in his more bitter moments, to be a brilliant general, but it was hard for him to accept the fact that this single German officer and a relatively small number of German troops had altered the whole aspect of the war in North Africa within a few weeks of their arrival there. Gloomily comparing Rommel, who was always in his tank at the head of the attacking columns, with Graziani, who had remained 'seventy feet underground in a Roman tomb', he could not view the victories in the desert without grumbling that they looked like German victories, not Italian ones. He ordered Graziani to face a court of inquiry, which censured the conduct of the man for whom he felt now nothing but contempt. The court's findings gave profound satisfaction to Badoglio, who heartily disliked his formerly more popular colleague; but both he and Mussolini knew that Graziani was not, in fact, alone to blame. Military intelligence, one of the few really successful organizations in the Italian Army, had intercepted American messages which showed how much weaker – both in numbers and in armour – the British were in North Africa. A less adequate general than Graziani could have stopped them with men who were properly trained to fight and wanted to fight and who had proper equipment with which to fight. But what could you do, Graziani asked his wife in an exasperated letter; 'you cannot break armour with finger-nails alone!' Badoglio, who as Chief-of-Staff since 1926 had been in charge of staff planning and armaments research for fifteen years, and Mussolini, who shut his eyes to Badoglio's evident incapacity, must both share in the responsibility for the Army's failure. But while Badoglio and Graziani blamed each other, Mussolini blamed them both and exacerbated his discontent by angry reflections on the Germans' success. When Rommel was promoted field-marshal he complained that it was a device of Hitler's to 'accentuate the German character of the battle' and retaliated by promoting General Count Ugo Cavallero, Badoglio's successor as Chief-of-Staff, a marshal, although his opinion of him was not much higher than that of his other generals. 'Cavallero is optimistic,' De Bono said. 'That's the only reason the Duce prefers him.' He was also, according to Ciano, grotesquely servile and 'would bow to the public lavatories if that would advance him'.[1]

Despite Mussolini's resentment and pique, however, Hitler remained understanding and friendly towards him personally. For whatever he thought of the Italians, his respect for their Duce was as yet but little dimmed. Even in November, when the situation in Greece was at its most chaotic, he had embarrassed Ciano by declaring with tears in his eyes: 'From this city of Vienna, on the day of the *Anschluss*, I sent Mussolini a telegram to assure him that I would never forget his help. I confirm it today. I am at his side with all my strength.' And after the North African disaster, at a conference at the Berghof in January, Hitler was as friendly as ever. Mussolini was so ashamed of his army's failure that he left for Germany in a state of high nervousness and dreaded the meeting. He had postponed it twice in the hope that better news would come from the Italian war fronts, and had made a half-hearted attempt to cancel it altogether. But it was so cordial that Ciano described Mussolini's subsequent mood of relief as one of elation – 'the normal reaction after a meeting with Hitler'. The Italian delegation arrived at Pusch station to find the Führer standing on the platform in the snow in his long leather greatcoat with his cap pulled down over his ears. Mussolini's Pullman coach stopped immediately opposite him, and the Duce got out slowly and walked towards his host, and for a moment as they shook hands they looked each other sternly in the eye. 'I haven't enough blood in my veins,' Mussolini had said a minute or two before in the cold train, 'to blush when I see him.' His features were set in a hard expression, the Italian Ambassador noticed, and then as Hitler spoke they relaxed into an artificial smile.

The Ambassador saw Mussolini alone for a moment before the conference began and told him that Hitler would be prepared to listen favourably to any request for help that he felt inclined to

1. Ciano's opinion in this case – as in many others – was biased. He was on intimate terms with (supposedly the lover of) Cavallero's daughter who was married to Francesco Jacomoni, the Governor of Albania. Indeed it was widely supposed in Rome at the time that Ciano had advocated the attack on Greece because he was personally interested in Albanian expansion there.

make to him. Mussolini interrupted him sharply. 'I have nothing to ask,' he said.

Nor did he ask. He allowed Hitler to do most of the talking, sitting quietly in one of the deep arm-chairs with which the German conference rooms were always filled, making only an occasional comment while the Führer demonstrated his knowledge of the military problems and outlined his schemes for their solution with a skill which deeply impressed Alfieri and Ciano and the fat little General Alfredo Guzzoni, acting in Cavallero's absence in North Africa as Chief-of-Staff. Hitler was in a contented mood, his mind already occupied with pleasant anticipatory thoughts about his forthcoming attack on Russia, which with his usual care he concealed from the Italians. But Mussolini's *amour-propre* had been so much upset by what he thought of as his country's disgrace, by the Germans' insistence that his attempts to improve relations with Moscow should be discontinued, and by their obvious hints that as Italy could not supply reliable soldiers she should supply more workers for German industry instead, that he could not bring himself to respond to Hitler's charm and reassuring confidence. The Führer was 'polite, friendly, and understanding', he admitted to the Italian Ambassador, but felt compelled to add 'too much so. The man is hysterical. When he told me that no one had lived through and shared my anguish more intensely than he had, there were tears in his eyes. It's all so exaggerated. He was too eager to make me feel and appreciate his kindness and generosity, his strength and superiority.'

At meal-times Mussolini seemed to concentrate on his food, bending over his plate with his napkin tucked into the top of his tunic, eating very little and very quickly. He listened to Hitler with that earnest display of concentration which so often conceals a deep embarrassment. On the rare occasions when he intervened in the discussion he did so in a mumble as though German were a language that he had forgotten how to speak. During tea on the first day he was a pathetic figure as he tried without success to push his chair back from the oppressive heat of the fire, sipping a cup of camomile tea while Hitler ate a large number of biscuits and jam tarts and Goering, splendid in a new dove-grey uniform, talked and talked.

The whole pattern of the conference was repeated six months

later, in August 1941, when Mussolini visited the Führer's headquarters on the Eastern Front to make a tour of the Russian battle-
fields. 'The Duce judged it opportune,' the Italian official record
of the meeting explained, 'to allow the Führer to develop his pro-
positions quite freely.' Hitler made the most of his opportunity
and on one day spoke for two and a half hours without stopping.
Mussolini's relief when they left for the front was obviously overwhelming.

Notice of the attack on Russia had been given to the Italians at
half-past four in the morning of 22 June. Alfieri was summoned
from bed to the *Auswärtige Amt*, where Ribbentrop told him that
at three o'clock that morning German troops had crossed the
Russian frontier. Mussolini was still in bed when the telephone
rang at his villa in Riccione. Rachele answered it and gave her
husband the message. He took the news badly, Rachele afterwards told the journalist Bruno d'Agostini, and he said to her
forlornly, 'My dear Rachele! This means the war is lost.' A few
hours later, however, Ciano telephoned Alfieri with a personal
message from the Duce to the Führer. Italy considered herself at
war with Russia as from three o'clock that morning, Ciano informed the Ambassador, and then asked him to do his 'utmost to
get the Germans to agree to the Duce's suggestion' that an Italian
expeditionary force should be sent to Russia.[1]

Although the offer of Italian troops was not welcomed in Berlin,
Mussolini was determined to send them, insisting in private that
it was not only his own pride which was involved. Italy must con-
tribute all she could to ensure 'a *blitz* victory. If Russia is not
defeated in the first six months,' he thought, 'she will never be
defeated at all.' Eventually a force of 200,000 Italian soldiers,
which might have altered the whole aspect of the war in North
Africa, was despatched – against the advice of every responsible
Italian general – to fight alongside the Germans on the Eastern
Front. And here their horror at the Nazis' treatment of Russian civilians and their own ill-treatment after the collapse at
Stalingrad, where the Germans commandeered most of the
available transport, as they did in North Africa in 1942, were

1. Mussolini had been similarly insistent that an Italian expeditionary force should
fight alongside the Germans in the invasion of England in 1940. Ten divisions and
thirty squadrons were offered to Hitler 'at the earnest wish of the Duce'.

to be yet further strains on the weakening military alliance.

Mussolini followed the movements of his troops in Russia with an interest which for days on end completely absorbed him. Their activities were reported in the most minute detail in the Press, and their successes were as over-stressed as the German successes were depreciated. The news that the German armies had come up against stiffening resistance at Minsk delighted him. 'I hope for only one thing,' he said, 'that in this war in the East the Germans will lose a lot of feathers.' This attitude was apparent throughout his tour of the Russian front. When he reviewed General Messe's Turin division, he was clearly annoyed that the men looked so clean and well-shaved as they drove past him in their requisitioned lorries, which, to the drivers' obvious embarrassment, skidded drunkenly on the mud-covered road, and he could not disguise his disappointment that Hitler had not seen them looking like the battle-scarred warriors of his imagination. In contrast the German troops looked rough and aggressive, and when Hitler went up to talk to them, making them laugh with dutiful heartiness at his heavy jokes, Mussolini was left talking to Field-Marshal Von Rundstedt. 'Hitler might have taken me with him when he went to speak to the troops,' he afterwards complained petulantly to Alfieri, 'instead of leaving me with that old Rundstedt. Did you notice how unsoldierly the Führer looked when he was talking to the men?'

Later on that day, as if to show that there was at least something he could do which Hitler could not, he went up to Bauer, Hitler's personal pilot, and, having asked him various questions about the aircraft in which they were travelling, he said that he would like to pilot it himself. When he asked Hitler if he might do so, the Führer looked around anxiously, not wanting to refuse but evidently hoping that one of his staff would find a reason for him to do so without hurting Mussolini's feelings. Bauer caught his eye and nodded slightly to reassure him. Hitler then agreed that the Duce should take the controls; but for the rest of the journey Hitler stared fixedly at Bauer's back 'as if to make sure', Alfieri thought, 'that the proximity of the Duce was not distracting his attention'.

In the subsequent official communiqués, by means of which the war aims of the Axis Powers and their New Order for Europe were announced as a counterblast to the recently published Anglo-American Atlantic Charter, Mussolini's prowess as a pilot was given prominence. 'You can add,' he told Alfieri as he gave him instructions for the Stefani news agency, 'that according to my reckoning I have travelled altogether 3,300 miles by rail, 1,250 by air, and 700 by road. And, as you can see, I'm quite ready to do it all over again.'

'His face was wreathed in smiles,' Alfieri said. 'He gazed at me with an expression of childlike contentment.'

Never again was a visit to Hitler to end on so pleasurable a note.

At the beginning of the following year Goering arrived in Rome wearing what Ciano described as 'a great sable coat, something between what motorists wore in 1906 and what a high-grade prostitute wears today' and suggested that Mussolini should make another trip to Germany. Hitler, concerned to put new spirit into the Duce, who must, he felt, have lost heart during the sad winter days, invited him to Schloss Klessheim. 'Hitler talks, talks, talks, talks,' Ciano wrote in an anguished description of this meeting. 'Mussolini suffers – he who is in the habit of talking himself and who instead has to remain silent. On the second day after lunch when everything had been said Hitler talked without interruption for an hour and forty minutes. He omitted absolutely no subject: war and peace, religion and philosophy, art and history. Mussolini automatically looked at his wrist-watch. I had my mind on my own business, and only Cavallero, who is a phenomenon of servility, pretended he was listening in ecstasy, continually nodding his head in approval. The Germans, however, dreaded the ordeal less than we did. Poor people, they have to endure it every day and I am sure there isn't a gesture, a word, a pause, which they don't know by heart. General Jodl after an epic struggle went to sleep finally on the divan. Keitel was yawning but succeeded in keeping his head up.'

Afterwards Hitler compared himself to Napoleon, and confided to the Duce that he 'was in the protection of Providence'. 'I really don't know,' Mussolini said on the way home, 'why the Führer asked me to go.'

Three months later he might well have asked a similar question about Cavallero. For over a year he had been awaiting a favourable opportunity to visit North Africa and had given General

Cavallero instructions to send him a telegram and the single word
'Tevere' when he was certain that the Italian Army had begun an
advance which would take them to the Suez Canal. The telegram
arrived on 27 June, when it was hoped that Rommel's counter-
attack, which had driven the British back across the Egyptian
frontier, was still in full impetus. But a cyclone prevented Mussolini's departure for two days, and by the time he arrived in
Libya the advance had already slowed down and was stopped at
El Alamein.[1] Furious with the military commander for making a
fool of him by calling him to the front at an unfavourable stage,
as had been done during the invasion of Greece, Mussolini spent
three unhappy weeks in Libya wandering about behind the lines,
followed by dispirited Italian generals whom he tried to encourage
with promises that every effort was being made to get supplies
across the Mediterranean and that one day soon a convoy would
get through. Plans were being prepared, he told them, for the
capture of Malta, and the Mediterranean routes would then be
kept open. But his listeners could not disguise their doubt.

On 20 July 1942 Mussolini returned to Rome. He looked
desperately tired and ill. It was announced that the exhaustion
caused by his strenuous duties had brought on an attack of amoebic
dysentery. He was taken to Rocca delle Caminate, and a rumour
flew round Rome that he had gone there to die. 'Perhaps he *is*
dying,' one of his Ministers said, 'but not of dysentery. It's a less
commonplace disease. It's called humiliation.'

It was an understandable diagnosis. So excited by the prospect
of victory in North Africa that he had been planning the details of
the Italo-German military government of Egypt, he was forced to
face a situation which even the blithely confident Cavallero
described as 'serious'. He was forced also to accept the abandon-
ment of the plans for the capture of Malta, which Hitler implied
could not now be carried out successfully owing to the low state of
Italian morale. He was obliged to accept severe cuts in the ship-
ment of coal and oil from Germany and Romania as the German
Government felt disinclined to 'throw good oil after bad', as an
attaché at the German Embassy in Rome brutally put it. He had,
as the cruel year went on, to read reports and to listen to accounts

1. In his *Storia di un anno* written two years later Mussolini gave the date 28 June
1942 as the turning-point of the war and of his own career.

of German units appropriating transport on the Russian front and leaving Italian units to retreat on foot through the snow. He had to face the fact that the Germans were not only losing confidence in the Italian will to fight but were actively taking steps to protect themselves from the consequences of an Italian collapse. The German Military Attaché in Rome was appointed a 'liaison officer' at Italian Army Headquarters; several German units entered Italy for 'training'; and Field-Marshal Kesselring was sent to Italy as 'Commander-in-Chief, South'. There were also alarming reports of German cells being formed in the larger Italian cities and of plans for the military occupation of the country and the establishment of a puppet Government under the slavishly Germanophil Roberto Farinacci.

Month by month the relationship between Italy and Germany deteriorated. The treatment of Italian workers in German labour camps; the resentment caused in Italy by the export of so many works of art to the Reich; the refusal of the Italians to be other than 'extremely lax', as Goebbels wrote in his diary, 'in their treatment of the Jews'; the continued reluctance of Hitler to agree to a more uncompromising policy towards France, whose Mediterranean possessions formed a perpetually rankling topic in Axis relations and caused Mussolini repeatedly to complain that the Germans had demonstrated typical unintelligence by not having 'occupied the whole of France at the armistice'; the perpetual and increasingly open complaints by the Germans – particularly by Goering, whose grumblings infuriated Mussolini, and later by Hitler, who put them into writing – that if Italy had not attacked Greece, Spain would have come into the war and Gibraltar would have fallen – all these jarring dissensions aggravated a relationship which had never been harmonious and eventually brought Mussolini to the exasperated conclusion that, if things went on as they were, Italy would soon be 'fighting the Germans as a matter of honour and historical duty'. Such bitter pronouncements were becoming habitual. Alternately raging at the Germans, already infected by 'the germs of collapse', for their 'senseless barbarity' and at his own people for their 'debilitating clemency', his outbursts of fretful ill-temper became as regular as his sudden changes of mood. One day criticizing Franco for his ingratitude, the next day praising him for his stand against German pressure; in the evening muttering gloomy prophecies about the progress of the war and in the morning accepting the re-assurances of his more confident advisers and talking with apparently genuine confidence in 'the most optimistic fashion', so Ciano said, 'of successes, offensive possibilities, and African recoveries', he seemed not merely erratic but no longer conscious of inconstancy. His threat of war against Germany was followed within a few days by his reaffirmation of his 'decision to march with Germany to the end'. Rommel was 'a madman' at one moment, and 'one of the great military leaders of our time' at another.

After the summer of 1942, Mussolini rarely appeared in public, and when he did people looked at him with a kind of shocked sympathy. He pushed out his jaw and opened wide his eyes in the grimly noble expression which he liked the photographers to catch, but the face had lost the spontaneous vitality that once had made it so arresting. As long as three years before, Sumner Welles had found a man looking 'fifteen years older than his actual age of fifty-six. He was ponderous and static rather than vital. He moved with an elephantine motion; every step appeared an effort. He was heavy for his weight and his face in repose fell in rolls of flesh. His close-cropped hair was snow-white.' A month after Welles's visit the new Secretary of the Party, Ettore Muti, was also shocked to find the Duce looking aged and haggard. Ciano was worried, too, but comforted himself with the reflection that it was 'a temporary condition'.

Ciano was wrong. By the summer of 1942 two years of war had so aggravated Mussolini's health that one of his doctors began to doubt that he had long to live. 'Somehow,' said a woman who saw him at Villa Torlonia towards the end of that summer, 'he didn't look real any more. It was like looking at a caricature – or even at a corpse.'

Part Three

The Fall of the Colossus

I   'The War is Going Badly'

> *Fate ! Statesmen only talk of fate when they
> have blundered.*

By the autumn of 1942, after more than two years of a hated war,
the opposition to the Germans and to the Fascist régime was
already widespread all over Italy. Intellectuals in Rome and Milan,
working-men in Naples and Sicily, were being arrested daily.
Strikes were common, and frequently the police fired over the
heads of angry crowds as the only way of dispersing them. Socialists in Genoa and Communists in Turin printed clandestine
news-sheets and scratched Fascist slogans from walls and pasted
in their place posters demanding liberty and peace. Non-Fascist
newspapers cautiously supported the opposition and fanned the
sparks of discontent by referring, although forbidden to do so, to
queues and shortages, until several of them – including *Oggi* –
were suppressed. Almost all foodstuffs including bread, vegetables, meat, rice, and eggs were rationed, and the police did not
any longer even attempt to interfere with the extensive and in-
tricate black market which had become uncontrollable since the
Government in a characteristically inept decree had decided to
cut all prices by 20 per cent.

In the south thousands of peasants were close to starvation, and
all over the country the poor were hungry and pulling in their
belts to the last hole, the one they called the '*foro Mussolini*' –
Mussolini's hole.[1] For it was his war and he had led them to it,
and these Germans who marched about everywhere, like the
soldiers of an occupying force, were his friends not theirs. They
would do anything to end the war, the Italians told each other,

---

1. It is a pun. *Foro* means forum as well as hole; and Mussolini's forum on the
outskirts of Rome was part of a grandiose scheme of his not yet completed when war
had been declared.

repeating with sardonic humour a favourite joke; as a last resort they would even try to win it. But most of them had already stopped thinking about victory and waited with a kind of hopeful resignation for defeat, listening to the broadcasts of the B.B.C. for any hint that it might soon be granted them.

Mussolini accepted their despondency and defeatism as a further manifestation of their unworthiness to be considered as anything other than 'a mediocre race of good-for-nothings' who were 'only capable of singing and eating ice-cream'. They were not as good as the Italians of 1914: this was a sad 'result of the régime, but an undeniable one'. As for the Army, it was 'useless', and the generals, almost to a man, were 'paralytic'. The admirals were worse. The *bourgeoisie*, of course, were 'selfish and decadent' and 'the worst possible type of Italian'. But although he permitted himself these frequent and varied attacks on his people, if the Germans showed signs of agreeing with him he was furious.

He was handed one day the transcript of an intercepted telephone conversation between a staff officer at the German Army Headquarters in Italy and another German officer in Berlin, in which the Italians had been referred to as '*macaroni*' and Italy as a country which ought soon to be occupied. For days afterwards he went about muttering the enigmatic threats which he never tired of making and told Ciano that he was preparing a dossier of German insults and crimes which was 'to be used when the right moment comes'.

In the meantime, however, he limited himself to frequent public references to Japanese virtues and triumphs, obviously intended as slights to Germany. Declaring that he was 'the foremost pro-Japanese in the world', he ended a speech by announcing that the Italian and Japanese soldiers would march side by side to victory with the other 'armies of the Tripartite Alliance', whose nationality he was careful not to mention. On another occasion after reading a report on the treatment of Italian labourers in the camps in Germany, where they were not only treated as unwelcome slave labour and denied even the pretence of hospitality but were even beaten for insubordination and laxness and guarded by watchdogs, he exploded with indignation. 'These things are bound to produce lasting hatred in my heart. In the end I shall square this account. I can wait many years to do so, but I will not permit the sons of a race which has given to humanity Caesar, Dante, and Michelangelo to be devoured by the bloodhounds of the Huns.'

He made no direct protest to the Germans himself, however, preferring to rely on the Germans to tap the telephone lines between Rome and Berlin, which for years had been the accepted method of conveying complaints to Germany. Indeed, he instructed Ciano to take the matter up with Mackensen, the German Ambassador, as if he were acting on his own personal initiative without orders from the Duce, who was 'to be supposed to have no knowledge of it'. This reluctance to intervene personally was symptomatic of an attitude of mind towards the Germans which was disastrous for Italy. They were 'uncouth barbarians' who were attempting to ride roughshod over Italy for their own ends; they were again now, as they had been in 1936, 'primitive degenerates' without 'taste or scruple'. They were 'dirty dogs' who were taking everything and leaving Italy with a heap of bones; 'untrustworthy humbugs' who ought to leave the Italians alone. 'They should remember,' he said, 'that through them we have lost an Empire. I have a thorn in my heart, because the defeated French still have their Empire, while we have lost ours. . . . We may be willing to give up our shirts, but the Germans remove even our hides.' The only hope for Italy, he admitted privately, was that the war would end in a compromise which would save Italian independence and at the same time be long enough to exhaust the grasping Germans. And yet he felt for them, despite these judgements and extravagant tirades of abuse, a continuously compelling admiration. So jealous of their military success that he could not disguise his pleasure when he heard of some German failure on the Russian front; so anxious not to give them cause for condescension that he could not bring himself to write what he could only conceive as a humiliating letter to Hitler asking for the grain that would have helped to feed millions of his hungry people; so angry at each fresh report of their high-handedness and cruelty, particularly in Alto Adige, that he foresaw 'an unavoidable conflict between Italy and Germany', he nevertheless succumbed to the irresistible attraction of their power, efficiency, and ruthlessness whenever in the presence of a German general or a German diplomat, or, above all, in the presence of their leader himself.

A few hours after a conversation with Field-Marshal Kesselring, the German Commander-in-Chief in Italy, he spoke of his own generals with profound contempt. He only liked one of them, he said, the one who had said to his soldiers in Albania, 'I have heard that you are good family men. That's all very well at home; but not here. Here you can't do too much thieving, murder, and rape.' 'I too will adopt the method of hostages,' Mussolini announced while in this ruthless mood. He had given orders, he said, that for every soldier wounded by Croatian rebels two hostages would be shot, for every one killed twenty hostages would be shot. But he knew, Ciano commented, that he would never enforce it. He was always threatening death and punishment; he rarely went beyond the threat.

In his compulsive determination to make his own people as hard and disciplined, as strong and indifferent to suffering, as the Germans, he introduced measures which the Italians considered merely absurd. Gratified, so he said, that Naples was having so many air-raids because they would help to harden the breed and make of the Neapolitans a Nordic race, he gave orders that every time there was an alarm there, the sirens would sound in Rome as well; and at the first opportunity the anti-aircraft batteries were to open fire to make the illusion of danger more exciting, more fearful, and more dramatic. With the same ends in view, new categories of civilians were pronounced fit for mobilization; punishments for political and military offences were to be made more severe; newspapers were ordered to print, without undue regard for truth, items which tended to inflame patriotism, loyalty to Fascism, and hatred for the enemy. Hitler, he told Ciano, had used big figures to impress people 'like that jackass of a Roosevelt. . . . (They are both big jackasses and belong to kindred races.)' But if the Germans falsified their communiqués, so would he. He had in fact always done so. When the British Navy had attacked the Italian battle fleet on 11 November 1940 at Taranto and put half of it, including the new *Littorio*, out of action, the papers had been ordered to discount this crushing defeat and to print instead fanciful commentaries on an air-raid which, through the pressing insistence of Mussolini, the Italian

Air Force had carried out on the same day on a convoy in the Medway – a raid which in fact caused little damage, cost the Italians eight bombers and five fighters, and was the first and last Italian raid on Britain. Later when a company of parachutists, numbering about 150 men, occupied one of the Ionian islands, Mussolini said that it should be announced that a division had landed there.

The Italians, however, were not impressed by the Duce's efforts to deceive them, to mould them into the people he would like them to be, to force upon them characteristics which were not their own. And as the months dragged on and the war seemed interminable and victory no longer possible, Mussolini began slowly but inexorably to slip from the favour of even those supporters who had enthusiastically accepted his declaration of war and had excused the disasters of its first two years. He was still cheered, of course, on the rare occasions when he was seen, still spoken of with admiration, and treated with that adulatory respect which he had by now accepted as his right; but the spontaneity of devotion and the overwhelming acclamations which, with rare exceptions, had swayed an entire nation were gone. The cheering seemed mechanical; the respect prescriptive.

There were other reasons, apart from the detested war and the hated German alliance, which were the cause of this.

Mussolini was now seriously ill. His presence was never dynamic and glowing as once it had constantly been. He had lost most of his former tireless energy, and his always mercurial temperament was no longer merely unpredictable but wildly erratic. Syphilis was responsible, his enemies said; inadequately treated in his youth, it was now entering its final stages, inducing feverish excitation and hallucinations. 'I remember,' Giuseppe Bottai, the Minister of National Education, said at this time, that Marshal Balbo 'called Mussolini a product of syphilis, and that I used to object to his words. I wonder now if this judgement on Mussolini wasn't correct, or at least very close to the truth. The Duce has decayed intellectually and physically. He doesn't attract me any more. He is not a man of action. He is presumptuous and ambitious and expects only to be admired, flattered, and betrayed.'

By October 1942 Mussolini was not merely decaying but often in violent pain, and his physician, Dr Pozzi, was constantly in attendance either at Villa Torlonia or Rocca delle Caminate. The wounds he had received in 1917 had opened up again. In addition, the ulcer which had intermittently been troubling him for years gave him so much pain that frequently during an interview he found it impossible to sit still and turned and twisted in his chair, fidgeting convulsively; and sometimes the pains were so bad that he had to press his hands against his mouth to prevent himself from crying out. According to Quinto Navarra, his personal attendant who acted as Chief Usher at Palazzo Venezia, he would on occasions abandon himself to his pain and throw himself on the floor to roll about, groaning in agony. No one could doubt his physical courage, but he was never a man to bear pain without complaint and he began increasingly to rely on the analgesic drugs and injections which Dr Pozzi gave him.

At the end of September Edda Ciano had written to her husband at the Foreign Ministry: 'My mother has no sense of humour. She says and does the most fantastic things. Anyway this is not why I am writing to you. My father is very ill. Stomach pains, irritability, depression, etc. My mother draws a dark picture. In my opinion it's the old ulcer again – his private life of the last few years gives one much to worry about, its effects, etc. Well, let's not talk about that. They made X-ray pictures of all kinds – all negative – but a specialist was never called. . . . Please will you do something . . . anything so that my father is seen and examined properly. Get in touch with my mother and help her. So far the only measures taken have been blasphemy and curses.'

Professor Cesare Frugoni, one of Italy's leading doctors, was eventually asked to examine the Duce and confirmed Edda Ciano's opinion by diagnosing severe duodenal ulcers. Mussolini was put on a mainly liquid diet, and this made him anaemic. In May 1943 he was found writhing on the floor at Rocca delle Caminate by a servant, who rushed up to Rachele's room shouting, '*Il Duce muore! Il Duce muore!* The Duce's dying!' Dr Pozzi came immediately and told Rachele that her husband must stay in bed and rest. He advised also that another specialist should be consulted in addition to Professor Frugoni and the three other doctors who had already been called, But Rachele wrote in her diary, 'the idea of too many doctors frightens me'. They all contradicted each other anyway. Frugoni, who at first diagnosed ulcers saying that one of his colleagues had 'a bee in his bonnet about dysentery', later agreed that acute dysentery was a complicating factor. Then he gave it as his opinion that the Duce was suffering from advanced cancer, only to be immediately contradicted by Professor Cesare Bianchi.

The real trouble, as both Ciano and Mussolini's eldest son Vittorio knew, was psychosomatic.[1] Although the Duce slept heavily, his days were spent in an almost continual state of excitement and anxiety. He would never recover so long as the war went so badly for Italy. As the news of each new disaster in North Africa and in the Mediterranean reached him, he wrought himself into a paroxysm of emotion as he inveighed against the Army, which was fighting with the 'calm and indifference of the professional instead of the fury of the fanatic'; against the Navy, to which he longed to send some signal 'like the one Churchill sent his admirals' but in eighteen months had given him no opportunity to do so; against the Italian people, who were not made for war like the Germans and Japanese and who were 'not mature or consistent enough for so grave and decisive a test'; against the English, whom he swore to hate 'for all time' for having taken his Empire from him and for having carried out the conquest of Abyssinia as a 'purely personal vendetta'; and against Roosevelt, for whom he reserved a scarcely less than pathological hatred. 'Never in the course of history,' he exclaimed maliciously, 'has a nation been guided by a paralytic. There have been bald kings, fat kings, handsome, even stupid kings; but never kings who in order to go to the bathroom and the dinner-table had to be supported by other men.' At Christmas he got angry about presents, which were the 'alibi of the rich to justify their good fortune in the eyes of the poor'. And then he even got angry about traditional holidays. What was New Year's Day, for instance, but 'the day of the circumcision of Christ – that is the celebration of a Hebrew rite which the Church itself has abolished'? And why did people complain so much about illiteracy? 'Even if there is illiteracy what does it matter?' he asked impatiently. 'In the fourteenth century Italy was

1. In May 1945 *Avanti !* published an article, '*Parla il dottore che misurò il cadavere di Mussolini*' by A. Astuni, which showed that the doctor who performed the autopsy on Mussolini's body could find no more than a slight scar as evidence of his ulcer. His heart and arteries were still sound. A knowledge of his glandular condition would doubtless be revealing.

populated by nothing but illiterates, but this did not prevent the flourishing of Dante Alighieri. Today when everyone knows how to read and write, whom do we have ? The poet Govoni!'

Mussolini, in fact, would take it out on everything and everybody, Ciano sourly commented, 'even on the Almighty, when things go wrong'.

But although increasingly vituperative, Mussolini was becoming noticeably more apathetic even on those days when his health seemed improved. His conversation was no longer forceful and sparkling, his ironic comments no longer entertaining but merely savagely ill-tempered. He contradicted himself frequently, lost his temper on the least provocation, roused himself to bursts of strenuous activity, only to relapse into a kind of absent-minded morbidity. His prejudices were more pronounced than they had ever been. He once dismissed a man from his personal staff because he wore a beard, 'that absurd fungus' which he had always detested as a mask 'for solemn humbugs and second-rate *arrivistes*'. He refused to employ another man because he did not like the look of his handwriting, for like most superstitious men he was convinced that graphology was an important guide to character, and he was proud of his own firm, idiosyncratic hand. ' I can tell a man's character as well by looking at his handwriting,' he once said, 'as by looking at his face.' For hours on end he would occupy himself with the details of propaganda which were often trivial and sometimes meaningless. Cutting out items from foreign newspapers, which he read with undiminished avidity, re-phrasing the headlines of his own newspapers, writing incongruously esoteric political articles, altering the style or content of the daily war bulletin before it was broadcast, releasing one item of news and increasing or minimizing the importance of another, he worked hard, but it was work which could well have been performed by any experienced journalist or official at the Ministry of Popular Culture. As editor of *Il Popolo d'Italia* he had amused himself by cutting out entertaining or fallacious items from other papers and sticking them on a wall of the office under the heading '*Colonna Infame*'; now, in imitation of this, he spent a great deal of time in looking for and cutting out inaccuracies and absurdities in foreign newspapers and having them reprinted in the Italian Press in what was called 'The Nonsense Column'. Before the war he had been known to issue as many as six orders a day to the newspapers instructing them on the handling of news; now even ten orders a day were not infrequent.

In the early days of the war journalists were invited to Villa Torlonia so that they could report the Spartan and energetic life which the Duce led – his habit of leaping from bed as soon as he awoke; his cold bath before reading his mail, and dictating his orders with the quick, mechanical ease of a teleprinter; his sudden breaks for riding, swimming, or a violent game of tennis; his simple meals, his refusal to rest, his voracious appetite for work. But now all had changed. The simple meals became medicinal slops; the riding and tennis were forbidden, and he took exercise by gently scything the long grass in the grounds of his villa; the vitality was contrived and the urgency simulated. The light in his office was kept on till late into the night, but this was to give an illusion of industry to those who passed the curtained window; the room beyond might well be empty. And the Duce himself in fact was now hardly ever seen.

Obsessed by the fear of defeat and failure, by doubts and uncertainties, overwhelmed by sudden bursts of anger which would be followed by days of despair, conscious of his sunken cheeks, thin neck, and darkly shadowed eyes, Mussolini became more and more reluctant to show himself in public and lived, so he told Giuseppe Bottai at Palazzo Venezia one day, 'a solitary life wrestling with my problems and deciding them all by myself'.

It would have been better, Bottai observed later, if he had, in fact, led a solitary life there. But, on most afternoons still – as in the past – Claretta Petacci lay waiting for him in the Cybo rooms, a flat on an upper floor of the palace. And Bottai was not the only Italian to suggest that the regular visits which he felt compelled to make to his mistress were at least partly responsible for the Duce's declining health. His visits, though, were in reality both shorter and rarer than before; and for hours on end Claretta lay on the divan bed in the sitting-room looking up at the signs of the Zodiac painted in gold on the blue vaulted ceiling and listening to gramophone records playing sentimental songs or dance tunes over and over again. Sometimes she would pass the time drawing designs for new clothes or painting romantic pictures of birds and flowers, or she would lie on the pillows reading love-stories, painting her nails, gazing at herself in the looking-glass or out of the window at the fountain in the courtyard. She filled a little book with descriptions of their happy days in the past – ski-ing at Terminillo, swimming at Rimini, picnics on the royal estate of Castelporziano – and with painful doubts about the future. For when her lover came to her now, he was often depressed, sometimes angry and glowering, nearly always irritable. On some evenings she waited until ten o'clock and he never came at all; and in her loneliness the resentments she harboured against those who blamed and despised her grew and festered. 'They are all his enemies,' she shouted to a servant one evening when she had waited five hours for him in vain. 'They betray him fifteen times a day.' The Fascists were 'traitors'; the generals 'silly old fools' – particularly that doddering idiot De Bono. 'Why does he pretend to be so scandalized,' she asked indignantly, 'when he makes love himself to an old countess on a black velvet sofa?'

Of course, the Duce himself, she felt convinced, was not only betrayed, but he in his turn was betraying her. She was haunted by the fear that he had found another mistress or had begun to make love again to one of his former ones. Margherita Sarfatti or Angela Curti, perhaps, were trying to take him from her, and there was a new woman now called Irma who was 'making a rag of him'. 'People say it's me,' she complained, 'but it's *her*, it's *her*.' When she dared to do so, she taxed Mussolini about his other mistresses, but he would then insult her or deride her so sarcastically that she began to cry, and that would make him angrier than ever. So she took to writing him letters in which appeals and accusations tumbled over each other in her fear that she was losing him. How could she make sure that she did not do so? she asked her brother's mistress, Zita Ritossa. By not making herself so readily available whenever the Duce wanted her, Zita Ritossa advised her. 'But if I tried that,' she said pathetically, 'he wouldn't bother about me at all.' It was probably true. Indeed, at this time he made a positive effort to end the affair which had now lasted for seven years – the longest liaison of his life. According to the Sicilian Princess di Gangi he confessed that he now found the woman 'revolting'. One afternoon in the spring of 1943 Claretta was told by an embarrassed policeman at the Via Astalli entrance to Palazzo Venezia that he had orders not to let her in. She lost her temper and pushed her way past him, only to be met by the Duce's cold, dispassionate stare. 'I consider,' he announced aloofly, using an expression which, she afterwards confessed, terrified her, for he had told her how often he had used it in dismissing other women in the past, 'I consider the cycle closed.' But he gave in. There were to be several more attempts to dismiss her, and he was always to give in. The tears poured down her face, streaking her white cheeks with the thick mascara she always wore as she begged him to forgive her and to take her back; and he did. Afterwards he would regret that he had done so and telephone to say she must not go to Palazzo Venezia again. 'Please leave me alone. The war is going badly,' he told her. 'The people might criticize me for my weakness.' 'There's already been one woman who made me do stupid things,' he said on another occasion, 'and I don't intend to put up with it again.' But he did. He insulted her, quarrelled with her, behaved towards her with studied indifference, 'just as if,' so she said herself, 'he had another woman who was taking everything out of him'. He quarrelled with her about her family, about her brother's disreputable financial speculations and the absurd memoranda he sent him on how to win the war, about her tall, hook-nosed, calculating mother, whose dangerous boasts and promises of patronage were earning her the contempt of Rome. Once when they were quarrelling about her brother he hit her so hard that she fell back against the wall and was only restored to consciousness by a strong injection of a stimulant given to her by her father. But there were days when, for a moment, their quarrels seemed unimportant and they found comfort in love and in the memory of happiness; and afterwards she would fill her diary with the trivialities of their conversation. 'I won't come in the day any more,' she whispered once. 'Just after dark. For a few minutes, just to see you and to kiss you. I don't want to cause a scandal.'

It *was* a scandal, though – a scandal which, in the words of an important police officer, was 'doing the Duce more harm than the loss of fifteen battles'. 'There is really much too much talk about the affair,' Ciano agreed, and he told his friend Serrano Suñer, the Spanish Foreign Minister, that there would be no objection to lots of mistresses, but this concentration on one and on her family was a serious scandal. The Petacci family, Angelo Cerica, a senior *carabinieri* officer, said, 'meddles in everything, grants political protection, threatens from above and intrigues from below'. But what could one do to warn the Duce, Ciano asked in exasperation, particularly as two of his most intimate colleagues, his private secretary De Cesare and his Under-Secretary of the Interior, Guido Buffarini-Guidi, were making plenty of money in 'this underworld setting'? Someone really must talk to him, though, Mussolini's sister Edvige insisted. It was all very well for her brother to protest to Alessandro Pavolini, the Minister of Popular Culture, that all the great men of the Italian Renaissance had had their love-affairs and that he gave nothing to Claretta except a few small presents now and again and occasionally 500 lire to buy a dress. This was true; but the people who saw her wearing the expensive clothes and smelling of the expensive scent with which artful Roman shopkeepers and calculating business-men were anxious to provide her, did not believe it was true and told each other that their exorbitant taxes were paying for her luxuries. They could not know that her large diamond ring was given to her by a banker who believed he owed the successful conclusion of a business deal to her intervention and that her mink coat was a gift from an acquaintance of her brother's who had been given a profitable contract by the Ministry of Works. In any event when people spoke, as they frequently and openly did speak, of the 'Petacci scandal' they were usually referring to the family's discreditable activities rather than to Claretta's. They knew her parents had built before the war a beautiful modern villa with black marble bathrooms in the expensive Camilluccia district, and they believed that Mussolini had paid for it or, at least, for Claretta's exotic bedroom, the walls of which were covered with looking-glass and whose enormous silk-covered bed was raised like a throne on a dais. But he had not paid for it, although the domineering Signora Petacci had told her daughter to ask him to do so. Claretta had refused even to suggest it, and when he saw the villa for the first time and was asked by its proud owners if he liked it, he replied gruffly, 'Not much.'

The most detested member of the family was Claretta's brother Marcello, a doctor in the Navy, who was reported to be making a fortune from smuggling gold through the diplomatic bag, from illegal trading in foreign currency, and from his widely self-advertised friendship with the Duce, which enabled him, so it was supposed, to place contracts and arrange profitable appointments. While it was untrue that the Duce helped Marcello to make money – he never directly helped anyone to make money, least of all himself – he was nevertheless ingenuous and careless enough to let the suspicion grow up that he had done. The truth was that he was not in the least interested in money and hardly ever thought about it. He was, indeed, according to Claretta, so innocent about it that he once inquired how she managed to live so well. 'Does your father earn a lot?' he asked her with an apparently genuine wish for enlightenment about something that had never before occurred to him. It was, of course, absurdly ingenuous of him not to realize that when Claretta, heavily made-up, over-dressed and over-scented, distributed money to the poor, her careless patronage would be resented. Ciano noted in his diary that the Director of Public Health had told him that Guido Buffarini-Guidi was allowing her 200,000 lire a month; but, as was natural, the poor to whom she distributed most of this largesse grumbled that it was the conscience-money of a spoiled tart.

It was, above all, absurd of Mussolini to suppose that his selection of friends and protégés of the Petaccis to fill the vacant posts at his disposal would not cause deep resentment. That he was surprised when his choices were resented seems certain, and that he remained as often as not unaware of the resentment seems equally so. No one greatly objected to his asking the newspaper *Il Messaggero* to appoint Claretta's father its medical correspondent: Dr Petacci was, after all, a competent physician. No one objected to his trying to ensure that Claretta's sister Miriam should have a successful film career; she was not a bad actress. But other displays of his haphazard patronage could not so easily be forgiven; and in particular his choice of Aldo Vidussoni, a young man of twenty-six and a friend of the Petaccis, for the important Secretaryship of the Fascist Party was universally regretted; and the semi-official explanation that Vidussoni had been appointed to exercise some sort of beneficial influence on the recalcitrant youth of the country convinced no one. Ciano was aghast at this particular choice of a man whom Vittorio Mussolini described as full of 'idiocy, ignorance, and malice' for so important an appointment, and said so – but not to the Duce.

Several leading Fascists approached Ciano and told him that as

Mussolini's closest adviser and as his son-in-law it was his duty to inform him how strong feelings in the Party were against the appointment and how fast resentment in the country generally was rising against the Petaccis. But Ciano dared not. Nor did anyone dare to mention to him the damaging gossip which was going round Rome concerning the influence that a somewhat disreputable architect named Pater was having on Donna Rachele, who, according to her daughter Edda, was going through her change of life. 'The fact was,' Bottai said, 'no one dared speak to Mussolini about anything.' When a friend had said to Ciano that the Duce was often in 'such obvious pain it was alarming' and he ought to do something about it, he asked, 'But what? . . . Who has the courage to speak to him about a personal matter?'

Who for that matter, as Bottai had said and as Ciano might well have added, had the courage to speak to him about any unpleasant matter? When the Ministry of the Interior prepared a documented report on the disturbing internal situation in Italy and the growth of anti-Fascism, Buffarini-Guidi dared not show it to the Duce. When the indignation of Raffaello Riccardi, the Minister of Commerce, eventually overcame his reluctance to speak to Mussolini about the Petaccis' illegal gold transactions, the Duce appeared indignant too, and even – so Riccardi thought – 'humiliated'. But Ciano did not think that the Minister's future in the Party was likely thereafter to be very successful. 'With Mussolini,' he commented astutely, 'it is extremely dangerous to believe that one is two steps above him.' Buffarini-Guidi agreed and said that the Duce's principal reaction was not one of indignation and certainly not of humiliation, but of anger with Riccardi for having made a scene. Count Cavallero took no such chances as Riccardi had done. He had found by experience that it was much easier to get on with the Duce if information which would displease him was suppressed. When asked to provide a list of military equipment being manufactured in Italy, he allowed the numbers of anti-tank guns to be deliberately exaggerated. Mussolini, although often willing to accept good news without the deeper inquiry which would perhaps prove disappointing, on this occasion questioned the high figures which Cavallero had supplied. The Count said that they represented theoretical possibilities of production rather than actual numbers, and altered them in pencil.

   This calculated withholding of information from the Duce was, of course, no new development in Fascist circles. It was, indeed, widely believed in Italy that for years the *gerarchi* had been concealing the true facts from him. In the past this belief had often worked to Mussolini's credit. When some local Fascist was thought guilty of corruption or an act of cruelty or malice, or when a Fascist decree was found to be harsh or intolerant, the people would say to each other, 'If only the Duce knew!' For the Duce was still a god then and not to be held responsible for the wrongs of his mortal followers; but this was an attitude which was rare now. By the end of 1942 most Italians had begun to suppose that the Duce must be a part of every rankling injustice, every defeat, every hardship, every fresh disaster that showed the Fascist system which he had created was not capable of dealing with the emergency into which he had plunged it. The war had gone on too long.

> *Why did not Caesar look at the list of the conspira-*
> *tors when it was thrust into his hand ? Maybe he*
> *allowed himself to be killed, feeling that he had*
> *reached the end of the tether.*

I

On 23 January 1943 units of the British Army occupied Tripoli. To many Italians then, the war appeared already lost and the only hope for Italy seemed to lie in a disengagement from the German alliance. Few of them expected, however, that the Axis would be broken so long as the Duce remained in power. It was an opinion which the Germans shared. Writing after the fall of Tripoli and when it seemed likely that Tunis also would be taken, Goebbels laid emphasis on this belief. 'The Duce has again assured the Führer and in a most emphatic way,' he wrote, 'that he will march with us through thick and thin and that he will always remain faithful to the Axis. This is absolutely true. As long as the Duce is in power in Italy, we can feel secure; the loyalty of Fascism is assured.'

How long, though, Goebbels wondered, could the Duce remain in power ? And how much power did he really possess ? 'The aristocracy and the Court,' he was sure, 'sabotaged all his deci-sions'; and the generals were constantly at odds with him.

The opposition, in fact, had already gone deeper than Goebbels knew. As early as November 1942, when General Montgomery's victory at El Alamein had presaged the ultimate defeat of the Italian armies in North Africa, the plotting had begun. It had at first been limited to vague and indeterminate suggestions and hints, secret conversations and meetings between the Court and various officers of the General Staff. But in time the conspiracies spread and multiplied, and the King himself became deeply involved in them; while both the Minister of his Royal Household, Duke Pietro d'Acquarone, and Princess Maria José, the wife of his son and heir Umberto, were known to be in touch with those generals who wanted to see the end of the Duce's dictatorship. Acquarone, indeed, had not limited his contacts to the generals, and three years before, in January 1940, he had approached Ciano on the golfcourse and said that the King felt that it might 'become necessary to give things a different direction'. He wanted to go deeper into the subject, Ciano thought, but he was given no opportunity to do so.

'I hear from several sources,' Marshal Caviglia, an old and respected anti-Fascist, wrote in his diary in the winter of 1942, 'that at the Palace they envisage a solution earlier than anyone supposes. The King is carefully considering what should be done.'

Those of Caviglia's fellow-generals, however, who were also considering what should be done, did not all agree that it was Mussolini alone who would have to be replaced. General Vittorio Ambrosio, for instance, a man who was later to play an important part in the dramatic events which were to lead to the Duce's arrest, believed that the King also might have to go, as he had been 'too identified with Fascism'. 'Visited Bonomi,' he recorded in a cryptic but nevertheless revealing note in his diary in February 1943, 'Badoglio's proposal – Abdication of the King. The Prince. Armistice. Cavallero.'

Ivanoe Bonomi, whose name is the first mentioned in this note, a Prime Minister before the Fascists came to power and a Prime Minister again after her débâcle, was one of those few Socialists whom the King trusted. His supposed loyalty to the Crown was, however, opportunist rather than inflexible. So was that of Marshal Badoglio, whose proposal that the King should abdicate was apparently the subject of the discussion to which General Ambrosio referred. Although he himself denied harbouring so presumptuous an aspiration, Badoglio was believed by Marshal Caviglia to have 'designs on Mussolini's succession', and he certainly admitted to a friend in April 1943 that he agreed with General Ambrosio that Italy must lose no time in breaking with Germany 'with or without the Monarchy' and that this would involve the removal of the Duce.

While Badoglio and Ambrosio, in concert with two other generals, Giuseppe Castellano and Pompeo Carboni, discussed their plans and assessed their chances of success, several of Mussolini's Fascist Ministers were also plotting the Duce's overthrow. The most influential and outspoken of these were Giuseppe Bottai, Minister of Education, and Count Dino Grandi, Minister of Justice. Dino Grandi, like Marshal Badoglio, was both ambitious and shrewd. He was also extremely intelligent, vain, and amusing, and, unlike most of Fascism's *gerarchi*, charming and comparatively cultured. He had a delightful smile and a manner at once expansive and equivocal. He was – and remains – an enigmatic figure whose motives were clear neither to his friends nor to his enemies. One of these enemies, Guido Buffarini-Guidi, the large and sensual Under-Secretary of the Interior whose craftiness was universally admitted and deplored, hoped that by bringing Grandi's conspiratorial activities to the Duce's notice he would bring himself into favour. He contrived to do so in a characteristically devious way. As the man responsible for the allowance of which Ciano had made note, Claretta Petacci had become dependent upon him. He had also taken care to ingratiate himself with Donna Rachele, and, although she was later to detest him, she was at this time disarmed by the flattery of his calculated attentions. A third woman whose friendship Buffarini-Guidi was careful to cultivate was Angela Curti, one of the Duce's former mistresses and still an influential confidante. Protesting much concern for Mussolini's safety, he persuaded Angela Curti to write to him and warn him about the plots which Grandi and Bottai were hatching. He intimated that Count Ciano and Roberto Farinacci were also showing signs of serious disloyalty.

Mussolini was not much disturbed. A few days after receiving Angela Curti's letter, he decided to make another 'change of the Guard', as the frequent reshuffles of the Ministries were termed in Fascist parlance. But all the important offices changed hands, so that there was no discrimination against those Ministers he had been warned about, and none of them was sent from Rome; Count Grandi was replaced as Minister of Justice, but he was allowed to retain the Presidency of the Chamber of Deputies. Giuseppe Bottai was replaced as Minister of Education, but he retained, as the others did, his seat on the Fascist Grand Council.

Count Ciano was replaced at the Ministry of Foreign Affairs by the Duce himself, with Giuseppe Bastianini, who had been Ambassador in London for some months before the war, as Under-Secretary; but Ciano was permitted to choose his next appointment and it was at his own request that he went as Ambassador to the Holy See. Mussolini, in fact, so Ciano wrote in his diary, was 'very much embarrassed' and said, 'You must consider you are going to have a period of rest. Then your turn will come again.' 'Our leave-taking was perfectly friendly,' Ciano added, 'and I am very glad of that, because I like Mussolini, like him very much, and what I shall miss most will be my contact with him.'

It seemed, indeed, that the reshuffle had taken place with the principal object of showing the Germans that their Axis partners were determined to prosecute the war with increased energy. On 31 January, six days before the Government changes were announced, Count Ugo Cavallero had been dismissed as Chief-of-Staff in consequence of the military defeats in North Africa. A new Cabinet was a logical corollary.

Mussolini's choice as successor to General Cavallero, a blind supporter of the German alliance, was, however, as ingenuous as his refusal to take seriously the defection of his Ministers. He chose as the new Chief-of-Staff General Ambrosio, one of the men most deeply implicated in the plots to overthrow him and, as it happened, a man both disliked and distrusted by Field-Marshal Kesselring, the German Commander-in-Chief in Italy, and by Hitler, who thought he would 'be happy if Italy could become a British Colony today'.

As the winter turned to spring, the plots developed and ramified. There were anti-Royalist plots, anti-Fascist plots, anti-German plots. Filippo Anfuso, on a visit to Rome from the Embassy in Budapest, found that Count Ciano, now working in his new office, was 'up to his neck' in them; and there were many others besides Ciano as deeply involved. It was difficult to discover, in fact, as Anfuso says, 'who was in what conspiracy'; but it was certain that each one, for a variety of conflicting reasons, was aimed at the displacement of the Duce.

Mussolini, however, continued to ignore the reports he was given about them. Rachele passed on the warnings she had received, but he told her not to fuss; his sister Edvige did the same, and he said that she was dramatizing the situation; in April the anxious Angela Curti went to tell him that the King was frequently receiving not only the dissident generals but anti-Fascist politicians as well, and Mussolini, confident that the Court was completely out of touch with liberal opinion, replied that he had complete faith in the King's loyalty to him; the Secretary of the Party gave Mussolini a similar warning a few weeks later, telling him that Badoglio's son had announced in Morocco that his father would soon succeed Mussolini and that there were reports from all over Italy that the Fascists were planning to destroy him, but again he did not take the warning seriously; even the Pope, so it seems, offered through an intermediary to receive him secretly and to provide him with information of which the Vatican felt sure the Duce must be ignorant, but Mussolini declined the offer. He had seen the King recently, he said, and His Majesty had assured him of his friendship.

Carefully concealing any anxiety which these repeated warnings may have given him, discounting the most alarming reports from the Minister of Commerce, dismissing the extensive strikes in the industrial north as 'the machinations of the *bourgeoisie*', Mussolini remained as indifferent towards his opponents as ever. He was too concerned about the war, he said, to bother with anything else. 'The political situation,' he felt sure, was 'entirely dependent upon the military one' – a victory in the field would silence all the opposition. And he continued to insist that a military victory was still possible, if only the Army would pull itself together. Rommel's retreat would undoubtedly prolong the war, but the ultimate result was not in doubt. The situation in Tunisia was serious but not yet irredeemable. The immediate necessity, he believed, was a negotiated peace with Russia, which would free Germany to concentrate on the threat in the Mediterranean. On 26 March he wrote to Hitler to congratulate him on having stabilized the Russian front after the battle of Stalingrad and to suggest that now that Russia was weakened 'to such a degree that she cannot hope, at any rate for a long time to come, to constitute a serious menace', he should 'end the Russian episode'. Hitler was in no mind to do so. He was, in the words of Dino Alfieri, the Italian Ambassador in Berlin, 'dominated and obsessed by his fanatical desire to defeat Russia'. Anxious about the Duce's attitude, by the reports of increasing anti-German feeling in Italy, by the replacement of General Cavallero by Ambrosio – 'an untrustworthy political general' – and by the persistent rumours that Ciano had gone to the Vatican as Ambassador in order to negotiate a separate peace, Hitler asked the Duce to come to Germany to discuss the whole situation. A meeting was accordingly arranged for 7 April at Klessheim Castle near Salzburg.

Mussolini did not want to go. He had not fully recovered from a particularly violent attack of his illness and was afraid that the Germans would despise him for having to travel with a doctor to give him his injections and a cook to prepare his special foods. He had already decided that he was 'sick and tired of being rung for', and the last time he had visited Germany he had only consented to go on condition that he would be allowed to eat his meals alone, not wanting 'a lot of ravenous Germans to notice' that he was compelled to live on a diet of rice and milk. This time he was sick several times on the journey and arrived looking, so Goebbels thought, like 'a broken old man'. His resolutions about insisting on the necessity for peace with Russia, about demanding the return of Italian troops from other fronts to defend the homeland, and about telling the Germans that Italy must have more military and economic help, were all forgotten. He never once mentioned the need for a new sort of European charter with a view to peace in the West, which he had discussed at length in Rome. He spoke half-heartedly and soon abandoned all attempts at talking himself to sit listening in morose silence to the Führer's endless expositions and diagnoses. He was thinking, Alfieri believed, of what Hitler's determination to launch a new offensive in Russia would mean to the Italian Army in Tunisia. On the second day he had to leave the conference room because of a sudden attack of stomach cramps, and in another room while he drank the medicine his doctor had given him to ease the pain he said sadly, 'The Führer wanted me to be examined by his own doctor. I refused. I've already diagnosed my illness myself. It's called "convoys".' He seemed so depressed and listless that for the first time Hitler expressed concern as to whether 'the Duce was determined,' as he said to Doenitz when the visit was over, 'to carry on to the end'.

On the return journey to Italy, however, he began to feel better, and as always when he had come home from Germany he spent

R—G

the first few days behaving as a dictator is expected to behave. He threatened various arrests and gave instructions for a new *confino* to be prepared for anti-Fascists; he dismissed Carmine Senise as Chief of Police, because he had not dealt sufficiently harshly either with the strikes in Milan and Turin or with the clandestine Press or the growing black market, and he appointed the more severe Renzo Chierici in his place. He also dismissed Aldo Vidussoni from the Secretaryship of the Party and replaced him by Carlo Scorza, a myrmidon of the Party's youth who had been implicated in the murder by Fascist thugs of the liberal leader Giovanni Amendola in 1925. He went over the plans for a series of regional rallies at which leading Fascists were to harangue the people and encourage them to fight to the death. 'They spread it about that I'm finished,' he said grimly to Bottai, indulging his passion for enigmatic menaces, 'fading away, done for. Well, they'll see –'

On the anniversary of the capture of Addis Ababa he went out on to the balcony of Palazzo Venezia to speak to the crowds in the square below. 'I feel your voices are vibrating with an incorruptible faith,' he shouted with the fire of his youth. 'Have no fear for ultimate victory. It is certain that your sacrifices will be rewarded. That is as true as it is true that God is just and that Italy is immortal.'

He came in from the balcony encouraged by the cheers of the people, and the windows closed behind him; although at the time it seemed impossible to believe that he had spoken publicly in Rome for the last time, they never opened for him again.

Two days later his momentary enthusiasm had collapsed. Within a fortnight all the Axis forces in Africa had been taken prisoner, and a landing on the other side of the Mediterranean was believed to be imminent. Hitler believed the attack would be made in Sardinia; Mussolini thought it would come in Sicily, and he told a meeting of his generals at Villa Torlonia that it would have to be fiercely resisted, for there was no question of a political settlement or a separate peace. On 10 July the attack was made after a violent bombardment of the coast-line. Within a few days the Allied armies were streaming across the plain of Catania, and for a week Mussolini alternated between periods of studied calm and unconcealed anger with the retreating Italian troops.

The King, after so many changes of mind and of mood that the conspirators had begun to doubt that he would ever take a determined stand, at last decided that he could delay no longer. Independently of the Fascists, with whom he had been in contact, he decided on the advice of General Castellano and the Duke Acquarone to arrest Mussolini on a Monday or a Thursday when he went to the Quirinale or the Villa Savoia for the usual audience. He asked Marshal Badoglio if he were prepared to succeed the Duce as Head of the Government and Badoglio agreed, suggesting a non-Fascist administration led by such men as the Socialist Ivanoe Bonomi and another former Prime Minister, Vittorio Emanuele Orlando. Castellano and d'Acquarone then met to discuss the details of the arrest and the action to be taken to ensure that no unmanageable opposition came from Mussolini's supporters and, in particular, from General Galbiati, who, largely on the recommendation of the Petaccis, now commanded the Fascist Militia.

Meanwhile the Fascist plotters also decided that they could wait no longer. Although separated by mutual suspicions and jealousies and by conflicting ambitions, they were at least agreed that in the extreme emergency which had been forced upon them by the invasion of Sicily it was essential that the Fascist Grand Council – the supreme constitutional authority of the State, created by the Duce but not convened since the war began – must meet again. On 16 July various important Party officials, who were to have spoken at the several regional rallies planned before the invasion of Sicily, met in Rome and insisted on the necessity of a meeting of the Council to obtain from Mussolini a report on the general situation, which was daily growing more alarming. At first Mussolini refused, but later consented and set the date of its meeting for the following week, Saturday 24 July.

On the Monday of that week Hitler asked Mussolini to meet him again for an urgent conference in Italy. More worried than ever by reports of anti-German feeling in Italy, of Italian Army units surrendering *en masse* in Sicily and of their refusing to co-operate with the German Army, he hoped to stiffen Italian resistance by persuading the Duce to agree that all Italian armies should be placed under the German High Command. Piloting his own aeroplane, Mussolini flew from Rimini to Treviso, where he met

Hitler on the airfield and accompanied him to Senator Achille Gaggia's villa at Feltre on the southern slopes of the Dolomites. The villa, as Mussolini described it, was 'a labyrinthine building which some people found almost uncanny. It was like a crossword puzzle frozen into a house.' The atmosphere was formal and strained.

This was their thirteenth meeting, and it followed the by now familiar pattern. For almost three hours, from eleven o'clock until nearly two, Hitler talked. What he had to say was simple and direct enough. There was only one thing to be done – to fight and to go on fighting, in Italy as well as in Russia, until the Axis was triumphant. It was no good thinking that this could be done without sacrifices. In Germany boys of fifteen were fighting in anti-aircraft batteries. In Italy there appeared to be a very different attitude. The troops had not fought as they should have done; the civil administration commanded insufficient respect; the people had abandoned themselves to defeatism; it would be necessary to adopt much more vigorous measures; cowards, traitors, and in-competents would have to be shot; the Italian armies must put themselves under German command. Mussolini sat listening silently, cross-legged on the edge of his big arm-chair, his hands clasped round his knees. He was obviously in pain and frequently he stretched his back and passed his hands against it with a sigh. Often he rubbed his lips with the back of his fingers, and occasionally he was obliged to wipe the sweat from his face with his handkerchief. But only twice did he speak – once to correct a misapprehension as to the population of Corsica and once when his secretary came in to hand him a piece of paper and he announced dramatically in German, 'At this moment the enemy is carrying out a heavy air attack on Rome.'

After a brief discussion on the subject of the air-raid between the Italians, Hitler's tirade continued; but Mussolini seemed scarcely to be listening any more, and as soon as the meeting broke up for lunch he said, 'I am extremely upset to think I am away from Rome at a time like this. What will the Romans think?'

Not interested in what the Romans would think of him, the three Italian delegates – Bastianini, the Under-Secretary of State at the Foreign Office; the Ambassador, Alfieri; and the Chief-of-Staff, General Ambrosio, pressed the Duce to answer the Führer's charges and to tell him that Italy was at the end of her tether and could not carry on much longer without extensive help. On the way to Feltre General Ambrosio had asked Field-Marshal Keitel bluntly what help Italy could expect to receive from Germany before it was too late. Sitting in the same car next to the German Ambassador, Alfieri listened to Ambrosio's direct and uncompromising questions with admiration. 'Here at last was a man,' he thought, 'who was not afraid to use the kind of language which I had waited so long to hear.' But it was no good. 'The two leaders will discuss these matters themselves, you know,' Keitel said coldly, refusing to be drawn.

Ambrosio had no more success with the Duce than he had had with Keitel. Mussolini listened silently to his advice and then suddenly burst out, 'Can you really suppose that I've not been tortured by the same thoughts as you ? Behind my mask of impassivity I am in an agony of spirit. But if we detach ourselves from Germany, what then ? One day at a specified hour we broadcast a message to the enemy. What would happen ? They would demand, quite justly, our capitulation. But can we give up so easily twenty years' work and abandon the realization of all our hopes ? And what do you think Hitler will do ? Do you really think he will leave us liberty of action ?'

He spoke in a voice which Alfieri described as 'trembling with emotion'. He seemed more profoundly upset than they had ever seen him before, and when Ambrosio, later on in the conversation made some remark to the effect that the war was not popular in Italy, he rounded on him furiously.

'Oh, don't let's have platitudes, for God's sake! No war ever has been or will be popular. Wars only become popular when they end in victory.'

Suddenly his anger evaporated, and after a moment's pause he calmly began a long political and historical dissertation which, the Ambassador thought, 'would have been interesting in any other place and at any other time'.

This long and ill-timed dissertation was interrupted by the appearance of his secretary, De Cesare, who told him that the Führer was waiting for him to join him for lunch. Mussolini walked down the corridor to the dining-room looking, so Alfieri said afterwards, 'strangely absent-minded'.

During the train journey back to Treviso the Italian delegates to the conference wondered what Mussolini and Hitler had talked about when left alone in the dining-room. 'I am certain,' Mackensen, the German Ambassador, assured them, 'that this time they will come to some most important decisions.' They watched the two men closely as they walked together from Treviso station and got into the car which was to take them back to the airfield. Both of them, in Alfieri's phrase, 'looked calm and satisfied' – perhaps the Duce had spoken out, after all. Ercole Boratto, the driver of the car, knew better. 'Mussolini had difficulty in concealing his worry,' he thought. 'During the drive the tension found expression in sudden outbursts on the part of the German and suppressed reactions from the Italian.'

As Hitler's Condor flew back to Germany, Mussolini stood alone on the air strip, stiffly at attention, his arm raised in salute. Then he turned abruptly away and walked to his own aeroplane. Ambrosio, Alfieri, and Bastianini hurried after him. He affected not to see them, slowly putting on his flying jacket and talking with great concentration to the Italian general who commanded the troops stationed at Treviso. Alfieri, afraid that he would leave without saying anything at all, overcame his diffidence and went forward to speak to him on the pretext of asking for some instructions to take back to the Embassy in Berlin. Mussolini waved him away. 'I had no need to speak to Hitler in the way you suggested,' he called above the roar of the engines. 'This time he promised faithfully to send all the assistance we ask for. Of course,' he added, turning to Ambrosio, 'our requests must be reasonable.'

It was the final disillusion. Ambrosio knew from what little Keitel had told him that even reasonable requests would be met only if the Italians agreed to conditions which Mussolini had admitted were wholly unacceptable. He felt sure that Mussolini was refusing to face his problems and doubted that he had so much as suggested to Hitler that Italy would soon be utterly incapable of fighting any longer. He knew that the letter which the Duce had once said he would write to Hitler, telling him that Italy must make peace, had not been sent and never would be sent. He returned to Rome fully convinced that the other generals were right, that the Duce would never be induced to break with Germany and that his removal from power was the only hope for Italy.

2

On his return from Feltre, Mussolini went to the King to give a report on the meeting. Before leaving for the Palace he told Senator Manlio Morgagni, president of the Stefani news agency, that the Germans were still strong enough to 'dam the tide and perhaps to solve the whole situation in Italy'. But to do so they would want 'effective command not only of the Italian front, but that of the interior as well. This is a condition that the people will not accept, the King will not accept and I cannot accept.'

Mussolini found the King, so he wrote afterwards, 'frowning and nervous. "A tense situation," he said. "It can't go on much longer. Sicily has gone now. The Germans will double-cross us. The discipline of the troops has broken down." This was the gist of the talk.' The King was violently opposed to the German conditions. He had already been told by Ambrosio what Hitler's attitude had been at Feltre, and he had been warned that Mussolini had appeared physically and morally incapable of presenting the Italian tragedy in its true light. During the audience he referred to the growing feeling in Italy against the Duce, and the reports of various conspiracies were also mentioned. But he was generally reassuring, and Mussolini left the Palace unconcerned for his safety as he had always been. A few hours later Roberto Farinacci warned him that General Cavallero had proof that both the Court and Count Grandi were plotting to overthrow him and, what was more important to Farinacci, were plotting to do so in order to break with Germany. It was impossible, Mussolini said. Why, that very morning the King had told him, 'These are fearful times for you, but you can rest assured you have a friend in me. It's absurd to suppose that everyone will abandon you after all you have done for Italy and in any event I would be the last to do so.' When Scorza came to give him another warning and to tell him that a telephone conversation between Badoglio and the Duke d'Acquarone had been intercepted, he seemed scarcely interested to hear what the conversation was about. It was about his being 'bundled up' one day when he left the King, Scorza insisted on telling him. 'I do not like cowards,' was Mussolini's only comment.

That evening he went to see the damage that had been caused by the air-raid on 19 July. The ruins were still smouldering, and the Duce looked at them, his chauffeur noticed, with a kind of piteous despair.

Filippo Anfuso used a similar phrase in describing his own feelings as he looked out of Ciano's drawing-room window in the Via Angelo Secchi and saw the clouds of dust drifting slowly away to the east. Those bombs, he afterwards decided, were the mainspring of the Roman conspiracies.

No one thought of anything but the conspiracies now. Even the troops of countesses and princesses who paraded in and out of Ciano's room, gossiping about their experiences in the raid, laughing at Anfuso, the emotional Sicilian, for suggesting that his native island should be defended at all costs, even they who usually talked of little but themselves like the 'inmates of a high-class harem' avidly picked on every detail which would help them solve what one of them called 'the mystery of the imminent fall of the Duce'. For nobody knew what would happen, just as nobody agreed about what ought to happen. Bastianini said that Mussolini had ruined Italy. Gaetano Polverelli, the new Minister for Popular Culture, thought that he was the only man who could save it. Vittorio Cini, the Minister of Communications, said that Mussolini had 'gone mad and must be put away'. Ermanno Amicucci thought that it was they who considered putting him away who were the imbeciles. 'I've no idea what they are all up to,' he said, 'but it's easy to see that they'll lead us to ruin.' Ciano, whom most of them believed had always considered himself to be the Duce's rightful successor, remained secretive and enigmatic. There was no doubt that even before his dismissal from the Foreign Office – since the beginning of the war in fact – he and Mussolini had not been as close as once they had been. In January 1941, when, like many other Ministers sent to fight by the Duce as an example to the nation, he had come to say good-bye at Palazzo Venezia before leaving to take command of an Air Force squadron at Bari, he had found the Duce distant and cold. All foreign policy matters were taken out of his hands, and he was not informed of what was happening in his absence. He lived at the Hotel d'Europa in Bari between missions, and the life he led there, while no wilder than that led by any extrovert Air Force officer, was maliciously criticized. Mussolini's refusal to support him in one particular scandal seemed to Ciano a piece of gratuitous spite. He often spoke of it to his friends; but if they ventured to criticize the Duce themselves, he would look at them disapprovingly. 'I wish I could be sure,' Bottai said anxiously, 'which way that cat would jump.' But no one could be sure about Ciano or, indeed, Anfuso frustratedly decided, 'about anything'. All that was certain was that the Duce was approaching disaster; and that Rome, dusty, expectant, and suffocatingly hot, felt – as Mussolini himself was to say – 'that a great drama was about to be performed'.

3 The Grand Council Meeting

I came to Rome to stay in power as long as possible.

I

On the afternoon of 21 July Dino Grandi went to Via Ferdinando di Savoia to call on Federzoni, then President of the Italian Academy. Federzoni was a fellow-Bolognese, and Grandi felt that he could trust him. Grandi handed him the draft of the resolution he intended to submit at the meeting of the Grand Council. At first sight the resolution seemed harmless enough. It was only in the last few sentences that its real purpose was revealed. After a long and rhetorical preamble, which recited a number of well-established facts and unexceptionable hopes, it declared that 'the immediate restoration is necessary of all State functions, allotting to the King, the Grand Council, the Government, Parliament and the corporations the tasks and responsibilities laid down by our statutory and constitutional laws'. It was also necessary, it declared, to invite 'The Head of the Government to request His Majesty the King – towards whom the heart of all the nation turns with faith and confidence – that he may be pleased, for the honour and salvation of the nation, to assume, together with the effective command of the Armed Forces . . . that supreme initiative of decision which our institutions attribute to him and which, in all our national history, has always been the glorious heritage of our august dynasty of Savoy.' In other words Mussolini was to resign his power.

Federzoni read the paper silently and carefully. Watching him read it with such quiet deliberation, Grandi began to think that he had gone too far in showing it to him. But then Grandi's mind was put at rest. 'We must try anything and everything,' Federzoni said as he handed it back, 'even the impossible, to save the nation from total ruin. Even if we fail in our attempt, our sacrifice will be the spark that will fire a rebellion and arouse the people from their apathy.'

Encouraged by Federzoni's reaction, Grandi then approached Giuseppe Bottai, Giuseppe Bastianini, and Umberto Albini, three other influential members of the Fascist Grand Council. All of them agreed to support his resolution at the meeting.

The most respected of the three was Bottai. He had been an early supporter of Fascism and was one of its few leaders who was an intellectual. He was a good writer, an adroit negotiator, and an able administrator. As Minister of Corporations he had been mainly responsible for the Fascist Labour Charter and as Minister of Education for the School Charter, which, when it was felt that Gentile's Act of 1923 was too liberal and anti-clerical, had brought the Italian education system more completely under Fascist supervision. He was clever, witty, malicious, and indiscreet. He made no secret of the fact that his former devotion to Mussolini had turned to sour disillusion and that he hated the war. The week before Mussolini declared war on France and Britain he told Ciano on the golf-course that a new party to rival the Fascist should be formed and that it should call itself the 'Party of the Interventionists in Bad Faith'. Two years later he was even more bitter. The only way to get on in Italy now, he said, was to get to know the Petaccis, so he had decided to accredit an ambassador to their Court. In the summer of 1942 he paid Ciano a visit. 'He has nothing to tell me,' Ciano wrote afterwards, 'but he is more anti-Mussolini than ever. If he talks this way to me, imagine what he must say among his own friends!' The following month, while staying with Ciano again, he was once more indulging in 'useless recriminations'. He spoke of Mussolini with angry resentment and said that the war was illegal because the Grand Council had not been consulted. The Duce in his opinion was 'a self-taught man who had had a bad teacher and was a worse student'.

It was on men like Bottai that Grandi felt able to rely for the unwavering support he would need when Mussolini himself must be faced at the Grand Council meeting. Of Bastianini and Albini he could not be so certain.

Bastianini, as Mussolini's choice as successor to Ciano at Palazzo Chigi, did not share Bottai's strongly antipathetic opinion of the Duce, but he was well aware that the war was leading Italy to disaster and that with the displacement of Mussolini as Head of the Government a separate peace might still be concluded. With this end in view he had already made some tentative soundings in neutral embassies. Cautious, precise, and methodical, he was not likely to make any forceful criticism of the Duce at the meeting, but it was not likely that he would fail to vote for Grandi's resolution if it seemed that it was gaining support.

Albini was Buffarini-Guidi's successor as Under-Secretary of State for the Interior in the recently reshuffled Cabinet, and he knew at first-hand the real extent of the disastrous situation on the home front. Like Bastianini he thought that Mussolini should be replaced, but also like Bastianini he could not be expected to take the aggressive stand that it was hoped Bottai would adopt.

The cautious and hesitant attitude of Bastianini and Albini was also assumed by several other members of the Grand Council whom Grandi, Federzoni, and Bottai then approached. De Bono and De Vecchi, since Balbo's death in an aeroplane accident the only two surviving members of the Quadrumviri who had led the March on Rome in 1922; Annio Bignardi, President of the National Fascist Confederation of Agricultural Workers; Count Giacomo Suardo, President of the Senate: Cianetti, Minister of Corporations; and De Stefani, a former Minister of Finance all agreed to support Grandi's resolution, but none of them would take the responsibility of committing themselves during the meeting unless the debate appeared to take a favourable turn.

To Grandi's surprise Carlo Scorza, Secretary of the Party, to whom he showed the resolution on Wednesday 21 July at the Fascist Party Headquarters, seemed prepared to support it. He took the precaution before committing himself, however, of taking a copy to Mussolini when he went to see him at noon that day to present his daily report. Mussolini read it quickly, not in the least alarmed. He handed it back with the laconic comment that it was 'inadmissible and contemptible'. Scorza, so Mussolini himself wrote later, 'put it back in his brief-case and did not press the matter further'. When he had left Palazzo Venezia, Scorza drafted his own resolution, which he intended to present to the Grand Council as an alternative to Grandi's.

2

Having now obtained the support of Federzoni, Bottai, Bastianini, Albini and, as he hoped, of Scorza, Grandi asked for an interview with the Duce. He did not, in his own phrase, 'wish to pass for a conspirator' and hoped that he might perhaps be able to persuade him to make some voluntary gesture which would render the meeting unnecessary. At five o'clock on the afternoon of 22 July, Grandi was received in the *Sala del Mappamondo* at Palazzo Venezia. The Duce was standing behind his enormous desk and watched Grandi with a cold impassivity as he approached him. He did not ask him to sit down. Grandi read out his resolution and then made the Duce a brief speech in support of it. Mussolini did not interrupt him, continuing to watch him with an expression of haughty contempt, and when the speech was over he merely said, 'Leave me now. We shall see one another at the Grand Council.'[1]

On his way out Grandi passed through the assembly hall where the palace servants were already arranging chairs for the meeting. On one of them, waiting for the Duce to receive him, sat Field-Marshal Kesselring. It was, as Grandi said afterwards, 'not a good sign.' He had, he admitted, become nervous. The Duce's impassivity and disdainful confidence were not merely enigmatic but alarming. He decided to ask Albini to arrange for two hundred police to be hidden in different parts of the building. He also decided to give way to Bottai, who suggested that Count Ciano should be brought into the conspiracy. Although Grandi did not altogether trust Ciano he had to agree with Bottai that if he were persuaded to support the revolt many wavering votes might be given to the resolution.

On the afternoon of the day before the meeting Bottai invited Grandi and Ciano to come to his house. His guests were not at

1. Count Grandi's account of this meeting does not differ materially from Mussolini's. Field-Marshal Kesselring, however (giving the date as 24 July and not 22 July), says that Mussolini was quite cheerful when he went into the *Sala del Mappamondo* after Grandi had gone. 'Grandi has just left me,' Mussolini said. 'We had a heart-to-heart talk. Our views are identical. He is loyally devoted to me.'

ease with each other and could not agree on a common policy. Ciano seemed to suspect that Grandi wished to displace Mussolini only to gain more power and influence for himself and Federzoni; Grandi felt that Ciano, despite any undertakings given beforehand, might at the last moment throw the weight of his influence on to the side of his father-in-law; Bottai believed that the political power which was to be wrested from Mussolini should be placed in the hands of the King together with the supreme command of the armed forces, but the others did not think that this was practicable. The conversation between the three men was long and inconclusive, and when Ciano left, Grandi and Bottai were not at all sure whether or not he intended to support them.

But by the following morning, he had apparently made up his mind. At noon Dino Alfieri, recalled from the Italian Embassy in Berlin to attend the meeting later on that day, paid a visit to the Foreign Ministry, where he found Bastianini 'silent and preoccupied'. He had been with Bastianini only a few minutes, however, when Count Ciano was announced, and the rather gloomy atmosphere immediately cleared. 'Ciano was cordial and friendly,' Alfieri wrote later, 'and he seemed excited. He was obviously pleased to see me.'

'I'm so glad you've come,' he said. 'We are all agreed that we must go to any length to save Italy. . . . "He" – the pig-headed one – simply refuses to understand the position. Today when the Grand Council meets, we have decided to speak out clearly and he'll be *made* to understand it.'

Ciano told Alfieri that he was on his way to promise Grandi his support and asked him to go with him. They found Grandi wearing a sports-shirt in his office at the Chamber of Deputies. He greeted them warmly and showed them the resolution. Alfieri read it quickly and said that while it seemed all right he would like one or two passages explained to him.

'No need to have any scruples or misgivings,' Ciano said, interrupting him impatiently. 'It's simply a memorandum. During the discussion we shall, as always, treat the Duce with the utmost respect and deference.'

And so Alfieri hesitantly gave way and Grandi wrote his name in blue pencil at the bottom of a list of his supporters.

With the exception of Federzoni, however, Grandi was not sure that he could trust anyone on the list absolutely, not even Bottai.

'In my heart of hearts,' he said afterwards, 'the only person I trusted completely was Federzoni.' He had begun to think it would have been better if he had staged a sudden *colpo di stato*. Now that Mussolini knew how far he had already gone in his efforts to undermine his authority, he was afraid that he might be arrested; and he felt sure that if he were arrested most of his supporters would desert him and align themselves with that strong group of devoted disciples on the Grand Council who would certainly stand by the Duce whatever happened.

When he had put on the black bush-shirt, known as the *Sahariana* which Mussolini had ordered all the members of the Council to wear, he put a pistol in his pocket and some hand-grenades in his brief-case. At half past four he left his flat and set out for Palazzo Venezia, where he found several companies of the Fascist Militia in the inner courtyard. Other militiamen were in the Palazzo itself. 'You did a fine thing by having that talk with him,' Bottai said angrily. 'This is the end for us.' Grandi thought so too. Indeed, he had begun to think that he would not get out alive.

Mussolini was already in his office. He had had lunch at Villa Torlonia, where 'everything,' as Rachele noted in her diary that evening, 'was as usual.' He seemed completely unmoved by the reports of the plots against him. Four days previously, while a maid was fastening his collar before dinner, Rachele told him that she had been given a list of names of men whom Bastianini had supplied with passports and that it was 'high time he did some-thing about Ciano, Grandi, Badoglio, and company'. But he would not be warned. He was worrying about the Americans' tanks, he said, not about the intrigues of a few Italians. Now, as he left for the Grand Council meeting, Rachele offered him her advice again. 'Have them all arrested before the opening,' she urged him. He kissed her at the door of the villa without replying and walked to the waiting car with a bulging brief-case under his arm'. 'He honestly believes that everything will work out for the best,' Rachele wrote in her diary after he had gone.

He strode into the meeting with his customary self-confidence, not looking at any of the members of the Council, who jumped to their feet when he came in to answer Scorza's shouted order 'Salute the Duce!' with a loud chorus of 'We salute him.' He showed no pleasure at being so readily accorded the ritual salute to the Duce of Fascism, and sat down at his table glowering. He flinched with pain as he settled himself in his chair. His ulcer had been troubling him in the night, and when Claretta Petacci had telephoned him he had mentioned it.

'What will happen if you are feeling ill on this day of all days?' she had asked him.

He had replied with that characteristically self-glorifying resolution which was never softened by irony. 'I shall be strong and dominate the situation in my usual way.'

As he sat in his chair, listening to Scorza calling the roll, pulling papers out of the brief-case which Navarra, the Chief Usher, had put on the table in front of him, frowning sternly with his chin thrust out so that he looked as one of his mistresses once said, as if his whole face was pushed forward by his ears, he seemed capable indeed of domination. Unlike the others in their black Saharan shirts, he was wearing the greyish-green uniform of the Fascist Militia, and this alone accentuated his aloofness, the acknowledged supremacy of *Il Duce*. The table at which he sat was on a dais higher than theirs, and this too created an illusion of spiritual superiority. And above all there were the habits, the attitudes, the memories and fears of two decades of Fascism. The man looking down at them so fiercely, Bottai could not help thinking, was Fascism incarnate.

For many of them – for most of them perhaps – he was, despite himself, still Italy's greatest son. And there were few of them there who had not once professed it; and fewer still, no doubt, unwilling, had they been given the cause, to profess it even now. Grandi himself had done so recently with a fervour which the Duce's most fanatical adherents would have found it difficult to match. 'My life, my faith, my soul are yours,' he had declared less than two months before.

But Mussolini, like his own faithful followers, had also become conditioned by the habits of the past. Obedience, adulation, unquestioning trust, had been for years accepted not as the pleasing reactions of a responsive people, but as the homage due to his genius. 'Mussolini is always right' – the slogan splashed on count-

1. Surrounded by members of the 'London Fascisti' in London in 1922

2. Rachele, Anna Maria, Romano, Benito, Edda, Bruno, Vittorio

3. Playing the violin at Villa Torlonia

4. On a visit to Gabriele D'Annunzio at Gardone

5. Giving the Fascist salute at a parade in Rome

6. Standing beside his writing-table in the Sala del Mappamondo at Palazzo Venezia

7. Reviewing troops home from Abyssinia in Piazza Venezia

8. Greeting the King during the Army manoeuvres in the Abruzzi in August 1938

9. Accepting a presentation from Count Grandi during the seventeenth anniversary celebrations of the March on Rome

10. With Bruno and Vittorio before the war

11. With Hitler and Ciano at the Brenner in October 1940

12. Making a speech from the balcony at Palazzo Venezia

13. Piazzale Loreto, Milan, 29 April 1945

a century ahead to secure its five meals a day. It wants to occupy Italy and to keep it occupied.'

It was a disastrous performance. The members of the Council looked at the Duce in a kind of shocked silence. Alfieri wrote afterwards of the feeling of appalled disillusionment that swept over them all. It was the most inept speech that they had ever heard him make, and in a sense the most decisive. When he had finished speaking, the Duce had already fallen.

For a few moments no one spoke. Then the sounds of shuffling feet, whispering, the clicking of brief-case catches, disturbed the embarrassed silence. At length Marshal De Bono stood up. His short speech was no more than a veiled attack on politicians who blamed the Army chiefs when they themselves should accept the blame for having chosen them. This was a view which his old fellow-monarchist, De Vecchi, now rose to support; but in supporting it he made some remark about Italy's allies which the violently Germanophil Roberto Farinacci found objectionable. Contradicting De Vecchi, Farinacci launched into a fanatical panegyric upon German strength and invincibility. Stung by his remarks, De Vecchi accused Farinacci of shirking military service in the First World War and of posing as having been a hero of the Abyssinian war after having been injured in a fishing accident.

Bottai, realizing that the meeting was in danger of breaking up in a petty squabble, interrupted De Vecchi to make the first authentic speech of the evening. The other members of the Council listened to his words and understood that for the first time Mussolini was being criticized in public and in his presence. Gathering courage from the spark that Bottai's words had struck, other members showed that they wished to speak; but it was Grandi who rose, and the others sat back to listen.

'I am going to repeat here before the Grand Council,' Grandi said in a low, grave voice which immediately commanded respect, 'what I told the Duce the day before yesterday, and I propose the following Order of the Day.'

He read out his resolution calmly and clearly, but when he had finished it his tone changed and he made a speech of passionate eloquence and savage indictment. He spoke bitterly of 'the restrictive and idiotic formula of the Fascist war', of the 'needlessly rigid insistence on the observation of petty formalities'; of the 'constant introduction of new regulations and the gradual suppression of personal freedom'. 'You have imposed a dictatorship on Italy,' he said in a voice breaking with emotion, 'which is historically immoral. For years you have kept in your own hands the three Service Ministries. And what have you done? You have destroyed the spirit of our Armed Forces. For years you've suffocated our personalities in these funereal clothes. For years when selecting someone from among several candidates for an important post, you have invariably selected the worst.'

For over an hour Grandi spoke. Mussolini sat listening in silence to the speech which he afterwards referred to as a 'violent philippic – the speech of a man who was at last giving vent to a long-cherished rancour'. He leaned over the table in a cramped posture as though he were still in pain, occasionally drawing doodles on a large sheet of paper, covering his eyes with his hand to shade them from the brilliant light of the chandelier in the middle of the ceiling. 'Those fearfully strong white lights,' he confessed later to Marinetti, 'made me terribly tired. I had to keep my hand in front of my face to shield them from my eyes. . . . Two hours before the meeting I had had a violent attack of my old complaint. I was still in pain then, my brain was very clear. I heard the speech of Grandi, the public prosecutor, distinctly, but all my energy was drained away. This is one of the effects of the disease: complete extinction of energy but a great clarity – one might almost call it transparency – of thought.'

He looked defeated, Bottai thought, and in despair. 'He didn't seem like a man any more, but the ghost of a man already on the other side of life.' Buffarini-Guidi described him as being like a man so far lost in thought 'that he was in another world. It seemed that he was covering his head as Caesar had done with his toga under the blows of Brutus and the conspirators.'

When Grandi stopped speaking he changed his position to slump back in his chair as he undid the collar of his shirt. His white face was seen to be running with sweat.

It was now that Ciano decided to speak. Under his father-in-law's baleful gaze he spoke in an almost gentle voice. He confined himself to a history of the Italo-German alliance which, to Farinacci's fury, seemed to reflect no credit on the Germans; but he left no room for doubt that he would support Grandi's resolution. At the end of his speech Farinacci rose again to contradict most of what he had said and to make a second and yet more passionate defence of the Germans. He offered the Council an alternative to Grandi's resolution in his own, which proclaimed the solidarity of Fascist Italy with National Socialist Germany and invited the Head of the Government to request the King to assume command of all the Armed Forces and 'thus to show the entire world that the whole population is fighting, united under his orders, for the salvation and dignity of Italy'. Expecting that the King would be more easily persuaded than Mussolini to delegate his powers to Kesselring, Farinacci's motives for wanting to displace the Duce were not the same as those of Grandi. But they were both agreed that Mussolini would have to go.

As the evening wore on it became apparent that a majority of the Council thought the same, while even those members who would not have hesitated to vote against a simple motion of censure were apparently prepared to support one which seemed to be so much less than that, so mild and so apparently innocuous. Few members questioned Grandi's motives. Gaetano Polverelli, Minister of Popular Culture; Antonino Tringali-Casanova, President of the Fascist Special Tribunal; Carlo Alberto Biggini, Minister of Education; and Enzo Galbiati, Chief-of-Staff of the Fascist Militia, spoke against his motion but with little conviction and less effect. More taken up with personal quarrels than reasoned argument, their speeches added to Mussolini's weariness while contributing nothing to his salvation.

After midnight, when the meeting had been going on for over seven hours, in a voice of utter exhaustion, 'low, humble, almost pathetic', as Bottai described it, Mussolini asked, 'What good are these reproaches now that we are alone and face to face with the power of three empires?' He proposed to Scorza that the meeting be suspended until the following day. He was unwell, he said, and must not overstrain himself.

'In the past,' Grandi said firmly, returning to his attack, 'you have kept us here till five o'clock in the morning discussing some trifle or other. We shall not leave here until my resolution has been discussed and voted on.' He would agree to an adjournment for ten minutes, but no more.

Mussolini gave a nod of assent. 'The arrogance of the dictator had given way,' Bottai noticed with pleasure, 'to the submission of the accused.' He left the room to go into his office, a lonely, dejected figure. As he passed the Ambassador to Germany he said to him, 'Come with me, Alfieri.'

'The vast room was in semi-darkness,' Alfieri remembers, 'only partly relieved by a feeble glimmer from a reading-lamp. Slowly he crossed to the table, gently pressed a tiny switch connected to the central chandelier, and glanced absent-mindedly through a few telegrams. He stood for a few moments in silence; then, as if he had only now become aware of my presence, he asked me, "What's happening in Germany?"'

Alfieri repeated what he had already told him at Feltre and in his reports, of the obvious signs of weariness in the German people, but also of their discipline and fatalistic fanaticism, their fear of the Gestapo, their belief in Goebbels's propaganda. 'In Berlin,' he added, 'people are following events here with particular interest and feel that as a result of recent military developments, the internal situation has become somewhat critical.'

'Who told you that?' Mussolini asked sharply, almost with annoyance, as if even now, after all that had happened and all that he had had to listen to during the last few hours, there could be any doubt that the internal situation was indeed critical.

'It's the general opinion in Berlin,' Alfieri said. 'And the prefects whom I spoke to on the way here confirmed it.'

But Mussolini would not be persuaded. He refused to accept the truth of facts that others had accepted long before. As he sipped a cup of sugared milk that had been placed on his table, he told Alfieri that the Germans were misinformed, adding that the bombing of Rome and other large cities would eventually have a beneficial effect on the Italian people, inspiring them 'with a sort of mystical heroism which makes men indifferent to danger and enables them to resign themselves to suffering, bereavement, and the destruction of their homes'.

'Believe me,' he said, 'you have been misinformed. Anyhow, the situation is not as grave as you make out. Time is still on our side.' He spooned out the remains of milk-sodden sugar in the bottom of his cup and then, wiping his lips on a napkin, he stood up. The few minutes' escape from the oppressive atmosphere of the adjoining room, the cup of milk, the opportunity to speak again, had restored some of Mussolini's lost confidence. For some time after the meeting had been resumed this regenerated mood persisted. When Galbiati made a flamboyant speech in his favour and cried out that all Italians were united round the Duce, he decided to make another speech himself.

'Among the accusations that are made against the régime,' he said with a sudden flash of anger, 'the one most current on the lips of the people is forgotten. I mean the fabulous riches which several of you have amassed. I have enough here,' he added, tapping his brief-case, 'to send you all to the gallows. You,' pointing to Ciano, 'more than anyone.'[1]

Encouraged by Mussolini's revival, Scorza now rose to say in a long and incoherent speech that the only thing wrong with the Duce was that he had not been dictator enough and that to give him more time for the discharge of his other duties he should give up the command of the Armed Forces to Graziani. Constantly interrupted by Bastianini, he tried to put forward his own motion, which seemed to suggest that the dictatorship of the Fascist Party should be more strictly enforced.

By this time the meeting had lost all semblance of order. 'Everyone was talking at once,' Bottai said. 'Everyone hurled insults.' Mussolini said that he had in his hand the key to the military situation, but he would not tell them what it was. 'If you get rid of me,' he called out, 'I shall have to renounce the secret weapon that can end this war. You'll lose at the same time the war, me, and your own heads.' While Farinacci looked at him in amazement, Grandi murmured 'Blackmail!'

Then Count Giacomo Suardo, President of the Senate, who had helped himself to a large glass of brandy during the few minutes' recess, astonished everyone by saying that he had decided to withdraw his support of Grandi's resolution and hoped that others would join him in voting for Scorza's. Tullio Cianetti, Minister of Corporations, said that that might well prove the better course. Ciano also began to waver. He proposed that a commission should be appointed to consider the resolutions of both Grandi and

---

1. During his years of power, however, he never seems to have paid any more attention to the dishonest financial speculations of the *gerarchi* than to those of anyone else. When Achille Starace became involved in a scandal of this sort, he was not much concerned, implying that the man's real sin was his wearing a Distinguished Service medal without authority.

Scorza and devise a third to combine the two. Bottai opposed this suggestion and spoke again of the necessity for immediate action, but his words were less confident than before and he was heard with obvious impatience. Before he had finished Polverelli stood up to say in a voice broken by emotion that he had always been and would die Mussolini's man. Grandi spoke again, with interruptions from Biggini. Carlo Pareschi, Minister of Agriculture, supported Grandi and was attacked for doing so by Buffarini-Guidi. The debate had become not merely confused but incoherent.

Grandi afterwards confessed that at this point he felt that he had lost. The supporters of Scorza – of war to the end and uncompromising devotion to the existing régime – and of Farinacci and his motion for unalterable loyalty to Germany, seemed to be gaining ground. At about a quarter past two Mussolini abruptly interrupted the discussion.

'The debate has been long and exhausting,' he said in a harsh, brusque voice. 'Three motions have been tabled. Grandi's takes precedence over the other two, so I'll put it to the vote. Scorza, call the names.'

As the Party Secretary called out the names on his roll, Mussolini leant forward in his chair, resting his elbows on the table, staring at each member as he gave his vote. 'His imperious eyes seemed to bore into the minds of us all,' Alfieri said afterwards, 'as if he sought to influence our decisions.'

There were twenty-eight members of the Grand Council present at the meeting. Of these Count Suardo was the only one who abstained from voting. Scorza voted against the resolution, as did Polverelli, Buffarini-Guidi, and Galbiati, but only three other members supported them. Farinacci voted for his own resolution. Nineteen votes were given for Grandi.

Mussolini quickly gathered together his papers and stood up. As he rose to his feet Scorza shouted out the order, 'Salute the Duce!' There was a mumble of embarrassed response, which Mussolini cut short with an angry gesture.

'I excuse you from that,' he snapped.

At the door he turned round, and in a quiet yet bitter voice, he added, 'You have provoked the crisis of the régime.'

He went into the Mappamondo room, where after a few moments Polverelli, Galbiati, Buffarini-Guidi, and Scorza joined him

Galbiati suggested that the traitors should be immediately arrested, but Mussolini seemed stunned by his defeat and spoke scarcely a word. When the others had been talking together for some time, he interrupted them, turned to Scorza, and said, 'Those gentlemen in there seemed very anxious to talk of peace. What they don't realize is that Churchill and Roosevelt don't merely want my overthrow but the suppression of Italy as a Mediterranean Power. . . . Without me,' he added with a sudden flash of vanity, 'it would not be a peace but a *Diktat*.'

At five o'clock he decided to go home, 'Come home with me,' he said to Scorza. 'I am very tired.'

'The streets were deserted,' he wrote later, 'but in the air, already almost light, for dawn was breaking, there seemed to be a feeling of inevitability.' As he went down Via Nomentana with Scorza at his side he murmured, 'Albini and Bastianini too. And Ciano even – the lovely forty-year-old!'

At Villa Torlonia his haggard face told Rachele that her fears were justified. She had waited up for him, and when someone rang from Palazzo Venezia to say that he was on his way home she went into the garden to meet him.

'Well,' she said to him with a kind of piteous anger. 'You've had them all arrested, I suppose.'

'No,' he replied, weary and unconvincing. 'But I will.'

It was no more than a conventional protest. It was as if already his will to resist was broken. He went into the house and looked at his wife in silence. 'There's nothing more I can do,' he said. 'They're set on our ruin. My orders don't count any more.'

He undressed and went to bed, but he could not sleep. At eight o'clock, when Dr Pozzi called to give him the analgesic injection which he had now every morning, he refused it. 'I don't want one today,' he protested. 'My blood's running too fast.'

3

An hour later, however, to Bastianini's amazement, he was sitting at his writing-table in Palazzo Venezia as though nothing had happened. He looked neither tired not worried. He asked to speak to Grandi on the telephone, but when he was told that he was not to be found and was thought to have gone to his country house, he suggested mildly that the staff should try to contact him there later.

At about half past nine Albini brought him the usual morning post, and he read it carefully, paying particular attention to the reports of a heavy air-raid on Bologna. Only when he had finished reading these reports did he remark to Albini in an almost conversational tone, 'Why did you vote for Grandi's motion last night ? You were a guest, not a member of the Grand Council.'

Albini blushed and muttered an excuse. He was not only embarrassed but seemed to regret his vote of the night before. 'I might have made a mistake,' he said. 'But no one can have any doubt about my devotion to you – not just now but always.' Others too were alarmed by what they had done. Scorza telephoned to say that 'the night had brought wisdom' and they were 'beginning to have qualms'.

'Too late,' Mussolini commented with one of those enigmatic threats which by now had become mechanical. He seemed almost cheerful. He asked Scorza to come round to Palazzo Venezia where the Party Secretary found him in a mood of complete confidence. He listened with obvious indifference to Scorza's anxious suggestions that he ought to act quickly against his enemies. There was no need for alarm, he said. He would issue instructions after he had seen the King. When a letter was handed to him from Cianetti, who wrote to withdraw his vote and to offer his resignation as Minister of Corporations, he read it without apparent surprise or pleasure, as if he had expected it, as if the other rebels would soon follow his example.

Just before lunch Bastianini arrived with the new Japanese Ambassador. Mussolini was 'particularly courteous and friendly', Bastianini said, expounding his views on foreign policy and military strategy in considerable detail. He spoke knowledgeably and flatteringly of Japan and her people while the Ambassador smiled and bowed with pleasure.

After Hidaka had gone, Bastianini remained with Mussolini to discuss various routine matters and the arrangements for the forthcoming visit of Reichsmarshal Goering. Not a word was said about the Grand Council meeting. Mussolini seemed to have dismissed it from his mind. Only when his secretary, De Cesare, told him that he had made an appointment for him to see the King at five o'clock at Villa Savoia did he make any sort of reference to his predicament. '1700 hours,' he said quietly. '17. That's an unlucky number.' By the time he left his office to return to Villa Torlonia for lunch, however, he had apparently overcome his momentary concern. Accompanied by General Galbiati he went by way of the Tiburtino quarter, which had been badly damaged in the air-raid of 19 July. As he got out of his car to walk about in the ruins, he was cheered by a large crowd of people. He raised his arms to them, basking in the comfort of their adulation, telling Galbiati to distribute all the money he had on him as his own pockets were, as usual, empty. When he got back into the car Galbiati advised him, as Scorza had already done, to have the nineteen dissident members of the Grand Council arrested. But again he refused.

After a late lunch at Villa Torlonia, at which he ate nothing but a bowl of soup, he changed into a dark blue suit for his audience with the King. Civilian clothes had been specified by the staff at Villa Savoia, his secretary had told him, and this in itself seemed suspicious to the wary Rachele.

'Don't go, Benito,' she pleaded with him. 'He's not to be trusted.'

That morning in his office Claretta had said the same thing. 'I begged him not to go,' she told Navarra, 'but he wouldn't listen.'

He would not listen to his wife either. He had no sense of danger. Perhaps the King would take over from him as Commander-in-Chief of the Armed Forces, but nothing would happen worse than that. It was not until three o'clock that he thought of suggesting to General Galbiati that some mechanized units of Blackshirts camping near Bracciano should move into Rome; but it was too late now. Several hours before, a division of *Granatieri* had been ordered to come to Rome by General Castellano, and Galbiati's order to the Blackshirts was intercepted and held.

At about half past three Galbiati left Villa Torlonia. Mussolini was still completely confident. His last comment to Galbiati was that he would get the King's agreement to appoint three new members of the Government. At a quarter past four he telephoned to Scorza, who had rung up earlier to leave a message that Marshal Graziani had promised Mussolini his continued support. 'Tell Graziani,' Mussolini said carefully, 'that I will see him after my audience with the King.' While he was still talking with Scorza on the telephone, De Cesare arrived at the villa. It would take them only a quarter of an hour to drive to their appointment, however, so Mussolini decided to wait until a quarter to five before setting out. Even on a week-day there was hardly any traffic in the streets because of the petrol shortage; on a Sunday they would be deserted.

Exactly at a quarter to five Mussolini picked up his black felt hat and went out with De Cesare to his waiting car. He did not take with him a brief-case full of papers as he usually did when going for an audience with the King, but only a document setting out the constitution and powers of the Grand Council, a copy of Grandi's motion, and Cianetti's letter of resignation.

4

While Mussolini was getting ready for his interview with the King at Villa Savoia, the King was making preparations to receive him there.

Early that morning Grandi had reported the results of the Grand Council meeting to Acquarone and had suggested that Marshal Caviglia, a distinguished soldier and a well-known anti-Fascist, should be nominated Head of the Government by the King and that diplomatic representatives should immediately be sent to Madrid to open negotiations for peace with the Allies. When Acquarone said that the King had decided to appoint Marshal Badoglio as Head of the Government, Grandi was dismayed. With scarcely another word he left the room and disappeared for ever from public life.[1] At six o'clock Acquarone woke up the King to pass on Grandi's report on the Grand Council voting. An hour

1. Grandi had spent part of that morning in his office at Montecitorio, where Ciano called on him with Filippo Anfuso. Anfuso's account of the events of that morning provides evidence of how little any of the conspirators knew about the plans of the Court and how little they trusted each other. At Montecitorio, Anfuso says, Grandi and Ciano 'went off and talked together in a corner.' Then they began arguing. 'It was clear that Grandi hid a lot from Ciano.' A little later, when Ciano and Anfuso had left Grandi and were going back together to Anfuso's house, Ciano showed that his knowledge of the Court's intentions was as uncertain as Grandi's. 'All is arranged, you'll see,' he said confidingly. 'The Ministry is already made. Pirelli will be Foreign Minister. I believe Vitetti is Under-Secretary. General Carboni is Minister of Propaganda. For the time being I shall stand aside, but we shall see. As for you, I don't want to say too much. You are known as a Germanophil. However, I'll speak to my friends.'

later he called on General Ambrosio, and together they went to
Badoglio to tell him what the King had decided to do. Although
Badoglio was later to lose much of his self-confidence, for the
moment he was overcome with excitement. He put on his Marshal's uniform and sent a servant down to the cellar for a bottle of
champagne. Then he cheerfully told his family that he had decided, in exercise of the powers shortly to be conferred upon him,
to have them all put under arrest.

Ambrosio, charged with the duty of arranging a less light-
hearted arrest, did not share Badoglio's high spirits. General
Castellano had been to see him that morning and had told him
that the King had given no definite orders for Mussolini's arrest.
'If Mussolini accepts his dismissal without protest,' Ambrosio
said, 'we'll let him go. But if he resists we'll have to arrest him.'

'But that's not possible,' Castellano objected. 'The King
doesn't want anyone with him when he talks to Mussolini. We
shan't know how he takes it. And if we let him get out of Villa
Savoia, we'll never catch him again.'

'All right,' said Ambrosio. 'Then we'll have to arrest him anyway.'

At about eleven o'clock Castellano left Ambrosio to go to the
office of the Commander of the *Carabinieri*. A week before he
would have had to contend with General Hazon who, although a
supporter of the conspiracy, would not have readily agreed to
Ambrosio's proposal. But Hazon had been killed during the air-
raids of 19 July, and the appointment of his second-in-command
General Pieche, a loyal Fascist, had been avoided by the machinations of General Antonio Sorice, Under-Secretary of State at the
Ministry of War, who persuaded Claretta Petacci to support the
candidature of General Cerica. Cerica agreed to do what Ambrosio
and Castellano wanted. He arrived at Villa Savoia with a colonel
and fifty officers and men of the *carabinieri* half an hour before
Mussolini was due.

'Do you want orders from the King in person?' Acquarone
asked him when he arrived.

'It's all right if you give me orders in the King's name,' said
Cerica. 'But I want it in writing.'

Acquarone went over to the King, who was walking in the
garden with his aide-de-camp, General Putoni, and said to him,

'The Commander of the *Carabinieri*, General Cerica, desires your Majesty, through me, to confirm the order to arrest *il cavaliere* Benito Mussolini.'

The King's voice was so soft that they could scarcely hear him as he replied, '*Va bene*.' When he turned away to continue his walk with General Putoni, his face was deadly white.

During the afternoon General Cerica was given a written order signed by Ambrosio and Acquarone. Cerica folded it up carefully and put it in his pocket. Even now, so he says, he could not believe that he would be given the opportunity of using it.

The Arrest at Villa Savoia

25 JULY 1943

One can't govern for so long and demand such heavy sacrifices from the people without provoking some sort of indignation.

Mussolini's car drove down the almost deserted Via Salaria in the burning heat of the silent Sunday afternoon and through the open iron gates into the grounds of Villa Savoia. It stopped outside the portico. The driver, Ercole Boratto, noticed with surprise that the King, accompanied by an aide-de-camp, was standing on the steps wearing the uniform of a Marshal of Italy. He walked down the steps to greet his visitor, which was something Boratto had never seen him do before, smiling and offering his hand. The King and Mussolini walked back to the villa together, followed by the aide-de-camp and De Cesare, while Boratto drove the car to the corner of the steps as usual. He watched the four men walk through the door of the villa and settled down to wait. It was insufferably hot in the car, but these interviews normally lasted no more than a quarter of an hour, and he comforted himself with the reflection that he would soon be home again. He had not been waiting long when a police officer, whose face was familiar, came up to the car and leant through the window to say, 'Ercole, you're wanted on the telephone. Hurry up! I'll come with you. I've got a call to make too.'

Boratto got out of the car and walked away with the police officer, wondering who could want him. It was not the first time that he had been called away to the telephone at Villa Savoia, but he felt a vague uneasiness. There were more *carabinieri* in the grounds than he had seen there before, and everyone, apart from the Duce, seemed tense and watchful. Mussolini, however, appeared quite unconcerned. He had been perfectly composed in the car.

He was behaving so still. Although he had not replied to the King's greeting, merely shaking his head as if to say, 'No, I am not very well, thank you,' when they walked into the drawing-room a servant heard him reply in a polite, conversational tone 'Yes, very,' to the King's comment 'Isn't it hot!' In the drawing-room, calmly and without undue emphasis, he reported the events that had taken place at the Grand Council meeting the night before. They were unimportant, he said, and by reference to various statutes added that he would prove that the vote against him had no legal force. He was quite confident in the merits of his case.

The King interrupted him. 'I immediately gave him to understand,' he said afterwards, 'that I did not share his opinion, pointing out that the Grand Council was an organ of State which he himself had created and which had the approval of both parliamentary chambers. Therefore, every decision taken by the Grand Council was highly important.'

'My dear Duce,' he continued, 'it isn't any good any more. Matters are very serious. Italy is in ruins. The Army is completely demoralized. The soldiers have no desire to go on fighting. The Alpine brigades have started singing a song to the effect that they will not go on fighting for Mussolini.' In Piedmontese dialect he quoted a chorus of the song which ended with the words, 'Down with Mussolini, who murdered the Alpini.'

Mussolini listened in silence.

'The Grand Council's vote is terrific,' the King went on. 'Nineteen votes for Grandi's motion and among them four holders of the Order of the Annunziata. You can certainly be under no illusion as regards Italy's feeling for you. At this moment you are the most hated man in the country. I am your only remaining friend. That is why I tell you that you need have no fears for your own safety. I will see you are protected.'

Mussolini still did not speak, and when the King brought his comments to an end by saying that Marshal Badoglio was an obvious successor, Mussolini sat down suddenly, without a word, as if he felt faint. All the colour had gone from his face. He appeared not to be listening any more; and after the King had said that Badoglio had the full confidence of the Army and also of the police, he repeated the words 'Also of the police', as though he had heard the sound of them but had not understood their sense.

'Then it's all over,' he muttered and, according to the King, he repeated the sentence three times.

At length he stood up.

'If your Majesty is right,' he said in a stronger voice, 'I should present my resignation.'

'Yes. And I have to tell you that I unconditionally accept your resignation as Head of the Government.'

'You are taking a decision pregnant with results. A crisis at the moment will cause the country to believe that peace is near, because the man who declared war has been removed. The blow to the Army's morale will be disastrous. . . . The crisis will be considered a triumph for the Churchill–Stalin set-up, especially for the latter, who will see it as the retirement of an antagonist who has fought against him for twenty years. I realize the people's hatred. I had no difficulty in recognizing it last night at the Grand Council. One can't govern for so long and demand such heavy sacrifices from the people without provoking some sort of indignation. I wish good luck to the man who takes over the Government at this stage.'

The interview was over. They walked together to the door. The King's face, Mussolini said afterwards, was 'yellow and he seemed even smaller, almost bent double'. He had conducted the interview with 'unusual agitation . . . in a jerky painful mumble', biting his nails, and at times his remarks had been 'incoherent'. But an aide-de-camp who saw him leave the room in which the interview had been held could see no alteration in the King's appearance or in his manner; and Badoglio, who saw him soon afterwards, described him as being 'very calm'.

Although the King, returning Mussolini's opinion of himself, said that the Head of his Government seemed smaller than before, 'almost shrunken', in fact Mussolini too was calm. Outside the drawing-room he offered the King his hand, and Victor Emmanuel took it in both his own and shook it warmly. They spoke again of the oppressive heat, and then the King was introduced to De Cesare, who had been waiting outside in the ante-room with Colonel Torella di Romagnano, one of the King's personal staff. Mussolini presented De Cesare with evident composure. He had accepted his dismissal as calmly as he had rejected the warnings about the King's intentions.

T–H

And despite all the warnings he had received, it is certain that he had not been in the least alarmed. The immediate shock of the Grand Council meeting had soon given way to a mood of blind confidence. 'My father's behaviour during those days,' Countess Ciano says, 'was completely incomprehensible. He knew that a *coup* was being prepared some fifteen days before it happened, but he did not treat it at all seriously. He thought it would be quite sufficient to change a few Ministers.' When his wife had warned him, he had turned on her and said that she herself was the mischief-maker. When Claretta had warned him, he had ignored her. When Scorza and Galbiati had warned him, he had paid no attention and had asked for no details. Even now as he came out on to the portico steps of Villa Savoia he had no sense of danger. He saw his car parked not in its usual place at the corner of the steps, but further away on the other side of the drive. He made a slight gesture of irritation and walked down the steps towards it. Captain Vigneri of the *carabinieri* went up to him, saluted smartly and said, 'Duce, we have heard you are in danger. I have orders to protect you.'

'There's no need for that,' Mussolini said with no more than a hint of either surprise or anger. 'I have my own escort.'

'My orders are,' Captain Vigneri insisted, 'that I must escort you.'

Mussolini had reached the bottom of the steps now and was walking across the drive towards his car. 'All right,' he said. 'If those are your orders. You had better come with me in my car.'

'No, Duce,' the captain told him. 'You must come with me.'

'But it is ridiculous. I never heard of such a thing.'

'It is an order, Duce.'

Vigneri pointed to an ambulance. Mussolini made no further protest and went towards it. The back doors were open, and as he came up to them he hesitated for a moment, for there was an armed guard inside. The captain took him gently by the elbow, and Mussolini, accepting the gesture as one of help rather than compulsion, climbed aboard. He sat down, pulling his hat over his eyes as De Cesare climbed in after him. Another officer and three *carabinieri* climbed in as well and two police officers in plain clothes carrying machine-pistols. The doors were loudly slammed shut. It never occurred to him that he had been arrested.

The Prisoner

Historia magistra vitae – but she has bad
pupils.

I

No one spoke in the ambulance. For half an hour, as it raced
through the streets, Mussolini sat crouched and silent, believing
the *carabinieri* captain's assurance that he was merely being protected from the danger of the mob. At six o'clock, when the ambulance came to a stop inside the courtyard of the *Carabinieri*'s
Podgora barracks in Via Quintino Sella, he stepped down as
though he had come on a tour of inspection, scowling about him,
his jaw thrust out, leaning forward slightly with his legs apart
and his hand on his hips in a stance which was as familiar as his
face.

He was shown into the officers' mess, which he noticed was
surrounded by *carabinieri* with fixed bayonets, and was left there
alone.

In the next room an officer watched him through the half-open
door, but they did not speak to each other. After three-quarters of
an hour Mussolini was taken out again to the ambulance, which
drove off at so great a speed that De Cesare protested that the fearful jolting would upset the Duce's stomach. But Mussolini himself
remained silent, and when the ambulance arrived at the barracks
of the *carabinieri* cadets in Via Legnano he got out again without
protest. De Cesare whispered that the unusual numbers of armed
carabinieri in the courtyard were surely not there only to see that
no harm came to him, but Mussolini refused to believe him. Even
when De Cesare was put in another room and he was left alone in
the Commandant's office he still believed that the rows of *carabinieri* in the corridors of the building had been posted there for

his protection. He seemed merely surprised when on going to the lavatory he was accompanied by an officer and several men, who guarded the door and then followed him back to the commandant's office.

He was offered a meal, and he refused it as if the very thought of food nauseated him. Although he did not complain, he looked so ill that the Commandant thought it would be wise to get a doctor to look at him. Dr Santillo came immediately and found him 'very pale, almost deathlike', with 'a very slow pulse'. He asked for a barber, and when he had been shaved he apologized, with unexpected embarrassment, that he did not have any money with which to pay him; but he would remember him, he said, and one day perhaps he would be able to make it up to him.

At eleven o'clock he put out the light and tried to sleep on the camp-bed which had been provided for him. But he was disturbed by the light shining through from the next room, where the officer on guard sat watching him intently, not even troubling to answer the telephone which rang with a maddening persistence.

2

Outside in the streets of Rome people had been gathering in little groups ever since dusk to discuss the latest rumours. At five o'clock the squares had filled with soldiers armed with machine-guns and even light artillery, but few people believed the semi-official explanation that these troops were preparing to resist an Allied parachute landing which was expected to take place at any moment in the suburbs of the city. No news of what had passed at the Grand Council meeting had reached the public or even the Press, and all that was known was that the meeting had lasted until the early hours of the morning and that some decision of importance had been taken. By nightfall the rumours had become more insistent, and they all centred upon the Duce. He was reported dead; to have flown to Germany; as having resigned and gone home to the Romagna. At a quarter to eleven, when thousands of people listened in silence for the expected announcement in news broadcast at that time, their wireless sets were silent. They waited anxiously. Usually a gramophone record was played when a programme did not run to time; but now they could hear only the hum and crackle of their sets. And then at last, with relief and excitement, they recognized the voice of the announcer:

'His Majesty the King-Emperor has accepted the resignation, from the office of Head of the Government and Chief Secretary of State, of his Excellency Cavaliere Benito Mussolini, and has nominated as Head of the Government and Chief Secretary of State Cavaliere Marshal of Italy Pietro Badoglio . . .'

For many listeners this was enough. They waited to hear no more. They ran down into the streets to shout and dance and sing. Mussolini had fallen; the war was as good as over. They kissed each other, held hands to run up and down the pavements calling up to the faces at open windows that Fascism was dead. They yelled curses at Mussolini like excited children who have been told after an enforced silence that they are allowed to scream. They ran to the Quirinale to cheer the King and to Via XX Settembre to cheer Badoglio. They broke into the offices of *Il Messaggero* and threw furniture, files, telephones, and enormous portraits of Mussolini out of the windows. They hacked Fascist emblems off buildings and tore Fascist badges out of the lapels of anyone foolhardy enough to wear them. Few badges, however, were still worn. Rowdies and toughs, looking for victims, could find none. Everyone, it seemed, had become anti-Fascist. Scorza, who had been waiting in vain for a message from Mussolini, had gone in desperation to Party Headquarters in Piazza Colonna, where he had ordered a mobilization of all Fascists in Rome. 'Something is happening,' he said to the Federal Secretary. 'I don't just know what, but I've got a feeling it's serious.' He had no more success, however, than Galbiati had had with the Militia. Less than fifty Fascists answered his call to duty; and even they could find little to do.

The houses of a few known Fascists were broken into, but their owners could not be found. The offices of a few Fascist organizations were set alight, but the fires were soon put out. A gang of demonstrators burst into Palazzo Venezia, shouting that they wanted the man who had oppressed them for twenty years, but they did not attempt to break down the locked door of the Mappamondo room and contented themselves by waving a red flag.

There was little violence and no one was killed. The mood was one of gaiety rather than of revenge. In Via del Tritone, Piazza

Colonna, Via Nazionale, and Piazza del Popolo crowds of people sang and danced as at a *festa*. 'Fascism is dead,' they called happily to each other. And it was true. Not a single man died in Rome that night in an effort to defend it.

Most of the population, however, sat at home in sad disillusionment. After the announcement that Mussolini had resigned came Badoglio's proclamation that the war would go on and that Italy would remain true to her allies. They had expected as much. The Germans were still in Rome. It might have been Mussolini's war, but it could not be ended yet. The German Army was still in control of most of Italy, and already orders had been issued by the German Command to ensure that this control should become a stranglehold. There seemed no hope yet of peace.

There were those as well who remembered how so many of those people outside, celebrating his fall with such exuberance, had once filled the air with their tautophonic chants, '*Duce! Duce! Duce!*' and their protestations of loyalty till death. But only one of those seemingly devoted disciples felt called upon to make any final gesture of constancy.

'The Duce has resigned,' Senator Manlio Morgagni wrote in a note which he left on his office desk. 'My life is finished. Long live Mussolini!' Then he shot himself.

3

At Villa Savoia the King was pacing up and down the paths of the garden talking cheerfully about the Grand Council meeting and Mussolini's arrest with an officer of his staff. The Queen was not so content. 'They could have arrested him where and when they wanted,' she complained later. 'But they should not have done it here. Here he was our guest. The laws of hospitality have been violated. It is a disgrace.'[1] She had thought Mussolini gross and vulgar when she had first met him, but she had grown to admire him and could find it in her heart to regret the suddenness and violence of his fall.

---

1. Prince Umberto also disapproved of the methods of the generals, some of whom, so he afterwards said, went so far as to propose that the fallen Duce should be executed immediately. He claims to have opposed the suggestion vehemently.

4

At one o'clock in the morning Lieutenant-Colonel Chirico went into the Commandant's office in the Vittorio Emanuele II barracks and said to Mussolini, 'General Ferone has just arrived with a message for you from Marshal Badoglio.'

Mussolini got off his camp-bed and went into the next room, where he found General Ferone wearing what he described as 'a strangely smug expression'. Ferone, a staff officer at the War Ministry, handed him the letter from Badoglio. Before reading it, Mussolini looked again at Ferone and said to him, 'General, we have met before, have we not?'

Ferone, who had commanded a division in Albania, had, in fact, once been introduced to Mussolini, but the meeting had been a hurried one and the Duce, whom he felt sure had forgotten it, had not appeared to pay him the least attention.

'We met in Albania,' Ferone said rather coldly.

'Quite right,' Mussolini replied, opening his eyes wide, suggesting that he was surprised that Ferone should have remembered it, implying, as Napoleon liked to do, that his memory for such things was infallible. 'Quite right, General. Don't forget I always appreciated you.'

Then he turned his attention to the letter.

To His Excellency Cavaliere Benito Mussolini [he read]. The undersigned Head of the Government wishes to inform your Excellency that what is being done is solely for your own safety and in the knowledge of reliable information from several quarters of serious plots against your life. He, therefore, wishes to inform you that he will give orders that you shall be safely escorted, with all due consideration, to any place you indicate. – The Head of the Government, Pietro Badoglio, Marshal.

Mussolini looked up at Ferone, who asked him where he would like to be taken.

It was not for him to say, Mussolini replied with a hint of proud disdain, he had no home of his own. He would be a guest wherever he went.

Ferone suggested Rocca delle Caminate, and Mussolini

seemed pleased. He had not presumed to suggest it himself, he said, as he had always considered the house not as his personal property but as belonging to the Head of the Government. He asked Ferone to convey his wish to Marshal Badoglio in a letter which he dictated slowly.

26 July 1943. One o'clock in the morning [he began in those tones of measured solemnity which were intended to give to his most mundane remarks a sense of inspiration and of destiny]. One: I thank Marshal Badoglio for his concern for my personal safety. Two: The only residence at my disposal is Rocca delle Caminate, where I am prepared to go at any time. Three: I desire to assure Marshal Badoglio, recalling our work together in days gone by, that there will be no difficulty on my part and I will cooperate in every way. Four: I am glad of the decision taken to continue the war with our ally as the honour and the interest of the country require it, and it is my heartfelt desire that success shall attend the grave task which Marshal Badoglio is undertaking in the name and on the order of H.M. the King whose faithful servant I have been for twenty years, and still remain.

He finished the dictation of this almost servile letter, asked to read through what had been written, and then at the foot of the page wrote in blue pencil, 'Long live Italy. Mussolini.'[1]

General Ferone left, and Mussolini went back to lie down on his camp-bed in the dreary little office. He lay awake for a long time, but before dawn he fell into a heavy sleep.

For the whole of the next day he remained in the room, lying for most of the time on his bed, occasionally getting up to look out of the window at the cars driving in and out of the barrack square below and at the cadets marching in front of the wall on which, painted in huge white letters, were the words: '*Credere ! Obbedire ! Combattere !*' the sempiternal slogan of his régime.

He was polite to his captors, 'desirous', so it seemed to one of them, 'of ingratiating himself with ready obedience to every request. He ate little and did not smoke.' When Dr Santillo called again to ask him if there was anything he wanted, he answered him almost deferentially. 'Only some toothpaste,' he said, 'and a pair of slippers.' The officer in charge of him said that he was 'resigned

1. When the letter was published Hitler said it was obvious from its meek tone that it had been forged. But Mussolini printed it in his *Storia di un Anno*.

and tranquil'. He had at last, he later confessed to Rachele, realized that he was a prisoner and that after twenty-one years of power he had lost it in a day. 'Dictators cannot slide from grace,' he said sadly to Dr Santillo. 'They must fall. But their fall makes no one happy.'

The next day he was allowed to visit De Cesare in a nearby room. They sat on De Cesare's bed talking to each other and drinking cup after cup of tea, which was brought to them by the Commandant's wife. At seven o'clock, on looking out of the window of his room, Mussolini saw two platoons, one of *carabinieri* and the other of metropolitan police, enter the barrack square and form up beside a group of lorries. An hour later more vehicles drove into the square with several officers. The *carabinieri* cadets, intrigued by the sight of such activity, craned out of the windows and filled the balconies as they looked down excitedly.

'All inside,' an officer shouted up at them. 'All inside! And close the windows!'

Soon afterwards the officer came into Mussolini's room and said to him. 'The order to leave has come.'

They went downstairs together to a waiting car. Mussolini got into the back, followed by a man who introduced himself as Brigadier-General Polito, Chief of Military Police. The car drove quickly out of the barracks led by a despatch-rider who raced on ahead to warn the *carabinieri* at the road blocks to let it through without question. The blinds of the car were drawn down, but through a crack Mussolini caught sight of the Santo Spirito hospital and realized that he was being taken not towards Rocca delle Caminate along Via Flaminia but south towards Via Appia. When the car reached Albano, his fears were confirmed.

'Where are we going?' he asked.

'Southwards.'

'Not to Rocca delle Caminate?'

'Another order came.'

'And who *are* you? I used to know of a police inspector called Polito.'

'That's me.'

'How do you come to be a general?'

'They gave me equivalent rank in the Army.'

Saverio Polito had, in Mussolini's own phrase, 'carried out

some brilliant operations during the years of the régime', and he spoke of them now – of his capture of Cesare Rossi, the former head of the Fascist Press Office, who had been arrested after the murder of Matteotti, and of his destruction of the Pintor gang in Sardinia. As the car raced down the Appian Way, through Velletri, Cisterna, and Terracina, Polito, smoking continuously, talked with animation, entertaining Mussolini with details of his adventures and of criminals he had known. And then, well after midnight, the car slowed down and General Polito pulled down the glass partition behind the driver's head and called out. 'Where are we?'

'Near Gaeta.'

The name filled Mussolini with a kind of bitter pride. Already he was thinking of himself as one of the tragic figures of history. This self-defensive compensation for his fall from grace was later to assume the force of an obsession, and he was to see in his own fate a reflection of the fate of those other great men whose lives had finished like his. Julius Caesar's end, Napoleon's, even that of Christ, were seen to have close affinities with his own. Now, when he saw the massive shape of the fort which dominates Gaeta harbour, he comforted himself with the reflection that Pius IX had taken refuge there in 1848 and that Mazzini had been interned there in 1870. 'I reflected,' he told a Swiss journalist the following year, 'that the same destiny was awaiting me. I was so convinced of this, that I question my Cerberus, Inspector Polito, asking if I was to have the honour of occupying the same cell as the great hero of our *Risorgimento*.'

'It has not been decided,' Polito said shortly.

The car came to a halt and a naval officer walked towards it, waving a torch. The instructions he gave to the driver disabused Mussolini of his hope of sharing the scene of his martyrdom with Mazzini. The officer pointed towards the docks, announcing the cruelly ironic name of the prisoner's destination – 'The Ciano Wharf'.

5

At five o'clock that afternoon Rear Admiral Franco Maugeri, the Chief of Naval Intelligence, had been told by the *Chef de Cabinet* of the Ministry of the Navy that he was to hold himself ready for a 'little escort duty'. He was to drive to Gaeta, where the corvette *Persefone* was waiting at the Costanzo Ciano Wharf. Two hours later General Cerica gave him his detailed orders. Mussolini, accompanied by General Polito, Colonel Pelaghi, and an armed escort, was leaving Rome that night for Gaeta. Maugeri's orders were to meet him there, take him aboard the *Persefone*, and give orders to her master, Captain Tazzari, to sail for Ventotene, an island thirty miles to the south. No one must know the identity of the prisoner until the *Persefone* was at sea. He was to be described to Tazzari and the officers at Gaeta Naval Headquarters as an 'important personage implicated in a serious charge of espionage'.

Maugeri had arrived at Gaeta at a quarter to eleven and for three hours waited for the arrival of the prisoner from Rome, first in the *Persefone*'s stifling ward-room, then walking up and down the quayside, endlessly smoking and talking to the other naval officers, one of whom believed that the Admiral had an appointment at sea to discuss with English or American envoys the possibility of an armistice. A few minutes after two o'clock in the morning Maugeri saw the headlights of three cars approaching rapidly down the road from Formia.

Maugeri has described, in his book *Mussolini mi ha detto*, how the leading car drew up in front of him a few yards from the gangway leading on board the *Persefone*. Lieutenant-Colonel Pelaghi of the *carabinieri* got out of it and came across the quayside towards him. General Polito got out of the following car and then Mussolini also stepped out onto the quay. Maugeri saluted and, as he did so, he met Mussolini's 'enormous eyes' as they came nearer to him 'shining in the surrounding darkness'.

Admiral Maugeri led the way on board and, followed by Polito, Colonel Pelaghi, and another *carabinieri* officer, took him as far as the door to Captain Tazzari's quarters. While Mussolini stopped to look at the barograph, Maugeri went back on deck where he found the Lieutenant of the corvette giving instructions to Mussolini's guards – six *carabinieri* armed with machine-guns.

The *Persefone* weighed anchor and left Gaeta astern. There was some trouble with the starboard engine which, however, eventually started up, throwing out a cloud of smoke that lasted throughout the voyage.

Visibility was poor and there was a slight sirocco. It was hot and humid and the clouds were low. Maugeri was happy to be at sea again but he remembered thinking that if there were to be an attack by bombers or submarines it wouldn't be 'much fun'.

Before reaching Ventotene, Captain Tazzari reduced speed and reversed course to wait for dawn; and at a quarter past five he dropped anchor a few hundred yards from the shore.

The crew remained at action stations while General Polito went ashore to discover if the island was suitable for Mussolini's exile. Admiral Maugeri watched him as he climbed into the *Persefone*'s motor-launch, and then went below again to make sure that 'everything was all right'.

'Also,' he admitted, 'I am compelled by a feeling of curiosity. I enter the cabin. Mussolini raised his great eyes to mine, as I say "Excellency" (what else could one call him?). "Do you want anything – a hot drink or a cup of coffee?"'

Mussolini refused the coffee. All he wanted, he said, was some information. How big was Ventotene? he asked.

Admiral Maugeri told him all that he could from memory and then sent for the chart-book.

'Ah, a small island,' Mussolini said, smiling.

He was thinking of Elba and St Helena, Maugeri realized, and the Admiral's thoughts too turned to Napoleon. He looked down at Mussolini with a kind of pity. He 'looks like a corpse', he noticed, as if seeing him for the first time. 'He is emaciated.'

'This is a corvette, isn't it?' Mussolini asked him, interrupting his thoughts, and they began to talk of the war at sea, the technical superiority of the British Navy, the battles that Maugeri had seen. The conversation flowed easily, Maugeri said. They spoke of the American, French, and Japanese Navies, and of the way of life in America and in Japan.

Mussolini said that he had recently been shown a film about a Japanese school of aviation. He had noticed that the Japanese were much taller than was generally believed and asked Maugeri if he knew why.

The Admiral thought that this was because they were very fond of sport and had inter-married much with Russians and Koreans.

The children were very pretty, Mussolini commented. His daughter who had been there had told him so.

The conversation turned again to America and of her capacity to absorb so many races. As he spoke Mussolini's face became less ashen and his eyes regained some of their sparkle, so that when Polito returned he seemed almost cheerful.

Polito said that Ventotene was out of the question as a place for Mussolini's internment, for the Police Commissioner on the island was not at all helpful and there was, in any case, a German garrison there. Admiral Maugeri immediately gave orders for the *Persefone* to sail away twenty-five miles north-west to Ponza, where she anchored in the roadstead soon after noon.

'Through some unexplained impulse,' Mussolini wrote – characteristically mistaking the natural curiosity of the islanders at the arrival of a warship for their extra-sensory recognition of the importance of the ship's passenger – 'all the windows and balconies were suddenly filled with men and women armed with binoculars who were watching the boat as it came ashore. In a flash the whole island knew of my arrival.'

One of those looking out towards the *Persefone* was Pietro Nenni, who recalled the day, thirty years before, when he and Mussolini had been prisoners together at Forlì. They had been friends then, Nenni remembered with a sudden access of sympathy. Standing next to Nenni was another anti-Fascist, Zaniboni, who shared his fellow-exile's pity.

'I shan't go for a walk again,' Zaniboni said as he saw the white face of Mussolini in the boat. 'I don't want to risk a quarrel with a ruined man.'

The sight of the scores of staring people in the harbour and along the mole, watching the motor-launch approach the island, filled Mussolini with dread. He felt, he said later, a terrified anxiety lest they should see him brought ashore a prisoner, and he asked to see Admiral Maugeri.

Maugeri, who had been smoking on deck, went below and found Mussolini, 'very agitated', although he was making an obvious effort not to appear so.

'I don't want to land by daylight,' he said. 'I don't want people to see me. . . . Admiral, why all these pointless annoyances?' Since the previous Sunday, he complained, he had been cut off completely. He had had no news of his family. He had only the clothes he stood up in. He referred to the letter in which Badoglio had spoken of a serious plot against him.

Maugeri told him that he had been ordered on the mission because the Navy had considered an officer of high rank should accompany Mussolini on his journey. But he had no authority to answer his complaints.

It was, nevertheless, Mussolini insisted but in a calmer, even petulant voice, most ungenerous treatment. It might have serious repercussions. It might even be dangerous, for Hitler had a strong sense of friendship.

He continued in this manner for some time, and the longer he spoke the less agitated and concerned he became. Soon Maugeri and he were talking again about the war and about the repercussions which his fall had had in Germany and England.

Was Churchill very harsh about him, Mussolini wanted to know, and suggested that the feeling against him personally in England was very strong.

Maugeri did not answer the question directly, but spoke in a general way of the 'colourless German comments' and the 'trend of English propaganda', which was advising the Italians to drive the Germans out if they wanted an honourable peace. Then he suggested that Mussolini should go up on deck as it would soon be time for him to land. Polito had returned to the *Persefone* from his reconnaissance of the island where orders had been given for a house in the village of Santa Maria to be prepared for the reception of 'an exalted personage'.

Mussolini walked up to the ship's rail with his hat – as he was usually to wear it now – pulled well down over his eyes. He looked across to the island and asked which was to be his house. He was shown an isolated, greyish, sad-looking, three-storeyed house with green shutters on the shore of a little bay between two high rocks. In front of it was a row of sailing-boats laid up on the beach. When someone began to describe the house to him, he said irritably, 'I understand. It is that little house above the sailing-boats with green windows.'

He was not told that it had also been the prison of Ras Imeru, the Abyssinian patriot.

He was overcome with depression and made sure his face was well concealed by his hat before climbing down the ladder into the launch. 'I don't want to go,' he protested, with the sudden desperate anger of a child, turning round, holding on to the rail. 'I don't want everyone to know what's happened.' But the anger subsided as quickly as it had risen, and he said good-bye to Admiral Maugeri with composure. 'Please pass on what I have told you,' he said in a voice so unnecessarily loud that a sailor standing nearby wondered if the words had been meant for him.

He smiled sadly, Maugeri noticed, and saluted in the Roman manner. He took his place in the motor-launch with his escort of *carabinieri*. The motor-launch drew away from the ship and the sailors remained silently at their stations.

It was ten o'clock when Mussolini landed on the beach of Santa Maria in Ponza. Before walking up to the house, he turned round and stood for a few moments looking back towards the sea.

'I am tired,' he said suddenly. 'I should like a bed to rest on.'

The bedroom had been freshly white-washed, and with its clinically austere walls and cheap wash-basin it gave the inescapable impression of a prison cell. The only furniture was a bare iron bedstead, a dirty wooden table from a wine-shop heavily scratched by knives, and a chair with the stuffing burst out of its seat. At sight of this lonely, comfortless room Mussolini was overcome again by that sudden anger of despair that he had felt on the *Persefone*. 'I have had enough of this,' he said, clenching his fists as he turned towards the window to pick up the chair, which he placed in the middle of the floor. He sat down on the chair and buried his face in his hands.

Sergeant-Major Marini of the Ponza *carabinieri*, who was standing in the doorway and had watched the scene with embarrassment, came into the room, gave a Roman salute, and remained standing at attention. He tried to say something, but the words caught in his throat. So nervous and unsure of himself did he look that Mussolini's mood immediately changed. He stood up and took the Sergeant-Major by the shoulders and said to him dramatically, 'Courage! I know what you must be feeling.'

'We didn't know you were coming to Ponza, Excellency. I was told barely half an hour ago.'

'Don't worry.'

'I so often wanted to meet you in the past to tell you things.'

'And now that you do meet me it doesn't matter any more.'

The Sergeant-Major left the room to fetch a mattress and some sheets, and when he returned the wife of one of his men came with him carrying a bowl of soup, an egg, and some peas. Mussolini was lying on the slats of the bed with the jacket of his suit for a pillow. He looked worn out. But when he had eaten he felt better and later on was able to talk with some semblance of his former animation to some fishermen who came to visit him and to give him a present of a few lobsters.

The next day, 29 July, was his birthday. He was sitting, dressed in his ill-fitting blue suit, by the window when Sergeant-Major Marini came into the room to give him four peaches.

'Sergeant-Major, you are very kind,' he said. 'I hope this doesn't mean that the population will go short of fruit?'

'No, no.'

'Good. Then I shall eat them between now and tomorrow.'

During the morning a few fishermen and *carabinieri* came to wish him a happy birthday, and in the afternoon a *carabinieri* officer handed him a telegram.

DUCE,

My wife and I send you our warmest and best wishes for today. Though circumstances have prevented my coming to Rome as I planned – in order to offer you a bust of Frederick the Great as well as my congratulations – the feelings I express to you today of complete solidarity and brotherly friendship are all the more cordial. Your work as a statesman will live in the history of our two nations, destined as they are to march towards a common fate. I should like to tell you that our thoughts are constantly with you. I want also to thank you for the charming hospitality which you formerly offered me, and I once more sign myself with invincible faith –

Yours,

GOERING.

It was the only message he received from the mainland.

Hitler, so Mackensen told Alfieri, was 'furious with the King and Badoglio because he could not find out where Mussolini was.' In an effort to discover his whereabouts he had instructed him as his Ambassador in Rome to go and see the King and ask for permission to visit him. But Badoglio regretted that he was 'unable, in the personal interest of H. E. Mussolini himself, to consent to the proposed visit'. He was, however, prepared to 'forward forthwith any letters which H. E. Ambassador may have for him and to transmit any answers'. Hitler thereupon decided to send to Mussolini a beautifully bound edition of the collected works of Nietzsche.

The books did not arrive while Mussolini was at Ponza, and he passed his time on the island by translating Carducci's *Odi Barbare* into German and in reading Giuseppe Ricciotti's *Life of Christ*, which he later gave to a priest on the island heavily annotated with comments indicative of the comfort he had received from the 'surprising analogies' between Christ's fate and his own. He had started annotating the book before his arrest, and it is evident from the notes made in Ponza in a different coloured pencil that those pages describing Christ's betrayal and arrest were now the most significant. Seeing him reading the book one day, Marini made some reference to the parallel which could be drawn between the betrayals of the founder of Christianity and of the founder of Fascism.

'You should not compare Him with me,' Mussolini said, but he could not disguise his pleasure.

There was comfort for him too in the reflection that Ponza had been the home of other exiles. 'Even since ancient times,' he wrote afterwards, 'famous people had been banished there – Nero's mother Agrippina, Augustus's daughter Julia, and to make up for these a saint – Flavia Domitilla and, in A.D. 538 a pope, St Sylvester the Martyr.' But this capacity to see himself against the background of history was no more than a cold consolation in the bleak sameness of his days.

He got up each morning at half past seven and had a glass of milk and an egg for breakfast; for lunch he had another egg, a few tomatoes, a piece of bread, and some fruit. He drank another glass of milk before he went to bed, which he did every evening as soon as it was dark. For hours on end he sat alone reading and writing or looking out of the window across the harbour bay, thinking, as he later confessed, about 'the miserable conspiracy which had got rid of me, convinced that all this would lead to capitulation and to my being handed over to the enemy.' He was allowed no newspapers and no visitors; nor was he allowed, so he told Rachele, to attend the Mass which he asked the parish priest of Ponza to say on the anniversary of Bruno's death. His only companions were the *carabinieri* who listened to him talk not only with bewilderment but also with embarrassment, for they had been forbidden to reply, Sergeant-Major Marini, and the parish priest, Luigi Maria Dies, who said afterwards that Mussolini's exile had turned this 'great man into a good Christian'.

He rarely left the house. When two new officers, Lieutenant-Colonel Meoli and Lieutenant Elio di Lorenzo came out to the island with Sergeant-Major Antichi to reinforce his guard, he was allowed to go swimming; and once, escorted by three *carabinieri*, he went to see the Roman remains on the island and the grottos where lampreys had been reared by the priests of the temple. But he did not like the villagers to see him, and for most of the time he preferred to stay indoors.

On 1 August a lobster fisherman came out from the mainland in his motor-boat *Maria Pace*, bringing him a box of fruit and two trunks which his family had been allowed to send him. Sergeant-Major Marini watched him unpack. There were three envelopes in the case, one containing a letter from Rachele and a photograph of Bruno, the second containing 10,000 lire, and the third a letter from Edda, which he read hastily and then threw under the bed. 'Do you want to reply to the letters?' Marini asked him. 'No,' he said, 'I'm not in a hurry for that.'

The clothes, however, gave him a momentary pleasure, and he changed immediately into a clean white shirt. A moment later he was seen to take the shirt off and to walk to the window with his chest bare and a yachting cap on his head; then suddenly he took the cap off and put his white shirt on again. He was bored and he was frustrated. The basin in his room did not work, and this alone was enough to drive him to despair. 'Tell me, Sergeant-Major,' he asked Marini with bitter petulence. 'Why is there never any water in this tap? I've spent a pretty penny on getting the pipes laid in Ponza, I can tell you.'

'Excellency, you spent a pretty penny all right, but the water from the spring still runs into the sea.'

'Are you speaking the truth, Sergeant-Major?'

'Yes, Excellency.'

'Ah, these Prefects! These Prefects!'

And so another discourse began.

After a week of this sad, dispiriting life, he became ill and Dr Silverio Martinelli, the Ponza doctor, was sent for.

'I know your complaint,' Martinelli said without examining him. 'I've brought you some medicine. I can't do more than that. You ought to be operated on.'

'Everyone in Italy knows my complaint,' Mussolini said angrily. 'Give me my medicine.' But when he was handed it, he said it was not enough and demanded a double dose. Even now he could not resist the opportunity for talking, and at great length expounded to the doctor his medical history. 'So there you are,' he added at the end of his monologue without self-consciousness, 'those are the physical sufferings of the Duce!'

Six days later, soon after dark, Mussolini saw a mysterious light flashing continuously on the hills behind the harbour. He watched it for some time, but was, however, fast asleep when shortly before dawn he was woken up abruptly and told that he was being moved from the island immediately.

'I collected my few things,' he wrote the following year, 'and, accompanied by my armed escort, went down to the beach, where a boat was waiting. The structure of a warship showed clearly in the distance at the entrance to the roadstead.' He was taken on board the *Panthère*, a ship which had formerly been in the French Navy, where he saw Admiral Maugeri again.

Maugeri found him looking better than before. 'He looks bolder, has more colour, less flaccid. . . . Still the same suit, still the same hat.'

'And where are we going to this time, Maugeri?' he asked almost cheerfully.

'To Maddalena Island.'

'More and more inaccessible.'

The thought seemed to please him. During the long conversation which he and Maugeri had in the captain's cabin, the Admiral admitted that the disconcerting impression began to grow in his mind that Mussolini was now considering himself as a 'third person and not as the principal actor in the gigantic tragedy of our nation'. Mussolini was speaking and yet it seemed to Maugeri that he was not speaking of himself and had nothing at all to do with the events he described.

Despite his aloofness and exalted dissociation he was, nevertheless, extremely anxious to know what had been happening in the world from which he had been cut off for ten days. Already he had been told by another naval officer on board that Badoglio had dissolved the Fascist Party. Now he heard with apparent interest that Farinacci had gone to Germany and spoken on Munich radio and that Ciano had been dismissed from his ambassadorship. 'Now there,' he commented in a 'decided and mournful voice', 'is a truly wretched figure . . . golf with his girl friends every day.' And when Maugeri told him that it was feared that German commandos had been preparing an attempt to remove him from Ponza he displayed a natural and real concern. It would be the greatest humiliation which could possibly be inflicted on him, he thought. And did people really think he would go off to Germany and try to seize power again with German help ? he asked, denying strongly that he ever would.

The thought that he was, indeed, not yet a historical figure, upon whom contemporary events could no longer have any influence, and the realization of what a raid by German commandos might mean, apparently filled him with indignation. Maugeri thought that the indignation was sincere. Certainly he seems not to have considered before the implications of a rescue by German troops, although he had discussed with Marini on Ponza the possibility of a British attack.

The following morning, when the ship, steaming at twenty-two knots in a strong westerly wind, was already half-way to Maddalena, Mussolini was composed again. There had been two alerts in the night when enemy aircraft had flown low over the ship, but no attacks had been made and afterwards he had been to sleep for a few hours. When Maugeri came in to see him he was rested and calm.

The sea was rough, breaking over the bows and across the deck and the strong wind carried the spray as far as the bridge. Visibility was poor. The mountains of Corsica could be seen through the mist on the port bow, but Sardinia was no more than an indeterminate blur. The *Panthère* steamed right up to the danger limit of the batteries so that the captain could take his bearings accurately. But there was nothing to be seen except Cape Figari and neither he nor Admiral Maugeri were absolutely certain of that. So the ship steamed slowly southwards keeping outside the limits of the minefields until Tavolara came clearly into sight and it was possible to identify the entrance to the estuary. Piloted by a motor-boat the *Panthère* went down the channel at four knots. Now that the worries of navigation were over, Admiral Maugeri felt calmer but the sight of Mussolini standing on deck with the *carabinieri* officers annoyed him. Colonel Meoli ought to have avoided this, he thought, for the crew might well have made some demonstration. They did not do so, however. They looked at him, of course, but they were silent and they did not stare.

At two o'clock a motor-launch, with Admiral Bruno Brivonesi aboard, drew alongside, and Mussolini climbed down towards it. He knew Brivonesi and did not like him. He had had him court-martialled after a naval incident in which he had lost three ships without inflicting any loss on the British cruisers which had attacked him. The sentence which the court had imposed was, in Mussolini's opinion, inadequate, and his subsequent appointment to command the naval base at La Maddalena a disgrace. He was married to an Englishwoman, Mussolini commented with evident distaste.

On Maddalena, Mussolini was given further irritation by being reminded of the English. He was taken to a house with a large garden overlooking the sea and surrounded by pine-trees. It was well furnished and had until the night before been used as a mess by E-boat officers. Mussolini was told that it belonged to an Englishman called Weber, behind whose desire for isolation he detected a sinister motive. Of all the places in the world where this Weber could have settled why did he have to choose 'the most stark and lonely island of all those to the north of Sardinia? The Secret Service? Possibly.'

Maddalena was even more lonely now. Nearly all the civilian population had been evacuated after a heavy air-raid which again Mussolini, with an increasingly paranoic insistence on betrayal and deceit, found 'mysterious', for the enemy had 'an exact knowledge of the targets'. The only people remaining were sailors, a few fishermen, and a force of *carabinieri* now increased to more than a hundred men.

The bleakness of the place had an immediate effect on Mussolini's spirits. He went out on to the terrace of the house from which he could see, through the depressing mist of the early afternoon, the hulks of the big ships sunk in the harbour and beyond the harbour the dark shapes of the Gallura mountains. He found the atmosphere 'menacing and hostile'. He came back into the house and Maugeri noticed how gloomy his face was. Barely nodding the Admiral farewell, he went into his room and shut the door.

Mussolini remained on the island for three weeks. It was a miserable time. The days at Ponza, he had complained, were long and lonely; here they seemed even longer, and 'the solitude still more rigorous'. That August was particularly hot; the sea was calm and there was no wind. 'Everything,' Mussolini afterwards wrote, 'seemed to be nailed down under the sun.' He showed no desire to leave the cool of the villa, only occasionally going for a short walk in the pine-wood with a *carabinieri* sergeant. Once again he was completely cut off from the outside world, receiving nothing but Hitler's present of the twenty-four volumes of Nietzsche's works, which he began carefully to read from the beginning, finding the early poems 'very beautiful'. He also began to write a diary, filling it with 'daily notes of a philosophical, political, and literary character'; but no one saw it except himself, and it was never afterwards found.[1] Most of the time he spent looking gloomily out to sea from the shade of the terrace.

One day General Polito came to the island, and Mussolini asked him what had become of Badoglio's promise to let him go to Rocca delle Caminate. It had been decided that it was too dangerous, Polito said; the Prefect of Forlì did not think he could guarantee his safety there.

'Nonsense,' Mussolini said crossly.

'It isn't nonsense,' Polito said. 'The Fascists seemed to have disappeared. There are signs of the reaction against them and against you everywhere. The offices of *Il Popolo d'Italia* have been attacked in Milan. I myself saw a bust of you on the floor of a public lavatory in Ancona.'

'What about the war?'

1. *Pensieri di Maddalena e di Ponza* published in translation in the *Salzburger Nachrichten* may perhaps have been this diary. A notebook containing the *Pensieri* was given to the *Salzburger Nachrichten*, so this paper says, by an SS officer a few days before the surrender. Colonel Skorzeny tells me that when Mussolini invited him to visit him in the summer of 1944 he asked him to bring back with him from Germany a diary which had been impounded by the Germans after the rescue from the Gran Sasso. Skorzeny persuaded the *Auswätige Amt* to let him take back the diary after photostat copies had been made. He believes that one of these copies may have been extracted from the files and sold to the *Salzburger Nachrichten*.

'Everyone is longing for it to be over. It's just as much a burden now for the civilian population as it is for those who are fighting – particularly for the old people, the women, and the children. This is why there is so strong a feeling against you.'

But although the Italians were indeed longing for the war to be over, Badoglio felt obliged to move towards an armistice with extreme caution. His policy was not a successful one. He had said, and continued to insist, that the new Government would remain faithful to Italy's allies. The Germans, however, openly doubting his word, were still pouring troops across the Brenner, while the Allies, antagonized by his declared object of continuing the fight, hardened their determination to batter Italy into defeat. On 6 August at the frontier station of Tarvisio, Ambrosio and the new Foreign Minister Raffaele Guariglia met Ribbentrop and Keitel and registered a formal protest against what was now in effect a military occupation of their country. 'We have a right,' Ambrosio told Keitel, 'to be given advance information about German troop movements.' It was no more than a formal objection. The delegates on both sides knew that the Axis had already collapsed. Kesselring was one of those few Germans – perhaps indeed the only one – who still believed that Badoglio would keep his word. At this meeting Ribbentrop, surrounded by an intimidating S S guard, made no secret of his own distrust and asked Guariglia how long the new Government had been negotiating with the Allies for a separate peace. Guariglia, shrewd and wily, looked back at Ribbentrop with an air of injured innocence and said in his strong Neapolitan accent, 'But we are your loyal allies!'

Less than a week later General Castellano was on his way to Lisbon to inform the British Ambassador there that the Italian Government was ready to surrender. For days the atmosphere in Rome had been electric. Diplomats watched each other warily, and at Palazzo Chigi the confusion was appalling as officials and messengers rushed from one office to another trying to learn what was happening. 'Telegrams kept pouring in from our embassies,' Alfieri said, 'urgently requesting instructions. In all the offices the telephones rang incessantly.' And over all there hung the fear of a sudden and savage German reaction, perhaps even a declaration of war. General Castellano heard officials repeatedly tell each other that there would soon be a 'new night of San Bartolomeo'.

After three weeks of furtive negotiations, on 3 September, in an army tent at Cassibile near Syracuse in Sicily, the surrender was signed. On that same day Badoglio assured the German Ambassador in Rome that Italy would fight alongside her 'ally Germany to the end'; and it was not until eight o'clock on the evening of 8 September, when the Allies had landed on the mainland at Sàlerno, that the armistice was revealed to the Germans and to the world.

Of the negotiations which ended the Pact of Steel Mussolini, of course, knew nothing. Looking out across the sea, so flat and motionless that it reminded him of an Alpine lake, he waited gloomily for news throughout the hot August days. He was sitting on the terrace of the Villa Weber as usual on the evening of 26 August when a German aircraft flew so low over the house that he could see the pilot's face. The next day a *carabinieri* officer came to warn him that he would be taken off the island the following morning. General Basso, the military commander in Sardinia, had advised that Maddalena could no longer be considered a safe *confino* for the 'high-ranking personage' held there. German submarines often passed very close to the island, and an attempted rescue was believed to be imminent.

In the early hours of 28 August Mussolini was taken from the Villa Weber down to the harbour where a Red Cross seaplane had been moored for some time. Accompanied by Lieutenant Faiola and Sergeant-Major Antichi, he stepped aboard, and after an hour and a half's flight the seaplane landed on the waters of Lake Bracciano. At Vigna di Valle he was met by a police inspector named Gueli, who, since Polito had been injured in a car crash, had been appointed his senior jailer, and by a *carabinieri* major. He was transferred to an ambulance, which then drove away fast in the direction of Rome.

6

On the Gran Sasso

Ah ! The highest prison in the world.

I

On reaching the Rome by-pass the ambulance turned left towards Via Flaminia, and crossing the iron bridge over the Tiber it made for the Sabine road. At Rieti the road turns sharp right across the valley which divides the Sabine mountains from the Abruzzi, and Mussolini realized with relief as the ambulance climbed up the Aquila road towards the Gran Sasso d'Italia that he was being taken to a part of Italy that he loved.

The rugged profile of the mountain rising to over 10,000 feet in the heart of Italy cannot easily be forgotten [he wrote in his *Storia di un anno*]. There is an indefinable aura about the people and the atmosphere of the Abruzzi which captures one's heart. ... At the beginning of September many flocks of sheep which had come up from the *campagna* in the spring and had been pasturing on the plateau were now slowly drifting away and preparing to go back. Sometimes the shepherds appeared on horseback and then vanished along the ridge of the mountain, standing out against the skyline like figures from another age.

Fifteen miles beyond Aquila the winding road up the Gran Sasso ends at the terminus of a funicular, which goes up a further 3,000 feet to the plateau known as the Campo Imperatore. This plateau, 6,500 feet above the sea, stretches for ten miles beneath the towering Monte Corno, the highest peak in the Apennines. It was to an isolated hotel on this high plateau that Mussolini was being taken.

For several days it had been known that 'an important person-age' was soon to visit this hotel, the Albergo-Rifugio, and the arrival there on 28 August of Private Francesco Grevetto, who was known to have been in the service of the Duce before his arrest, left little room for doubt who that visitor was to be. As the hotel was still full, the Villetta inn at the bottom of the funicular was prepared for Mussolini's reception until the Albergo-Rifugio had been cleared of its guests.

Flavia Iurato, the manageress of the hotel, who had come down the funicular to supervise the preparations for Mussolini's reception at La Villetta was in the village square when the Red Cross Ambulance drew up. 'From it emerged a heavily built man,' she said afterwards. 'He was wearing a dark suit, overcoat, and black hat – Mussolini. There was no longer anything of the well-fed, self-assured dictator about him. Indeed he looked anxiously about him as if he feared some trap, rolling his eyes which stood out from his emaciated face.'

There had been an air-raid warning on the drive from Cittaducale. 'Groups of soldiers in their shirt sleeves fled shouting in all directions,' Mussolini himself wrote later with undisguised contempt. 'And the civilians followed their example. So did the officers.' But some of the officers noticed that Mussolini himself was as anxious to reach the safety of the ditch as any of them.

His lonely days on Ponza and Maddalena and his declining health had sapped the vigour of his spirit as well as of his body. To those who saw him now he seemed not only a sick man but a defeated one. His physical courage had never been seriously doubted before, and was not to be doubted again, but for the moment he seemed almost timid.

In his second-floor room at La Villetta Mussolini sat listlessly gazing upwards at the mountains. He was allowed for the first time to listen to the wireless, but the privilege seemed a not particularly welcome one. So depressed, indeed, did he appear to his warders, Faiola and Gueli, that after each meal they quickly removed the knives and even the forks from the table as they feared he might try to use them on himself.

At the beginning of September he was taken to the funicular station for the last stage of his journey. He did not want to go, but his protest was no more than mild.

'Is this funicular safe?' he asked the station-master nervously. And then added quickly, correcting himself with a touch of his former pride, 'Not for my sake, you understand, because my life is over. But for those who accompany me.'

He comforted himself with the thought that it was built, like the Albergo-Rifugio itself, 'during the twenty years of Fascism'.

How high up was the hotel? he asked: 2,112 metres, someone told him.

His comment was predictable and somehow touching in the guileless simplicity of its childlike pride: 'Ah! The highest prison in the world.'

2

Seen from the top of the funicular railway, the Albergo-Rifugio certainly gives the impression of a prison. Its plain curved walls and small windows are uncompromisingly functional. But Mussolini seemed pleased with its appearance, Gueli thought, as though considering its bleak bareness a worthy setting for the tragedy of exile. Once inside, however, his pleasure was dispelled. He was shown into a suite on the first floor which was lavishly furnished and included a room for his servant, Grevetto. Immediately he knelt down on the floor of the sitting-room and rolled up the carpets.

'If I am a prisoner,' he said to a group of *carabinieri* and some members of the hotel staff who seemed disposed to treat him with a deference ill-suited to the role in which he had cast himself, 'if I am a prisoner, treat me as such. If I am not, I would like to go to Rocca delle Caminate.'

He was, in fact, treated more like a guest than a prisoner. His day, the manageress of the hotel said, 'became that of any peaceful citizen on holiday. . . . At his own request he took his meals in his own rooms – in the sitting-room, to be exact. He was on a strict diet due to his illness, that is, almost entirely plain rice, eggs, boiled onions, very little meat, some milk, and a lot of fruit. Indeed he really did a grape cure, because he ate about seven pounds of them each day.' Every afternoon he went for a walk with Sergeant-Major Antichi and every afternoon, when he returned, Gueli went up to the sitting-room to talk to him. Those conversations with a man 'of such brains', Gueli said, were 'the best hours of my life'.

He had dinner at seven o'clock and then went down to the hotel dining-room to play *scopone* with Antichi, Gueli, and Faiola.

Before going back to his suite he was allowed to listen to the wireless. He heard not only Italian news broadcasts but German and English ones as well, and whenever his name was mentioned, sometimes with praise, more often with abuse, the others looked at him to see what his reaction might be, but behind his expression of hard impassivity it was impossible to detect either pleasure or pain.

He listened without apparent emotion to the news of what he now called the 'sham war', which daily grew more serious and tragic. He heard of the increasingly violent air-raids on Italian cities and the appalling numbers of casualties; of the armies falling back; of the rapid conquest of Sicily and the reports of hundreds of thousands of homeless and almost starving refugees; of the destruction of crops and the shortage of wheat and the sudden stoppage of coal shipments from Germany; of the bewildered Italian armies in Croatia, Greece, and France giving up their arms without protest to the Germans; of the capitulation and the armistice; of the increased flow of German troops from the north and the precipitate flight of the King and Badoglio's Government from Rome to Pescara and then to Brindisi. And he listened to all these things with the same expression of cold, dispassionate inappetence. It was as if the whole course of history had already been decided, or that without his hand to guide them contemporary events had for him no interest or meaning.

'What judgement will history pass on me?' he asked Gueli one day; and it was for him the one important question. For the rest he appeared to care nothing. This impassive dissociation had become almost habitual. He displayed no interest in the increasingly elaborate security measures on the Campo Imperatore, in the armed guards now placed at his door, the machine-guns on the terrace. 'He showed neither sorrow nor humiliation,' the manageress noticed, 'only sometimes when he saw he was being watched he composed his face in a studiedly thoughtful expression. . . . He did not spend his time in either reading or writing. . . . . He was often to be seen at the window, looking at the majestic Gran Sasso with field-glasses or sitting on the low wall by the courtyard, gazing abstractedly into the distance like the traditional oleograph of Napoleon on St Helena.'

Sometimes he would go out of his way to be kind or gracious, but there was always something consciously paternal in his manner, a compelling necessity to compare the misfortunes of others with his own. When, for instance, the chambermaid, Lisa Miscordi, who did his washing for him complained of a painful ankle, he immediately went to look for ointment and bandages.

'Be brave, my child,' he told her soothingly. 'Remember that I have been in pain for eighteen years.'

On another occasion he heard one of the *carabinieri* guards arguing with a shepherd who had come to the hotel to buy a bottle of wine. No civilians were allowed into the hotel, the *carabiniere* said, but the shepherd refused to be turned away. Mussolini told the guard to let the shepherd in and he took him to a table, where he sat down, not in the least concerned to find himself in the unexpected company of his former Duce.

What improvements, Mussolini asked him, had Fascism brought about in the sheep-farming industry?

The shepherd could not think of any, and said so. And then, leaning forward across the table to put a roughly confidential hand on Mussolini's shoulder and addressing him with the familiar *tu*, he added, 'You were wrong. You taxed us too heavily; and you let them steal too much for the wool and cheese State Pools.'

Changing the subject, Mussolini asked him about the war. What did he think of that, now it had ended so badly?

'Too many thieves about,' the shepherd said with the conscious knowledgability of his kind. 'The bread had to fatten too many people before it got to the soldiers' mouths.'

At length when he had finished his wine he got to his feet, patted Mussolini on the shoulder, and then shook him by the hand.

'Take care of yourself, Mussolini,' he said with easy familiarity. 'And thanks for the wine.'

Instead of angering him, as the onlookers feared, the strange interview put Mussolini in a cheerful mood. After supper that evening when he came down for the usual game of cards he asked enthusiastically when the first snow would fall. Sometimes there was snow up there at the beginning of October, he was told. 'Let's hope it snows soon,' he said, looking pleased. 'I should love to put on skis again.'

The mood was only momentary. An hour or so later the full

terms of the armistice which Badoglio had signed with the Allies were announced on the wireless. It was a Berlin transmission repeating a news item which had been broadcast by Algiers Radio.

'It is officially announced,' Mussolini heard, 'that one of the conditions of the armistice is that Mussolini shall be handed over to the Allies.'

At three o'clock the following morning Private Grevetto handed Lieutenant Faiola a letter which Mussolini had asked him to deliver.

In the few days that you have been with me [Faiola read], I have realized that you are a true friend. You are a soldier, and know better than I what it means to fall into the hands of the enemy. I learned from the Berlin radio that one of the armistice terms speaks of handing me over alive to the English. I shall never submit to such a humiliation, and I ask you to let me have your revolver.

Faiola jumped out of bed and rushed to Mussolini's room, where he found his prisoner sitting on the bed, 'awkwardly waving a Gillette razor-blade, as if he were trying to slit the veins of his wrist'.

According to Mussolini's own account, Faiola, 'after removing any remaining metal or other sharp objects' from the room, including all the razor-blades, repeated what he had promised previously; 'I was taken prisoner at Tobruk, where I was badly wounded. I witnessed the British cruelty to Italians and I shall never hand an Italian over to the English.' Then he burst into tears. But it was not only, as he later confessed, the fear that he would be ordered to hand Mussolini over to the English that distressed Faiola. A more urgent fear was that the Germans would make it impossible for him to do so; for in that event, so he said, his instructions were categoric. 'The Germans,' he had been ordered, 'must not take Mussolini alive.'

7

The Rescue from Gran Sasso

12 SEPTEMBER 1943

*I knew that my friend Adolf Hitler would not
desert me.*

I

On the afternoon of 26 July Otto Skorzeny, a young captain in the
Friedenthal Special Formation of the Waffen S S, was sitting in the
Hotel Eden in Berlin drinking coffee with an old friend from
Vienna. Without understanding why, he was conscious of a
vague feeling of apprehension.

He decided to telephone his office, and was immediately glad
that he had done so. His secretary had been trying to find him for
two hours; he was urgently wanted at the Führer's Headquarters;
a plane would be waiting for him at five o'clock at the Tempelhof
airfield.

'Radl must go to my room at once,' Skorzeny said, 'pack a uniform and linen and go straight to the airfield.'

Obersturmführer Karl Radl, his second-in-command, was
waiting there when Skorzeny arrived. What was it all about?
Skorzeny asked him. But Radl had no idea either.

As they walked on to the tarmac a Junkers 52 came down the
runway, and a few minutes later Skorzeny was flying over Berlin
with a glass of brandy in his hand. Three hours later the Junkers
came in to land on an airfield at the edge of a lake near Lotzen in
East Prussia. A Mercedes was waiting for him, and he was driven
through the forest in the gathering darkness. The car slowed down
at a barrier, and Skorzeny's papers were inspected. The barrier
was raised, and the car drove on through a birch-wood to another
barrier, where his papers were inspected again. Once more the car
moved on and entered now an enclosure surrounded by barbed
wire where sheds and huts covered with grass and camouflage

nets stood in muddled confusion at the side of the winding tracks.

Skorzeny was taken to a wooden building and shown into an ante-room, comfortably furnished with a Boucle carpet on the floor. There were five other officers in the room, and a Waffen S S captain introduced him to each of them in turn. He was nervous and did not listen to the names, and when the captain had gone he lit a cigarette. After a few moments the captain came back again and said, 'I'll take you to the Führer, gentlemen. You'll be introduced and must tell him of your military careers. He may have some questions to ask you. Please come this way.'

Skorzeny put his cigarette out and began to tremble as he followed the others through another and larger ante-room into a room where there was a massive table covered with maps. In his excitement his eyes picked out details which seemed curiously vivid: a picture by Dürer in a silver frame, bright curtains at the windows, a row of coloured pencils lying exactly parallel on a writing table.

A door opened, and the Führer came in. The officers clicked their heels. The Führer gave the Nazi salute and came slowly towards them. He was wearing a white shirt and black tie and the Iron Cross First Class on the field-grey coat of his uniform. The officers were introduced to him in turn. He asked each a question and then moved on to the next. Having spoken to Skorzeny, who, as the junior of the five, was on the left of the line, he stepped back and said suddenly, 'Which of you knows Italy?'

Skorzeny was the only one to reply. He had been to Naples twice, he said.

'What do you think of Italy?'

The officers hesitated before making the conventional replies which such a question was likely to evoke. In the mumble of uncertain voices talking about the Axis and Fascism, Skorzeny's voice sounded sharp and definite.

'I am Austrian, my Führer,' he said dramatically.

Hitler looked at him as the other voices fell into silence.

'The other gentlemen may go,' he announced at length. 'I want you to stay, Captain Skorzeny.'

When they were alone the Führer began to talk with that growing animation rising to excitement which the sound of his own voice always aroused in him.

'I have a very important task for you,' he began. 'Mussolini, my friend and our loyal comrade-in-arms, was betrayed yesterday by his King and arrested by his own countrymen. I cannot and will not fail Italy's greatest son in his hour of need. To me the Duce is the incarnation of the ancient grandeur of Rome. Italy under the new Government will desert us. I will keep faith with my old ally and dear friend. He must be rescued promptly.'

There seemed so real a warmth and so sincere a sympathy in Hitler's tone, Skorzeny said afterwards, that he was both disconcerted and moved. And when the Führer began to give him his instructions, he found his words and manner so convincing that he did not doubt for a moment that he would succeed in his mission.

'I fully understand, my Führer,' he said, as intense and emotional as Hitler himself. 'I will do my best.'

Not once during the interview had Hitler's eyes moved from his face. As he left the room he turned at the door to salute, and Hitler was still watching him. He felt dizzy and for a long time afterwards he had difficulty in collecting his thoughts.

He had not recovered from the effect of Hitler's hypnotic presence when he was called into another room to discuss the details of his assignment with General Student and Reichsführer Himmler. Himmler was irritable and on edge. He was sure that the defection of the Badoglio Government was only a matter of time. Italian representatives were already in Portugal attempting to negotiate a separate peace. He quickly recited a list of Italians, giving his views on their reliability. When Skorzeny took out his pen to make a note of the names, most of which he had never heard before, Himmler turned on him furiously. 'You must be mad to put anything on paper!' he shouted. 'This is top secret. You must remember the names.' Not even Field-Marshal Kesselring, the Commander-in-Chief in Italy, nor the German Ambassador knew anything of the Führer's plan.

Later Himmler again rounded on him angrily when he saw him smoking. 'These eternal weeds!' he said, glaring at Skorzeny through the thick lenses of his rimless spectacles. 'Can't you do anything without a cigarette in your mouth? I can see you're not at all the sort of man we need for this job.'

General Student was more friendly. When Himmler had gone

they made their plans. Skorzeny would fly to Rome as Student's *aide-de-camp* at eight o'clock the next morning. At the same time fifty men of Skorzeny's unit were to fly from Berlin to the South of France and then on to Rome to join the 1st Parachute Division which was also to be sent to Italy.

It was already midnight. The next few hours Skorzeny spent preparing lists of equipment, explosives, and weapons, wireless equipment, medical supplies, and civilian disguises – even priests' cassocks and black hair dye; choosing the officers who were to go with him; making telephone calls to Berlin; writing messages for the teletypist. Then he tried to sleep, but he could not. At six o'clock he got up and made his will.

That evening in the uniform of an officer of the Parachute Corps he was dining at Field-Marshal Kesselring's villa as Frascati. The conversation was mainly concerned with the arrest of the Duce. An officer said that he had asked an important Italian officer if he knew where the Duce was, but the Italian had replied that he did not know and that none of the other generals knew either.

'I should doubt whether that can be true,' Skorzeny said, hoping that one of the other officers might be provoked into betraying a confidence.

'I believe it absolutely,' Kesselring said quickly, annoyed by the imputation to the honour of professional officers who were his colleagues and allies. 'I have no reason to doubt the word of honour to an Italian officer, and it would be as well for you to feel the same, Captain.'

Kesselring himself had asked Crown Prince Umberto where the Duce was, he said. Umberto had replied that he had no idea Mussolini had vanished.

There were rumours, of course, Skorzeny soon discovered. It was widely believed that the Duce had had a stroke and was closely guarded in a sanatorium in the north. He was also reported to have committed suicide and to have escaped to fight with the Blackshirt brigade at the front. It was even said that he had been flown to Spain. Each rumour contradicted the last, and for days Skorzeny remained in ignorance of the truth and began to doubt that he would ever find it. In Berlin astrologers were consulted, and in Rome agents of *Amt* VI of the Security Service were told to do their utmost to find the Duce. There was a brief hope when the Police Attaché at the German Embassy was told by an officer of the *carabinieri* that Mussolini had been taken from the Villa Savoia in an ambulance and that on 25 July, at least, he was in a *carabinieri* barracks. But it was now well on into August and, so far as Skorzeny could discover, Mussolini was no longer there.

And then at last in a restaurant in Rome, Skorzeny received by chance his first real clue. A fellow-customer of the restaurant, who paid frequent business trips to Terracina on the Gulf of Gaeta, told him an interesting story. The maid of a man he knew at Terracina had a lover in the *carabinieri* who was stationed on the island of Ponza. The *carabiniere* who did not get much time off to visit the mainland, wrote often to his mistress. In one of his letters he had mentioned the presence of 'a very important prisoner' on the island.

It was later confirmed by an Italian naval officer that the prisoner was, in fact, Mussolini. But by this time the Duce had already been moved. A few days later, though, Skorzeny had discovered where the new hiding-place was. A German liaison officer with the Italian Navy in Sardinia had reported the presence of a mysterious prisoner on the island of Maddalena. Skorzeny decided to go there immediately, taking with him one of his officers, Lieutenant Warger, whose Italian was fluent. Warger was ordered to frequent the dockside taverns in the guise of a heavy-drinking German sailor. As soon as he heard Mussolini's name mentioned he was to say the Duce was dead. If he were to be contradicted, he must bet on it.

One evening a market-gardener, who had mentioned Mussolini's name, accepted the bet and to prove that he had won it he took Warger to a house adjoining the Villa Weber and pointed with satisfaction to the huddled figure of a man sitting alone on the terrace. It was not, however, until Skorzeny had paid a second visit to the Führer's headquarters that the German Command was persuaded that the man Warger had seen was, in fact, Mussolini. Admiral Canaris had reported that the Duce was held prisoner on a small island near Elba and orders had already arrived for a parachute attack on the island when Skorzeny convinced Hitler that the prisoner was held a hundred miles further to the south.

'I believe you, Captain Skorzeny,' Hitler said, abruptly

standing up to shake his hand when he had finished speaking. 'You're right. I withdraw my order for the parachute attack. Have you a plan for a similar operation on Maddalena? If you have, tell us about it.'

Skorzeny propounded a plan, which was immediately accepted.

'You will succeed, Skorzeny,' Hitler said dismissively, and once more Skorzeny felt the power of the Führer's hypnotic confidence.

In less than a week the whole operation – involving the use of a flotilla of E-boats, several R- and M-boats, a company of volunteers from the S S Brigade in Corsica as well as Skorzeny's own unit – had been planned in its every detail. The attack was to be made at daybreak on 27 August. On the morning of the day before, while the German troops were actually embarking, Mussolini was flown back to the mainland, and once again the search for him began. This time, however, they had less difficulty in tracking him to his next hiding-place. The Red Cross seaplane was seen landing on the Lago di Bracciano, and a few days later Skorzeny was handed an intercepted code message intended for the Ministry of the Interior which read, 'Security measures around Gran Sasso completed.' The message was signed 'Gueli'.

The preparations for his rescue began once more. Aerial photographs were taken, and to ensure that an Intelligence report that he had received about the hotel on the Gran Sasso was correct Skorzeny arranged for a German staff surgeon to inspect it, ostensibly to inquire about its suitability for a hospital for malarial cases. The surgeon, not knowing the real purpose behind his visit, reached Aquila without difficulty, but in the valley below the Albergo-Rifugio he found the road closed and the station of the cable railway guarded by a detachment of *carabinieri*. He persuaded them to let him telephone the hotel, where an officer told him that the Campo Imperatore was now a military training area and closed to all visitors and that the hotel itself had been cleared of its guests and prepared for the reception of two hundred soldiers.

The surgeon noticed a wireless truck in the valley and a good deal of activity on the cable railway. Some Italians he spoke to later said they thought the reason for the activity might be that

Mussolini was being held prisoner at the hotel. That, of course, was only a rumour, the surgeon insisted, and he did not suppose that it was at all likely to be correct.

If he did not make haste with his plans, Skorzeny thought, the surgeon's supposition might well soon prove true. There was now not only the danger that the Duce might be moved again, but also, since the recent announcement of the armistice, the further danger that he might be handed over to the Allies and thus lost to the Germans for ever.

Skorzeny had three alternatives: a ground attack, a landing by parachute, or a landing by glider. A ground attack was ruled out because of the number of troops that would be needed. The idea of a parachute assault was also discarded because of the danger of dropping through thin air at such high altitudes and the difficulty of getting the parachutists to land on the plateau in a compact and manoeuvrable mass. A landing by glider, therefore, seemed the only workable solution. This too was dangerous because the single possible landing-ground was a small triangular field just behind the hotel. Indeed, the Chief-of-Staff to the Parachute Corps and his senior staff officer both thought that a landing on so small and unprepared a space would result in the loss of well over three-quarters of the force and that the few who survived would not be enough to complete the operation. When asked to suggest an alternative plan, however, they could not; and ultimately they were obliged to agree that gliders would have to be used. General Student decided that twelve gliders should be brought from the South of France to Rome and while Skorzeny's force landed in these, the lower station of the funicular should simultaneously be seized by a battalion of parachutists. The operation was to be carried out at dawn on 6 September.

While discussing the details of the operation with Skorzeny, his second-in-command, Karl Radl, made a suggestion which he hoped would increase the effect of surprise, an essential pre-requisite to the success of the plan. He proposed that they take with them an Italian officer, whose presence would mislead the *cara-binieri* and help to prevent them carrying out any orders they might have received to kill Mussolini rather than let him fall into German hands. The officer chosen was General Soleti. He was told by General Student that Hitler had personally requested

that he should take part in the operation in order to prevent unnecessary bloodshed. General Soleti immediately accepted the
invitation, which Skorzeny thought had greatly flattered him.

Owing to a delay in the arrival of the gliders the date fixed for
the operation had to be postponed. It was eventually fixed for two
o'clock in the afternoon of Sunday, 12 September. At one o'clock
that day the gliders of Skorzeny's force were circling above the
Pratica di Mare airfield, slowly gaining height. The weather
was perfect. Banks of white cloud hung steadily in the air at about
ten thousand feet, and when the gliders rose above them they came
into the brilliant sunshine. Inside the gliders it was insufferably
hot. Behind Skorzeny a corporal was being sick; next to him,
crouching on the narrow board that ran through the centre of the
fragile canvas-covered skeleton of the craft, General Soleti looked
anxious and ill. A few minutes before two o'clock Skorzeny,
looking through a hole he had cut in the canvas of the glider, saw
beyond the edge of a cloud below him the roof of the hotel.

'Helmets on!' he shouted, and then; 'Slip the tow ropes!'

The gliders fell towards the earth in a sudden silence. Both the
pilot and Skorzeny could see the triangular space behind the
Albergo-Rifugio, but as they dropped down towards it they saw
that it was not the flat ground that they had supposed but a very
steep hillside. A landing there was impossible. They would
have to crash-land on the rough ground in front of the hotel.

2

Hearing the roar of the aircraft Mussolini, sitting with his arms
folded by the open window of his sitting-room, looked up into
the cloud-filled sky and saw the gliders swooping down on to the
rock immediately in front of the hotel. As the nearest glider came
to ground with a crash of tearing canvas and splintering wood, he
saw several men fall out of the wrecked fuselage, pick themselves
up, and run towards him. At first, although they were less than
thirty yards from the hotel door, he could not see who they were;
but then he saw that one of them was an Italian officer, who was
shouting at the top of his voice to the stupefied *carabinieri*, 'Don't
shoot! Don't shoot!'

'Don't fire!' Mussolini himself shouted through the open

window. 'There's an Italian general there. Everything's all right!'

'Excellency! Excellency!' Lieutenant Faiola called out breathlessly as he ran up the stairs to Mussolini's room. 'Excellency! The Germans!'

He burst into the room, and at the sight of his prisoner leaning out of the open window he screamed, close to hysteria, 'Shut the window and don't move.'

Below them Skorzeny had dashed across the rough ground in front of the hotel and through the first open door he had seen. Kicking the chair from beneath a wireless operator, he smashed the set and looked around for a way out of the room into the hotel. But there was none. He ran outside again and raced along the side of the building until he came to a terrace about nine feet above the ground. Jumping on to the back of one of his men he leapt to the top of the terrace and looked anxiously upwards at the curved wall of the building with its rows of small square windows. At one of these on the first floor he saw the face of Mussolini gazing down towards him.

'Get away from the window,' he shouted and ran on into the entrance hall of the hotel. 'Here,' one of the staff said later, 'all was confusion. No one thought of giving orders.' The place was filled with *carabinieri*, who had left their machine-gun posts at the first sight of the German commandos and rushed for shelter, many of them dropping their rifles and grenades on the way. With unnecessary shouts of '*Mani in alto!*' Skorzeny's men pushed their way into the building while Skorzeny himself beat a path through the *carabinieri* with the butt end of his machine-pistol to reach the staircase, which he ran up three steps at a time. At the top he turned left along a corridor and threw open the door of the room he hoped was the one he wanted.

Facing him, in the middle of the room, stood Mussolini. With him was Lieutenant Faiola and another Italian officer, who were both taken out into the corridor by a young *Untersturmführer*. Below the windows outside, the other gliders had now crashed on to the rock and more SS men were streaming across the rocks towards the hotel. So far not a shot had been fired.

Skorzeny put his head out into the corridor and shouted for the officer in command of the hotel. An Italian colonel appeared and was summoned to surrender. He asked for time to consider the summons, and Skorzeny gave him a minute. In less time than that he returned with a goblet of red wine. Bowing politely he held it out towards Skorzeny and said solemnly, 'To the victor.'

In the somewhat formal atmosphere that had now been created Skorzeny turned round to introduce himself to Mussolini.

'Duce!' he announced, standing stiffly to attention. 'The Führer has sent me! You are free!' He was sweating heavily, Mussolini noticed, and 'seemed deeply moved'.

The Duce put out his arms and for a moment held Skorzeny to his breast.

'I knew,' he said, 'that my friend Adolf Hitler would not desert me.'

He spoke in a clear voice, but Skorzeny was shocked by his appearance. He wore a shabby, badly fitting suit and looked very ill. He was unshaven and seemed to have aged many years since Skorzeny had last seen him, standing proudly on the balcony of Palazzo Venezia. Looking down now on the stubbly hairs of his head, the Austrian was reminded of its former smooth and massive grandeur. Only his large, dark eyes seemed to be those of a man of power and influence. General Spoleti said afterwards that he looked haggard and that his only wish seemed to be to return home to Rocca delle Caminate.

Skorzeny's immediate problem, however, was to get him away at all. It had been arranged that he should leave in a Heinkel from Aquila airfield, which was to be captured by paratroopers; but the wireless operator could not make contact with the Luftwaffe to call the Heinkel up from Rome. An alternative plan had been to use a lighter aircraft, which could land and take off in the valley. This aircraft had managed to land, but in doing so had damaged its landing gear so badly that it was no longer serviceable. Finally, if all else failed, it had been planned to land a Fieseler-Storch spotter plane on the plateau. Captain Gerlach, General Student's highly skilful personal pilot, had managed to bring the Storch down. He was frankly doubtful, however, that he would be able to get it up again.

As yet unaware of Gerlach's apprehension, Mussolini came out into the open air wearing a pair of heavy ski-boots. As always in the presence of Germans, he looked sternly resolute. Domenico

Antonelli, who had taken over as manager of the hotel the day before, thought that he had already reassumed the manners of a dictator. 'He moved with more determination, he spoke with confidence, he thrust out his jaw.'

He asked Gueli and Faiola to go with him. At first they both agreed, but when the time for departure came Faiola hesitantly asked if he might have a word with the Duce.

'Go on then,' Mussolini said impatiently. 'Go on! Go on!'

'Duce,' said Faiola, with obvious nervousness. 'I have a wife and child. If you don't mind I would rather stay here.'

'Very well, then, stay.'

Antonelli noticed how harsh his words were.

Outside the hotel the staff were lined up as servants once were in country-houses to bid farewell to an honoured guest. Mussolini shook hands with each one in turn, saying a few words with a dictator's condescension, at once gracious and remote. They had expected this proud and aloof courtesy from the first, but he had not previously shown it.

'Thank you very much,' he said finally and distantly to them all. 'I shall never forget you.'

He walked away to the Storch while the German soldiers, and the *carabinieri* too, stood stiffly at attention, saluting him in the Fascist manner, shouting loudly '*Duce! Duce! Duce!*'

'The captain who was to pilot me came forward,' Mussolini said when describing this dramatic moment. 'A very young man called Gerlach, an ace. Before getting into the machine I turned to wave to the group of my guards. They all seemed stunned. Many of them were sincerely disturbed. Some even had tears in their eyes.'

Gerlach was too worried to appreciate the drama. He had only managed to land on so short and roughly prepared a strip with the greatest difficulty, he insisted, and did not think he could possibly take off with a passenger. When Skorzeny said that he was coming too, Gerlach was aghast. It was quite impossible, he said. One passenger was bad enough, two would be disastrous. If the aircraft ever got into the air it would never stay there. But Skorzeny was insistent. 'If there was a disaster,' he wrote afterwards, admitting his concern for his own interest, 'all that would be left for me would be a bullet from my own revolver. Adolf Hitler would never forgive such an end to our venture. As there was no other way of getting the Duce safely to Rome it was better to share the danger with him, even though my presence added to it. If we failed, the same fate would overtake us all.'

Mussolini confessed later that he shared Gerlach's apprehension, but he did not mention it. A *carabiniere* watched him as he stooped to enter the small aircraft. He looked old and frail in a winter overcoat which was too big for him and a black, wide-brimmed felt hat pulled down low over his eyes; and the *carabiniere* felt a sudden pity for him and an admiration for his courage. Skorzeny noticed that he hesitated slightly before climbing into the rear seat and respected him for making no protest.

The Fieseler-Storch's engine roared to full power as twelve men tugged hard against its pull and then, as Gerlach dropped his hand, let go to send it hurtling over the rocky plateau. The aircraft gathered speed as it approached the end of the cleared strip, but the wheels did not leave the ground. The edge of the plateau drew closer and it seemed that the Storch would surely dive down the declivities of an approaching gully when suddenly it rose from the ground. A moment later it fell again and one of its wheels hit a rock, sending the machine toppling to the left and over the edge and down towards the valley. It fell dizzily through the thin air, and the wind roared in Mussolini's ears, as Gerlach tried to pull the Storch out of its dive and into level flight. 'It was a moment of real terror for me,' Mussolini admitted to a Swiss journalist the following year.

The *carabinieri* and S S men ran forward towards the shelf of the plateau and watched the machine falling helplessly towards the dark rocks of the valley. And then, as if from the beginning the pilot had intended this spectacular take-off, his machine came out of its dive and flew away to the south-west towards the Avezzano valley less than a hundred feet above the ground.

For some time no one in the aircraft spoke. Crouched close to Skorzeny, Mussolini looked not so much afraid as sad and troubled. As though to reassure him Skorzeny placed his hand on his shoulder, and when the Duce turned round his face was paler even than before. But after a few moments he began to speak, pointing out features of the countryside below, telling Skorzeny what had happened to him in the towns and villages over which they had passed. On the Pratica di Mare airfield Gerlach's passengers were transferred to a Heinkel, the engines of which were so loud that Mussolini could no longer make himself heard. He sat back with his eyes closed and then appeared to sleep.

It was already dark when the Heinkel came down at Aspern airfield in Vienna, and Mussolini came out of it looking exhausted. On his arrival at the Hotel Continental, where a suite had been prepared for him, Hitler telephoned to congratulate him on his escape; but he was in no mood for conversation. He thanked the Führer briefly. 'I am tired,' he said. 'Very tired. And I need to rest.'

Hitler's obvious concern for his welfare, however, and his expressions of delighted pleasure had a restorative effect and when later on Skorzeny took him a pair of pyjamas which had been provided for him by Gruppenführer Quermer, the S S chief in Vienna he refused them quite gaily. 'It's unhealthy to sleep in night clothes,' he said with a suggestively prurient smile which Skorzeny took as indicative of the 'Duce's wide experience of life'. 'I never wear anything at night and I should advise you to do the same.'

In the morning Mussolini was obviously refreshed. He had his beard and scalp shaved, and he received numerous callers. The excited congratulations, the adulatory respect, the infectious enthusiasm, affected him deeply. He spoke no longer of retirement to Rocca delle Caminate, but of the future of Fascism and of the necessity for making it a republican party.

'I made one great mistake,' he said, 'and have had to pay the price. I never understood that the Italian Royal House was my enemy and would remain so. I should have made Italy a republic after the end of the Abyssinian campaign.' Once again he seemed to Skorzeny a man of hope and of resolution.

At midday on 13 September he left Vienna for Munich, where Rachele and the children met him at Reem airport. Rachele was 'shaken by his deathly pallor'. But he walked up to her 'in his usual sprightly fashion' and when she asked him what he intended to do now he began immediately to talk of his future plans. 'I am determined not to abandon my course of action and to do what may still be possible to save the Italian people,' he said. He spoke very fast as if afraid, Rachele thought, that she would interrupt or argue with him. They left the airfield together and drove to the Karl Platz, where a suite had been prepared for him. But it was so luxurious that he refused to sleep in the bedroom and spent the night instead in the more modest room which had been given to Rachele. He agreed, however, to have a bath. He badly needed it, Rachele said. 'His socks were sticking to his feet.'

The next morning Edda came to see him. The meeting was a difficult one, for Galeazzo too was in Munich. Helped by the Germans and against the orders of Marshal Badoglio, he had left Rome with Edda and the children on 23 August. He had tried to obtain from the Germans a visa to go to Spain or South America, and after long delays was given one on condition he travelled via Munich. But the Germans, and in particular Ribbentrop, whose dislike had turned to hate, did not want him to escape them. Ciano, himself, seems not to have been aware of the extent of the feeling against him and he left for Germany without undue apprehension. Filippo Anfuso, his former Principal Private Secretary, has described how he warned Ciano not to go to Germany. Ciano broke down and wept. 'Mussolini is a great man,' he said. 'A real genius.' The son-in-law did not doubt that he would be forgiven. But on his arrival in Munich difficulties were put in the way of his continuing his journey. Both he and Edda were diligently watched and reported on by the Gestapo, whose men waited in the corridor outside Mussolini's room while the interview between the Duce and Countess Ciano was taking place.

Edda begged her father to see Galeazzo. He had a full explanation of his conduct, she said. But, persuaded by Rachele, Mussolini refused to meet his son-in-law. Later, however, he relented and said that he would grant Galeazzo a short interview in a few days' time. Nothing, though, would make his wife change her mind. 'I hate him,' she said with Romagnol passion and implacability. 'I would like to kill him.'

Before the interview between the two men took place, Mussolini was flown from Munich for a meeting with Hitler at the Führer's headquarters in East Prussia. The conversation he had with him there decided Ciano's fate for ever.

8

The Meeting at the Führer's Headquarters

15 SEPTEMBER 1943

I have come for my instructions.

The JU 52 came down on to the headquarters airfield in dazzling sunshine. As Mussolini climbed out, Hitler came towards him with tears in his eyes. They shook hands, looking at each other silently; and for a long time they stood together alone holding hands, like David and Jonathan in the wilderness of Ziph. It was obvious that Hitler at least was deeply moved.

Immediately afterwards, however, when they met in private the atmosphere was very different. Mussolini's ambitions, reawakened by the compliments and adulation in Vienna and Munich, had died away again. Hitler found him depressed and listless. The interview began, so Mussolini said later, by Hitler 'recalling him to realities', as the King had done in July.

What, Hitler asked sharply, did the Duce intend to do now? When Mussolini suggested that it might be best to retire from public life so as to avoid a civil war in Italy, Hitler said, 'Nonsense!' That was quite out of the question. It would show to the world that the Duce no longer believed in a German victory. The Duce must reconsider the question. Without a strong Fascist Government back in power in northern Italy there was no telling what might happen to the Italian people. The German armies would be compelled to govern by merciless martial law, they would have to fall back to the Po or even to the Alps, leaving the earth scorched behind them. 'Only barbaric measures,' Hitler had already decided, 'can now save Italy.' It had been suggested that a Fascist Government in Italy should be formed under the leadership of one of those Italians who had escaped to Germany – Pavolini, Farinacci, Renato Ricci, Preziosi, or even Vittorio Mussolini – but these men were not acceptable to the Führer. The *Governo Nazionale Fascista* which had been announced on the German wireless from the forest of Rastenberg on 9 September was no more than a stop-gap and would come to nothing without the Duce's leadership. The Duce, himself, must go back, place the traitors of 25 July on trial, and have them executed. He must allow Germany to occupy the north-eastern provinces of Italy, Alto Adige, Venezia Giulia, and the Trentino as a safeguard against an attack through Yugoslavia. The world must be given reaffirmation of the solidarity of the Axis. Hitler went on talking for about an hour, and Mussolini felt too tired and weak to resist him. At the end of his speech Hitler turned to the newly appointed German Ambassador, Rudolf Rahn, who was present at the interview, and ordered him peremptorily to assist in the drafting of the new Republic's Constitution. Mussolini left the Führer's room in a daze. Countess Ciano, who saw him a few days afterwards, described him as a man deprived of his will. Hitler, in telling Goebbels of his interview, did not disguise his disappointment in the Mussolini that Skorzeny had brought back from Italy, saying that he seemed a much smaller man than before.

The main cause of Hitler's disillusionment, Goebbels thought, was Mussolini's apparent lack of determination to hound the traitors of 25 July to their deaths. 'Punishment of the Fascist traitors,' Goebbels wrote, 'is indispensable to any resurgence of Fascism.' But the Duce, 'too much bound to his family', seemed unwilling to punish anybody. He seemed to blame the King for his catastrophe more than anyone else, certainly more than Ciano, a particularly hated figure at the German headquarters. When Mussolini had made reference to the fact that Ciano was after all his daughter's husband, Hitler had snapped, 'That makes his treachery all the graver. I must be very clear. The apparent condonement of treachery in Italy would have profound effects elsewhere.' This, Germany would not allow. An example of condign punishment must be given to the world.

Ciano, it was known, had been promised an interview with Mussolini on his return to Munich. 'That means this poisonous mushroom is again planted in the midst of the new Fascist Republican Party,' Goebbels commented in disgust. 'Ciano intends to write his memoirs. The Führer rightly suspects that such memoirs can only be written in a manner derogatory to us, for otherwise he could not dispose of them in the international market. There is, therefore, no thought of authorizing Ciano to leave the Reich. He will remain in our custody.'

'The Duce,' Goebbels added in another passage of his diary, 'has not drawn the conclusions from Italy's catastrophe which the Führer expected. He was naturally overjoyed to see the Führer and to be at liberty again. But the Führer expected the first thing the Duce would do would be to wreak full vengeance on his betrayers. He gave no such indication, however, which showed his real limitations. He is not a revolutionary like the Führer or Stalin. He is so bound to his own Italian people that he lacks the broad qualities of a world-wide revolutionary and insurrectionist.'

The Führer's attitude pleased Goebbels. 'We may consider him,' he wrote, 'absolutely disillusioned concerning the Duce's personality, although there was no actual quarrel.' Jealous of the Führer's former friendship with Mussolini, he had never been able to like him himself and had obviously been pleased when those Fascists who had already fled to Germany spoke to Hitler of his weakness or his lack of force as an anti-Semite. Goebbels had recognized the Duce's fall as a serious blow to German propaganda, but had soon comforted himself with the thought that he had never accorded him the Führer's fulsome admiration. Now he thought that Hitler too was disenchanted, he sat back in the chair in his office, intoning, '*Duce! Duce! Duce!*' with malicious pleasure. 'In the last analysis,' he thought, 'he is nothing but an Italian, and he can't get away from that heritage.'

And it was because he was an Italian, Mussolini said afterwards, that he accepted Hitler's terms. Cruel as they were, he believed that to refuse them would be to condemn Italy to destruction. Already Kesselring had announced that the whole of Italy behind the German front line was a war zone subject to martial law and that various acts calculated to injure the successful prosecution of the war, including the organization of industrial strikes, were capital offences. It was, Mussolini later maintained, in order to protect Italy from further enslavement by German orders such as these, and to ensure that those violently Germanophil Fascists who had fled from Italy after his arrest did not inherit his power, that he went back to Hitler and told him that he had decided to return to active political life. 'I have come,' he said bitterly, 'for my instructions.'

Hitler, taking no notice of the Duce's sad implication of pro-test, immediately gave him them. The Duce would, of course, understand that in exchange for the re-establishment of Fascism, Germany would need 'territorial security to prevent any further crisis'. The security required would involve reorganization of the whole of Alto Adige and in particular the handing over to the Third Reich of the province of Bolzano and eventually, after a plebiscite under German supervision, of the districts of Trento and Belluno. These areas would form part of the new and enlarged Austria, which was to become one of the Federated States of Great Germany like Czechoslovakia, Hungary, and Poland. Later on Italy might have to give up Dalmatia, Trieste, and Istria. As Germany was now fighting virtually alone on Italy's behalf, there would have to be reorganization too in the economic and industrial fields. Installations and industrial machinery would have to be evacuated north of the Alps, more Italian labour would have to be supplied to German farms and factories, and German reparations eventually paid. More immediately, certain Fascists would have to be removed from their offices, and, of course, the traitors of 25 July tried and executed.

As always when he spoke of his future plans to change the course of history and alter the shape of Europe, Hitler became feverishly excited and seemed to detect in the mere power of his own words a transcending significance. Mussolini listened, as he had become used to listening, making no comment of either agreement or dissent. Even when Hitler stopped, Mussolini's questions were mild to the point of diffidence.

Would it not be desirable, he wondered, to enter into negoti-ations with Russia so as to smash the Allied *bloc*? No, it would not. What about Corsica? There might be discussions about Tunis, but otherwise Italy had forfeited her claims against France. Would it not be advisable to allow Poland and Czechoslovakia the same autonomy which would be allowed to other nations of the European *bloc*? No. The only concession which Mussolini was able to obtain was freedom of action in Italian internal affairs; but even this freedom was to be carefully controlled.

He was, and he looked, a defeated figure. His clothes hung about him in folds, and his untidy collar sagged loosely from his neck. Hitler, having got his way with him, became sympathetic and insisted that he should be examined by Professor Morell, a gross and dirty quack who had once been a specialist in venereal diseases. Morell, who gave Hitler daily injections and regular doses of drugs containing a haphazard variety of narcotics, diluted poisons, stimulants, and aphrodisiacs, examined Mussolini and found him fairly healthy with slight blood-pressure, nervous exhaustion, and weak bowels. 'In fact, just about what we've all got,' Goebbels commented impatiently. But Hitler, despite his dependence on Morell, did not altogether trust him, and, professing himself dissatisfied with his diagnosis, he asked Mussolini to take Professor Zachariae, another German doctor, back to Italy with him.

Mussolini returned to Munich on 17 September. 'Physically he looks a little better,' his wife wrote in her diary. 'But there is a bitter expression in his eyes which betrays his mental torment.' As usual he did not discuss his dilemma with her, saying merely that he had spent 'three days of intensive work with Hitler'. Late on the afternoon of the next day he shut himself up in his room to prepare the speech to the Italian people which he was to broadcast over the Munich radio that evening.

'I went with him,' Rachele said, 'into the little transmission room fixed up in the Karl Platz. It may seem strange, but this was only the second time he had broadcast. In the past his speeches were always made in public, though they were relayed by radio. He was not at his best, and before he began his eyes held mine. After a pause, which it seemed would never end, he began to speak.'

His voice sounded feverish and his words were slurred, often mispronounced, and sometimes unintelligible. He told his listeners about his imprisonment and dramatic escape in a way which even a neo-Fascist admirer has felt compelled to call 'journalistic'. Then, in an attempt to recapture the powerful accents of the past, he recalled his people to their duty and enjoined them to follow him in the march to victory.

But neither Goebbels nor Hitler expected them to follow him. Italy had abdicated 'as a people and as a nation'; and although Goebbels, in contrast with other listeners, thought that the Duce had spoken 'quite coolly, realistically, and without exaggerated pathos', he had shown himself 'incapable of staging a great come-back'. In any event 'old Hindenburg was undoubtedly right when he said that even Mussolini would never be able to make anything but Italians out of the Italians.'

9

The President at Gargnano
– The First Year

Hitler and I have surrendered ourselves to our illusions like a couple of lunatics. We have only one hope left – to create a myth.

I

Mussolini remained in Germany for ten days, first in Munich, but when the air-raids became heavy he was moved fifty miles away from the town to Schloss Hirschberg, a castle at the foot of the Bavarian Alps near Garmisch. Here he planned the organization of his new Government and the reconstruction of Fascism.

By six Orders of the Day, dated from Rastenberg between 15 and 17 September 1943, the *Repubblica Sociale Italiana* had already been announced. These orders provided for the Duce's resumption of 'the supreme direction of Fascism in Italy'; for the reconstitution of the Fascist Party under its new name of '*Partito Fascista Repubblicano*'; for the restoration of the Militia; for collaboration with the Germans and for the punishment of traitors. Of the several Fascists who had fled from Badoglio's Italy only two were mentioned in these Orders – Alessandro Pavolini, a political fanatic and former secretary of the Duce's, who was made the Secretary of the new Party, which he was determined should be one of an intransigent and powerful minority; and Renato Ricci, who was appointed to command the Militia, into which, despite his determined efforts, he was never able to enlist more than a few worthwhile men. Roberto Farinacci, violently Germanophil, and Giovanni Preziosi, unshakably anti-Semitic, both of whom had been endeavouring to ingratiate themselves with the Germans at Mussolini's expense, were disappointed in their hopes of being given important office.[1] Vittorio Mussolini told his father that neither of them had hesitated to provide Hitler with their versions of the Duce's weaknesses and failings – his anti-German outbursts, his absurd tolerance towards his political enemies, his equivocal attitude towards National Socialism, above all his irresponsible views on anti-Semitism. They had spoken to the Germans, too, of his increasing lack of virility and his declining health.

It seemed, indeed, that their criticisms might be justified. It was obvious certainly to the Germans that talk as he would at this time of a new approach, fresh ideas, opportunity of learning from past mistakes, a cleansed Fascism, he spoke without inner conviction. He was tired and depressed and seemed – although better than he had been on his arrival in Vienna – still desperately ill. He was habitually nervous and on edge. He came down to work in the mornings looking as exhausted as he had done the night before. For the first time in his life he could not sleep, and on the rare occasions when he did manage to fall into a restless slumber he would wake up suddenly, the nurse who attended him says, in the agonies of cramp. 'He eats very little,' Dr Zachariae reported to Berlin. 'Cramps in his stomach prevent him from sleeping. He has very low blood-pressure, a dry skin; his abdomen has become excessively thin, and his liver is swollen.' After a careful analysis of his blood, however, Zachariae had decided that he was not affected by any syphilitic infection, although Farinacci had told Ribbentrop that the Duce was 'obviously in the tertiary stage'.

Farinacci's verdict was understandable. A sudden brief mood of high excitement would collapse without warning into a period of apparently blank despair. The report of a serious disaster on the Italian Front would seem to affect him not at all, and then a trifling irritation would throw him into a deep despondency. He would appear to be in a momentarily cheerful mood as he discussed the revival of Fascism, and then the mere sight of a German uniform would drain away his evanescent enthusiasm.

For the influence of the Germans was pervasive and inescapable, and he knew in his heart what the revival of Fascism really

---

1. They had annoyed Hitler by flying to Germany after Mussolini's arrest instead of organizing a counter-revolt which could have resulted in forcing the King to hand over command of the Armed Forces to the Germans. 'There's nothing to be done,' Hitler exclaimed in exasperation 'with these dagos!'

meant. On 27 September, accompanied by General Karl Wolff, Chief of the S S in Italy, he returned to Rocca delle Caminate, where several members of his newly formed Government came to swear allegiance to him as President. As if to emphasize the nature of the power from whom they derived their authority, these Ministers were brought to the house by Himmler's most trusted S S agent in Italy, Colonel Eugen Dollmann.

Although they did not include the extremists, Roberto Farinacci, who went sulkily back to Cremona to give his newspaper, *Regime Fascista*, a veiled anti-Mussolini bias, or Giovanni Preziosi, they were all men who were prepared to uphold the German alliance. Guido Buffarini-Guidi, who was appointed Minister of the Interior, was already well known in Fascist circles as a cunning and evasive intriguer, but his claims to office were supported by the Germans, for whom he was careful to display an obvious admiration. Another admirer of the German spirit, Fernando Mezzasoma, was given the important office of Minister of Popular Culture. A young, small, pale man, whose eyes seemed abnormally large behind the thick lenses of his spectacles, Mezzasoma was Fascism's last able recruit. He spoke of the rebirth of the Party, and its new role as a revolutionary system which was to combine totalitarianism and social radicalism, with a burning enthusiasm which Mussolini seems to have found as tiring as Pavolini's theatrical outbursts and Buffarini-Guidi's calculated demands for harsh reprisals against the enemies of the Axis. It was these three men – Pavolini, Mezzasoma, and Buffarini-Guidi – whom the Germans were relying upon to ensure that the Social Republic took the course which they wanted it to take. A fourth member of the Government, whose loyalty to the German alliance was unquestioned, was Marshal Rodolfo Graziani. 'I have never been a Fascist,' he told a German officer, 'but a soldier who has always obeyed his orders.' And although he confessed to a disappointment that Mussolini had been returned to power, his dislike of Badoglio and his contempt for the political intrigues of the Army staff were so intense that it was felt his political shortcomings could be discounted. The Government was given an aura of respectability by his appointment to it as Minister of Defence. The other Ministries were allocated to men of no remarkable talent or reputation. Antonino Tringali-Casanova became

Minister of Justice; Domenico Pellegrini of Finance; Silvio Gai of Economics; Edorado Moroni of Agriculture; Carlo Alberto Biggini of Education, and Giuseppe Peverelli of Communications. Francesco Maria Barracu was appointed *Sottosegretario alla Presidenza del Consiglio*. Mussolini, himself, took over the direction of what Foreign Affairs the Republic was entitled to have and gave the Under-Secretaryship to Count Serafino Mazzolini. Zealous, intense, and hysterical, Mazzolini, whose body was wasted by the effects of tuberculosis and diabetes, fitted well into the atmosphere of intrigue and unreality which was to characterize the Republic.

For most of its life Mussolini took pains to avoid the company of these Ministers who formed its Government, characteristically preferring to talk to men who were political outsiders. Two such men were Carlo Silvestri, a Socialist journalist, and Nicola Bombacci, a former Communist and Vice-Secretary of the Italian Socialist Party, whom he had known since 1902 when they had been schoolmasters together at Gualtieri. Although Bombacci, the friend of his youth, had become his political enemy, Mussolini had gone out of his way to help him and his family when he was out of work in 1937. It was a gesture which the impressionable Bombacci never forgot. 'I shall share his fate,' he said when asked what he intended to do if the German armies collapsed. 'I shall never forget what he did for my family when they were starving.'

Mussolini, he decided, was himself in need of help and sympathy now, and he went to stay with him at Rocca delle Caminate and listened with patience and understanding to his long complaints and diatribes against the Germans, whose influence was as pervasive here as it had been in Germany.

SS troops patrolled the grounds continually and even stood watching him balefully when he tried to recover his lost strength and fitness by chopping up wood in the garden. When, on German advice, it was decided that the headquarters of the new Government should be at Salò on Lake Garda rather than at Rome, which might have to be abandoned to the Allies, and Mussolini moved to Villa Feltrinelli in the little lakeside town of Gargnano a few miles north of Salò, German guards patrolled the grounds there too.[1]

1. It was one of the principal weaknesses of the Salò Republic that for reasons of military exigence it was established so far north. By abandoning Rome, the historical

Specially chosen from the *Volksdeutsche* and with little knowledge of German, let alone Italian, these foreign guards depressed Mussolini beyond measure. 'I don't want everyone to think I am a prisoner,' he complained angrily. But his status was almost that. 'He is fantastically guarded,' a young German officer, Fürst Urach, wrote home. 'I always sing or whistle when I cross the garden as there is an S S man with a pistol behind every tree. There are a few Italian Blackshirts there as well in order to keep up appearances.'

German soldiers followed him in lorries when he went out in his car and German agents listened in to his telephone calls, which had to be made through a German Army exchange. General Wolff, the Ambassador Rahn, the doctor Zachariae, and Colonel Dollmann, who had received personally from Himmler orders never to go far from Mussolini's side, were all regular visitors. 'Wolff and Dollmann are my jailers,' he grumbled, and whenever he looked from his window he saw a German helmet. 'They are always there,' he said, 'like the spots of the leopard.'

To his Italian visitors he was always grumbling like this; but he did not do so to Hitler. Once he wrote to him to complain of the high-handed conduct of German troops, of their arrogant occupation of north-eastern Italy, which amounted almost to annexation, and of the attitude of the German Government, which seemed to regard his own as completely servile. But he received no satisfaction and never repeated his protests so unequivocally, deriving some sort of comfort from the knowledge that he had at least once made them and frequently re-reading, with a pleasure that one of his secretaries thought pitiable, the carbon copy of the letter which he kept in a drawer of his desk.

Against the trial of the traitors of 25 July, which Hitler had imposed upon him, he made no such protest. He accepted Hitler's terms and issued orders that these men must be found and brought to trial. The world must be shown, he said, that there had been an underhand plot against him in which the King had been involved; and the world must also know that he still had the power and the relentless implacability of the Duce of Fascism. His secretaries

capital of the country, the Fascist Government lost what little prestige it could hope to have in the particular circumstances of its creation and accentuated the impression of its precariousness.

have described how, when the names of the traitors were mentioned, his face would assume the marble-like expression of the Emperor Caracalla, at once merciless and passionless. They could only guess what he was thinking. Was he hiding behind that façade of cold impassivity a shame for his weakness in not resisting Hitler's demands? Was he hiding a human concern for Edda's children, whom, until the beginning of December, the Germans still held in Munich, by implication as hostages? Was he hoping to regain his reputation for stern justice and impartiality? Did he really believe, as he told Serafino Mazzolini, that the trials were necessary for 'pure reasons of State'? Was it true, as he later told the journalist Ivanoe Fossani, that he had not wanted the trial himself, but the Party had insisted and the Germans had been determined to have it as 'it was necessary to restore faith in the alliance'.

Whatever his reasons might have been, there was no doubt that having on 24 November 1943 issued a decree establishing the special tribunal, he never wavered in his determination to abide by his promises to Hitler. The decisions of the Tribunal were 'to be guided by justice' but 'also by the highest interests of the country now at war'. Its President was to proceed 'without regard to anybody whosoever he might be'; and there was no doubt who was meant by that anonymous description.

Soon after his return to Italy Edda came to see her father. Exhausted by a long journey on a slow military train, she became almost hysterical as she begged him to save Galeazzo from the Germans. '*Non agitarsi troppo*,' Mussolini told her impatiently. 'Don't get so upset.' He advised her to go into a nursing-home; there was nothing he could do to help her. Ribbentrop had provided him with 'documentary evidence' that established fully 'Galeazzo's perfidy, particularly in regard to the English', and he could not for the sake of Italy forgive him.

He had seen Ciano, in fulfilment of the promise he had given in Munich, before coming back to Italy, and the interview had been short and painful. 'The poisonous mushroom', as Goebbels had called him, endeavoured to explain his conduct at the Grand Council meeting to the Duce, whose face took on its most granitic expression. He seemed scarcely even to hear Galeazzo's voice as he looked at him with a cold distaste, unforgiving and inexorable.

He remained standing by the fireplace when Ciano left and he did not wish him good-bye. It was as if he had already come to his decision to show that he too, like the man who had become his master, was implacable; that the betrayal of Fascism's Duce was treason and the only punishment for treason was death. 'I feel myself akin to Dante,' he had said years before, 'owing to his partisanship, his irreconcilability. He would not even forgive his enemies in Hell.'

After this interview Ciano had tried again to get away to Spain, but once more the Germans prevented him. They had, however, given him permission to return to Italy, and in the belief that he was being allowed his freedom he flew from Munich to Verona, where he was immediately arrested by a force of German and Italian police.

Having failed to break down her father's stony resolution, Edda had been to see Hitler, but he too refused to intervene to save her husband's life. She threatened to reveal things which would shock the whole world, and Hitler, so Mussolini told Mazzolini, was 'very much upset' by Edda's threats and even more by a letter which she had subsequently written to him. Certainly a request was made through the German Embassy that the trial should be postponed. But Mussolini, characterizing the role for which he had cast himself, was adamant. He would 'not delay the trial by a single day'. When the jurist Rolando Ricci, who had helped to devise the Constitution for the Social Republic, advised him against the trial, he rejected the advice with the same inflexibility; and when Edda made a passionate plea to him as her father and her children's grandfather, he replied, 'Before the supreme necessity of Rome, Roman fathers never for a moment hesitated in sacrificing their sons. Here there is neither father nor grandfather. There is only Fascism's Duce.' Edda burst into tears and ran out of the room.

At this time on the edge of a nervous breakdown, she had taken her father's advice and had gone to live in a nursing-home at Ramiola near Parma, under the name of Elsa Santos. Giovanni Dolfin, one of Mussolini's secretaries, has described her visit to Villa Feltrinelli. Dolfin had not seen her before and was impressed by her extraordinary resemblance to her father. 'She is very different from her photographs,' he wrote in his diary. 'She is exactly like her father. *E una Mussolini inconfondibile.*' They had the same eyes, the same expression, the same gestures, the same vivacity when talking. They even had the same nervous habit of suddenly throwing the head back in the middle of a sentence, and the same way of looking with an almost hypnotic intentness at the person to whom they were talking. Although she tried to disguise her agitation, Edda was close to distraction. Untidy, pale, and thin, she looked as ill as her father had done a few weeks before, and when she left Villa Feltrinelli, having failed in her mission, a servant noticed that the tears were streaming down her face. Two days later the German officer in command of the villa guards was summoned to Verona to explain why he had allowed Countess Ciano, who was known to be Mussolini's favourite child, to enter the villa.

The Germans' concern was unfounded. The preparations for Ciano's trial continued. Mussolini appointed as President of the Tribunal Aldo Vecchini, an old lawyer who shared Rolando Ricci's doubts about the validity of the evidence which could be brought against the prisoners, but was obliged to overcome them. The eight other members of the Tribunal had no doubts at all: five of them at least were devoted Fascists. Of the nineteen accused only six were present in court, the remainder – including their leader, Grandi, who had flown to Spain soon after Mussolini had been arrested – had managed to escape abroad or were successfully hidden in Italy. Those present were Emilio De Bono, Tullio Cianetti, Giovanni Marinelli, Luciano Gottardi, Carlo Pareschi, and Ciano.

The trial began at nine o'clock in the morning of Saturday, 8 January 1944 in the hall of Castelvecchio in Verona. The members of the Tribunal, all wearing black shirts, sat at a table on a dais behind which hung a black cloth on which had been embroidered the symbol of Fascism. Each of them the night before had received the anonymous present of a miniature coffin.

To their left was a bench where the six prisoners sat; to their right a table for journalists and film cameramen; in front a bench for counsel and behind this bench the public seats. Outside the rain had turned to snow, and the spectators came in from the cold in silence.

The Clerk read the indictment in an ugly nasal voice. The

prisoners were accused of 'having, on the occasion of the vote taken by the Grand Council of Fascism on 25 July 1943 in Rome, conspired among themselves and attempted to destroy the independence of the State and of having thwarted, by the encouragement of illusions of easy terms of peace, not only the moral resistance of the nation but military operations also and, by so doing, of having given aid and comfort to the enemy.'

The first of the accused called upon to answer this charge was the seventy-eight-year-old Marshal De Bono. He stood up to face the court in his military uniform, wearing all the decorations he had earned before and since the March on Rome. He had at first refused to consider himself in any danger. The King and Badoglio might have been well advised to move south to Brindisi, but he had served Mussolini faithfully for more than twenty years and no harm would come to him. He rejected with scorn the suggestions of his friends that he should go into hiding or shave off his distinctive beard. Even when he was arrested he thought the whole matter would be cleared up in a few days and did not take the opportunity to abscond which had been given him when he contracted bronchitis and was allowed to return to his country estate on parole. He arrived in Verona in his own car and told his chauffeur to wait for him as he would not be kept long. There was something, however, in the forbidding atmosphere of the courtroom that told him that he had been wrong. He had an old man's premonition of death. Suddenly in the middle of his examination he interrupted the proceedings and said impatiently, 'All this is so futile! Someone has apparently decided that I must die. I am old, very old. So you rob me of nothing. But please be quick.' He went to the bench amidst a murmur of sympathy from the public seats and sat down; and, although he had not been dismissed, neither the President of the Tribunal nor the prosecuting counsel felt able to recall him.

The Tribunal's efforts to establish 'the existence of a premeditated plot' were no more successful when the next prisoner, Carlo Pareschi, was called. Pareschi had been Minister of Agriculture and had been attending his first meeting of the Grand Council. He was a young and inexperienced man whom a journalist described as looking 'dazed by his predicament', but to the prosecuting counsel's suggestions that there had been a plot to overthrow the Duce in order to come to terms with the enemy, he replied with calm denials. 'All responsible Italians were against Mussolini,' he ended by saying bravely, 'and against the war. But amongst the members of the Grand Council there was no agreement and no plot such as you describe. It was just that the cup was full to the brim and Grandi poured in the drop that made it spill over.'

Cianetti was called next. He had withdrawn his support of Grandi's resolution immediately after he had given it, he said, and his faith in the Duce was undimmed. He gave no hint of a premeditated plot. Nor did Gottardi, the former President of the Fascist Confederation of Industrial Workers, who had voted for Grandi's resolution only because he hoped it would 'liberate the Duce from the grave responsibilities of military command when the war was taking such a bad turn'. Nor did Marinelli, who for many years had been Treasurer of the Party. He was sixty-five and very deaf – so deaf, in fact, that he had, so he maintained, only caught snatches of the speeches made at the meeting and had gained the impression that the resolution contained nothing that would harm either the Duce or Fascism, being led to suppose even that the resolution had been approved by Mussolini himself. Nor finally, when he was called, did Ciano give any hint of a conspiracy to overthrow Fascism and the Duce. 'Grandi never suggested,' Ciano explained, 'and I never imagined that the resolution would cause the fall of the régime.'

'You signed Grandi's Order of the Day,' Counsel persisted, 'before it was presented at the meeting.'

'Yes, a few hours before. But I knew – Grandi had told me – that Scorza had taken a copy of the text to the Duce. When one is plotting to overthrow someone by treason one does not as a rule forewarn him, nor does one inform him of the means that are to be employed.'

'But why didn't you personally inform your father-in-law? In view of your personal relationship with him it would seem normal.'

'Mussolini, even for me, was totally unapproachable. For six months I had been unable to see him alone.'

For the whole of that day the prisoners were examined and re-examined and their depositions read; but not once was the prosecuting counsel able to uncover even a hint of the conspiracy which it was his duty to expose. The following morning, however, when the trial was resumed a document was placed before the court which went a long way to show that the actions of the accused might not be as guileless as the prisoners had insisted they had been the day before. The document, which the President read out with a careful emphasis, was a paper written by General Count Ugo Cavallero, the former Chief of the General Staff. Cavallero had been found dead on a garden bench in the early morning of 14 September, a few hours after having had dinner at Field-Marshal Kesselring's Headquarters at Frascati. A pistol lay on the bench beside him; and although the bullet holes in the left side of his head were in a curious position for a man who had committed suicide, there now seems no reason to doubt the verdict of the German Embassy that Cavallero had shot himself. He had been arrested on Badoglio's orders on the day of the Grand Council meeting and had previously been dismissed by Mussolini in favour of Ambrosio. Neither side trusted him, and he knew that if he worked for either, the other would condemn him as a traitor. He had been involved in some indeterminate way in the plots to overthrow Mussolini, and Kesselring says that it was the thought that he might have to meet the Duce again that drove him to suicide. The document he had written was found, so the President of the Tribunal said, in Badoglio's office after the flight of the Government to Brindisi. In its detailed descriptions of the plots against the Duce, beginning as early as November 1942, it was exactly what the prosecution required. Its genuineness was accordingly doubted – and in view of its late introduction into the proceedings the scepticism was natural – although its contents have since been shown to be largely true. It revealed that the General Staff in league with the King had been seriously discussing the overthrow of Mussolini for nine months before the Grand Council meeting; and that Ambrosio and Badoglio had agreed that the Grand Council should be made the instrument of their designs, which would thus be given a clothing of constitutionality.

Accepting Cavallero's document as evidence, the members of the Tribunal felt able to agree that the prosecution's case had been made. That afternoon and the following day were spent in listening to the cautious pleas made on behalf of the prisoners by their counsel; but the result was not now – nor perhaps ever had been – in doubt. At half past one on Monday the President of the Tribunal returned to pronounce that, with the exception of Cianetti, who was sentenced to thirty years' imprisonment, all the accused were condemned to death.

Cianetti murmured, '*Grazie, grazie.*' Marinelli fainted. De Bono gave a shout of 'Long live Italy', in which Pareschi, Gottardi, and Ciano joined.

At ten o'clock that night the priest who heard confessions at the Degli Scalzi prison came to see the condemned men. The German guards would not at first let him into Ciano's cell, but after telephoning the Gestapo command he eventually obtained permission to administer the Last Sacraments to him.

Some nights before, Ciano had had a very different companion in his cell. She was a good-looking girl with blonde hair who, the Gestapo hoped, would be able to persuade the susceptible Ciano (in a moment of passion or desire) to reveal where he had hidden his diaries. This improbable and outmoded device had an unexpected result. Donna Felicita was not only unable to persuade Ciano to tell her anything but, according to Colonel Dollmann, she fell in love with him, wept bitterly when he was condemned to death, and eventually became an agent for the Allies.

For Ciano there was some comfort in his last hours. A message was smuggled through to him that his wife, helped by her lover, Marquis Emilio Pucci, had managed to escape across the border into Switzerland with some notebooks containing his later diaries concealed in a belt round her waist, leaving the earlier diaries, together with some important documents dealing with Italo-German relations, which Ciano had extracted from the files at Palazzo Chigi, in the care of one of the doctors at the Ramiola nursing-home. Edda had collected these notebooks and papers from their hiding-place in Rome and had at one time hoped that she might exchange them with the Germans for her husband's life. Negotiations were, in fact, begun with the Gestapo in Italy, but when Himmler heard about them he persuaded Hitler to put an end to them. Ciano, himself, seems never to have believed in the possibility of their success and told the priest who visited him on the night before his execution that he was convinced that the Germans would arrange in some way for him to be killed.

Having given Ciano his Last Sacraments the priest obtained permission for him to join the other condemned men in De Bono's cell. Marinelli had had a heart attack and lay on the bed while the others sat talking to the priest. 'We did not talk about the life that was past,' the priest said afterwards, 'but about the life to come, about God and the immortality of the soul. . . . It was a pleasant night, almost Socratic.' Pareschi read extracts from Plato, which the others discussed with him. Once someone mentioned Mussolini and for a moment the conversation returned to their trial. As traitors, Gottardi supposed, they would be shot in the back. 'It's too much,' De Bono suddenly exclaimed with an anger that was close to tears. 'For sixty-two years I've worn a soldier's uniform without ever bringing a stain on it.'

At dawn news came that the execution had been delayed. They had all signed an appeal for mercy the night before, which Pavolini had undertaken to hand to Mussolini, and it was expected that De Bono, at least, would be reprieved. The prisoners began to have hope again until De Bono shook his head and said, 'It's an empty hope. We have Galeazzo with us.' Pavolini, in fact, had taken care to withhold the appeal so that Mussolini, in Pavolini's own phrase, would be spared the 'necessity of confirming the death-sentence'.

At eight o'clock a German officer came to the prison to say that the 'technical difficulties' had been overcome and the executions were to take place within the hour a few miles outside Verona at Fort Procolo. The five prisoners were taken there by a car under a German escort. In an uncontrollable access of rage Ciano began to curse Mussolini to damnation, until De Bono put a hand on his shoulder and told him he should try to die in a state of forgiveness.

It was a cold morning, and De Bono rubbed his hands vigorously as he walked from the car to the row of school chairs to which he and the others were to be tied with their backs to the firing squad. Ciano, perfectly composed again now, pointed to the right-hand chair and said to him, 'That is your seat by right, Marshal.'

'On the journey we are about to take,' De Bono answered, 'I cannot believe that precedence is of any importance.'

They both asked the police officer who commanded the firing

squad if they might face the rifles; but their request was refused. Marinelli had fainted again and had to be carried to his chair; Pareschi took off his fur-lined coat and offered it to the soldier who was tying him up; Gottardi murmured to himself, perhaps in prayer. The sky was dull and overcast, and Muller the U F A camera-man doubted that his pictures would come out very well. While he was adjusting his lens, De Bono shouted, 'Long live Italy!'

'Long live Italy!' Ciano answered him.

And then the order to fire was given, and the five men were shot. At the last moment Ciano managed to struggle free of his ropes and turned to face his executioners. Their aim was bad, and Ciano was not dead when the commander of the firing squad walked up to him to put a bullet through his head. Muler's photograph was clear enough to show a face completely calm, almost serene.

'We were all swept away by the same storm,' Ciano had said to the priest. 'Let my children know I died without bitterness to anyone.'

2

Two hours later Mussolini presided over a meeting of Ministers and said to them tonelessly, 'Justice has been done.'

He had, as was usual now, spent a sleepless night. His secretary, Giovanni Dolfin, says that at one o'clock in the morning he had made a muddled telephone call to ask for news of Edda and of the condemned men in Verona. At six o'clock he telephoned General Wolff. Apparently anxious to appear calm and dispassionate, he spoke to him for an hour 'in a perfectly friendly way' and, according to both Colonel Dollmann and Möllhausen, the head of the political section at the German Embassy, he did not once 'mention the imminent tragedy'. Wolff told Möllhausen that he thought Mussolini had made the call as a 'means of getting through the critical hours and of preventing himself from weakening'.

When Dolfin had come in to tell him that the execution had been postponed, he had murmured an acknowledgement and carried on writing at his desk. The secretary was conscious of the great effort he was making to maintain a façade of indifference. An hour later he was told that the traitors had been executed, and he accepted the news in silence, trying not to betray the deep emotion which – Dolfin thought – he was obviously feeling. 'I have never been blood-thirsty,' he had said the night before with a kind of angry apology. 'So far as I am concerned Ciano has been dead for ages.' Now he said briefly and sternly that he was glad to know that his son-in-law and the others had died like good Italians and Fascists; but when he left for his office, having eaten nothing all morning, Rachele said that he was 'weeping tears of despair'. 'We will lose the sympathy of the Italian people,' he said desperately to Dolfin, the stony mask broken at last. 'They will never understand my torment.'

After the trial at Verona the changes of mood which during the last few years had been an essential trait of an increasingly unstable temperament became more sudden and pronounced than ever. On the day after the executions Mussolini said to the Minister for Foreign Affairs, 'Now that we've started rolling heads in the dust we'll carry on to the end,' and he gave to Tamburini, his Chief of Police, a list of untrustworthy Fascists who were to be arrested. A few days later, however, he had changed his mind. He cancelled the instructions he had given Tamburini and spoke instead of pardon and forgiveness. Indeed, he seemed, on occasions, to have lost altogether his wish to govern and wanted only to think of his past and of his place in history. Photographers and journalists who came to see him to prove that he was still alive, tried to indicate also that he had lost nothing of his spiritual fire; but they admitted in private that he seemed listless and defeated. He looked in much better health than he had done at the time of his rescue from the Gran Sasso; he gave brave answers to their questions and stared with familiar force into the camera's lens, but when the photograph was taken and the notebook shut he seemed to sink into lethargy. One day he asked Colonel Dollmann if it were really true that no one in Rome had moved a finger to help him after his arrest, and when Dollmann had to admit that it was so, he said with a flash of anger that he could never forgive such ingratitude. 'No man has done more for Rome,' he went on, 'since Julius Caesar. I will never go to Palazzo Venezia unless as a conqueror.' The next day his anger and claims were forgotten, and he was sunk again into lethargy.

T — K

He spent hours reading newspapers and looking eagerly for references to himself, cutting out those articles which directly concerned him, even those printed in Rome newspapers during his captivity which gave sensations and spurious descriptions of his private life and his supposed mistresses. He carefully numbered each item and annotated most of them with coloured pencils. He was constantly making excuses for his failure and the loss of the Empire. He blamed alternately the British and the Americans, the Germans and the Italians, the Freemasons, the *bourgeoisie*, the Jews, the conspirators of 25 July, above all the King. 'If the *colpo di Stato* had not taken place,' he once told a parade of Fascist soldiers in Guardia, 'I should not now be standing in a suburb of Brescia, but in a square in Cairo.'

'He thinks only of history,' his Minister for Popular Culture, Fernando Mezzasoma, wrote, 'and how he will appear in it.'

He spent hours too in lecturing and haranguing his Ministers and visitors on historical and political themes, using the grandiose gestures and phrases of his youth. Once at the Party headquarters at Villa Cavallero he got up from a conference which was boring him and walked round the room, abruptly stopping with his arms crossed on his chest to ask intently, 'What is Fascism?'

It was obviously a rhetorical question and he went on to answer it himself. 'It can be answered in only one way. Fascism is Mussolinism. Let us not delude ourselves. As a doctrine Fascism contains nothing new. It is a product of the modern crisis – the crisis of man who can no longer remain within the normal bounds of the existing laws. One could call it irrationalism.' He had not created Fascism, he maintained another day, he had merely exploited the Italians' latent and inborn Fascist tendencies. 'If this had not been so I would not have been followed for twenty years. The Italians are a most fickle people. When I am gone I am confident that the historians and the psychologists will ask how a man had the power to lead such a people for so long. If I had done nothing else this masterpiece would be enough to prevent me being swallowed up in oblivion. Others will conquer with sword and fire, perhaps, but certainly not with consent as I did. . . . When people say that we were the white guard of the *bourgeoisie* they lie shamelessly. I have promoted – and I say with a clear conscience – the progress of the workers more than anyone. . . . I have made dictatorship noble. I have not, in fact, been a dictator, because my power was no more than the will of the Italian people.'

And on he went, becoming more convoluted, more obscnre, until his hearers could not understand what he was talking about and doubted that he could himself. On another occasion, when the defence of Rome was being discussed, he gave a long dissertation upon the 'biological decadence of France'. At other times he would talk as he had done years before as a Socialist, dismissing the recent development of Fascism as a political calamity. 'We've lost completely,' he said to Nicola Bombacci, 'without the possibility of appeal. One day history will judge us and say that many buildings were built, that many bridges were thrown across many rivers; but it will be forced to conclude that as far as the spirit is concerned we were only common pawns in the recent crisis of human conscience, and that we remained pawns to the end.'

It was becoming a frequently voiced assessment. 'Hitler and I,' he admitted in one of these moments of self-analysis, 'have surrendered ourselves to our illusions like a couple of lunatics. We have only one hope left; to create a myth.' Others had not needed to do so; their work had survived. He often spoke of these men: of Frederick the Great, Napoleon, Washington, Bismarck, of his Italians – Garibaldi, Mazzini, Giolitti, and particularly of Crispi, whose career offers so many parallels with his own. He spoke frequently too of his contemporaries: of Pietro Nenni, who 'when all was said and done remained a good Italian'; of Dino Grandi, who 'despite everything' was 'the finest man Fascism produced'; of Briand, 'perhaps the only statesman who wished to create a European federation without resorting to arms'; of Eden, whom he hated; of Roosevelt, whom he despised; of Lansbury, Hoare, and Lloyd George, whom he had liked; of Stalin, whom he envied; and often of Churchill, whom he greatly admired. He was, however, sometimes unable to disguise his jealousy of Churchill's success. He 'does not have the European spirit' he once decided, 'and doesn't really understand anything except the necessity of those English. But he is the man of the moment because he hates the Germans.' Churchill's great merit, of course, was that he was not so much a politician as a buccaneer. 'He is an obdurate and obstinate old man,' he once told Mezzasoma with a respect which was almost affectionate. 'In some respects he is like my father.'

He did not always speak with so detached and tolerant an air, and occasionally the mere mention of a man's name would induce in him a sudden surge of fury. Farinacci was one of these names that he could not bear to hear discussed. 'Don't talk about him,' he once told Dollmann angrily. 'He wants to be my successor.' 'Don't mention his name,' he snapped on another occasion when the conversation turned to another Fascist whom he did not like; 'the very *sound* of it,' he added, scratching his fingers feverishly, 'makes me itch all over.' In an effort to bring Mussolini's mind to a favourite topic Mezzasoma asked him one day when he was plainly beside himself with irritation, 'And you, Duce? How about yourself?'

'I?' Mussolini said, smiling that consciously enigmatic smile which he was apt to use before delivering himself of one of his celebrated neologisms. 'I? I am not a statesman. I am more like a mad poet.'

He would have liked to have been one just as Hitler would have liked to have been a great painter – most dictators are, it seems, artists *manqués*. He would have liked to have had D'Annunzio's bizarre gifts, or Baudelaire's or Rimbaud's, and he spoke of these men with veneration, if not always with discrimination. But he was not a poet, not even in the sense that he thought he was. He wrote a great deal as he had always done. He formed a news agency *Corrispondenza Repubblicana*, which issued reams of his polemical writings; he wrote a series of autobiographical articles for the *Corriere della Sera*, which were eventually expanded into a book; he translated an Italian version of *Walküre* back into German to see how it compared with the original; he even wrote for a schoolboys' magazine. But none of these writings was the work of a mad poet.

He felt nearer to this ideal, perhaps, when he played his violin. 'It leads me to a glimpse of eternity,' he said. 'And when I play the world slips away from me.' He played without grace but with a kind of emphatic power, sometimes with a wild hysteria that suggested the agony of a great mind distraught. 'He was dictatorial even when music was concerned,' Margherita Sarfatti says, 'and had no respect for style or form. He had expression and technique, but he played everything in his own way.' Often in the evenings at

Villa Feltrinelli he would shut himself away to practise his favourite pieces by Beethoven, Wagner, Schubert, and Verdi, and sometimes he would stand alone in the garden with the pink marble walls of the villa for a backcloth playing with an abandoned force that the German guards took for genius. Once in a bombed house after an air-raid he played parts of the Beethoven Violin Concerto to some German officers, and when he had finished and they applauded him he closed his eyes as if in ecstasy.

He felt a particular need now for the sort of emotional escape that his playing gave him, for his family suffocatingly surrounded him. They were all at the villa for most of the time from the beginning of January 1944 onwards – the unpopular and arrogant Vittorio with his wife and children, Bruno's widow Gina and her children, the schoolboy Romano, his third son, and Anna Maria, his youngest daughter. Professor Zachariae lived in the house as well, together with Lieutenant Dicheroff, a twenty-two-year-old liaison officer who was there on Hitler's orders. In her autobiography Rachele describes the atmosphere as a happy one, but the Germans did not find it so. Romano was learning to play the accordion and filled the house with his strident discords; the daughters-in-law quarrelled; Vittorio induced his father to employ two of his friends as well as himself and his cousin Vito as additional and incompetent private secretaries; the grandchildren screamed and squabbled and rushed round the house shouting for 'Grandpa Duce'; while Rachele, herself, indulged her discontent by sulking silently or breaking out into torrents of recrimination or complaint. The trouble for her was that she had been told in anonymous letters that Claretta Petacci, whom she had hoped had gone from her husband's life for ever, had now come back to him and was living in a villa near the lake. She had only heard about Claretta on the night of 25 July when she had left Villa Torlonia for fear of the mob and had taken shelter in the gatekeeper's lodge, where a servant had commiserated with her about her husband's long-standing infidelity. 'I wish I had not told her,' the servant said afterwards. 'I was amazed that she did not know.'

Claretta had moved with her family from Rome on hearing of Mussolini's arrest, and on 12 August she had been arrested at the villa of her sister Miriam's husband, Marquis Boggiano, on Lake Maggiore. Together with her parents and Miriam she had been shut up in the prison of the Visconti Castle in Novara, where she had passed the time by scribbling convulsively in her diary about her sadness and her great love for Ben. 'I feel like a swallow,' she wrote one day in an entry typical of many, 'a swallow which, by mistake, has got into an attic and knocks its head against the walls in terror.' Not content with making long and romantic entries such as this in her diary, she wrote almost every day to Palazzo Venezia, hoping that by some means Mussolini might receive her letters. 'I wonder if you'll get this letter of mine,' she wrote, 'or will they read it. I don't know and I don't care if they do. Because although I used to be too shy to tell you that I loved you, today I'm telling all the world and shouting it from the roof-tops. I love you more than ever.'

She was still in prison writing with the insatiability of a grapho-mane when her lover flew back to Italy from Munich. She was determined to rejoin him. The nuns who had been looking after her smuggled a letter out of the prison to her brother, Marcello, who went to the German headquarters in Novara. The whole family was immediately released, and a few days later a German staff car took her from the hotel in Merano, where she was staying, to see Mussolini. She returned to the Hotel Parco ecstatically happy. She would be allowed to return to him, she said, and when a house had been found for her on Lake Garda she would be able to see him every day. Soon after this Buffarini-Guidi arranged for her family to move to Villa Fiordaliso in the grounds of D'Annunzio's villa, the Vittoriale, a big, mournful house which had been turned into a museum. She herself was given a sitting-room high up in a tower of the Vittoriale itself and, as an additional security against an attack by partisans, a German officer for a bodyguard. Although she wrote in gratitude of the Germans' thoughtfulness in providing her with so young and charming a guard and told her sister how much she liked him, Major Franz Spögler was not so much an escort as a spy. One of his principal duties was to send a weekly report on Claretta Petacci to the Gestapo headquarters in Vienna, where it was supposed that her influence on the Duce might not be a beneficial one.

In fact, Mussolini saw little of his mistress. Rachele's outbursts of jealous rage were becoming insufferable, and in consequence he visited Claretta less and less. Only occasionally in the evenings, when it was getting dark, did he go to the Vittoriale, but he never stayed long. He drove there in a small Fiat, leaving his official Alfa Romeo in front of the main door of his office in Villa delle Orsoline. The meetings were sad and unsatisfactory, Claretta said. The Vittoriale was damp and cold, the woods outside it full of German soldiers. There was no happiness anywhere and no seclusion. Twice he told her that he did not want to come to see her any more; but she began to cry and begged him not to abandon her, and he gave in and said that he would come again soon.

One day Rachele, unable to control her jealousy any longer exacerbated Claretta's misery by insisting that Buffarini-Guidi should take her to see her husband's mistress. Rachele arrived at the Vittoriale trembling with anger. Claretta kept her waiting and eventually came down in a dressing-gown accompanied by Major Spögler. She looked pale and ill and sat in an arm-chair twisting a scarf between her fingers and did not answer when Rachele told her to leave her husband alone. Her silence irritated Rachele, who came towards her and grabbed hold of the sleeve of her dressing-gown. At this Claretta burst out, 'The Duce loves you, signora. I have never been allowed to say a word against you.'

For a moment Rachele seemed placated, but when Claretta offered her typed copies of the letters Mussolini had written to her she flew into another rage.

'I don't want typed copies,' she shouted. 'That's not why I came.'

'Why did you come, signora?' Claretta asked her.

She did not reply for the moment. 'She stood looking at me,' Claretta said afterwards, 'her hands on her hips. Then she started to insult me. Her face got redder and redder.'

Claretta decided to ring up Mussolini.

'Ben,' she said, 'your wife is here. What shall I do?'

Rachele snatched the telephone from her hand and made her husband admit that he knew she was coming. She was angrier than ever by now. She told Claretta that she was hated by the Fascists even more than by the partisans, and twice Claretta fainted and Buffarini-Guidi had to run away to fetch some smelling-salts. When she was revived she sat in her chair crying helplessly. Rachele too, Spögler thought, was crying when she left.

With his mistress and his wife squabbling over him, his

daughters-in-law irritating him, his Ministers bothering him with details which no longer interested him, Mussolini was more and more anxious to be left alone. During the first few weeks at Gargnano he had stayed in bed until ten o'clock in the morning and had not left for his office in Villa delle Orsoline until half-past eleven or twelve. But by the spring of 1944 he was getting up earlier and earlier every day and was often in his office by eight o'clock. He stayed there until two o'clock, when he returned to Villa Feltrinelli for a light lunch, which, like all his meals, was eaten so quickly that he had often finished and left the room before the others had begun. By three he was back again in his office, or in the ill-furnished and tastelessly decorated sitting-room where he saw his visitors, and he did not go home again until eight or nine o'clock.

Although he spent so many hours at his desk, the questions which really concerned him were of a philosophical or personal nature rather than a practical one. Only occasionally did a problem of government occupy and absorb his mind, and even then it was usually one which did not appear to deserve the sudden interest which he took in it.

He was, for instance, passionate in his determination to obtain the formal recognition of the Vatican for his régime. He could not carry on, he once exclaimed in exasperation, without this recognition, although his Government's functioning was not likely to be any the more successful with it. It was a matter of personal pride, and he began to feel himself insulted by the Pope's reluctance, which became so much an obsession with him that he declared that his patience was exhausted and he would denounce the Lateran Pacts and set up a schismatic Church. He went so far as to consider the qualifications of certain politically sound priests for new bishoprics and was only dissuaded from his reckless course by the Germans, who did not want their bad relations with the Papacy made any worse than they already were.

The only other matter which excited in him, at this time, a comparable interest was his recognition of himself as a man who had never in his heart lost the Socialist principles of his youth. Although most of his Ministers privately condemned this renewed belief in authoritative Socialism as a misguided one, they could not doubt the sincerity with which he held it. It was certainly not a passing enthusiasm, but remained with him to the end. 'Social-ism,' he was fond of saying, 'is the cornerstone of the Republic.' Such pronouncements were heard with alarm by the Germans and by the new *élite* of Fascism and in particular by men such as Farinacci, Pavolini, and Buffarini-Guidi, who viewed with pro-found misgivings Mussolini's endeavours to widen the appeal of the *Partito Fascista Repubblicano* by making what they took to be servile concessions to the Left: concessions amounting almost to the abrogation of the Fascist ideal and – even more tragic to some of them – the rejection of the myth of the Duce as Superman.

The ideological pattern for the Social Republic had been set at Verona on 14 November, when the first congress of the Republi-can Fascist Party met to define the principles upon which it would govern. The proceedings were opened by the reading of a letter from the Duce in which the importance of returning to 'the origi-nal intentions of the Fascist revolution' was stressed. Indeed the *Manifesto di Verona* which was ultimately issued was largely a recapitulation of the aspirations of 1919 with the added reference, which had become almost obligatory in Fascist circles, to the 'decadence of the monarchy'. So far as Mussolini himself was concerned its most important points were those dealing with the welfare of the workers; and he refused to accept the suggestion that this aspect of Socialism was a newly discovered interest.

Any accusation, particularly in the newspapers which he still read so avidly, that Fascism had not in the past been seriously concerned with the good of the working-class and that it had been maintained in power by bourgeois capitalists, aroused in Musso-lini an anger and contempt that seemed otherwise reserved for Roosevelt, the King, and Anthony Eden. Having read one day a report of a meeting of the General Confederation of Workers in Naples where a delegate had alleged that the social laws of the Fascist régime had proved of no benefit to the workers, he im-mediately wrote a passionate reply for the *Corrispondenza Re-pubblicana* in which he listed the laws he had enacted on their behalf, the number of hospitals he had built for them, the pensions he had provided, the scales of minimum wages he had introduced. 'These charges,' he insisted, were made by 'Communists and other enemies of our country who use the workers as pawns in their devilish games.' But the 'workers themselves knew them to be false'.

'It is impossible,' he said during a subsequent discussion on the same subject, 'to corrupt the proletariat. The workers are not capable of the sort of betrayal that the bourgeois are. The bourgeois with their materialistic mentality and greed are the ruin of Italy. I am an old Socialist at heart.'

Certainly it was true that while other aspects of his Government's business received scant attention, he was determined to show that with what little power and funds it possessed the Social Republic should live up to its name. In the last month of his life, when the Gothic Line was broken and the complete overthrow of the shattered Axis and of his Government seemed certain, he was still giving his attention to such, by then irrelevant, matters as the possibility of introducing collective farming as a means of saving the small peasant and the reorganization of hospitals for impoverished victims of tuberculosis. Möllhausen told Rahn that even at this hour Mussolini – despite his detachment and his attitudinizing protestations that he and his work were already a part of history – was dominated by an ingenuous concern to leave behind him some sort of framework on which a Welfare State could be built.

But few problems concerned him as deeply as this, and for most of the time he seemed content to sit quietly reading or writing in his office, to be left alone and to become less and less the dictator and more and more the 'university professor' which the admiring Doctor Zachariae had decided he so much resembled. His office was a small stuffy room with a majolica stove disproportionately large and a desk set across the corner, and he sat there by himself for hours on end reading and writing and looking out of the window into the garden. When a secretary entered the room he would look up slowly, not troubling to remove the spectacles the necessity for which he would have strongly denied a year before; but he had no pride of that sort now. His eyelids were often swollen and inflamed and he admitted without compunction that his sight was getting worse and worse every day.

He did not trouble either to foster the impression of a great mind at work as he had done at Palazzo Venezia, where his enormous desk had sometimes been completely bare to show how his mind contained all that he needed to know and sometimes littered with documents to show how busy he was. At Villa delle Orsoline it was merely untidy. Newspaper cuttings, papers and books, jars of coloured pencils and photographs, were piled higgledy-piggledy upon it without regard to order or, more unusually, effect. A journalist once looked at the spines of the books to see what the Duce was reading. They were a characteristically disparate selection – Dostoevsky, Tolstoy, Hemingway, Plato, Sappho, Kant, Sholokov's *Quiet Flows the Don*, Nietzsche, Emil Ludwig's *Napoleon*, Sorel's *Reflexions sur la Violence*, Goethe, Schopenhauer, books about Christ, about Frederick the Great, about Beethoven – and they all had bits of paper stuck between the pages to mark a significant passage or pencilled notes scribbled in the margins. So engrossed did he become on occasions that visitors and officials, particularly German ones, were dismissed with an impatient order to go and see Graziani or the Minister of Popular Culture or his Principal Private Secretary. 'Mussolini tends to withdraw from all questions of Government,' the young German officer Fürst Urach wrote home. 'If a German General comes to him with some request he says, "Oh, do talk to Graziani." If Leyers or some economic expert comes he says, "Oh, do see my Economics Minister, won't you?"' When one visitor, more importunate than the rest, insisted that the Duce's decision was vital, Mussolini replied that if the decision really were a vital one he could not possibly make it. The Germans must: he himself was merely Mayor of Gargnano.

But however vindictively he spoke against the Germans, those 'criminals by birth', as he referred to them on one occasion, those 'barbaric vandals, cruel, unjust, violent, and rapacious', as he called them on another, he could not escape from the spell of their leader.

On 21 April 1944 he went to Germany to see him. Hitler received him warmly at Salzburg, and Mussolini assured him more than once of his unshadowed belief in an ultimate German victory. The atmosphere was friendly and comforting, and encouraged by that and by the support of Graziani and Mazzolini, who had come to Germany with him, and of Filippo Anfuso, his new Ambassador in Berlin, Mussolini went so far as to protest against the German occupation of Alto Adige and Trieste, which he had mentioned in his letters, and to call Hitler's attention to the ill-treatment of Italian workers in Germany. Hitler seemed sympathetic and said that he would see what could be done. Little was done, however, and three months later, when Mussolini went to see Hitler again, the atmosphere was very different and at the beginning seemed unaccountably tense. Hitler came towards him, limping across the station platform, looking very pale. He held his right arm stiffly against his chest and offered Mussolini his left hand. He had had a slight accident, he apologized. Later on he took Mussolini to the still smoking ruins of the hut where Colonel Graf Claus von Stauffenberg's bomb had just exploded, killing four men. Stauffenberg had brought the bomb into the conference room inside his brief-case, which he had placed under the table where the maps were spread out in front of the Führer, but finding the brief-case in his way an operations officer had pushed it away from Hitler with his foot. Providence had saved him once again, Hitler said, and had shown him that he was destined to triumph over his enemies. 'I am absolutely of your opinion,' Mussolini politely replied, 'this was a sign from Heaven.' The Führer seemed quite calm, Mussolini thought, but he was much quieter than usual, and when the conference with the Duce was over he sat down next to Ribbentrop and Goering on one side of the tea-table and said nothing, abstractedly staring at the wall in front of him and swallowing from time to time one of his brightly coloured pills. For the first hour Mussolini and Graziani had to listen to the Germans arguing amongst themselves about the reasons why the war had not yet been won and to Goering grumbling at Keitel and making threatening gestures at the Foreign Minister with his baton. A reference was made to Roehm and the purge of 1934 and at this Hitler suddenly jumped to his feet and began to speak, insisting that Providence by intervening to save him from death had again demonstrated that he was the Man of Destiny chosen to save Europe and the World. It was his duty to spare no one in pursuit of his revenge. He went on in this vein for half an hour, while the Germans fell into silence and Mussolini gazed at him as if mesmerized, looking appalled by the shouted threats and hysterics. At last the stewards came in with the tea, and the Führer lapsed once more into the silent reverie from which the mention of Roehm had roused him.

Mussolini seemed deeply shocked by Hitler's behaviour, and when he said good-bye on his return to Italy he did not respond to Hitler's emotional words as once he might have done. Undeterred by the Duce's withdrawn coolness, however, Hitler prolonged the farewell and stood holding his hand and staring into his eyes. He looked, Rahn told Möllhausen when they got back to Lake Garda, like a bemused lover and everyone was thoroughly embarrassed. ' I know I can count on you,' Hitler had said emotionally. 'Believe me, you are the finest, indeed perhaps the only, friend I have in the world.' As soon as the Duce had gone, Hitler gave orders that an air-raid shelter should be built in the grounds of Villa Feltrinelli, but Mussolini only visited it once and then merely to congratulate the workmen who had built it.

The meeting between the two men had been valueless. Mussolini had repeated none of the protests he had found the courage to mention in April and he returned to Italy gloomy and silent. People had become used to him coming back from Germany infused by Hitler's confidence and spirit, but this time if there was a change in him it was for the worse. He had been given some statistics by an Embassy official concerning the Italians in Germany and they had appalled him.[1]

He returned to the inconsequential routine of his work with even less energy and enthusiasm than before. Earlier in that summer he had played an occasional game of tennis, but his opponents always let him win and he became bored with the game and confined his exercise to riding a bicycle round the shores of the lake, and to walking in the woods either alone or with Romano, but followed always by his German guards. He also gave up the German lessons which he had previously been having three times a week; he could always make himself understood, and the expert fluency which he had hoped to achieve seemed no longer necessary. He left for the office earlier than ever now, sometimes before eight o'clock, in order to escape from the squabbling household, and returned home late to spend the evening, whenever he could, reading alone in his room or sitting outside in a garden chair with his hands clasped behind his head staring out over the lake until the sun went down.

1. Salvatorelli and Mira say that in all 700,000 Italian soldiers were sent to Germany during the war for various non-combatant duties and that 30,000 of them died.

He hated the twilight. As soon as it grew dark, he went indoors and switched on the light in his room. One evening the current had failed and Quinto Navarra, who had returned to Mussolini's service, brought in a candle. 'But he couldn't stand its low light,' Navarra said, 'so he went out into the garden until the electric light came on again, and stood by the lake throwing stones into the water.'

Either his Italian physician or Professor Zachariae called on him every morning to satisfy themselves that the diet they had recommended him to follow was having the required effect. He was excessively pale, Zachariae noticed, and his dark eyes were on occasions almost feverish as they gazed out of a head that seemed curiously gaunt. He had no more than a cup of tea for breakfast, a very light lunch, and dinner. He never drank milk although in the past he had had as many as six pints a day. The plain uniform of the Fascist Militia, which he wore habitually, though usually well pressed seemed to hang about him, and the black collars of his shirts were much too big, revealing his formerly massive neck as lined and wrinkled like the neck of a tortoise. He took care to see that his skull was always well shaved and twice a month a girl came from Gardone to manicure his nails, but these were his only concessions to a personal vanity which had once been compulsive. 'Only rarely,' Navarra said, 'was he in a good humour, and these rare moments were always followed by long, black hours of sadness.'

The month after his visit to Hitler in Prussia he decided to make a tour of inspection of the front. Encouraged by the regimented cheers that greeted him he spent five days touring the lines, giving advice to the generals which they did not take and suggesting counter-offensives which were obviously impractical. Kesselring listened politely, but to Mussolini's annoyance made it clear that his suggestions were not considered of undue importance. 'That Kesselring,' Mussolini had already decided crossly, 'is not worth a fig.'

The cheers which had greeted him, however, from both Italian and German troops, had an invigoratingly restorative effect. He returned to Gargnano with new confidence and hope and told Rachele over and over again how the soldiers had displayed their spontaneous affection. The Germans in particular, he said, had 'gone wild with excitement and' – a seemingly incompatible reaction – 'stiffened to attention in the cramped space of their dugouts.' But the mood did not last. Within a week he had relapsed into his former despondency.

In June Otto Skorzeny went to visit him and found him lethargic and pessimistic. 'Mussolini was really quiet,' Colonel Skorzeny says, 'and he seemed to me to have resigned completely. He was not any more the strong chief directing his Ministers, but he let them go their own way. . . . He seemed to be a philosopher and no longer the chief of a Government. He talked to me about German history, with which he was very familiar, and about the philosophical basis of Fascism and how it would have to be changed in the future. He tried not to show his pessimism to his family.' But he did not succeed.

'As the days passed he became more thoughtful than ever,' Rachele said. 'I could tell by the way he talked from time to time that the deadly struggle between Italians behind the lines was a constant torment to him. Even at meals he sat gloomy and distraught. He would sometimes listen to me in silence and then ask suddenly, "What did you say?"'

There was no doubt that this struggle, to which Rachele referred 'as a constant torment', had by the end of 1944 begun to assume the proportions of a civil war.

I have decided that the Party must no longer
remain a political organization but must
become exclusively military.

Long before the Social Republic came into existence the plans for organized resistance to the Germans were being made. By the end of 1943 clandestine Committees of National Liberation had been established in most of the larger towns in northern Italy, and bands of partisans had been formed. Composed not only of brave and selfless anti-Fascists, but of deserters from the Italian Army, which had virtually disintegrated after the armistice, even of professional criminals and adventurers, of self-styled anti-Fascists more interested in settling personal grudges than in helping to drive out the Germans, some of these bands were at first little better than the 'groups of ruffians' which Mussolini was later to call them. Soon, however, their character changed. They were joined by many more sincere enemies of Fascism, by genuine patriots who saw that in the defeat of Germany lay the only hope of their country's future, and by regular officers who considered that the army of the Social Republic which Graziani was trying hard to create would never be more than a German satellite or even a police force for the coercive imposition of anti-Royalist and Fascist measures.[1] These officers gave to many partisan brigades an aura of respectability, and one of them, General Raffaele Cadorna, the son of Marshal Count Luigi Cadorna, a former Commander-

1. Graziani's difficulties were increased by the Germans' attempts to hamper the creation of an independent Italian army which they could never bring themselves to trust, and by their encouragement of the formation of several almost autonomous units such as the Decima Mas which did not come directly under his control and of various independent armed police forces which served the same purpose of 'divide and rule'. When it was decided that four divisions of Italian troops should be formed, arrangements were made for them to be equipped and trained in Germany. Hitler never made any secret of the fact that he thought that Italy's contribution to the manpower of the Axis should be in labourers rather than in soldiers.

in-Chief of the Italian Army, ultimately became their leader. But neither they nor the other unselfish patriots who joined the partisan movement were able to exercise over it an overriding control.

In November 1943 a meeting was held at Monchiero in Piedmont which, typical of many others held that winter, revealed the main direction that many partisan activities were to take. At the meeting, which was conducted by Luigi Longo, subsequently to become deputy leader of the Italian Communist Party, it was decided that the most effective way of increasing the power and influence of their organization – the Volunteer Freedom Corps – would be by inciting the Germans and Fascists to take reprisals against the Italian people. German soldiers and Fascist officials were, therefore, to be assassinated in order to provoke retaliation which would in its turn provoke hatred. For the same reason bridges and railway lines, electricity and telephone cables, must be blown up whether or not they were of strategic importance.

From the first Communist influence in most partisan brigades was strong. In many of them it was dominating. Some bands were composed entirely of Communists and were led by Party members with political commissars on the Soviet model to ensure that they did not operate on deviationary lines. Other bands, although only a few of their number were Communists, were eventually obliged to accept the appointment of a political commissar. These commissars 'were proposed and introduced by Communists,' Luigi Longo said afterwards, 'and were at first opposed by all the others. They were not understood save in the manner described by Fascist lies and libels. The military officers saw in them an intolerable outrage to their own dignity and prestige; the politicians recognized them as a Communist innovation, designed to secure control of the bands and to exploit them for Party purposes. . . . But we strove to the bitter end to support the institution of political commissars. Gradually they were introduced into nearly all the formations, even if under other names such as that of representatives of the Committee of National Liberation or of civilian delegates, but always with their duties recommended by us.' Even in some of those bands which professed themselves to be Socialist and called themselves Matteotti Brigades there were Communist members, some of whom went so far as to advocate secretly that the arms and supplies which the Allies parachuted to them should not all be used against the Germans but that some of them at least should be concealed until the war was over and the workers' revolution began.

During the winter of 1943–4 the partisans began their work as *agents provocateurs*. At first few incidents occurred. There were some isolated murders, acts of sabotage, and reprisal; but the Fascist régime in German-occupied Italy did not seem yet in any real danger from its political enemies. On 23 March, the anniversary of the Foundation of Fascism, however, the Rome Committee of National Liberation arranged for a massacre which was to act as an inspiration to the committees of the north. On the afternoon of that day a rubbish cart filled with explosives was blown up in Via Rasella beside a lorry taking a squad of German soldiers to their quarters. Thirty-three Germans and a few Italian passers-by were killed. As a reprisal 335 hostages were shot the following day on the Ardea road and buried in the Fosse Ardeatine caves.

The news of this outrage spread rapidly in Italy, and during that spring and early summer the activities of the partisans in the north were greatly increased and reprisals became more and more savage. In May nearly a hundred miners were shot by the Germans in a single small village; a few weeks later the execution of 400 prisoners and 110 deserters was announced; shortly afterwards 2,000 men were forcibly deported to Germany for blowing up a bridge over a river in Piedmont. The acts of sabotage increased after the collapse of the Gustave Line and the fall of Cassino until, at the time Rome was liberated in June 1944, they were of almost daily occurrence. On 21 June Mussolini declared that the Fascist Party could no longer remain a political one, but must become '*un organismo di tipo eclusivamente militare*'. From 1 July all members between the ages of nineteen and sixty who did not belong to the Armed Forces of the Republic were to become armed Blackshirts in order to safeguard 'public order and the peaceful life of the citizens against the cut-throats and those who were collaborating with the enemy'.

It was interpreted as a declaration of civil war. The outrages which these *Brigate Nere* provoked and the reprisals which they carried out against the partisans, although not on so extensive a scale, were often as violent as those taken by the Germans. And although it was the German SS who took reprisals in the grand manner, massacring the entire village of Sant' Anna di Stazzema in August 1944 and between 28 and 30 September killing almost 700 people at Marzabotto south of Bologna, the *Brigate Nere* were guilty of many less-well-known acts of savage inhumanity. Composed for the most part of worse riff-raff than even the most unruly of the partisan brigades, they performed their duties with a high-handed insolence and cruelty, torturing prisoners without compunction as Blackshirts themselves were sometimes tortured by the Communist partisans who captured them. Even when the Germans managed to rally north of Florence and settled down for the winter along the Gothic Line from Rimini to Spezia, the violence behind the German lines was only slightly abated.

Mussolini observed the increased savagery of Fascists and anti-Fascists alike with gloomy concern, occasionally giving way to outbursts of anger in which he would insist that 'the days for mercy are past'. But despite these flashes of exasperation and despite his call for more *Brigate Nere*, in the end he was forced to come to the belief that the only hope for the Republic was an attitude of conciliation. He instructed the Prefect of Turin to meet General Operti, a former quartermaster-general of the Italian IV Army and now a leading partisan leader, and to try to negotiate an amnesty with him. The negotiations dragged on for some time, but in the end only fifty-seven partisan officers, who had already been arrested by the Fascist authorities, accepted the terms of surrender. Pavolini, Farinacci, and Buffarini-Guidi were constantly complaining of Mussolini's unrealistic belief in the possibility of a reconciliation between Fascist and anti-Fascist and of his refusal, when the time came for a final decision, to endorse the stern measures which they proposed and to which earlier he had himself agreed. He had issued a decree on 25 April 1944 providing that the death penalty should be inflicted on all partisans arrested after that date, but he granted at the same time a free pardon to any who surrendered within a month and was afterwards easily persuaded to grant pardons in other cases. Sometimes he would make a show of harshness, but a day later he would relent and become forgiving again. Giovanni Dolfin recorded in his diary the many occasions upon which he intervened to save the life of a man condemned to death. Known Communists he could not forgive, particularly those acting under Tito's orders in Venezia Giulia, and many of these were executed as traitors, but when once a letter containing the names of the leaders of various illicit non-Communist political parties came into his hands, he did no more than make threats which no one took seriously and which he himself had forgotten the following day. One of the names in this intercepted letter was Ferruccio Parri, leader of the left-wing *Partito d'Azione*, against whom Mussolini's Minister of Justice had given repeated warnings. Mussolini, however, refused to order Parri's arrest, believing him to be an 'honest man at heart', and the Minister exclaimed in exasperation to Carlo Silvestri, 'How many times have I done my best to save him!' 'He refuses to save himself,' Farinacci said on a different occasion. 'He can only succeed by ruthlessness, not by conciliation.'

In his efforts to win over the people of the north by the socialization of industry he was no more successful. The laws which brought about his policy of Socialism and which attempted to solve the Republic's economic problems would, he felt sure, ensure the support of the northern workers. And when in early March the Rome Committee of National Liberation ordered a general strike throughout the territories of the Social Republic he did not consider the danger a great one. Certainly it was not the general strike that the Rome Communists had wanted and asked for, but Mezzasoma's office was obliged to admit that several factories had had to close down and that 250,000 men had come out, while the Communists claimed that more than a million men were on strike. Urged by the Germans to take drastic measures against the strikers, Mussolini refused. He had had enough of Italians fighting Italians, he said, and would not risk more of it.[1]

The danger of a full-scale civil war was not the only one caused by the existence of a Fascist Government and the division of Italy. There was the danger too that Italians might find themselves fighting their own countrymen at the front. This fear seemed constantly in Mussolini's mind. He marked on a map the movements

1. That widespread civil war might, in fact, break out in northern Italy was, so the German Embassy believed, the Allies' constant hope. The head of the political section suggested that this was the reason why the Government offices on Lake Garda were never bombed. The Americans knew exactly where each office was, he said, but only the villas occupied by the German Ambassador or by German troops were ever attacked. So long as a Fascist Government remained in power the advantages of a festering opposition to it could be reaped by the Allies.

of Italian units fighting with the Germans and repeatedly asked for information concerning units which Badoglio had made available to the Allies. There were three Italian units still fighting the Allies in Italy – the Barbarigo battalion on the Anzio front, a Blackshirt battalion fighting Tito in Croatia, and a Bersagliere battalion fighting the Slav partisans on the Carso. Another Bersagliere battalion was in action against the Germans, and Mazzolini once heard Mussolini say how pleased he was to learn from a communiqué broadcast by Bari radio that they were doing well.

'But they are Badoglio's troops!' Mazzolini exclaimed in amazement. 'They are fighting the Germans!'

'They are Italians,' Mussolini said contentedly, 'and they are fighting bravely. That is all that matters.'

Mazzolini noticed how for the rest of that day the Duce was almost happy. During the evening he seemed genuinely to believe that the war might yet be won; but two days later, in conformity with the predictable pattern of his life, he was depressed again.

The President at Gargnano – The Final Mouth

I am like the captain of a ship in a storm; the ship is broken up and I find myself in the furious ocean on a raft which it is impossible to guide or to govern.

In December 1944 Mussolini was raised to a pitch of exaltation which lasted for several days. He had gone to Milan with Wolff and Rahn for a brief visit when abruptly, and for once spontaneously, his car was surrounded by a crowd of people cheering him as vociferously as if he had just announced that the war was over. Occasionally he was cheered at Gargnano, but he had never been received like this. The crowds increased as the car drove slowly on through the streets, until even anti-Fascist observers had to admit that as many as 40,000 people were excitedly shouting, '*Duce! Duce! Duce!*' at the top of their voices. 'Had I not heard the frantic cheering on the radio,' Rachele said, 'I could scarcely have believed Benito's account of his experiences when he got back. It simply cannot be true that the whole country is against Fascism, or that everyone hates him.'

'In twenty years of Fascism,' he told her proudly, 'I have never had such a welcome. For some odd reason General Montagna, the Chief of Police, had not been told of my visit till the day before. The proceedings at the Lirico were broadcast so that all Italy suddenly knew of my presence. When I had finished speaking the ovation was thrilling – an absolute triumph. As for the crowds, they were like a tidal wave. It was wonderful to be among the people, standing up in the car and to hear their shouts of loyalty.'

He continued to speak of his reception for more than a week, and the Germans professed themselves astounded by it. There was no doubt, Rahn thought, that it had taken everyone completely by surprise. 'It was an astonishing ovation.' It was the more surprising because the speech which the Duce had made at the Teatro Lirico was a far from powerful one. He spoke slowly from notes which without his spectacles he had obvious difficulty in reading and promised further reforms in politics and industry. He said that it would soon no longer be necessary for workers to hold the Fascist Party ticket and that soon other political parties would be recognized. But only when he spoke of the inevitability of German victory and hinted at secret weapons of immense force did his voice catch the accents of its former power.

He had been told something of these weapons when he had visited Hitler in July, and soon after this triumphal visit to Milan he went to Germany again to receive from the Führer a report on them which drove him into a paroxysm of excitement. His train stopped outside Munich and waited in a siding for Hitler's train to come down from the north. The two men greeted each other with the warmth of their more happy days and drove away in a car to see the new weapons – 'extremely delicate machines', as Mussolini afterwards described them, 'evolved by laboratory research'. He believed without question all that the Germans told him about them.[1] They would 'amaze the whole world', he told Major Fortunato Albonetti, commander of his bodyguard, 'and would alter the course of the war within a few days'. Mussolini's excitement lasted all the way back to Gargnano, and Möllhausen said that as he was driving down the lakeside road to Villa Feltrinelli he shouted out cheerfully to a group of militiamen, 'Keep at it, lads. We've won the war.'

It was his last show of confidence. As the bitter winter turned to spring, he sank more deeply than ever into despair and relapsed again into that 'state of moral and physical collapse, absolutely devoid of energy' which Professor Zachariae had described before his final visit to Hitler. The details of government concerned him less than ever, the intrigues, the petty squabbles, and the discussions about the immediate future of Fascism, hardly at all. In the past he had occasionally made a successful protest against German demands; now he rarely did. In his first year as President

---

1. He was always wonderfully credulous about secret weapons, as he was about so many other things. When he heard that an Italian inventor was working on a 'death-ray' which would bring victory to Fascism, he was readily persuaded to invest money in its development; and as early as February 1939 he was talking of a secret weapon 'which could affect the whole course of the war'.

he had resisted strong German pressure to replace the lira by the mark as the Republic's currency; later he had also successfully resisted many demands for the dismantling of Italian industry and its transference behind the barrier of the Alps. But now his resistance was spasmodic and ineffectual, and the ultimate credit for keeping the factories out of German control must go to the combined efforts of the workers and employers themselves. For a time he refused to replace the Chief of Police, Tamburini, who had given offence to the Germans; but he did not maintain his refusal for long and allowed Buffarini-Guidi to persuade him to give way. When Count Mazzolini died of blood-poisoning following an insulin injection, and Preziosi tried behind Mussolini's back to obtain the German Embassy's support for his attempt to get the vacant appointment at the Ministry of Foreign Affairs, Mussolini said petulantly, when told of the intrigue, 'What does Preziosi want the job for anyway ? He will never have anything to do.'

'One thing is certain,' Hitler had written to him in his last New Year's letter, 'and that is that neither Fascism nor National Socialism will ever be replaced in Europe by Democracy.' Mussolini, however, no longer had patience with such claims or with the people who made them. He heard of the activities of rebel Fascists who were endeavouring to obtain German help for his overthrow and to have him replaced by a new Fascist leader whose views were sternly authoritarian and not tainted by Socialism; he heard that others were advocating a faster slide into democracy; he was told that Farinacci and Buffarini-Guidi were constantly reporting to the Germans that Mussolini had become too soft to remain even as a figurehead. But he heard these things with a calm which was close to indifference. One day Farinacci's newspaper *Regime Fascista* carried the headline, 'Duce's excessive kindness to Zaniboni', and attacked Mussolini for permitting this man, who had tried to assassinate him in 1925, to remain alive. Rachele says that he brought the paper home with him from the office and threw it down on the table with a tired comment that he would have found it impossible to make in the days of his power. 'Kindness,' he said, 'can never be excessive.' Eventually, mainly on the pressing insistence of Rachele, who had grown to hate him because of his contact with the Petaccis, he agreed to dismiss Buffarini-Guidi from the Ministry of the Interior; but he told one of his secretaries that he had only dismissed him to gratify Rachele and to irritate the Germans, not because he thought the Government would be strengthened or his own position more secure.

He seemed drained of all hope. He had no illusions left. Previously he had been able to retain them by succumbing to his own propaganda that the Germans' secret weapons and their new secret army would soon turn the fortunes of war, that the Allies' losses were more than they could bear, that the discord between the Russians and Americans would result in war between them, or at least make it possible for him to make a separate peace with one or other of them, preferring if it came to that, so he told both his Finance Minister and Preziosi, that Italy should become a Soviet Republic rather than an Anglo-American colony. But now he derived comfort only from the reflection that even if the British did win the war they would lose their Empire after it, just as he had done. When his Ministers tried to give him encouragement, he smiled at them ironically. When Graziani told him of his latest quarrel with Kesselring he shrugged his shoulders with indifference. One day after Mezzasoma had burst into his office to announce that 'wonderful news' had just come in of a successful German counter-attack on the Meuse, Mussolini remarked, without interest, as if indeed he had not understood what the excitable young man had said. 'That's good.' And he made a gesture of dismissal, not troubling to ask for any details.

On the anniversary of D'Annunzio's death he went to the Vittoriale and, standing beside the poet's tomb, he made a sad, almost despairing speech which one of his audience described as being 'short and mysterious, grave with a sense of tragedy'. His face was pale and sad and 'looked like stone', and the sky was grey and the atmosphere oppressive. 'You are not dead, my friend,' he said, 'and you will not die so long as there remains, standing in the Mediterranean, an island called Italy. You are not dead and you will not die so long as in the centre of Italy there is a city to which we shall return – a city called Rome.'

'He lives by dreams, in dreams, and through dreams,' Mezzasoma said. 'He does not have the least contact with reality. He lives and functions in a world which he builds for himself, a completely fantastic world. He lives outside time. His reactions, his enthusiasms, his breakdowns, never have any relation to life. They come at any moment and without any definite reason.'

Sometimes, indeed, he talked and behaved as if he had in fact become the mad poet which the year before he had claimed to be.

The journalist Ivanoe Fossani has described a revealing interview which Mussolini gave him at this time. It took place in the middle of Lake Garda on the island of Trimellone under a night sky brilliant with stars. A ferocious police dog was barking savagely, and Mussolini went up to it and took its lower jaw in one hand so that he could stroke it with the other. He gazed into its eyes, Fossani said, as he told it to be quiet, and after a few moments it stopped barking and lay down at his feet and went to sleep, and Mussolini began talking to Fossani. He spoke so fast and at such length that when he had finished and went back to Gargnano in his motor-boat, Fossani wrote furiously for three hours without stopping, in an effort to record everything that Mussolini had said. Fossani himself during the whole interview only spoke one word – 'Tell' – the name of the police dog. 'I suspected from the beginning,' he said, 'that the sound of my voice would have dammed the flow of talk of a man who had decided to confess to the stars.'

Away from the guards, and the Germans and the arguments of his Ministers, the tantrums of his wife and the tears of his mistress, Mussolini felt a sudden liberation which was close to delirium. 'If it were a summer's day,' he said, 'I would take off my coat and roll in the grass like a wildly happy child.' He spoke of the stars, and the mysterious power of the soil, of his dead son and his brother Arnaldo, of the inconsequence of human life and of the life of the soul. He spoke like a feverish prophet, spinning a web of argument and fantasy and unrelated fact, catching a thread in one train of thought to leap away to another, suddenly breaking through the muddle of contradiction, extravagant metaphor, and half-formed ideas to make an observation of striking truth and clarity, or a prophecy of deep prescience. He tried to analyse the reasons for his successes and failures. He was not infallible, he said. He had made mistakes. He could see them now and recognize them. It had not been easy for he had been surrounded for years by idolators. 'I heard the word genius,' he said with a kind of bitter disgust, 'a hundred times a day.' But others had made greater mistakes, and all his own would have been forgotten if the war, forced upon him by the diabolical foreign policy of the English, had been conducted by the Germans with restraint. The attack on Russia had been made against his strong advice, and now Germany was almost destroyed and the Russians would soon be in a position in Central Europe from which it would be impossible to dislodge them. If the same mistakes were committed in the East, China too would help to strangle the world. 'How can England and America fail to see so enormous a danger?'

This reference to the English aroused in him a fresh burst of invective. He attacked them and the French for failing to support him in his demands for a revision of the Treaty of Versailles, for the cancellation of war debts and reparations, and in his stand against Germany in the early 1930s. He attacked the King and the reactionary Court which surrounded him, he attacked the *bourgeoisie* who had infused a false spirit into the faith of Fascism, he attacked the General Staff for betraying the soldiers, he attacked the sordid industrial and financial groups who had outrageously ill-treated the workers whom he himself had 'always loved and love still. They are good and indestructible,' he said, 'and infinitely superior to all the false prophets who pretend to represent them.' And the thought of them brought a new mood of sadness. 'I have been a prisoner ever since I was arrested in the King's villa,' he said, in a quieter voice. 'There is no longer any escape. To our enemies we are those who must surrender unconditionally, to the others we are traitors. . . . I have no illusions about my fate. Life is only a short span in eternity. After the struggle is over they will spit on me, but later perhaps they will come to wipe me clean. And then I shall smile because I shall be at peace with my people.'

He stood up at last and shook Fossani silently by the hand. And as he walked back to his boat, the journalist, deeply impressed by the calm dignity of this 'great, unfortunate man in his hour of tragedy', says that the police dog 'leapt on to a rock where it let out a long, shrill howl'.

But if it were possible to recognize the greatness of this tragic figure in a moment of ecstatic pity beneath the purity of the stars, it was more difficult to do so in the stuffy little room in Villa delle Orsoline where most journalists saw him. One of these, Madeleine Mollier, found a man she scarcely recognized, a man who looked like a convict with his white face and shaven head and black,

lack-lustre eyes. He was not so much resigned as humble. His resignation and calm acceptance of his fate had an almost apologetic, self-pitying air.

'What do you want to know?' he asked her. 'Seven years ago I remember you came to Rome. I was an interesting person then. Now I am defunct. But I am not afraid any more. Death is a thank-you to God who has suffered so much. This morning in my room a little swallow was trapped. It flew around desperately in the room until it fell exhausted on my bed. I picked it up with care so as not to frighten it, opened my window, then opened my hand. It did not understand at first and looked around, before opening its wings and flying, with a little cry of joy, out to freedom. I shall never forget that cry of joy. But for me, the window will never open except to let me out to death. And it is right. I have made mistakes and I shall pay for them, if my poor life is worth the payment. I have never made mistakes when I have followed my instincts, but often when I have obeyed my reason. . . .

'Yes, signora, I am finished. My star has set. I still work, but I know that everything is a farce. I await the end of the tragedy, strangely detached from it all. I don't feel well and for a year have eaten nothing but slops. I don't drink. I don't smoke. . . . Perhaps I was, after all, only destined to indicate the road to my people. But then have you ever heard of a prudent, calculating dictator?'

He only derived comfort now, he said, from his books, the works of the great philosophers. He did not want to do anything except read and go on reading as he waited for the end.

'I have been dying,' he said when asked a question about Ciano, 'since that January morning when he too met his destiny. The agony is atrociously long. I am like the captain of a ship in a storm; the ship is broken up and I find myself in the furious ocean on a raft which it is impossible to guide or to govern. No one hears my voice any more. But one day perhaps the world will listen to me.'

To everyone who came to see him now he spoke in this way – consciously tragic, sometimes mystical, occasionally obscure, often lyrical. To the young writer Pierre Pascal, who had translated his *Parlo con Bruno*, he said: 'Have you noticed on your way here this morning the violent colours of the lake? The deep blue? I look at it when it is red at sunset or grey in the wintriness of the dawn and I see it as if for the first time. The beauties of Italy are profound.' Then, changing the subject suddenly, not waiting for an answer, he asked Pascal if he believed in God. He was not certain, himself, and wished that he could be so. Darting from God to Napoleon, to Charles Maurras, to the Italian painters, to Dante, to D'Annunzio, he avoided any mention of politics until Pascal made an observation about the necessity of uniting Europe so that it could defend itself from the intervention of the English. 'That will be the task of your generation,' Mussolini said, dismissing the unwelcome thought of the English, who had contributed so much to his ruin, 'and of the next one.' He was not in the mood for a talk about politics, and after Pascal had made a few remarks about the partisans in Italy and the maquis in France the conversation came to an abrupt end.

Another writer, Pia Reggidori Corti, found him equally unwilling to discuss contemporary events. He preferred to talk of Mazzini, Garibaldi, of philosophy, and of sexual love. Every love died, he said, sooner or later through the impossibility of lovers to understand each other; and when Corti replied that disillusion only came when simple infatuation was mistaken for love, Mussolini referred to Plato and ended the interview by saying that for his part he was convinced that to live was to suffer.

He would even interrupt an important conference with his Ministers or the Germans to talk of philosophy or history or religion. On 6 April when the last offensive of the Allies had already begun, when Massa had been occupied and the German armies were retreating fast through Tuscany, he shocked Colonel Dollmann, who was only concerned with the problems of withdrawal and surrender, by suddenly saying to him in the middle of an urgent discussion, 'Tell me, Colonel, do you believe in God? General Wolff does.'

The Germans Surrender

FEBRUARY–APRIL 1945

> *Surely I have the right to be at least
> informed of what is going on.*

Unknown to Mussolini, Colonel Dollmann and General Wolff of
the SS had for some time now been negotiating with the Allies for
the surrender of the German armies in Italy. Their mediator was
Cardinal Idelfonso Schuster, the worldly-wise Archbishop of
Milan, who had been in contact with them since the beginning of
February, when he had suggested that to save Italy and to prevent
the useless sacrifice of thousands of men they should allow him to
come to terms on their behalf with the partisans. The partisans,
the Cardinal said, were growing more numerous and better organized every day, and every day the Allies were sending them
arms and supplies. Colonel Dollmann discussed the Cardinal's
suggestion with General Wolff, and the two German officers
agreed that Schuster should send a representative to the partisan
headquarters to see General Cadorna. Schuster chose a tough, intelligent priest, Don Giuseppe Bicchierai, who had been a military chaplain.

Meanwhile Colonel Dollmann arranged for Baron Luigi
Parilli, a former representative of an American business concern in Italy, to be provided with a visa for Switzerland, where
he was ostensibly going for reasons of health, but in fact to
make contact with the Americans in Lucerne. On 3 March
Dollmann himself arrived in Switzerland and met Parilli who
introduced him to an American representative of Mr Allen
Dulles.

As a test of his good faith Dollmann was asked to arrange for
the release of Ferruccio Parri, the most important prisoner in
Fascist hands, and one other resistance leader.

Just over a week later Ferruccio Parri, his wife, and Usmiani, an anti-Fascist who had been under sentence of death in Verona, were in Switzerland.

On 8 March General Wolff himself came to Switzerland. He was introduced to Allen Dulles, who still made no promises but intimated that Wolff's future might well be assured by a successful end to the negotiations. On his return to Italy, however, Wolff heard that in his absence Field-Marshal Kesselring, on whose good sense he had felt able to rely, had been flown north with instructions to replace Rundstedt as Commander-in-Chief West and to keep intact the crumbling German front. Wolff did not know how far he could trust Kesselring's successor, General Vietinghoff; but he continued with the negotiations, hoping that Vietinghoff and the other Wehrmacht officers would accept what terms he could arrange for them. On 19 March he met the British Major-General Airey and the American General Lemnitzer close to the Italian–Swiss frontier at Ascona on Lake Maggiore and discussed with them the terms of surrender. But when he arrived back at his headquarters, Wolff was again given unpleasant news. This time Himmler telephoned from Berlin to say that the General's family and Frau Dollmann had all been brought under 'the personal supervision' of the Gestapo. General Wolff was forbidden to leave Italy again, and Himmler would telephone now and again to ask how he was and to give him news of his family. Wolff, however, agreed to maintain contact with the Allies by means of a radio transmitter in his aide-de-camp's bedroom, and on the last day of March he obtained Vietninghoff's agreement to the surrender. But on 13 April he was called to Berlin. He said good-bye to his friends and made his will.

Less than a week later, however, he was back in Italy. Himmler had not wanted to commit himself and had told Wolff to make a personal report on the Italian situation to Hitler. At half past four in the morning of 18 April Hitler, already in the bunker at the Chancellery, had listened to his report, as Wolff said later, in a kind of dazed, exhausted silence and finally had spoken not of Italy but of the chance that even now Russia might be separated from the British and Americans. Wolff, himself, knew this to be most unlikely, as a guarded suggestion that the remaining Axis troops in Italy should be allowed to cross the Alps unmolested so as to be free to fight against the Russians had been quickly and firmly rejected at the beginning of the negotiations by the Allied representatives, who insisted that the Russian alliance was indissoluble. But when he left the bunker, he felt that for Hitler the only remaining hope was that his enemies would quarrel. Italy had already been discarded from his mind.

Within a week of his return to Italy, Wolff had met the Allied representatives at the Swiss frontier for the last time and had agreed with them the final details for the unconditional surrender of the German armies and the action he should take against any Wehrmacht generals who failed to conform to them. The day after he got back from Chiasso, Wolff went with Dollmann to Cardinal Schuster's palace in Milan to meet the representatives of the partisans, who confirmed their acceptance of the terms agreed with the Allies and told the Germans that the Committee of National Liberation for North Italy had given orders for a general insurrection against Mussolini's Government on 25 April. It was also confirmed that a few hours before the insurrection was due to begin General Wolff would give Colonel Rauff, the Gestapo Chief in Milan, an order forbidding SS troops to interfere in what was recognized to be an Italian matter.

Of all this Mussolini was told nothing. Rumours, of course, had reached Gargnano. General Wolff had himself hinted at some sort of contact with the Allies in Switzerland at an unfriendly interview with a stony-faced Mussolini as early as 27 February. And on 5 March in a conversation with Alberto Mellini, an official at the Foreign Ministry, Mussolini admitted that he was suspicious. He believed that 'Schuster was up to something', and that the Germans were in touch with the Committee of National Liberation in Milan. But Rahn, while acknowledging that there was some sort of contact between the partisans and the SS, protested that the subjects discussed were confined to matters of a very limited sort and denied that he, or any other German, was negotiating with Cardinal Schuster. The release of Parri, Mussolini was assured, had been ordered purely in the interests of the Italian people, who would benefit by the lessening of tension which such a gesture would bring about. Mussolini accepted this assurance and told Mellini that he was not opposed to the man's release, but he could not believe that the rumours he had heard about the German overtures were unfounded. 'I feel sure they are treating with the Committee of Liberation,' he said. 'Rahn and Wolff would do well to tell me what they are up to. Surely,' he added petulantly, 'I have the right to be at least informed of what is going on.'

On 13 March he decided to make an overture himself. He sent his son Vittorio to Cardinal Schuster with a letter proposing some sort of guarantee for the civilian population in the event of a complete German retreat from Italy and a withdrawal of Fascist forces to a defensive position in the Alps. It was a hopelessly inadequate gesture, as Cardinal Schuster realized, but the Apostolic Nuncio at Berne was asked to transmit it to the Allied Forces Headquarters at Caserta, where it was immediately rejected. Only unconditional surrender would be entertained. Mussolini refused to consider unconditional surrender, still reluctant to believe that the Germans had in fact already agreed to it. On 6 April he received a report that certain German units had received orders to prepare for an evacuation of the country, but a day or two later he allowed General Vietinghoff to persuade him that his allies would fight to the death. Any rumours he might have heard about a German surrender, he was assured, 'were spread by Allied propaganda'.

13

The Move to Milan

19–25 APRIL 1945

I have gambled right up to the end and I have been beaten.

On 13 April Mussolini received the Under-Secretary of the Interior.

'Tell me,' he asked him bluntly, 'what do you think about the war now?'

'There is no doubt,' the Minister replied, 'that it's lost.'

But, Mussolini protested, in Germany resistance was hardening; every inch of ground was being contested.

'The last spasms cannot affect the final outcome,' the Minister said.

Mussolini became silent. And then he said softly, 'Yes, you are right. It is so. There is nothing else to be done.'

This fatalism, broken by one last eruption of hope, was now to remain with him to the end. Victory was at last accepted as being no longer possible; his only thought was the manner of his apotheosis. Some of his Ministers suggested a last stand at Trieste; some, supported by the German commander of the Milan garrison, General Wening, advocated a determined defence of Milan, which would become an Italian Stalingrad; others felt that the myth of Fascism would be more dramatically served by a fight to the death in the Alps. On 14 April Pavolini came to a meeting at Villa delle Orsoline to put forward his plans for this final gesture of faith and defiance, which was to be made in the Valtellina north of Bergamo. None of the Germans, including General Wolff, who were present at this meeting raised any objections to Pavolini's plans, and the possibility of a German surrender was not mentioned.

Mussolini spoke little. He seemed prepared to accept Pavolini's decisions without question, thinking of other things, as if already he were preparing himself for death. When Graziani spoke against the final stand in the Valtellina and attacked Pavolini for not having made more detailed preparations, Mussolini said quietly, 'No one is obliged to go to the Valtellina. Each one of you must decide for yourself.'

The following day when Father Eusebio, an Army chaplain who had had several conversations with him before at Gargnano, came to see him for the last time, he spoke like a dying man making his last confession. He was completely convinced of defeat, Father Eusebio thought, and had a presentiment of his own violent death.[1] 'Say good-bye to me now, Father,' he said to Don Pancino, another priest who visited him two days later. 'Thank you for the prayers you say for me. Please go on with them, for I have need of them. I know I shall be shot.' He gave the same impression of despair and resignation to Dinale, an old revolutionary whom he had known since his days in Switzerland. 'Gloomy and bitter presages of misfortune are in the air,' he told him, claiming to sense the same portents of disaster in the atmosphere that he had sensed in the air of Rome the day before his arrest. 'I am crucified by my destiny. I have provoked fortune and it has turned against me. The believers – and I have never envied them as much as I do now – would point to the hand of divine justice. For me the events are merely historical. I have gambled right up to the end and I have been beaten. I leave life without recriminations, without hate, without pride. *Addio.*'

'*Arrivederci,*' Dinale replied.

'No! No more illusions. *Addio.*'

On 16 April the Ministers of the Social Republic met for the last time. The next meeting, Mussolini told them, would be called in Milan, which he said, with a final and unconsciously ironic challenge to his enemies, thinking of his recent triumph there five months before, must be 'Decemberized'. 'I have never liked this *cul-de-sac* in which I find myself cut off from all contact with the people,' he had confided to Mellini earlier. 'Now Rome is lost, Milan is the only capital of the Italian Republic.'[2]

---

1. 'Poor Mazzolini,' he had said to his sister when talking of the Under-Secretary's death. 'But he died in his bed, as he wanted to. Who knows where we shall die and where our bones will be thrown?'
2. Previously he had wanted to move the seat of the Government south to a more central position at Monza, but the Germans had refused permission. They now

In the early evening of 19 April he prepared, ignoring the advice of Wolff and Rahn, to leave for Milan accompanied by an escort of German troops under Captain Otto Kisnatt of the *Sicherheits-dienst* and Lieutenant Fritz Birzer of the S S, a sad-looking young man who was told not to let the Duce out of his sight for an instant.

As the sun was setting Mussolini said good-bye to Rachele in the garden of Villa Feltrinelli, saying he would be back for her later. 'He also mentioned the possibility of a last stand in the Valtellina,' Rachele said, 'I could not find it in me to argue with him.' With Edvige, his sister, he was more explicit. Germany was at the end of her tether and after the war would be divided between the Russians and the Western Allies. As for himself, he added, unable even then to resist the pleasure of rhetoric, he was ready to 'enter into the grand silence of death'.

In Milan Mussolini established his office in a first-floor room in the Prefecture at Palazzo Monforte, where for five days he received an endless stream of visitors. The constant talk, the atmosphere of excitement and almost hysteria, had a restorative effect on him. He had arrived nervous and depressed, hopelessly uncaring. By 20 April he was calm and almost confident. He even spoke of the resistance in the Valtellina lasting for a month, which would give him time to form a stable Government and to arrange for an honourable peace. He energetically discussed the possibility of establishing a new anti-monarchical front with the Socialists. The journalist G. G. Cabella, who was accorded an interview on 20 April, found him 'in very good health as opposed to what people were saying'. He looked fatter than when Cabella had seen him last and seemed almost cheerful as he asked the journalist what he could do for him. 'I would like a signed photograph,' Cabella said, and Mussolini gave him one dating it proudly as was his habit 'Year XXIII of the Fascist Era' as if the régime were close to its birth and not its death. His career was over, he said, but neither Italy nor Fascism would ever die.

'Do you really trust Schuster?' Cabella asked him.

Mussolini looked out of the window spreading his hands wide in

advised against leaving for Milan on the grounds that Lake Garda would be on the main line of the Army's withdrawal, whereas in Milan they would not be able to provide the Fascists with adequate protection against the partisans.

MAP OF THE LAKE COMO AREA

a familiar gesture, the palms towards the ceiling. 'He is a little glib,' he said. 'But one must trust a man of God.'

'And are there really any secret weapons?' Cabella asked him.

'There are,' Mussolini replied emphatically. 'I had news a few days ago.' The plot against Hitler's life had put things back, but the tide would soon turn. He told Cabella that he would like an opportunity of correcting the proofs of his article before it appeared in *Il Popolo di Alessandria*, and some time later he was discovered doing so with his accustomed care.

On 21 April when Rahn called to see him he was still 'seemingly imperturbable and serene'. But the Ambassador thought that he saw in his eyes the knowledge of his tragic death. On the desk was a book of poems by Mörike. And it was, of course, a mood which could not last. Every hour there came news of a military disaster, a fallen town, a continued retreat. On 20 April he had heard that Bologna had been overrun and had to cancel the plans he had made to celebrate the anniversary of the birth of Rome by a speech to the people after High Mass in the Cathedral; on 22 April he learned of the advance along the Po and the fall of Modena and Reggio; the next day news arrived that Parma had fallen and contact was lost with Cremona and Mantua; in the evening Genoa was occupied by the partisans and Fiume by Tito.

With the enemy only sixty miles away and the Germans retreating headlong before them, Mussolini could no longer hope for a stand on the Alps lasting for a month. Graziani, indeed, insisted that the whole idea from a military point of view was quite inept. But Mussolini and Pavolini would not be dissuaded. It was not in any case a military triumph that they wanted but a moral triumph for Fascism. When Buffarini-Guidi advised the Duce to escape to Switzerland or Spain, he angrily rejected the idea as he had rejected the suggestion of Francesca Lavagnini, a former mistress, who had sent a message from the Argentine urging him to join her there, and as he had rejected the suggestion of Claretta Petacci that he should allow her to stage a car accident in which, it could be announced, Mussolini had been killed. He was angry, too, when one of his secretaries and Dr Zachariae suggested he should fly to Spain and when Tamburini proposed a flight to Polynesia. He was determined to die in the Valtellina. He was finished but Fascism was not. In a final speech to several officers who had been brought to see him he spoke with a flash of his former power of '*l'immortalità della patria e del Fascismo*'.

His family, however, must be got to safety. On 23 April he telephoned Rachele at Gargnano to tell her that he would come to make arrangements for her flight to Switzerland. But a few hours later he had to telephone again. Mantua had fallen, he told her, and Brescia was threatened; he would not be able to get through. She must go to Monza, where Barracu would meet her at the royal villa. He would get in touch with her again there. He tried also to persuade Claretta to escape, and went to see her at the house in Milan to which she and her family had been taken by Major Spögler. The rest of the family were planning to fly to Spain; but Claretta could not be persuaded to go with them. 'I am following my destiny,' she wrote to a friend, using one of her lover's favourite expressions. 'What will happen to me I don't know, but I cannot question my fate.'

Throughout 25 April Mussolini remained in Milan. Repeatedly rejecting all ideas that he should fly out of the country, he appeared placid and, on occasions, apathetic. Sometimes he would make an angry remark about the Germans, the King, or the English; but for most of the day he worked uncomplainingly and unhurriedly, collecting his papers together, receiving visitors, making preparations for his journey north. There were rumours that he would leave Milan that day, and during the morning Lieutenant Birzer called to remind him nervously that he had promised not to leave until Captain Kisnatt returned from Gargnano, where he had gone to collect their men's baggage. 'The situation is very changed,' Mussolini said coldly, and told him to go to the Muti barracks to fetch some lorries and petrol for their journey. He seemed upset that Birzer should imply he had broken his word to Kisnatt, but not in the least agitated by his own predicament.

During the late afternoon General Montagna, Chief of Police in Milan, and Graziani called at the Prefecture to discuss plans for all the retreating Republican troops to be re-formed north of Milan. But Mussolini told them that he was going to Cardinal Schuster, to ask him to arrange a meeting with the leaders of the Committee of National Liberation to find out their terms for a surrender. He had decided that he would 'spare the Army any further sacrifice'.

Soon after five Mussolini left for the archiepiscopal palace, leaving Graziani to follow on later. The streets were strangely quiet, the public buildings shut, most shops and offices locked and shuttered. Earlier on in the afternoon the factory sirens had screamed, announcing the beginning of the general strike.

'Mussolini entered my reception room,' Cardinal Schuster said, 'with such a dejected air that the impression he gave me was of a man benumbed by an immense catastrophe. I received him with episcopal charity, and while waiting for the arrival of the persons whom he had wanted to meet I tried to cheer him a little by starting a conversation.'

The conversation was difficult and spasmodic. Mussolini 'seemed extremely tired' and indisposed to talk. Cardinal Schuster insisted on his taking some refreshment as he was 'so very dejected', and 'out of politeness he accepted a small glass of liqueur and a biscuit. . . . He was like a man bereft of will, listlessly accepting his fate.'

Only when the Cardinal begged him to spare Italy useless havoc and to accept an honourable surrender did Mussolini momentarily recover his strength of will. His problem was twofold, he said, and would be carried out in two moves. The Army and the Republican Militia would be dissolved, and he himself would retire into the Valtellina with three thousand Blackshirts to continue the war in the mountains.

'Duce, do not have any illusions,' Cardinal Schuster told him. 'I know the Blackshirts who are going to follow you are rather three hundred than three thousand as some would have you believe.'

'Perhaps a few more,' Mussolini admitted with grim resignation. 'Not many, though. I have no illusions.'

Even with 300, however, Schuster believed that Mussolini would still go to his last ditch in the mountains. He was 'resolute in his determination', the Cardinal thought, and he did not venture to reply. They spoke of other things, but the brief fire in Mussolini had died, and it was the Cardinal who did most of the talking. He spoke of expiation and atonement, of imprisonment and exile; but Mussolini might not have been listening, although once when Schuster mentioned Napoleon there was a glint of pleasure in the tired eyes, and once when he spoke of God's forgiveness they filled with tears. The Cardinal gave him a copy of the *Storia di San Benedetto* and he accepted it gravely, carefully putting it into a brown envelope.

At six o'clock General Cadorna arrived with another delegate of the National Liberation Committee, Achille Marazza, a lawyer who was a Christian Democrat, and Riccardo Lombardi, an engineer who belonged to the *Partito d'Azione*, was already there. A few minutes later they were shown into Cardinal Schuster's room by Don Giuseppe Bicchierai. The Cardinal offered them his hand so that they could kiss his ring. When they had done so he introduced them to Mussolini, who walked quickly towards them, smiling with what Marazza thought was a vague sort of condescension. He held out his hand to each of them in turn, and uncertainly they shook it. Then he sat down next to Schuster on a sofa while the others remained standing.

There was an atmosphere of restraint and embarrassment which increased when the Social Republic delegates, Graziani, Barracu, and Paolo Zerbino, the Minister of the Interior, joined them. Mussolini was taking a part he had never learned to play and stared intently at the heavy crimson damask on the walls, avoiding the eyes of the others. It was very quiet in the street below the partly open window.

'Shall we sit down over there?'

Cardinal Schuster pointed to a large oval table in the middle of the room on which were several glasses, a decanter of marsala, and a plate of biscuits. He sat himself at one end of the table next to Mussolini. Cadorna and Marazza and Lombardi sat on their left; Graziani, Zerbino, and Barracu on the right. Graziani, Cadorna says, was looking very angry.

'Well, then,' Mussolini began in a sharp, impatient voice as if the initiative were unquestionably his. 'Well, then. What are your proposals?'

He had addressed the question to Cadorna, who, unwilling to answer it, turned to Marazza.

'My instructions are limited and precise,' Marazza said. 'I have only to ask and to accept your surrender.'

'I'm not here for that,' Mussolini snapped, turning indignantly to Cardinal Schuster. 'I was told that we were to meet and to discuss conditions. That's why I came – to safeguard my men, their families, and the Fascist Militia. I must know what's to become of them. The families of the members of my Government must be given protection. Also I was assured that the Militia would be handed over to the enemy as prisoners of war.'

Mussolini's indignation rose as he spoke. He would have said more had not Lombardi interrupted him to say, 'These are details. I believe we have authority to settle them.'

'Very well,' said Mussolini in the aggrieved but reluctantly satisfied tone of voice of a man who has won a point in an argument. 'In that case we can come to some agreement.'

The discussion then began in earnest and at first gave promise of success. The delegates of the Liberation Committee agreed that the Fascist forces when taken prisoner would be treated in accordance with the rules of The Hague Convention, that the families of Fascists would not be victimized, and that diplomats accredited to the Social Republic would be given the protection of international law. But as Mussolini seemed by his unaccustomed silence to be giving his assent to the Committee's terms, when the matter of war criminals was mentioned Marshal Graziani suddenly rose to his feet.

'No, no, Duce!' he protested. 'Let me remind you that we have obligations of loyalty to our ally. We can't abandon the Germans and negotiate a capitulation independently like this. We cannot sign an agreement without the Germans. We can't forget the laws of duty and honour.'

'I am afraid the Germans don't seem to have been troubled by the same scruples,' Cadorna said slowly, emphasizing each word and looking at Mussolini as he spoke. 'We have been discussing terms of surrender for the past four days. We've already agreed on all details, and we are expecting news of the signed treaty at any moment.' Marazza had no doubt that the news was a great shock to Mussolini. He appeared to wince as if he were in pain. 'Haven't they even bothered to inform your Government?' Marazza said with a pretence of surprise.

'Impossible!' Mussolini said angrily. 'Show me the treaty.'

It was not impossible, Zerbino interposed, for Don Bicchierai had told him as much in the ante-room. Mussolini turned to Cardinal Schuster, who later admitted to feeling annoyed that Don Bicchierai had violated a diplomatic secret. 'It was useless now, however,' the Cardinal said, 'to keep a secret which had become common knowledge. . . . I explained that, in fact, General Wolff, chief of the S S in Italy, was negotiating with me through the German Ambassador and Colonel Rauff. Mussolini, giving way to a sudden impulse of indignation, declared himself to have been betrayed by the Germans, who had always treated us as their slaves. He threatened to resume his freedom of action since, he said, "They have acted behind my back."'

Cardinal Schuster and Graziani tried without appreciable success to calm him down while the discussion was resumed. But he was obviously no longer in a mood for negotiations and he soon rose to his feet to say that he would agree to nothing until he had had an opportunity of talking to the German Consul. 'This time,' he said, 'we shall be able to say that Germany has betrayed Italy.' He asked for an hour in which to consider the Committee's demand for surrender, and the delegates agreed to give it to him. He left the room, so Graziani said, muttering threats to announce the German betrayal on the radio. Cardinal Schuster saw him to the ante-chamber and wished him good-bye and a safe return within the hour. Mussolini answered him 'with no special interest'.

Half an hour later the German Consul arrived and asked what had happened. Soon he was arguing heatedly with several of the Italians. Standing quietly in a corner was Carlo Tiengo, a former Fascist Prefect of Turin, who had been asked by General Diamanti of the Fascist Militia to try to find out what was happening. A quarter of an hour before Mussolini's answer was due Alessandro Pertini, the Secretary of the Socialist Party, burst into the room. He had come from a meeting at the O.M. motor factory, where there had been a riot of armed workers.

'Where's Mussolini?' he shouted. 'Why all this talk? Once Mussolini has been handed over to us, two days will be ample to set up a People's Tribunal. Summary justice is what we need. We've had enough of this chattering.'

While Marazza was objecting to Pertini's advocacy of violence, Tiengo crept from the room and ran to warn Mussolini of his danger. He found the courtyard of the Prefecture full of vehicles and excited men rushing up and down the steps. Inside the noise was appalling.

'Where's Mussolini?' Tiengo shouted, echoing Pertini's words at the archiepiscopal palace.

Someone told him that the Duce had gone into his office, turned everyone else out, and locked the door. Perhaps he was going to shoot himself. He had a revolver; he was in a wild mood. Dr Zachariae had noticed how deathly pale and curiously contracted his features were. When the German General Wening, commander of the Milan garrison, offered him an armed escort, he had yelled at him that the Germans were traitors and cowards and he would rather die than ask for their protection.

Immediately on his return from the palace Mussolini had gone up to a map on his table and pointing at it with a trembling finger he had announced, 'We leave Milan immediately. Destination Como.' It was not the most direct route to the Valtellina, but there were reports that the Americans were advancing fast along the Bergamo road and that the partisans had cut the road to Lecco. No one knew what the Duce intended to do when he got to Como. Perhaps, some of them thought, he would go on to Chiasso and try to escape across the frontier into Switzerland; and others have afterwards maintained that this was, in fact, his intention, and that he was glad that the Germans' betrayal had given him a chance to do so with honour.

But Vittorio, like most of them close to him at this time, did not think that he was considering escape. Earlier in the day he had told his father that there were still some aircraft on the Ghedi airfield and there was even now time to escape. The suggestion seemed to infuriate him. He stood up and snapped at his son so violently that Vittorio afterwards confessed, 'The words froze my blood.' 'No one told you to tell me what to do,' he said savagely. 'I am going to meet my fate in Italy.' Vittorio found courage to repeat his advice now; but again the idea was angrily rejected.

Mussolini stormed out of his office, and in the corridor Tiengo told him not to go back to the palace as his enemies would be sure to kill him. Carlo Borsani, a devoted disciple who had been blinded in Albania, begged him not to leave Milan, holding out his arms to the Duce, with tears in his sightless eyes. Buffarini-Guidi and Renato Ricci told him to accept Vittorio's advice and fly to Spain, while others called out, 'Don't go, Duce! Don't go.' A secretary ran up to him with papers for him to sign, but he brushed them away, not even looking at them. Someone advised him to try to get through to his bodyguard, who were still at Gardone. Bombacci, dressed in a black shirt and black breeches, said that the scene reminded him of a day in Petrograd when with Lenin he had watched the flight of Jadenic's troops. 'The cannon made the windows tremble,' he remembered. 'It was much like this; except this is worse.'

'They want to have another 25 July,' Mussolini shouted, paying no attention to any of them, infected by the hysteria around him. 'But this time they won't succeed. They won't succeed!'

He was wearing the uniform of the Fascist Militia, and there was a machine-gun over his shoulder. He was carrying two leather bags full of secret documents, which he gave with some money to Carradori, a trusted Blackshirt. He went up to Silvestri and Borsani and embraced them both silently. Suddenly he stood back and announced with melodramatic force, 'To the Valtellina!' and then he went down the steps to his car.

A squad of Blackshirts forced a path through the crowd, and the convoy slowly set off down Corso Monforte and into Corso del Littorio, making for the Como road. Luigi Gatti, Mussolini's young secretary, led the way, sitting on the bonnet of his car in a black leather jacket with a machine-gun held between his knees. Behind him Mussolini sat next to Bombacci in the back of an open Alfa-Romeo, and then followed about thirty other cars and lorries. In one of these, another Alfa-Romeo with Spanish number-plates, Claretta Petacci travelled with her brother Marcello and his wife and two children. Close behind were two lorries of S S soldiers commanded by Lieutenant Birzer, whom General Wening, despite Mussolini's theatrical protests, had ordered to continue his duties as escort. The last car of all was driven by Vittorio Mussolini.

Several Ministers of the Republican Government had decided to remain in Milan, but most of them went after the Duce too.

'Where are we going to?' one of them asked Mezzasoma.

'God knows,' Mezzasoma said with prophetic gloom. 'Perhaps to our death.'

14

The Flight from Milan

*I shall go to the mountains. Surely it's not
possible that five hundred men cannot be found
who will follow me.*

I

Mussolini arrived in Como about ten o'clock.

He hurried up the steps of the Prefecture, where he intended waiting for Pavolini, who had promised to bring 3,000 loyal Fascists to support him in his last stand in the mountains. But the news at Como was not encouraging. The telephone was still working and every few minutes it rang stridently in the corridor and a frightened voice would give an account of some new disaster. All the Milan suburbs were in the hands of armed workers; the Americans were still advancing; the Germans were in full retreat. The Republican troops had been stopped from entering Milan by groups of partisans who were blocking the Melegnano and Treviglio roads. Mezzasoma telephoned the offices of the *Corriere della Sera* and was told that the partisans had already taken the building over. There was no news at all of Pavolini.

At about half past ten the Prefect's wife cooked supper and served it in her husband's office, but Mussolini could not eat. He listened silently while his Ministers, close to panic, continued to give him contradictory advice. Paolo Porta, Inspector of the Fascist Party in Lombardy, said that he should wait no longer for Pavolini but withdraw to Cadenabbia. Buffarini-Guidi urged him to join him in an attempt to cross into Switzerland at Chiasso, where the frontier guards would be sure to let them through. Graziani, who had consulted the commander of the German garrison in Como, said that he thought a flight to Switzerland was out of the question. Then General Mische of the Republican Army telephoned to say that he was expecting the Duce at Sondrio.

'I shall go to the mountains,' he announced finally. 'Surely it's not possible that five hundred men cannot be found who will follow me.'

He appeared to be desperately concerned about his files. Apart from the two leather bags of papers that he had handed to Carradori in Milan, there were other documents in a lorry which had not yet reached Como with the rest of the convoy. He sent back Gatti and Colonel Casalinuovo to try to find what had become of them, while he himself carefully read through yet another collection of documents which he kept in two large brief-cases that he never let out of his sight. Exactly what all these papers were no one knew nor ever afterwards discovered, although several attempts to describe them have been, and doubtless will be, made. Carlo Silvestri, who had helped him fill two bags with them in Milan, believed they contained much that would help the Duce's defence in any trial which he might have to face after the war. They included, he says, proof of how much the Social Republic had done to save northern Italy from the ravages of the Germans and from civil war; evidence of the control which the Communists had gained over the activities of the partisans, diplomatic papers concerning 'England's responsibility for the war', papers about Umberto, Hitler, and the trial at Verona. They had certainly been selected with care. For several weeks before he left Gargnano Mussolini had been gathering together the most important and secret ones, and on the night of his departure for Milan one of his secretaries took a motor-boat on to Lake Garda and threw overboard all those which he had decided not to preserve.

When Gatti and Casalinuovo returned to Como to report that the lorry had been intercepted by partisans on its way north from Milan, Mussolini seemed more distressed by this calamity than any other. In addition to his documents, the lorry had also been carrying part of what was later to be known as the 'Dongo Treasure' – gold bars, objects of art, and money belonging to the Social Republican Government or its Ministers and amounting, it was afterwards suggested, to several thousand million lire.[1] But

---

1. According to a cashier at the Social Republic's Finance Ministry, this included a large amount of foreign currency removed to Mussolini's office in February. £2,675

Mussolini showed a complete indifference to the loss of this treasure. The loss of the documents, on the other hand, he mentioned repeatedly during the remaining two days he had left to live.

While awaiting the return of Gatti and Casalinuovo, Mussolini wrote his last letter to Rachele, who had left the royal villa at Monza and was now with Romano and Anna Maria at the Villa Montero at Cernobbio, where several times he had tried to telephone her without success. It was two o'clock in the morning when Rachele received the letter. She was lying on a bed in the villa guarded by some Blackshirts, whom her husband had sent to Cernobbio for her protection, when she 'heard footsteps and excited voices at the door'. A Blackshirt tiptoed into the room. 'There's a letter for you from the Duce,' he said.

'I started to my feet,' she remembers, 'and snatched the envelope, recognizing Benito's handwriting and the blue and red pencil he had been using lately for his private correspondence.'

She went to wake the children and read the letter with them. Before destroying it she made them learn it by heart. So far as they can remember, it said:

DEAR RACHELE

Here I am at the last stages of my life, the last page of my book. We two may never meet again. That is why I am sending you this letter. I ask your forgiveness for all the harm I have unwittingly done to you. . . . Take the children with you and try to get to the Swiss frontier. There you can build a new life. I do not think they will refuse to let you in, for I have always been helpful to them, and you have had nothing to do with politics. Should they refuse, surrender to the Allies, who may be more generous than the Italians. Take care of Anna and Romano, especially Anna who needs it so badly. You know how I love them. Bruno in heaven will help you.

My dearest love to you and the children,

Your

BENITO

Como, 27 April 1945   *Year XXIII of the Fascist Era*

She left the children to read the letter through again and again

in Bank of England notes, 2,150 sovereigns, 149,000 American dollars, 278,000 Swiss francs, and 18 million French francs were at that time placed in Mussolini's safe. As it is believed that most of this money eventually passed into the hands of the Italian Communist Party, the Romans have called the headquarters of the Party 'Palazzo Dongo' after the small lakeside town in which Mussolini was arrested.

while she asked a Blackshirt to try once more to telephone the Prefecture at Como. This time he managed to obtain a connexion. Gatti answered the telephone, but the receiver was taken from his hand and she heard Mussolini's voice.

'Rachele, it's you at last!'

His voice was quiet and resigned. He told her not to think of him but of her own safety and the children's. She had 'never heard him so apathetic'.

'But what about your safety?' she protested. 'I follow my destiny,' he said using once more that self-consciously dramatic phrase. 'But you must take the children somewhere safe. I can only repeat what I said in my letter. Forgive me for all the harm I have done you. Your life might have been quiet and happy without me.'

'There are plenty left who are ready to fight for you and Italy,' she told him in a hopeless attempt at encouragement. 'You have lots of followers and the men around you will do anything for you.'

'They're all gone, I'm afraid,' he said. 'I'm alone, Rachele, and I realize quite well that all is over.'

He asked to speak to the children, and Romano begged him not to leave them.

Rachele took the receiver from her son to say good-bye again to her husband. But as soon as she had done so, she decided not to make straight for Switzerland as he had suggested, but to try to see him once more at Como. When she arrived there he gave her various papers from his carefully guarded collection, including some letters he had received from Winston Churchill, which he hoped would help her to get across the frontier.

'If they try to stop you or harm you,' he told her, 'ask to be handed over to the English.'

2

At about half past four in the morning a German sentry, looking across to the Prefecture in the early light of the dawn, saw Mussolini come back down the steps and walk across towards his car with Bombacci, Marshal Graziani, and some other Italians he did not recognize.

Tired of waiting for Pavolini, Mussolini had decided to move further north along the lakeside road towards Menaggio, leaving instructions for Pavolini to follow him. Lieutenant Birzer, however, was determined that the Duce should not move without the escort that he had been ordered to provide. On hearing a warning shout from his sentry he ran to his car and drove it across the road, blocking Mussolini's way out of the square. He then went up to the Duce, clicked his heels, saluted, and said:

'Duce, you must not depart without an escort.'

'Please leave me alone,' Mussolini told him curtly. 'I can do what I want and go where I like. Get out of the way!'

'You must not go without an escort,' Birzer insisted, still standing stiffly at attention.

'Get out of the way,' Graziani repeated. 'The Duce can go where he likes.'

'Not without an escort, Marshal. Those are my orders.'

A group of Italians forced themselves between the Duce and the insistent German officer, but when some of Birzer's men came up behind Birzer, their fingers on the triggers of their rifles, the Italians gave way. Again Birzer clicked his heels, saluted, and said, 'You must not depart without an escort, Duce.'

And at last Mussolini gave a tired gesture of resigned acceptance.

He arrived at Menaggio in a dreary drizzle of rain about half past five in the morning. With his machine-gun still slung across his back and his head bent low between his shoulders he walked up and down for a few minutes in front of a school which had been turned into a barracks for the Blackshirts and then went to the villa of Emilio Castelli, secretary of the local Fascist Party, where he lay down and tried to sleep. While he was resting the other cars and lorries that had followed him from Como drove into Menaggio escorted by several companies of Republican soldiers and two armoured cars equipped with 20-mm. machine-guns. The long convoy came to a halt behind Birzer's lorry. Claretta Petacci was in one of the cars, and Colonel Casalinuovo took her to Mussolini at the Villa Castelli.

Luigi Gatti, afraid that the concentration of so large a number of vehicles would soon be reported to the partisans, ordered most of them to go back a little way down the road to Cadenabbia. The order was obeyed reluctantly. 'We have come to die with the

Duce,' someone shouted. Another man was heard to grumble loudly, as he turned his truck round in the narrow road, that the Duce had abandoned them and wanted to escape alone across the frontier into Switzerland. It was a growing apprehension. Birzer felt certain that this was what the Duce intended to do when, after three hours' rest, he came out of the Villa Castelli and gave the orders for the remaining vehicles to move off the lakeside road to the village of Grandola, where they would not be so conspicuous while they waited for Pavolini's force of loyal Fascists to join them. Grandola is only fourteen kilometres from the Swiss frontier, and as soon as Mussolini had given the order for the convoy to go there Birzer went up to him and asked, stiffly courteous as ever but with evident suspicion, 'Duce, where are we going now?'

'Follow me,' Mussolini said, 'and you'll find out.'

The Italian cars drove very fast up the steep and winding road into the mountains, and Birzer had difficulty in keeping them in sight. On the outskirts of Grandola one of the Alfa-Romeos in the Italian convoy turned sharply off the main road and raced up a narrow track towards an isolated villa. Birzer could not see whether or not the car was Mussolini's, but he suspected that it was and felt suddenly afraid that the Duce had escaped him. A minute or two later he was surprised and relieved to find him in the hall of the Miravalle Hotel. He had been walking in the garden with Claretta Petacci and three of his Ministers when a German sentry had insisted that they return indoors.

By the early afternoon the grounds of the hotel were packed with vehicles and the hotel itself was crowded with nervous and excited Fascists asking each other what on earth had happened to Pavolini. Mussolini had seen him for a few minutes during the morning in Menaggio, but no one was sure what they had said to each other. It was known that he had collected together between two and three thousand Blackshirts from all over Lombardy and from as far away as Turin and Alessandria and that these men, many of them with their wives and children, were now concentrated around the Stazione della Ferrovia Nord in Como. But Pavolini had had more than enough time to return there and bring these Blackshirts back with him; and yet nothing had been heard of him for more than four hours.

While the others anxiously ate a hurried meal, Mussolini continued to sort through his documents, annotating them carefully, picking out those which dealt with the negotiations between the Ministry of Foreign Affairs and the Swiss Government concerning a free passage across the frontier for the families of his Government officials and staff.

It was a wet and miserable afternoon, dark and foreboding. In the hotel the wireless was turned on constantly, and occasional broadcasts gave news of a general uprising of the people of the north of Italy, the collapse of resistance all along the front, and of the enemy's advance. To escape from the depressing atmosphere Mussolini went out into the garden to walk bareheaded in the rain with a young girl who had joined the convoy at Como. She was Elena Curti Cucciati, the pretty, fair-haired daughter of Angela Curti, his former mistress who had warned him so anxiously and so vainly about the plots to overthrow him. His pleasure at seeing Elena and the comfort which her company obviously gave him drove Claretta to a passionate outburst of jealousy. When he returned to the hotel she screamed at him, 'What is that woman doing here? You must get rid of her at once. You must! You must!'

He tried to calm her, but she went on screaming hysterically, and a group of people collected outside the dining-room window. One of them saw Mussolini's tortured face as he strode across to the window, shut it violently, and shouted, 'Stop!' in a voice not so much angry as despairing. She turned towards him and in doing so slipped on the carpet and fell, bruising her knee. He left her sobbing uncontrollably and went out into the garden again.

In an effort to give him hope Elena Curti Cucciati offered to go back to Como on a bicycle to find out what had happened to Pavolini. If he did not come soon, he had told her, everyone would desert him; several of those who had followed him from Como and Milan showed signs of doing so already. He continued to insist that Fascism must be saved by the example of a last stand in the mountains, but there were not many left who agreed with him now. When Buffarini-Guidi, who had taken to smuggling after his dismissal from the Government and knew the Grandola route well, said that he would try to break across the frontier into Switzerland through Porlezza, two of those who had previously agreed to go to the Valtellina, Angelo Tarchi and Fabiani, protested that they were not going to run the risk of falling into the hands of the partisans and agreed to go with him. Provided with false passports, they left soon after two o'clock without wishing Mussolini good-bye. Graziani also did not wish him good-bye when he left during the afternoon to join an Army unit at Mandello. They would soon all go, he said to Elena Cucciati, and there would be no one left but himself.

In the dining-room of the hotel a Blackshirt suggested that those who were still left ought to follow Buffarini-Guidi's example and ask the Swiss authorities to protect them until the Allies arrived and they could give themselves up to them. The frontier, however, was closed. Rachele and the children had already been turned back at Chiasso and been forced to return to Como; now Fabiani came running back to the Hotel Miravalle to say that the car in which he had been hoping to get through into Switzerland with Buffarini-Guidi and Tarchi had been stopped at Porlezza by frontier guards who had joined forces with the partisans. He had managed to escape, but the others had been captured.

Mussolini asked Lieutenant Birzer to go to their help, but Birzer said his orders were to protect the Duce and he was not concerned with anyone else. Recriminations, threats, and insults flew round the room as its frightened occupants argued about what they should do. Mussolini took no part in these angry discussions, but continued sorting out his documents; and then as the light of the dismal afternoon began to fail he called to Lieutenant Birzer and told him that he had decided to wait no longer for Pavolini, but to go back to Menaggio and then north along the lakeside road towards the Valtellina. They would leave a message for Pavolini's men to meet them in Merano. Birzer did not agree. He said with cold respect that his men were worn out and that they should not be asked to break through the blockades which the partisans would surely have erected north of Menaggio until they had had some sleep. With a shrug of resignation Mussolini gave way and ordered them all to stay the night at Grandola and to move off to Menaggio at five o'clock in the morning. Pavolini's three thousand men would have got there by then, he said. He spoke without conviction, and no one believed him.

In the early hours of the morning of 27 April Pavolini arrived in an armoured car from Como. It was still raining, and as he came into the hotel Elena Cucciati remembers how the water dripped down his white face. The Blackshirts in Como had signed a surrender with the partisans. He had only been able to bring a few men with him.

'How many?' Mussolini asked him anxiously.

Pavolini hesitated.

'Well, tell me. How many?'

'Twelve.'

It was the end of hope.

Soon afterwards Mussolini allowed Lieutenant Birzer to arrange for him and his few remaining followers to join a German convoy, of about forty trucks commanded by Lieutenant Fallmeyer, retreating north along the lakeside road towards Innsbruck.

Mussolini, driving himself in his Alfa-Romeo, followed Birzer; Pavolini, threatening to shoot his way through any road blocks the partisans might have erected on the road, drove in the armoured car with Barracu, Bombacci, Casalinuovo, Pietro Salustri, a young officer in the Air Force, Idreno Utimperghe, a Blackshirt, Elena Curti Cucciati, and Carradori, who was still clutching the two leather bags of documents and money which Mussolini had given him in Milan. Marcello Petacci and Claretta were further behind in the car which ostensibly belonged to the Spanish Ambassador.

For a few miles the convoy drove north without being challenged. Mussolini had recovered his confidence. 'With two hundred Germans,' he said, 'we can go to the top of the world.' On the far side of Menaggio his car slowed down, and he leaned out of the window and called to a man walking along by the side of the road, 'Are there any partisans round here?'

There were partisans everywhere, the man said.

The convoy moved on again, but after about a few hundred yards Mussolini stopped his car and walked back to Pavolini, who suggested that the Duce would be safer in the armoured car. Mussolini, after consulting Birzer, agreed and climbed in. Once more the convoy moved on. The lakeside road was unnervingly quiet. The men in the armoured car sat hunched up in silence. And then suddenly at seven o'clock in the morning about six miles north of Menaggio three shots rang out, and a moment later the convoy was halted by an enormous tree trunk and several boulders which had been dragged across the road. To the right was the lake, to the left an immense and thickly wooded wall of rock which was known by the name, aptly ironic, of the Rocca di Musso.

Fire opened again on the armoured car both from the mountains, where the partisans had placed two 12-mm. machine-guns, and from a bend in the road in front. The guns of the armoured car returned the fire, killing one of the partisans, a builder's foreman, and then a white flag was waved violently above the tree trunk and three men advanced towards the convoy. Two of them were partisans, the third was a German-Swiss, Luigi Hoffmann, who lived on the shores of the lake in a villa which belonged to his wife, the daughter of a rich silk-manufacturer from Como.

As the three men approached Barracu got out of the armoured car and went up to talk to them with Fallmeyer and Birzer. Using Hoffmann as his interpreter, one of the partisans, Davide Barbieri, a captain in the 52nd Garibaldi Brigade, told the German officers that to save unnecessary bloodshed he would allow their soldiers through the road block, but that his men had orders to let no Fascists through. Fallmeyer protested and asked to speak to the local partisan commander. Barbieri said that he would merely get the same answer, but if he wanted to speak to him he could go to the Command Headquarters at Morbegno to do so.

The partisan captain was playing for time. His men were no match, he realized, for the well-armed Germans if it came to a serious fight, for most of them only had shot-guns. An hour or two's respite would give an opportunity for other partisan units to come to their help. The Germans did not want to fight either. For them the war in Italy was over, and they were anxious to return home. One of them, a Protestant pastor in civilian life, went up to Don Mainetti, the parish priest, who had come down from his church at the sound of firing, and asked him in Latin to see what he could do to arrange a safe transit, 'in the name of Christian charity'.

Were there any Italians in the lorries? the priest asked him.

The soldier did not reply, but one of the German officers gave Don Mainetti his word of honour as a soldier that there were not; and the priest said that he would do what he could. As he was leaving, however, another soldier came up to him, an Austrian Catholic who had been educated at Padua, and whispered in Italian, 'There *are* Italians. Don't believe the officer. Have the lorries searched.'

The priest went up the path into the mountains to the local partisan headquarters. But when he arrived there he was told that the matter was now in the hands of the Command Headquarters at Morbegno and there was nothing to be done until further orders were received.

It was eight o'clock when Fallmeyer left for Morbegno, and it was not until after two that he returned to Musso. In those six hours of waiting the Italians in the convoy became more and more anxious and distraught. Pavolini proposed that they should shoot their way through; someone else suggested they ought to turn back and try to get round the road block by another road; but most of them thought that it would be madness to try to do anything until Fallmeyer got back. As the morning wore on, however, and the German officer did not return, some of the Fascists decided to seek the help and protection of the parish priest. Don Mainetti had returned from the mountains and was just about to have his midday meal when a man came up to his house and said 'I am Bombacci. I am ready to give myself up to the partisans. Will you help me, Father?' Bombacci later told his captors that he had become disillusioned with Mussolini at Menaggio because he believed, as Lieutenant Birzer did, that he had planned to make his escape into Switzerland alone with Petacci and that only when he had been given proof that the frontier was impassable did he make an attempt to get to the Valtellina. Several others of the Duce's followers believed that Bombacci's suspicions might be justified. And his example in giving himself up to the protection of the parish priest 'was soon followed by others', so Mainetti told his bishop afterwards. 'In my dining-room,' his report went on, 'were gathered the Ministers Zerbino, Augusto Liverani, Fernando Mezzasoma, nervously wiping his spectacles, and Ruggero Romano with his fifteen-year-old son Constantino. . . . It was now past one o'clock. I managed to get some soup for the fugitives. Partisans arrived at the house with Captain Barbieri in command. Barbieri tries to discover if Mussolini is in the lorries. Romano says he was with us in Menaggio, but since then he has vanished.

Bombacci, however, approaches my sister and says, "He is with us. It is not fair that he should get away."'

He was making no attempt to do so. He sat in the armoured car, reading his documents and listening to the intermittent broadcasts of news on the wireless, deriving a brief hope from the report that he had been arrested in a town far away from Musso. Elena Curti Cucciati has described how, while he sat calmly waiting for Fallmeyer to return, a small figure in blue overalls and a crash-helmet appeared at the window of the armoured car. Elena thought it was a boy and wondered what he was doing there until the helmet was removed, long black hair tumbled down around a woman's anxious face and she recognized Claretta Petacci with her 'beautiful luminous eyes'. Mussolini spoke to her 'tenderly' as he tried to comfort her.

While he was still talking to Claretta in a low voice, Fallmeyer returned to the armoured car and told him that he had not been able to negotiate a passage for the Italians, but that all the German lorries could pass through provided that it was agreed that they should be searched at Dongo to see if any Fascists were hiding in them. Birzer suggested that Mussolini should put on a German soldier's overcoat and get into the back of one of the trucks. Translating for the others Mussolini said, 'He says I could get through too, disguised as a German.'

'Go on, Duce,' Claretta said immediately. 'Go on, save yourself.' She was almost in tears.

But he did not want to move. He thought that Fallmeyer had perhaps made a deal with the partisans, agreeing to hand him over to them in exchange for a free passage back to Germany for himself and his soldiers.

'I'm afraid we've been betrayed, Lieutenant,' he said to Birzer.

'No, Duce. Put on a German overcoat and helmet and hide in one of Lieutenant Fallmeyer's lorries. They will be searched, but it is your only hope.'

'Very well. But remember your orders are to defend me.'

'Of course, Duce.'

Birzer walked away to separate the Germans from the Italians. When he returned Mussolini was still in the armoured car, and Claretta Petacci was sitting on the roof, crying bitterly.

'Lieutenant,' Mussolini said angrily as Birzer came up to him.

'If my Ministers cannot have the same protection that you are affording me, I refuse to move.'

'But, Duce, it is impossible. The conditions are signed. All Italians must remain behind.'

'But at least my friend can come with me.'

'That is impossible as well.'

Mussolini remained seated, his mouth set in a stubborn line, refusing to move. But after Birzer had left to bring the lorry, in which Mussolini was to hide, alongside the armoured car, the others persuaded him to change his mind. When Birzer drove up with the lorry and said, 'Duce, this is your last chance,' he climbed out silently and, helped by Carradori, he put on the German overcoat and helmet and stepped up into the lorry.

As it drove away Claretta ran after her lover and frantically tried to jump on to one of the other lorries, and Birzer had to use all his strength to drag her off the tail-board.

So Mussolini went on into Dongo alone. The partisans, warned of his presence in the convoy by a bicyclist who had seen him in the armoured car and by Don Mainetti, were waiting for him in the square.

15

The Capture

27 APRIL 1945

I never want to see a German uniform again.

I

It was about three o'clock when Mussolini, crouching in the back
of a German lorry, was driven away towards Dongo. Marcello
Petacci's car with its diplomatic badges and the Spanish flag
flying from its bonnet was the only Italian one permitted to
follow.

As soon as the Germans had driven away the partisans came
cautiously forward to capture the Ministers and officials who were
still standing by the other cars in the road. Most of them surrendered without a struggle. The Ministers in the priest's house
also allowed themselves to be arrested, but those in the armoured
car were still determined to resist.

As the Germans drove past him, Barracu, his face a fearful
white, stood up in the driver's seat shouting 'Cowards! Traitors!'
at the top of his voice. Then he disappeared behind the armour,
and with considerable difficulty the heavy vehicle turned round
on the narrow road; but as soon as it had succeeded in doing so the
partisans opened fire on it again and one of them threw a grenade
beneath its wheels. For a few moments the armoured car returned
the fire until a white flag was pushed up through its turret and
Pavolini jumped out and ran down towards the lake, shouting to
the others to follow him and throw everything into the water.
Carradori, his arms full of papers, ran after him. They both dived
in and swam under an overhanging part of the bank where the
partisans could not see them.

The others did not get so far. Casalinuovo and Utimperghe
were caught before they had covered a few yards, and Barracu was
shot in the leg. An hour later Carradori and Pavolini were dragged

out of the lake, after a struggle in which both of them were wounded, and were sent on to Dongo.

Mussolini was already there. The inspection of the lorries had begun. Accompanied by Fallmeyer, the partisans started with the one in front, but they found nothing suspicious there nor in the one behind it. Sitting near the driver in one of those further back, however, a partisan, Giuseppe Negri, who had once been a sailor, found a German soldier who appeared to be either drunk or asleep. He was squatting beside two tins of petrol, wearing a German steel helmet and the overcoat of a corporal in an anti-aircraft unit. According to another partisan – one of those ten people who afterwards claimed for themselves the honour of being the first to discover him – the man was also wearing large dark glasses. Negri had not troubled to climb inside the other lorries, but, pushed forward by a sergeant of the customs guard, he went into this one and looked more closely at the man crouching down at the front of it. He noticed a machine-gun between his knees, and when the other German soldiers said that he was a drunken comrade he affected to believe them. He jumped down from the lorry and ran away to find the deputy political commissar of the brigade, Urbano Lazzaro.

'Come here,' he shouted to Lazzaro as soon as he saw him. 'I think it's him.'

Lazzaro ran over to the lorry and climbed up into it. He pushed his way through to the front where the figure in the corporal's overcoat was squatting. 'Aren't you an Italian?' he asked. There was a slight pause and then Mussolini looked up and said emphatically, 'Yes, I am an Italian.'

'Excellency!' Lazzaro exclaimed, so taken aback by the Duce's suddenly directed gaze that the deferential title escaped from him unthinkingly. 'You *are* here!'

Mussolini's 'face was ashen', Lazzaro noticed. 'It was also expressionless. The stubble on his chin was dark and thick, accentuating the pallor of his cheeks. The whites of his eyes were yellowish. One read by his eyes that he was extremely tired, but not afraid. Spiritual death. He no longer had anything to do among men.'

He had told the German soldiers not to risk their lives by attempting to save him from capture, and he made no attempt himself to use his gun. Helped by Lazzaro he stumbled out of the lorry and did not protest when the gun was taken from him or when the German helmet was removed from his head. The crowd of people in the square began to cheer when they realized who the prisoner was.

'Have you any other weapons?' Lazzaro asked him. But Mussolini did not answer him, so the partisans searched him and took from his pocket a loaded revolver. Again he made no protest. When a partisan tried to take from him his two brief-cases, however, he turned round sharply. 'Be careful,' he said, 'those cases contain secret documents of great importance both historically and for the future of Italy.'

It was an isolated outburst. He seemed resigned and broken and looked weak and old and ill. As he walked across the square to the mayor's office in the handsome but crumbling building beneath the overhanging slopes of Monte Bregagno, Lazzaro said to him, 'Keep calm, we will not hurt you.'

The mayor, Dr Giuseppe Rubini, also tried to comfort him. 'Don't worry,' he said, 'you will be all right.'

'I know,' Mussolini replied with a sort of ingratiating condescension. 'The lake people are kind-hearted.'

He was allowed to sit down in the mayor's office and the partisans and townspeople crowded round him asking questions which he answered with indignation, offended pride, or a misguided eagerness to please.

'Why did you betray Socialism?'

'I did not betray it. Socialism betrayed itself.'

'Why did you murder Matteotti?'

'I had nothing to do with that.'

'Why did you stab France in the back?'

'It would take too long to explain why Italy had to enter the war.'

'Did you make the speech after your release from the Gran Sasso of your own free will, or were you forced to make it?'

'It was forced on me.'

'Why did you allow such stern measures to be taken against the partisans? Some were tortured, did you know that?'

'My hands were tied. There was very little possibility of opposing Kesselring and Wolff in what they did. Again and again in conversation with General Wolff I mentioned that stories of people being tortured and other brutal deeds had come to my ears. One day Wolff replied that it was the only means of extracting the truth, and even the dead spoke the truth in his torture-chambers.'

The questions were thrown at him one after the other, and he answered them all. Talking made his mouth dry, and he asked for a drink. He was given a glass of water and then a cup of coffee. He drank eagerly and then fell into silence with his hands on his knees, staring at the wall. He had taken off the German greatcoat and thrown it to the floor and sat bareheaded in the uniform of the Fascist Militia.

Outside the German convoy was allowed to continue its journey to the north, and soon afterwards one of the partisans' political commissars, Francesco Terzi, sent a message in the opposite direction to Como to report the capture of Mussolini and to ask the local Committee of National Liberation what should be done with him.

2

It was now about half past three. It would be some time before the partisan who had gone to Como could be expected to return with the instructions of the Committee of National Liberation. The young partisan commander in Dongo, Count Pierluigi Bellini Delle Stelle, decided that he would have to move his important prisoner to a safer hiding-place in case an attempt was made to rescue him. By seven o'clock he had made up his mind to take Mussolini further up the mountainside, to the frontier guards' barracks at Germasino.

A heavy rain was falling again now, and it had become much colder. One of the partisans guarding him asked Mussolini if he wanted to put the German greatcoat back on. 'I never want to see a German uniform again,' he said and instead put on a pair of blue overalls he found lying in a corner of the room. In the car which took him up to Germasino he began to shiver feverishly. It was a slow journey, for the rain poured blindingly down, splashing against the windscreen so violently that the driver could scarcely see the road in front of him.

'This is the second time you have been a prisoner,' said one of the guards making a nervous attempt at conversation.

'That's life, my dear boy,' Mussolini replied with a hint of cynical gaiety. 'That's my fate, from dust to power and from power back to dust.'

He had recovered some of his lost spirit now, as if he had found encouragement in the idea of martyrdom. At Germasino he seemed almost happy. As the guards lit a fire for him and prepared a meal he talked to them as if he were their guest and not their prisoner and when he was asked to sign a piece of paper attesting that he was being treated well, he did so willingly. 'The 52nd Garibaldi Brigade arrested me today, Friday, 27 April, in the square of Dongo,' he wrote, the words sprawling loosely across the page. 'The treatment I received during and after the arrest was correct.'

Mussolini sat down at the dinner-table. He was hungry and ate with pleasure. During and after the meal he spoke to the guards at length as a garrulous don might have spoken to a party of nervous students. It was not a conversation so much as a lecture. He told the young men about his visit to Russia and of his flight across the limitless waste of steppe; he spoke of Stalin as one of the greatest men living and of Russia as the real victor of the war; he expounded the natures of Bolshevism and of National Socialism; he foretold the collapse of the British Empire. They listened and they did not interrupt him. Whatever he had become it was impossible to forget that for more than twenty years he had ruled them. One of them, a young man named Marioni, says that 'sometimes he looked worried but never frightened. He did not seem concerned about his fate. He said to me and my mate, "Youth is beautiful, beautiful!" My mate smiled at this, and he said, "Yes, yes I mean it. Youth is beautiful. I love the young even when they bear arms against me." Then he took out a gold watch and offered it to us. "Take it in memory of me," he said.'

At eleven o'clock he said he was tired and asked if he could go to bed. They took him upstairs to a small room where a bed had been made up beneath a barred window. Giorgio Buffelli, the guard who had spoken to him in the car, saw a small black object sticking out of his pocket and pointed to it diffidently. He had noticed it some time before and he had persuaded himself it was the handle of a pistol. Mussolini took it out obediently and showed it to him. It was a spectacle-case. Buffelli closed the door and shot home the bolt.

Back in Dongo, Count Bellini had found Claretta Petacci in a room at the Town Hall, where she had been locked up separately from her brother as she had no passport to substantiate her claim to Spanish nationality. She was still insisting that she was the sister of the Spanish Ambassador to the Salò Republic and had gone so far as to ask some of the village girls what they thought would happen to Claretta Petacci if the partisans caught her; and now that Count Bellini told her that Mussolini was his prisoner, she said that she had never met him.

'I know who you are,' Count Bellini said.

They had also discovered, he said, that the man masquerading as the Spanish Ambassador was Marcello. She could pretend no more. She asked Count Bellini how Mussolini was. He was alone and safe, Bellini said. Claretta looked at him closely for a moment and then she asked him, 'Who are you? Are you a friend?'

'An enemy,' Bellini said.

'I understand,' she said, biting a finger-nail that had been broken during the journey. 'You all hate me. You think I went after him for his money and his power. It isn't true. My love has not been selfish. I have sacrificed myself for him. I have tried to be good for him.' Then she asked impetuously. 'Will you do something for me?'

'What?'

'I want you to lock me up in the same place with him. I want to share his fate. If you kill him, kill me too.'

Count Bellini looked at her as closely as she had looked at him. He was surprised. He had not expected this. He left the room without replying.

3

The young partisan sent from Dongo with the news of Mussolini's arrest had arrived in Como at half past six. Unable to find any members of the local Committee of National Liberation he had given the information to Gino Bertinelli, a lawyer, who a few hours previously had become Prefect. 'Go back at once,' Bertinelli had told him, 'and tell your commander to take Mussolini somewhere safe up in the mountains, otherwise he will be found and rescued again. I will try to get in touch with Milan.' The messenger hurried back to Dongo to give these instructions to Count Bellini, who had already made the arrangements for Mussolini's removal to Germasino.

Later on that night the information that Mussolini had been taken up to Germasino was received in Como by a close friend of General Cadorna, Colonel Baron Giovanni Sardagna, who had recently been appointed commander of the town by the Committee of National Liberation. Sardagna put an urgent call through to Cadorna and after a long delay, and on a very indistinct line, he was able to talk to Cadorna's chief-of-staff, Colonel Palombo.

'Mussolini has been arrested this afternoon near Dongo,' Sardagna told Palombo. 'What shall we do? They're asking me for orders. What shall I tell them?'

'I can't say exactly yet. We've already been told about the arrest. I'll call you up and give you orders later.'

'All right. But we'll have to be quick about this.'

'Of course. But I can't tell you anything definite now. I'll ring and tell you later.'

At about half past eleven Sardagna's telephone rang. It was not Palombo to speak to him, but a telegram from the Committee of National Liberation in Milan. The message read: 'Bring Mussolini and the *gerarchi* to Milan as soon as possible.'

Before acting on these orders, Sardagna telephoned again to Palombo.

'Listen,' he said when at last he got through to him. 'I can understand your order, but I would like you to confirm it verbally.' To bring Mussolini to Milan was easier said than done, he protested. There were not many men he could trust. So it would have to be done by a few picked men secretly at night. They would be sure to run into road blocks. Of course, they might be able to take him by water as far as Como, but it would not be easy to find a suitable boat. 'I must confess,' he said firmly, 'the whole thing seems extremely risky.'

'Well, surely,' Palombo insisted, 'you can at least find a safe place where he could be hidden for a while.'

T — M

And so it was decided that he should be taken from Germasino to Blevio, a village seven kilometres north of Como, where a friend of Baron Sardagna's, a rich industrialist named Remo Cadematori, had a large secluded villa with a long frontage to the lake. Sardagna telephoned Cadematori and told him that he needed his villa to hide someone in. The man would be brought across the lake from Moltrasio during the night. If he was asked who it was, he must say that it was an English officer who had been wounded. Cadematori asked no questions, but he knew instinctively that the man was Mussolini. He went out into the cold night to sit on the steps of his boat-house and waited there, with his old gardener for company, looking out across the dark waters of the lake.

<h2 style="text-align:center">4</h2>

The order for Mussolini's removal from Germasino to Cadematori's villa at Blevio was passed on to Count Bellini Delle Stelle at about half past eleven. Two hours later he had collected his prisoner from the barracks at Germasino, and at half past two in the morning, near the Ponte della Falk, his car met the car which had brought Claretta Petacci from Dongo. It was still pouring with rain, but everyone got out of the cars and Mussolini, a blanket slung over his shoulders and his face partly concealed by a bandage so that he should look like a wounded man on his way to hospital, walked towards Claretta. They greeted each other with a formality which was both pathetic and absurd.

'Good evening, Your Excellency.'

'You, signora! Why are you here?'

'I would rather be with you.'

That was all that was said. The cars splashed off through the rain towards Moltrasio. Next to the driver of the leading car was Luigi Canali – a partisan who called himself 'Captain Neri' – and in the back Claretta sat between two other young partisans, Giuseppe Frangi and Guglielmo Cantoni, who were both fishermen. In the second car Mussolini sat between Count Bellini and Canali's mistress, Giuseppina Tuissi, who was pretending to be a nurse. In front, beside the driver, was Michele Moretti, known to his fellow-partisans as 'Pietro Gatti'.

The slippery roads twisted in and out of the rock beside the lake. Sometimes the cars stopped at a road block, and men would come out of the darkness with lanterns swinging in the slanting rain; often the sky was suddenly and brilliantly illuminated by flares and the quick light of shells exploding in the distance. Once they were fired on from the hills to their right, and Count Bellini jumped out of the car, shouting and waving his arms. At Moltrasio the cars stopped near the Hotel Imperiale, and Count Bellini got out again and walked away with Luigi Canali.

Mussolini sat still, not speaking. It was very quiet in Moltrasio, but seven kilometres to the south rockets were flying through the air above Como and there was the sound of firing in the streets. The Americans advancing fast across the Plain of Lombardy had already reached the Bergamo Alps.

After a quarter of a hour Luigi Canali and Count Bellini came back to the cars. 'I certainly did not intend,' Bellini said afterwards, 'that I should run the risk of having to hand Mussolini over to the Americans.' The plan of taking him across the lake to Remo Cadematori's villa at Blevio was abandoned. Canali suggested that Mussolini and Petacci would be more safely hidden if they were to be taken back through Azzano to a farm near Bonzanigo where he knew a peasant and his wife, Giacomo and Lia De Maria, who had sheltered partisans on the run from Fascist troops. This couple would take them in and ask no questions. Count Bellini agreed to this, and the cars turned round and drove back north again.

The prisoners reached Azzano at about a quarter past three in the morning. The De Marias' house was some way up the steep mountainside, and Canali told the others that they would have to leave the cars and walk. He led the way up a narrow path flanked by stone walls. It was still raining hard, and the water rushed down the path as if it were the bed of a mountain stream. Mussolini's spirits had fallen. The rain had soaked through the blanket which he still wore over his shoulders. Claretta held his arm tightly. Despite the heavy rain a full moon shone dimly through the clouds so that when they reached the outskirts of Bonsanigo they could see the white walls of the farmhouse in front of them.

Canali called to the De Marias, making the sound – coaxing, penetrating, and repetitive – that farmers use to call their animals.

It was the partisans' signal, and in a few moments the door opened. Giacomo De Maria stood in the doorway with his wife, holding an oil lamp, behind him. They recognized Canali and stood aside to let him in. Mussolini followed him and slumped down on a bench in the kitchen with Claretta next to him, her arm through his.

'They are prisoners,' Canali said. 'Treat them well. Let them sleep.'

He left the two young fishermen, Cantoni and Frangi, to guard them and went back to the cars with Count Bellini, Giuseppina Tuissi, and Michele Moretti.

Giacomo De Maria lit a fire and offered the two prisoners something to eat. He did not yet know who either of them was.

'What can I get the gentleman?' he asked Claretta, unwilling to address directly the huddled figure with the bandaged head next to her.

'*Niente,*' Mussolini mumbled, shaking his head, not looking up from the fire, his hands deep in the pockets of the blue overalls.

'Coffee for me, please,' Claretta said.

'We haven't any real,' De Maria said apologetically, 'but I could make you some from flavoured powder.'

'I don't mind.'

He heated the coffee in silence. No one spoke. At length his wife came down from an upstairs bedroom, where she had turned her two sons out of a double bed and sent them into the loft. She said the room was ready if the gentleman would like to go upstairs. Mussolini did not answer her and he did not move.

'The room is ready,' Claretta said softly. 'Shall we go up?'

He stood up then, but still he said nothing as he followed Signora De Maria up the steep stone steps to the whitewashed bedroom on the top floor, where an immense walnut bed was the only furniture apart from two chairs with straw seats and a washstand. Mussolini walked towards the window, and De Maria, who had followed him up the stairs, thought that he meant to escape and quickly came up behind him to close the shutters. Claretta went over to the bed and felt it, as if she were in a hotel, but when she asked for another pillow she did so diffidently.

'He is used to two,' she said. It seemed to Lia De Maria that she was shy. And she noticed when she gave her another pillow that she looked at a darn in the linen closely and then put it on her side of the bed. The other two pillows she put on the side nearer the window where Mussolini liked to sleep.

He was sitting on the bed now, undoing his bandage. Signora De Maria watched him. As the white muslin unwound from his forehead she began to recognize the familiar face of the Duce. She stared at it, bewildered and alarmed, and the sound of Claretta's voice, asking if she might wash, made her jump.

'We are mountain people,' she said nervously. 'You must excuse us. You will have to go downstairs to wash.'

Claretta followed her downstairs to an outhouse, where she washed with one of the fishermen looking through a crack in the door. She had a good body with nice breasts, he said afterwards, and was not surprised that Mussolini had taken to her. He followed her back to the room when she had finished and told her that the door would have to be left ajar.

She finished undressing in the dim electric light and got into bed beside her lover. She murmured something to him and he replied. Cantoni and Frangi, listening through the partly open doorway, tried to hear what they were talking about, but they could not. They thought they heard the names 'Pavolini' and 'Graziani' and they believed that Mussolini said, 'I'm sure they won't kill me,' and then something like 'Can you forgive me?' and later on, when she had answered him, he murmured, 'That doesn't matter any more.' At one point when the talking stopped, the two youths became nervous and thought that perhaps the prisoners were planning to escape. They threw open the door suddenly and sprang into the room. Claretta pulled the sheet over her face and cringed down beside Mussolini, who sat up and said to them in a voice of mild reproof, 'Go away, boys. You needn't behave like that. Don't be tiresome.' They noticed how exhausted he seemed and how haggard and despairing his face was.

They left the room and squatted down once more outside on the landing. The light was switched out; and soon afterwards, above the continuous murmur of the wind and rain beyond the landing window, they heard the sounds of Mussolini's heavy breathing. All night long he slept, the closed shutters in front of the window of his room muffling the roar of thunder and hiding from him the strangely phosphorescent glow of the almost continuous lightning. At dawn the two young guards slept too; and as they slept the storm abated.

At about eleven o'clock Signora De Maria went out into the fields. It was a lovely morning. The earth was sodden, but the air was warm and clear. There was a gentle breeze from the south. She looked back at the house and saw the Duce leaning out of the window looking across towards the snow-covered mountains beyond the Lago di Lecco and pointing out the peaks to his mistress. Lia De Maria finished her work in the fields before returning to the house.

Her husband went up to the bedroom to ask if the prisoners would like something to eat. It would have to be simple food, he added with a peasant's defensive humility. Claretta asked for *polenta* with milk, knowing that to be the food of the *alpigiani* and hoping perhaps that the man would be pleased at being asked for it. Mussolini said gruffly he did not mind what he had. He was depressed to the point of despair. His eyes were bloodshot and his face was paper white beneath the grey stubble of his beard. He did not ask if he might wash or shave.

De Maria brought a box into the bedroom, and his wife covered it with a white table-cloth. Claretta ate the *polenta* and seemed to enjoy it, but Mussolini was not hungry. He spent a long time silently eating a piece of bread and a slice of *salame*. He kept putting the bread down and picking up a glass of water, from which he took little sips as he stared at the red flowers embroidered on the table-cloth. Was it true that the Americans had taken Como? he asked his young guards. They said it was, and he nodded resignedly.

When she had finished her *polenta* Claretta went back to lie on the bed. She pulled the covers up to her chin and shut her eyes, but she did not seem to be sleeping. Mussolini sat on the edge of the bed with his back to her, looking out of the window at the mountains.

A clock in the village struck the hours as the long day wore on.

27–8 APRIL 1945

> *However much the killing of one man by*
> *another is profoundly repugnant to my con-*
> *victions, I find, nevertheless, that violence*
> *from below in response to violence from above,*
> *although regrettable, is sometimes necessary.*
> *When all the roads are closed it is necessary*
> *to open up a passage, even at the cost of*
> *blood.*

The night before, on hearing of Mussolini's arrest, various members of the Committee of National Liberation for North Italy and senior representatives of the Volunteer Freedom Corps had met in Milan.

The reports of the meeting, which began soon after eleven o'clock, are contradictory and unreliable. It is at least certain that the decisions taken at various times during the night were taken by six or seven men acting in the name of the Committee of National Liberation, but not with its full authority. Two of these men were Luigi Longo, the dedicated Communist who had worked hard to make the partisan movement a political one, and Walter Audisio, a tall, pale, thirty-six-year-old book-keeper and former anti-Fascist volunteer in Spain, who called himself 'Giovanbattista di Cesare Magnoli' or, more simply and more often, 'Colonel Valerio'.

In the presence of more scrupulous and less politically committed members of the Committee it had been decided to give Walter Audisio the mission of bringing Mussolini back to Milan. Later on, however, when the others had gone, the 'particulars of this mission' were discussed. These 'particulars' involved Mussolini's being brought back dead. The execution had, in fact, already been ordered by Palmiro Togliatti in a mandate given – as he said later in the Milan Communist newspaper *Unità* – 'as head of the Communist Party and as Vice-Premier of Italy'. This order, Togliatti admitted, was that Mussolini and all his Ministers were to be shot as soon as they had been captured and identified. But it was never revealed to the non-Communist members of the Committee of National Liberation, who felt bound by the terms of the armistice which provided that Mussolini should be handed over to the Allies; and Ivanoe Bonomi, indeed, Badoglio's successor as Premier, said that he had never even heard of it. The Communist members of the Committee were, however, its most powerful ones, and some of them were known to sympathize with the views of the Piedmontese Committee, which had gone so far as to draft a penal code of its own whereby not only all members of Mussolini's Government, but all other Fascists regarded as guilty of 'the suppression of liberty' as well, were to be executed without trial if they did not surrender before the proclamation of a general insurrection in northern Italy.

In order to avoid so summary an execution of Mussolini three attempts – two by Americans and one by the Government in the south – had already been made to find him. None of them had been successful, but the members of the Milan Committee who had decided to have him shot knew that other attempts were being planned. Accordingly, at three o'clock in the morning a telegram was sent from Milan to the Allied Headquarters at Siena. This is what it said: 'The Committee of National Liberation regret not able to hand over Mussolini who having been tried by Popular Tribunal has been shot in the same place where fifteen patriots were shot by Fascists Stop.'

An hour later General Cadorna handed to A⊥disio a pass which, with the help of Dr Guastoni, an intermediary between the partisans and the Allies, he had obtained from Captain Emilio Q. Daddario of the American Army, a liaison officer with the Committee, who had been involved in one of the unsuccessful American attempts to find Mussolini. The pass was written in English and read:

Colonel Valerio (otherwise known as Magnoli Giovanbattista di Cesare) is an Italian officer belonging to the General Command of the Volunteers of Liberty. He is sent on a mission by the National Liberation Committee for north Italy, in Como and its province and

must therefore be allowed to circulate freely with his armed escort.
E. Q. Daddario, Captain.

Armed with this and another pass bearing the stamp – in the
shape of a five-pointed star – of the Volunteer Freedom Corps,
Audisio left Milan in a small car at seven o'clock in the morning of
28 April. He was accompanied by Aldo Lampredi, a workman
who also had the rank of Colonel in the Volunteer Freedom Corps,
and was followed in a lorry by twelve partisans commanded by
Riccardo Mordini, who had fought with the International Brigade in Spain. They were armed with Stens or Beretta machine-
guns and were wearing, not the civilian clothes they usually wore
on their missions, but nondescript khaki uniforms. Audisio was
wearing a long brown mackintosh and a red, green, and white
scarf.

He arrived in Como at eight o'clock and, quickly jumping out of
his car, ran up the steps of the Prefecture with Aldo Lampredi. Inside the building the first person he saw was Gino Bertinelli, the
new Prefect. Bertinelli noticed how nervous and agitated he
looked and immediately asked to see his papers. With an irritated
gesture Audisio brought out the one stamped by the Volunteer
Freedom Corps; but Bertinelli, who had seen scores of similar
ones in the last few days, was not impressed. So Audisio produced the one signed by Daddario. This had more effect on the
Prefect, but before promising his cooperation he wanted to know
exactly what Audisio's mission was. When he was told that it was
to take Mussolini and the other Fascists captured in Dongo to
Milan, Bertinelli was more guarded than ever. He knew that the
local partisans in Como would not want to be deprived of the
credit for the capture of so valuable a prisoner by handing him
over to these two unknown 'colonels' from Milan. The prison of
San Donnino in Como had already been prepared for Mussolini's
reception, and plans were being made for him to be taken there.

In their obvious anxiety to give nothing away, Bertinelli and his
associates – according to one of the various contradictory accounts
that Audisio subsequently gave of the events of this day – betrayed
'the petty jealousies of a bourgeois spirit'. And by ten o'clock the
conversation had become acrimonious. Audisio, however, was unable to persuade either Bertinelli or the Como Committee of
National Liberation to give way, and he demanded to be taken to

Baron Sardagna; but the Baron had disappeared and no one knew where he could be found. He then demanded to telephone Milan, and furiously waved his pistol as he told everyone to leave the room while he did so. During his conversation with Milan his fellow-colonel, Aldo Lampredi, and Ricardo Mordini, the commander of his escort, went on to Dongo without him, leaving no message.

Eventually a compromise was reached. It was agreed that the Fascists would be handed over to Audisio provided he signed a receipt for them; and it was also agreed that he would be allowed to take the transport he needed to Dongo, provided two representatives from the Como Committee of National Liberation accompanied him there. And so at last, at a quarter past twelve, Audisio prepared to leave Como. At the last minute, however, Commander Giovanni Dessì, an Italian intelligence officer, who had been asked by the Americans to find Mussolini for them, and another agent who called himself 'Carletto', attached themselves to the party. By this time Audisio was furiously impatient and determined to put up with no further obstruction. When the car in which the two agents were travelling stopped for petrol on the outskirts of the town, he drove up quickly beside it and, with a machine-gun in his hand, gave them the peremptory order: '*Scendere !*' and reluctantly they both did so.

Having got rid of two of his unwanted companions, Audisio, followed by the other two – the representatives of the Como partisans – drove fast along the road to Dongo. On the way he commandeered a big removal van, and it was in this that at ten minutes past two he drove with his escort into the square of Dongo.

Mistaking him and his companions for escaping Fascists or the leaders of an attempt to liberate their prisoners, the partisans in Dongo fired on him.

'I am sent by the General Command,' Audisio shouted at the top of his voice as he jumped down into the middle of the square waving his arms above his head. 'Who's in command here? Take me to him at once.'

After some delay a message, which he took to be insolent, was given to him. The partisan commander was in the Town Hall, he was told, and if the colonel cared to come up he would be received. Audisio lost his temper. He shouted furiously that he had given an order and that he intended it to be carried out. He marched across the square to the Town Hall surrounded by his escort; and Count Bellini came down the steps to meet him. The colonel could come in, he said, but the escort would have to remain outside.

In Count Bellini's room at the Town Hall, Audisio found his colleague Aldo Lampredi and he asked him to leave the room while he spoke to the Count alone. The conversation between the two men was cool and unfriendly, although Audisio did at least succeed in persuading Bellini that the two representatives of the Como Committee of National Liberation were suspected Fascists. Having agreed to lock them up, however, Bellini gave Audisio no hope that he would prove any more amenable than Bertinelli, the Prefect of Como, had been. He was determined not to be hurried into doing something which he would regret, and Audisio wrote afterwards that he was obliged to speak to the young partisan commander 'very frankly'. A partisan named Sauro Gnesi, whose sister was Bellini's mistress, said that he saw the colonel from Milan hand the Count a yellow envelope in which there was a sheet of paper signed by a single member of the Committee of National Liberation for North Italy, on which was written the sentence: 'Colonel Valerio is empowered to bring the war criminal Benito Mussolini to Milan.' Later on, however, when Count Bellini's fellow-partisans had been allowed to return to the room where the discussion was taking place, Audisio put all pretence aside and announced his real intention.

'I have come,' he said, 'to shoot Mussolini and the *gerarchi*.'

Bellini and his partisans, as the Count afterwards said, were dumbfounded. At length Bellini protested that Audisio's plan was 'most irregular'. Only that morning he had arranged with the National Liberation Committee in Como to transport all the Fascists, including Mussolini, there. What was all this, he asked, about shooting them in Dongo? He was the local partisan commander and he did not think he could allow it. The argument continued until three o'clock, when Count Bellini thought of an excuse for gaining time. As some of the Fascist prisoners were at Germasino, he proposed that he should leave to go and get them. Only he, Michele Moretti, and Luigi Canali knew where Mussolini was, and he believed that while he was away from Dongo there would be no possibility of Audisio's discovering his hiding-place.

He was wrong. Both Moretti and Canali were in the Town Hall when he left it and both of them were fervent Communists. Moretti in addition knew the other colonel from Milan, Aldo Lampredi, very well, as they had fought together in the past. Within ten minutes of Count Bellini's departure the two colonels, Audisio and Lampredi, drove quickly out of Dongo. Sitting in the front of the car, next to the driver, was Michele Moretti.[1]

1. The subsequent history of these men is illuminating. Walter Audisio, alias 'Colonel Valerio', alias 'Giovanbattista di Cesare Magnoli', is a Communist member of the Chamber of Deputies. Aldo Lampredi, alias, 'Guido', is also alive, but he has refused to talk about the events leading up to Mussolini's death. Michele Moretti, alias 'Pietro Gatti' although described by previous writers as either dead or living in luxury abroad on his share of the Dongo loot, is in fact still living, poorly and simply, on the outskirts of Cernobbio. He is still a Communist and after speaking to a few fellow-partisans and villagers immediately after Mussolini was killed now refuses to say any more. Giuseppe Frangi, alias 'Lino', also spoke to various people after Mussolini's death and then died in mysterious circumstances on 5 May 1945. His friend Guglielmo Cantoni, alias 'Sandrino', disappeared for some time and was believed to be in Switzerland. He gave some information to a journalist, but it was clear that at the time Mussolini was shot he was some way away from the others and could not be sure what happened. He is now living in a small village on the hills above the lake. Luigi Canali, alias 'Captain Neri', has disappeared. He seems to have asked a number of unwelcome questions concerning the ultimate destination of the 'Donga Treasure' and to have insisted that receipts should be given to the partisans for the money which was handed over to the Communist Party. His mistress, Giuseppina Tuissi, alias 'Gianna', made inquiries about him, and she too disappeared. Her friend Anna Bianchi asked about Giuseppina, and she was beaten up and her dead body was afterwards thrown into Lake Como. Anna's father swore to find and kill her murderers, and finally he also was killed. For political reasons it was not until 1957 that an investigation into these murders was held at Padua. But like so many other recent Italian scandals, notably the Montesi case, the truth about the affair appears to be by now so completely clouded by lies, evasions, and the silence of fear that it cannot be discovered.

17

Death at Villa Belmonte

No one can deny fate twice and every one
dies the death which befits his character.

I

Soon after four o'clock the silence in the bedroom at the De Marias' farmhouse was broken by the sound of quick footsteps in the yard outside. A tall man in a brown mackintosh came into the house and ran up the stairs. The door of the bedroom was thrown open, and the man burst in.

'Hurry up,' he said abruptly to Mussolini. 'I have come to rescue you.'

'Really!' Mussolini said with heavy sarcasm, managing for the first time that day to smile ironically as he looked at the tall, thin man with the machine-gun in his hand. 'How kind of you!'

'Are you armed?' Audisio asked him.

'No.'

Audisio turned away from him and looked at Claretta still lying on the bed with her face to the wall. 'You too,' he said, 'get up quickly. Hurry up!'

She got off the bed and began rummaging amongst the clothes.

'What are you looking for?' Audisio asked her angrily.

'My knickers,' she said.

'Don't worry about them. Come on, hurry up.'

She left the bed, and as Mussolini put on the grey jacket of his Militia uniform she picked up her handbag and another bag shaped like a bucket. Mussolini asked Audisio for news of Vittorio. He had been rescued too, Audisio said. 'And Zerbino and Mezzasoma?' Mussolini asked. 'Where are they?'

'We are looking after them also.'

Mussolini, Audisio said, 'gave a sigh of relief'.

'Quickly! Quickly!' Audisio urged them, almost pushing them down the stairs in his anxiety to get out of the house.

Lia De Maria watched them through the window as they were taken away out of sight down the steep lane to the road. She crossed herself when they had gone, for she had liked the woman, as the two young fishermen had also done, and admired her courage. She turned back into the room and went towards the bed. She had put clean sheets on it the night before and noticed that both they and the darned pillow were smeared with the grey marks of mascara-stained tears.

Claretta was not crying now, but her eyes were red and her lids swollen. She held Mussolini's arm tightly as she stumbled down the rough path in her high-heeled shoes; carrying her two bags with two coats – one of fur and the other of camel-hair – over her arm; but he had no strength left to support her. He stumbled too in the steep lane and put out his hand to steady himself against the wall and Claretta tried to help him, but he shrugged her off angrily as a resentful cripple might have done. They did not speak to each other.

They were taken down into the village, and as they walked across the square three women, who were beating their clothes noisily against the sides of a stone washing-trough, looked up at them. An old peasant was walking down the mountainside with a basket on his back and a woman was strolling along the road with a little boy. It was a quiet afternoon. The rain had stopped.

They turned left in the square and walked under an archway towards the asphalt road where the car had been left. Signora Rosita Barbarita was taking her two dogs for a walk, and when she came up to the car she went across to it to talk to the driver, whose name was Geminazza. He was nervous and did not want to talk. 'Be on your guard,' he had been told. 'You will soon see some people whom you cannot fail to recognize. But forget them immediately. If you don't forget you won't lose just your memory, but your head.'

As Signora Barbarita left him, she saw a group of people coming up the road towards her. A man in a brown mackintosh said, 'Go away! Go away!' and so she walked quickly back away from them. It seemed that they were having an argument although she could not hear what they said. She saw a woman throw her arms round the neck of an old man, who was pushed roughly into the car by the man in the mackintosh.

The car drove on towards the village to turn round in the square, and when it came back past her Signora Barbariti saw that the old man was Mussolini. Only he and Claretta were in the car with the driver. The man in the mackintosh sat on one of the mud-guards and the other two men·stood on the running-board. As the car moved slowly away up the hill, the two young fishermen, Cantoni and Frangi, ran after it.

The driver, Geminazza, could see them in his mirror. He could also see Mussolini and Claretta. 'They were close together,' he said years later, 'with their heads almost touching. Mussolini was pale and the Signora tranquil. It seemed to me that she showed no particular signs of fear. . . . We stopped at the gate of Villa Belmonte.'

2

It was a large villa standing back from the road behind a stone wall. Two families of evacuees lived here – Bernardo Bellini, an engineer, with his wife Teresa, and Rinaldo Oppizzi with his wife Aminta and their two little girls Lelia and Bianca. When Audisio's car stopped outside the wrought-iron gates of the villa, Signora Bellini was sitting on the terrace of the villa looking out over the lake. Her husband was inside listening to the wireless with Rinaldo Oppizzi. Below her in the garden Lelia Oppizzi was reading a book and the Bellinis' maid, Giuseppina Cordazzo, was weeding one of the flower-beds. Suddenly they heard a man's voice shout out, 'Get inside! Go indoors!'

Teresa Bellini caught sight of a heavily built man getting out of the car wearing what she thought was a black beret and holding the lapels of his coat. He looked 'like a mountaineer', she says, 'holding on to the straps of his rucksack'.

Audisio ordered Claretta to follow Mussolini out of the car, and the driver watched him as he levelled his machine-gun at them both and 'pronounced a few words very quickly'. The driver thought they referred to an order Audisio had received and to a sentence of death he had been ordered to execute, but 'everything happened so quickly' he was not sure. Mussolini remained completely motionless and impassive, but Claretta lost control of herself and threw her arms around him, jumping up and down and shouting, 'No! No! You mustn't do it. You mustn't!'

In a voice which Geminazza described as 'dry and nervous', the colonel said, 'Leave him alone, otherwise you'll get shot too.' But Claretta paid no attention and went on jumping up and down convulsively as she clung to Mussolini. Audisio squeezed the trigger and Claretta rushed at him, grabbing the barrel of the gun in both her hands and shouting, 'You cannot kill us like this.'

Audisio shot again. Geminazza saw the sweat pouring down his face. He squeezed the trigger a third time, but the gun was jammed and he pulled his pistol from his pocket. That would not fire either, and he shouted to Moretti, 'Bring me your gun.' Moretti gave him his French machine-gun and he pointed it at Mussolini, who faced him squarely, holding back the lapels of his jacket. 'Shoot me in the chest,' he said. Geminazza heard the words distinctly. They were the last Mussolini spoke.

3

The first shot which Audisio fired from Moretti's gun killed Claretta, who fell to the ground without a sound. The next hit Mussolini, who stumbled back against the stone wall of the villa, where he slid slowly to the ground with his legs bent under him. He was not dead and lay on the ground, breathing heavily. Audisio went up to him and shot him again in the chest. Mussolini's body jerked violently and then lay still. Audisio looked at it in silence for a moment and then said to Geminazza, 'Look at his expression. Doesn't it suit him?'

Moretti came up to them and made a gesture at Geminazza, as if to say, 'Accidents can't be helped.' Audisio offered them cigarettes and, although he did not usually smoke, Geminazza took one. He felt 'very shocked' and hoped it would soothe his nerves. He helped the others pick up the empty cartridge-cases from the road and then he got into the car to drive the two colonels and Michele Moretti back to Dongo. The two fishermen were left to guard the bodies. It was twenty minutes past four.

Less than a minute had passed since the car had stopped beside the villa gates. As it drove away again there was a sudden roll of thunder, and a few seconds later a torrential rain began to fall.

The people in the villa heard the shots and agreed that in all there were ten; but a high hedge which grew above the level of the wall had prevented them from seeing what had happened. The maid, Giuseppina, pretending that she wanted to pick some radishes, went up quietly to peep through the hedge; but a voice called out, *'Via! Via!'* and she went away without having seen anything.

At six o'clock Geminazza drove back from Dongo, where Audisio had attended to the execution of fifteen of the men who had been captured at Musso.[1] The bodies of Mussolini and Claretta were put in the back of the car, which then drove away in the rain to the main road at Azzano. Here the removal van was waiting to take them on to Milan, and they were thrown into it on top of the other corpses.

1. The fifteen executed men were Marcello Petacci, Fernando Mezzasoma, Nicola Bombacci, Alessandro Pavolini, Paolo Zerbino (Minister of the Interior), Ruggero Romano (Minister of Public Works), Augusto Liverani (Minister of Communications), Paolo Porta (Inspector of the Fascist Party in Lombardy), Luigi Gatti (Mussolini's secretary), Alfredo Coppolo (President of the Institute of Fascist Culture), Ernesto Daquanno (Director of the 'Stefani' Agency), Mario Nudi (President of the Fascist Agricultural Association), Colonel Vito Casalinuovo, Pietro Salustri (a captain in the Air Force), and Hintermayer, a propagandist.

18

The Piazzale Loreto

29 APRIL 1945

Here is the epitaph I want on my tomb:
Here lies one of the most intelligent animals
that ever appeared on the face of the earth.

In the early morning of 29 April 1945 the removal van, having passed through several American road-blocks, stopped in front of a half-built garage in Piazzale Loreto, where the fifteen hostages had been shot by the Germans nine months before. It was a Sunday. The corpses were tipped out and lay in a tumbled confusion until dawn, when a passer-by arranged them in some sort of order. Mussolini was laid out a little way apart from the others with his head and shoulders on Claretta's breasts. Two young men came up and kicked Mussolini repeatedly and savagely on the jaw. When they left him his face was appallingly disfigured. His mouth was open and his upper lip pulled back from his teeth so that he looked as if he were about to speak. Someone put a stick in his hand and squeezed his fingers round it.

By nine o'clock a large crowd had gathered and the people in it were shouting and jumping up and down to get a closer view. Some of them were calling out obscenities and curses, or shooting at the bodies with pistols and shot-guns; others were peering forward silently with a kind of fascinated satisfaction or a pitying disgust; a few were laughing hysterically. One woman fired five shots into Mussolini's body to 'avenge her five dead sons'. The crowd grew, and those in front were pushed forward so that they trampled over the bodies, and the partisans guarding them fired over the heads of the surging mass and then turned a hose on them in an attempt to drive them back.

'Who is it you want to see?' an immense partisan, his bare arms covered with blood, called out to the screaming people.

'Pavolini', a man called back. Then another voice shouted

'Bombacci', and others 'Mussolini', 'Petacci', 'Buffarini-Guidi'. The partisan lifted each up in turn, gripping them under the armpits, holding them high above his head.

'Higher!' the crowd shouted. 'Higher! Higher! We can't see.' 'String them up!' a loud voice called authoritatively.

Ropes were found and tied round the corpses' ankles. Mussolini was pulled up first, the soles of his split boots pointing upwards towards the overhanging girders of the garage roof, his head about six feet from the ground. His face was the colour of putty and splashed with red stains, and his mouth was open still. The crowd cheered wildly, and those in the front row spat at him and threw what filth they could find. Achille Starace was forced to stand up in a lorry to watch, and then he was dragged to a wall and shot and his body was thrown on to the pile to await its turn to be displayed.

Claretta Petacci was drawn up next. Several woman screamed. And then for a few seconds, as the bodies swung heavily in the clear morning light, a strange silence fell on the square. The jeering and shouting died away, the watching faces became for a moment calm and thoughtful, the air seemed filled, says a man who was there, with 'an oppressive quality, an atmosphere of expectancy, as if the whole thing was a dream from which we would awake to find the world unchanged. It was as if we had all in those few seconds shared the realization that the Duce was really dead at last, that he had been slaughtered without trial, and that there had been a time when we would have given his dead body, not insults and degradation, but the honours due to a hero and prayers worthy of a saint'.

The mood soon changed. Claretta's skirt had fallen down over her face revealing her naked thighs and hips, and when a partisan stood on a box and reached up to tuck the torn material between her tightly roped legs there were jeers and shouts from the mob. A man came up towards the body and poked it obscenely with a stick, and it rocked stiffly and twisted around at the end of the rope like a mechanical doll dancing, holding out its jointless arms towards an imagined partner. But Claretta's face was not that of a doll. Men were struck by its beauty beneath the dirt and the smears of blood. Her eyes, which were open when she was first tied up, had closed slowly. She looked gentle and at peace. She seemed even to be smiling.

Mussolini's tortured features expressed no such contentment. Some men thought they saw in the line of his swollen mouth and in the sightless, staring eyes a look of hopeless despair, but most of them could see no more than the ghastly travesty of a mud-splashed face.

Notes on Sources

In most cases the source for both direct and indirect quotations is indicated in the text. Where this has not been done the authorities are given below.

GENERAL

The most comprehensive biography of Mussolini is the four-volume *Mussolini: l'uomo e l'opera* by Giorgio Pini and Duilio Susmel. I have found this of particular value in describing Mussolini's life at Gargnano. A more recent biography in two volumes, *Il figlio del fabbro* by Mino Caudana, was published in 1960. It adds little of importance to the earlier work, however, and although painstakingly prepared and not inaccurate it is ill-written and partisan. But there are several details in it which I have not discovered elsewhere. Neither of these two books has been translated into English. Paolo Monelli's *Mussolini: Piccolo Borghese* has been translated as *Mussolini: An Intimate Life*, and, although Monelli has been careful to paint a portrait to suit the title of his book, his is the best short life of Mussolini which has yet been written. Monelli, an expert journalist, interviewed a number of Italians both for this and for an earlier book, *Roma 1943* (this has not been translated as a whole, but certain parts of it were incorporated in the translation of *Mussolini: Piccolo Borghese*), and has been able to provide much new evidence about Mussolini. I have acknowledged my debt to him and to Pini and Susmel and Caudana below. Richard Wichtering's *Mussolini* is an interesting account of him as seen through German eyes. Georges Roux's *Mussolini*, the most recent biography, is a long and careful one, but contains many dubious interpretations of the facts.

Mussolini's own *My Autobiography* is of little interest except as a sort of psychological case-book. It purports to be a translation by Richard Washburn Child, the American Ambassador in Rome from 1921 to 1924, but was in fact written by Child from notes taken during conversations with Mussolini. It is not merely untrustworthy but boring. Emil Ludwig's *Gespräche mit Mussolini* (translated as *Talks with Mussolini*), also written after lengthy interviews with Mussolini, is a much more interesting and revealing book. Where I have quoted from this I have acknowledged the source in the text. Mussolini's *Autobiografia*, written in prison in 1912, was published in 1947 with many notes and additions as *La mia vita*. Parts of it had already been incorporated in an otherwise worthless biography by Rossato which was published before the March on Rome.

The best of the early and semi-official biographies of Mussolini is Margherita Sarfatti's *Dux* (translated as *The Life of Benito Mussolini*). Margherita Sarfatti knew Mussolini intimately and although she admired him profoundly – at least until Claretta Petacci began to take up so much of his time – her book, if evasive on occasions, is not unduly prejudiced and is sometimes frank. She is an extremely intelligent woman and a gifted writer.

By far the most reliable history of Fascism is *Storia d'Italia nel periodo fascista* by Luigi Salvatorelli and Giovanni Mira. My quotations from this book are taken from the third edition (Einaudi 1959). I have found it extremely useful. The most recent account of modern Italian history available in English is *Italy* by Denis Mack Smith.

All the quotations throughout the book from Mussolini's public utterances can be found in *Scritti e discorsi*, and all the quotations from Mussolini's correspondence with Hitler in *Hitler e Mussolini: lettere e documenti*.

MUSSOLINI'S RISE TO POWER, PART ONE

An essential book on the young Mussolini, particularly on his life in Switzerland and the Trentino, is Gaudens Megaro's *Mussolini in the Making*. Megaro was at pains to refute much of what Mussolini's adulatory biographers had written about this period of his life and was able, after extensive research, to publish extracts from many of his early writings which the Duce would have liked to suppress. All the quotations from *Il Trentino*, *La Vita Trentina*,

La Lotta di Classe, L'Avvenire del Lavoratore, L'Avanguardia Socialista, Avanti !, and *Il Popolo d'Italia* in the first three chapters of my book are taken from this excellent study. I have also taken from it the account of Mussolini's behaviour at his mother's funeral as described by *Il Pensiero Romagnolo*.

Angelica Balabanoff's disparaging account of Mussolini's behaviour and appearance in Switzerland and Milan are from her *My Life as a Rebel*. The letter which Mussolini wrote to a friend from Lausanne and from which I have quoted in Chapter I was previously quoted in Sarfatti; and his own accounts of his childhood and the countryside of his birth and his journey to school are from *La mia vita* and *Vita di Sandro e di Arnaldo*. For details of his behaviour as a schoolboy at Dovia, Faenza, and Forlimpopoli, as a teacher at Gualtieri and Caneva, and as a lover everywhere I have drawn upon the conversations which Paolo Monelli and I have had with people who knew him at these times. The account of Mussolini's discovery of syphilitic symptoms was given to Monelli by Dr Riccardo Pascoli of Tolmezzo, who had the story from his uncle, Dante Marpillero, the man who persuaded him to see a doctor; and the account of Rachele Mussolini as a housewife in Milan was given to Monelli by Aldo Parini. The account of Mussolini's demanding to live with Rachele Guidi and of his early life in Via Merenda is taken from Rachele Mussolini's *La mia vita con Benito* (translated as *My Life with Mussolini*). This is an interesting but unsatisfactory and fundamentally inaccurate book. Bruno d'Agostini's *Colloqui con Rachele Mussolini* covers the same ground but is fresher and more evocative, and most of my quotations from Rachele are taken from d'Agostini except where I have shown otherwise. The history of Mussolini's fight for power has b..en written by Guido Dorso in *Mussolini alla conquista del potere*, and I have found this the most useful book for the period between 1913 and 1922. Other books I have found of particular use for these years are G. A. Chiruco's *Storia della rivoluzione fascista*, Cesare Rossi's *Mussolini com'era*, Edoardo Susmel's *Mussolini e il suo tempo*, and Alatri's *Le origini del fascismo*. Italo Balbo's *Diario* 1922 suffers from having been published in Italy in 1932, when much of what he would have liked to say was suppressed.

Mussolini's conversation with Michele Campana on their way

back from Cattolica is taken from Monelli, who was told about it by Campana himself. My account of Mussolini's superstitions and lack of interest in art comes mainly from Sarfatti; the comments of Alberto Moravia on Fascist censorship from the *Paris Review*, Salvatorelli's comments on Staracian discipline from *Storia d'Italia nel periodo fascista*. The two stories relating to Mussolini's sentimentality come from M. H. H. Macartney's *One Man Alone* and G. Ward Price's *I Know These Dictators*. Mussolini's comment after being shot by Miss Gibson also comes from Ward Price, and the King's comment after being shot at in Tirana from Ciano. The sources for the accounts of Mussolini's sexual activities after becoming Head of the Government are two of his former mistresses to whom I spoke in Rome; a pornographic book published in Paris after the Magda Coraboeuf scandal and attributed to her; the reminiscences of other women whose evidence has been used by previous writers, including Monelli and (less frankly) Nino D'Aroma; and the evidence of servants such as Quinto Navarra. All these sources are necessarily suspect, but they all bear out the general picture which I have drawn.

The full history of Mussolini's years in power is contained in Salvatorelli and Mira. Particular aspects are dealt with in more detail in Carlo Silvestri's *Matteotti, Mussolini e il dramma italiano* and Guido Leto's *O.V.R.A. Fascismo e antifascismo*. I have found the most interesting books written in English on Fascism or Fascist policies, G. A. Borgese's *Goliath*, Cecil Sprigge's *The Development of Modern Italy*, and J. S. Barnes's *The Universal Aspects of Fascism*. An excellent recent account of Mussolini's Italy has been provided by Roy MacGregor-Hastie in *The Day of the Lion*. Roberto Farinacci's *Storia del fascismo* gives a Fascist view and Ignazio Silone's *The School for Dictators* an anti-Fascist view. Silone and Anthony Rhodes, in his splendid book *The Poet as Superman*, give wonderful impressions of the trappings of Fascism.

MUSSOLINI'S FOREIGN POLICY, PART TWO,
CHAPTER I

From 1937 Ciano's diaries are, of course, essential. All Mussolini's comments in these chapters are taken from this source except where I have indicated otherwise. The diaries are amplified by the Diplomatic Papers, which are gradually being superseded by the monumental *Documenti Diplomatici Italiani*, although at the time I write (May 1961) the ninth series (1939–43) has only reached Volume IV, which does not go beyond the declaration of war. Bernardo Attolico, his daughter tells me, kept no private notes or diaries other than those which are now amongst the official documents. These documents, dealing with the period of his ambassadorship, are put into a more human context by Magistrati's *L'Italia a Berlino*; and this story is continued by Simoni's *Berlino – Ambasciata d'Italia*, Anfuso's *Da Palazzo Venezia al Lago di Garda*, and Alfieri's *Due dittatori di fronte* (translated as *Dictators Face to Face*). Quotations by Magistrati, Simoni, Anfuso, and Alfieri are all taken from these books. Mussolini's ideas and policies as described by Schuschnigg and Starhemberg are taken from Schuschnigg's *Austrian Requiem* and Starhemberg's *Between Hitler and Mussolini*. The most valuable German authority for the meetings between Hitler and Mussolini is Paul Schmidt. My quotations have been taken from the Italian version of his book *Da Versaglia a Norimberga*.

The 1952 edition of *Mussolini diplomatico* by Gaetano Salvemini and Mario Donasti's *Mussolini e l'Europa* are, I think, the best accounts of the development of Mussolini's foreign policy. Luigi Villari's *Italian Foreign Policy under Mussolini* is a skilful essay in apologetics. Elizabeth Wiskemann's *Rome–Berlin Axis* is by far the most reliable as well as the most entertaining study in English. Alan Bullock's masterly *Hitler* and William Shirer's *The Rise and Fall of the Third Reich* give excellent accounts from the German viewpoint. A. J. P. Taylor's alarming study *The Origins of the Second World War* contains particularly valuable passages on the Abyssinian crisis and on Italo-German relations over Austria. André François-Poncet's *Souvenirs d'une ambassade à Berlin* gives some interesting personal details. Quoted comments by François-Poncet are taken from this book. When I have quoted from Winston Churchill, Lord Vansittart, and Duff Cooper, I have done so from their books *The Second World War*, *The Mist Procession*, and *Old Men Forget*. Neville Chamberlain's observations on Mussolini at Munich are taken from a letter in Keith Feiling's biography.

The views expressed abroad about Mussolini in the early 1930s come from *What to do with Italy* by Gaetano Salvemini and George La Piana and from Michael Foot's *The Trial of Mussolini*. Lord Lloyd's British Council pamphlet is also taken from Michael Foot.

Hitler's letter to Mussolini before the *Anschluss* comes from Documents on German Foreign Policy, and Hitler's subsequent conversation with Prince Philip of Hesse comes from the Nuremberg Documents, I have taken both these from Alan Bullock's life of Hitler. For several details about the diplomatic exchanges which led to the signing of the Pact of Steel, for the meeting between Hitler and his military commanders after the signing of the Pact, and for the translation of the Pact itself I am indebted to Elizabeth Wiskemann's *Rome–Berlin Axis*. My descriptions of the meeting between Badoglio, Balbo, and Mussolini on 28 May comes from Badoglio's *L'Italia nella seconda guerra mondiale* and of Rome on the eve of war from M. H. H. Macartney's *One Man Alone*. I am grateful to the late Sir Percy Loraine for talking to me about the events which led up to Mussolini's declaration of war and to Sir Ivone Kirkpatrick for answering some questions concerning Mussolini's behaviour at Munich. Sir Noel Charles has been good enough to give me his views on the events which led to Italy's declaration of war.

THE WAR, PART TWO, CHAPTER 2, AND PART THREE, CHAPTER I

Italy's unpreparedness for war and her unsuccessful conduct of it are best exemplified in Ciano, Quirino Armellini's *Diario di guerra*, Emilio Canevari's *Graziani mi ha detto*, G. Carboni's *Memorie segrete*, Ugo Cavallero's *Comando supremo*, Carlo Favagrossa's *Perchè perdemmo la guerra*, Albert Kesselring's *Memoirs*, Von Rintelen's *Mussolini l'alleato*, Mario Roatta's *Otto milioni di baionette*, and Antonio Trizzino's *Navi e poltroni*. Badoglio's *L'Italia nella seconda guerra mondiale* does not seem to be very reliable. Nor are all of his self-exculpatory passages substantiated by the official documents which have so far been published. The same comments may be made on Rodolfo Graziani's *Ho difeso la patria*.Interesting sidelights on Mussolini's personal life during the war are contained in d'Agostini and Arnaldo Pozzi's *Come li ho visti io*. It seems necessary to treat both Quinto Navarra's *Memorie del cameriere di Mussolini* and Claretta Petacci's *Il mio diario* with caution, but there is much in them which is obviously authentic and has been corroborated by others. The Petacci scandal is well covered in Leto's *O.V.R.A. Fascismo e antifascismo*.

THE CONSPIRACIES AND THE GRAND COUNCIL MEETING AND THE ARREST, PART THREE, CHAPTERS 2 AND 3

The most authentic accounts of the conspiracies are in Attilio Tamaro's *Due anni di storia*, and in Pini and Susmel. I have based my account on these and on Marshal Caviglia's diary and on Anfuso, Cassinelli's *Appunti sul 25 luglio 1943*, Galbiati's *Il 25 luglio e la M.V.S.N.*, Carboni's *Memorie segrete*, and Viana's *La monarchia e il fascismo*. No stenographer was present and no official record was kept of the Grand Council Meeting. My account is based on an amalgam of conflicting reports by Giuseppe Bottai, Dino Grandi, Enzio Galbiati, Buffarini-Guidi, Dino Alfieri, the prisoners at the Verona trial, and (least reliable) by Mussolini himself. Piero Saporiti in *Empty Balcony* gives a good account based on Bottai and on the facts which Count Grandi gave the author in Portugal. The conversations which Mussolini had after the meeting with Scorza, Albini, and De Cesare are from Caudana.

The accounts of the events which led up to the arrest and of the arrest itself are also confused and contradictory. The most convincing versions are in Caudana, and Pini and Susmel. I have taken from Caudana the conversations between Castellano and Ambrosio, between Acquarone and the King, and between Mussolini and Captain Vigneri. Montenelli's and Lualdi's articles in the *Corriere della Sera*, Canevari's article in *Meridiano d'Italia*, and the article from *Epoca* listed in the bibliography all add interesting but minor details of which I have made use. The account of the interview between the King and Mussolini is based on Mussolini's two accounts – one given in a broadcast during the following September (quoted in *Dal 25 luglio al 10 settembre*) and the other in his *Storia di un anno* – and on the versions which the

King subsequently gave to members of his staff and which are recounted by Monelli.

Count Grandi's meeting with Ciano at Montecitorio is recounted by Anfuso. His actions and feelings before the Grand Council meeting have been described by Saporiti and in *'Dino Grandi Explains'* in *Life*.

My account of Rome after the arrest of Mussolini is based on Monelli's *Roma 1943* and Anfuso's *Da Palazzo Venezia al Lago di Garda*.

IMPRISONMENT AND RESCUE, PART THREE, CHAPTERS 5–7

Mussolini has given an account of these events in his *Storia di un anno (Benito Mussolini: Memoirs 1942–1943* contains a translation of this, also of Admiral Maugeri's report and the evidence of Domenico Antonelli, the manager, and Flavia Iurato, the manageress of the Albergo-Rifugio). Appended to Maugeri's *Mussolini mi ha detto* is a chapter based on information supplied by Vero Roberti, special correspondent of the *Resto del Carlino*, and this – also translated in *Benito Mussolini: Memoirs 1942–1943* – forms the basis of my account of Mussolini at Ponza and Maddalena. This has been supplemented by Caudana (to whom I am in particular indebted for the comments of Dr Santillo, some further details of conversation between Mussolini and Marini, Zaniboni's comment on seeing Mussolini approach Ponza, and Polito's conversation with Mussolini), Pini and Susmel, the Ponza priest Luigi Maria Dies and his little book *Istantanea mussoliniana a Ponza*, and *I dodici giorni di Mussolini a Ponza* by Muratore and Persia. General Castellano's remark on the atmosphere at Palazzo Chigi after Mussolini's arrest comes from his book *Come firmai l'armistizio di Cassabile*. Mussolini's life on the Gran Sasso is based on the reports of Domenico Antonelli and Flavia Iurato and on conversations I have had with Ernesto Ricci, one of Mussolini's guards. I have also referred to the article *Un pecoraio del Gran Sasso fu il confidente di Mussolini* by Vincenzo Rovi in *Tempo* and Gino Cesaretti's article *La commedia di Campo Imperatore* in *Europeo*. Colonel Otto Skorzeny's operation is described in his *Geheimkommando (Skorzeny's Secret Missions* is an abridged translation), and my account has been amplified by information given to me by Colonel Skorzeny himself. The article in *Avanti ! 'Come Mussolini fu liberato da Campo Imperatore'*, is based on information supplied by General Soleti, and I have found this useful also.

THE RESTORATION OF FASCISM, PART THREE, CHAPTER 8

The source for the interview between Mussolini and Hitler is Fernando Mezzasoma, whose record of a conversation he had with the Duce at the beginning of 1945 forms the basis of the accounts given by Roman Dombrowski in his *Mussolini: Twilight and Fall* and by Elizabeth Wiskemann. Mezzasoma's account has been largely corroborated by Rudolf Rahn. The German attitude to Mussolini's rescue is best exemplified by the Goebbels diaries from which I have quoted. Colonel Skorzeny has told me of the conversation he had with Mussolini after the rescue, and these have been incorporated in my narrative. Skorzeny was a witness of Mussolini's final meeting with Ciano.

THE SALÒ REPUBLIC, PART THREE, CHAPTERS 9 AND 11

The most interesting account is in Pini and Susmel (Vol IV). Others that I have found useful are Attilio Tamaro's *Due anni di storia*, Bruno Spampanato's *Contromemoriale*, Edmondo Cione's *Storia della repubblica souale italiana*, Felice Bellotti's *La repubblica di Mussolini*, Rodolfo Graziani's *Ho difeso la patria*, and Ermanno Amicucci's *I 600 giorni di Mussolini*. Giovanni Dolfin's descriptions of Edda Ciano, of Mussolini's behaviour at the time of the Verona trial, and the various conversations he had with him at this and other times are taken from his book, *Con Mussolini nella tragedia*. The descriptions of Mussolini's daily life at Gargnano comes from Rachele Mussolini and, more often, from Professor Georg Zachariae's *Mussolini si confessa*. Other accounts of Mussolini's life and politics at Gargnano have been provided for me by Eugen Dollmann's *Roma Nazista*, E. F. Möllhausen's *La carta perdente*, Rudolf Rahn's *Ambasciatore di Hitler a Vichy e a Salò*, and General Wolff's memoirs published in *Tempo*. Both Zacharie and Rahn mention Mussolini's quarrels with Rachele. Ivanoe Fossani's interview with Mussolini comes from *Mussolini si confessa alle stelle*, Madeleine Mollier's from her article 'Così era Mussolini all vigilia dell'ultimo tracolla' in *La Nazione*, Pierre Pascal's from *Mussolini alla vigilia della sua morte*, and Pia Reggidori Corti's from '*L'ultima intervista di Mussolini*' in *L'Ariete*. Remarks attributed to Mussolini in conversation with Carlo Silvestri come from *Mussolini, Graziani e l'antifascismo*, with Ottavio Dinale from *Quarant'anni di colloqui con lui*, with Edvige Mussolini from her *Mio fratello Benito*, with Alberto Mellini from *Guerra diplomatica a Salò*, and in conversation with Mazzolini from *Due anni di storia*. My authorities for the various Ministerial intrigues are Möllhausen, Dollmann, and Rahn. The German opinion as to why Salò was not bombed by the Allies is given in Möllhausen. Graziani's comment on Mussolini's return to power is contained in Dollmann, as is Mussolini's irritated comment about Farinacci.

THE VERONA TRIAL, PART THREE, CHAPTER 9

The best accounts are Domenico Mayer's *La verità sul processo di Verona*, Zenone Benini's *Vigilia a Verona*, and Renzo Montagna's *Mussolini e il processo di Verona*. The fullest account in English is in Saporiti. For Edda Ciano's part I have relied on Caudana, Duilio, and Susmel and on the articles in *Il Giornale del Mattino*, *L'Italia Libera*, *Oggi*, and *Le Soir* listed in the bibliography. For Mussolini's attitude I have relied on Zachariae, Wolff, Dolfin, Dollmann, Rahn, Möllhausen, and Mazzolini. The account of the German attitude to Ciano comes from Dollman and of Mussolini's telephone conversation with Wolff on the morning of the executions from Wolff and Möllhausen. The story about Donna Felicita comes from Dollmann. The account of the meeting between Hitler and Mussolini after the Stauffenberg bomb plot also comes fom Dollmann and from Allen Dulles's *Germany's Underground*.

CIVIL WAR, PART THREE, CHAPTER 10

General Cadorna, Ferrucio Parri, and Battaglia give the most reliable personal accounts in *La Riscossa, Il movimento di liberazione e gli alleati*, and *Storia della resistenza italiana* respectively. Luigi Villari's *The Liberation of Italy* is bitterly anti-British and frankly propagandist but so far as the facts are concerned generally reliable. I have extracted from this Luigi Longo's account of Communist influence in the Partisan brigades. Mussolini's visit to Germany in February 1945 was described by Major Albonetti to Michele Campana, who described it in turn to Monelli.

Since this book was written Professor Charles F. Delzell's excellent *Mussolini's Enemies: The Italian Anti-Fascist Resistance* has been published. I have accordingly in this edition revised my account of the anti-Fascist movement. It seems only right to add, though, that while I write with some personal (and highly fragmentary) knowledge of the partisans, many critics would still contend that I have unduly emphasized Communist influence in the movement at the end of the War.

THE GERMAN SURRENDER, PART THREE, CHAPTER 12

I have based my account on Saporiti, who has made use of a series of articles in the Zürich weekly paper *Die Weltwoche*, and on Dollmann and Wolff. The view that Mussolini was not kept informed by the Germans of their negotiations is supported by Silvestri, from whom I have taken the quoted assurances of General Vietinghoff.

MUSSOLINI IN MILAN, PART THREE, CHAPTER 13

Father Eusebio's and Don Pancino's talks with Mussolini come from Pini and Susmel, Ottavio Dinale's from *Quarant'anni di colloqui con lui*, Edvige Mussolini's from *Mio fratello Benito*, Vittorio Mussolini's from *Vita con mio padre*. The Cabella interview is from *Testamento politico di Mussolini*. The account of the interview with

Cardinal Schuster is from *Gli ultimi tempi di un regime* and from a translation of 'My Last Meeting with Mussolini' in *Benito Mussolini: Memoirs 1942–43*. Other accounts upon which I have relied for my record of this meeting are those of Cadorna and of Achille Marazza, whose account appears in Saporiti. Full descriptions are provided by Caudana and by Pini and Susmel.

In the autumn of 1962 much new light was thrown upon the death throes of Italian Fascism by the publication of captured archives in F. W. Deakin's scholarly and extremely interesting *The Brutal Friendship*.

THE LAST DAYS, PART THREE, CHAPTERS 14–18

Numerous accounts have been written in Italian of Mussolini's last few days. The most interesting are *Le ultime giornate di Mussolini e di Claretta Petacci* (n.d.) by Storicus, *La notte di Dongo* by Ezio Saini, the final chapters of Bruno Spampanato's *Contromemoriale* (Vol III), and Attilio Tamaro's *Due anni di storia*. Personal stories are told by Vanni Teodorani in his article in *Asso di Bastoni* and by Vittorio Mussolini. A more recent book, *Le ultime 95 ore di Mussolini* by Franco Bandini, offers not only a careful analysis of all the existing evidence but some new evidence besides. I do not agree with many of Bandini's conclusions, but his is an extremely useful book. I have made use of his accounts of the actions and comments of the inhabitants of the Villa Belmonte and of the driver Geminazza. I have also used his account of Sardagna's conversation with Palombo which he (and Sardagna) mistakenly believed was with Cadorna. Birzer's story appeared in *Tempo* in 1951 and has been corroborated for me by Herr Hans Pächter. Kisnatt's story was published in *Epoca* in 1954. Don Mainetti's story appeared in *Europeo* in 1956, and a somewhat different version is to be found in translation in Saporiti. I have used Monelli's version of the De Marias' story, and Elena Curti Cucciati's story is from her articles in *Oggi*. Mussolini's letter to Rachele (the authenticity of which is doubted by Bandini but accepted by Monelli) is taken from *La mia vita con Benito*, Giorgio Buffelli's story from *Tempo*, the conversation of the young frontier guards from Pini and Susmel, and the evidence of Count Bellini and Urbano Lazzaro from a series of articles written under their joint names in the *Corriere della Sera*. The frontier guards Francesco Nanci, Antonio Scappin, Antonio Spadea, and Francesco di Paolo all wrote short accounts of their experiences, but none of them contain much of interest. For details regarding Mussolini's documents I have referred to Emilio Re's *Storia di un archivio*, Carlo Silvestri, Bandini, and the article in *Il Risorgimento Liberale* mentioned in the bibliography.

Walter Audisio has provided three different versions of his activities: the first in a report dictated in Milan on 29 April 1945 which was subsequently published by *Il Corriere d'Informazione* in October 1945; the second in a series of articles in *Unità* in November and December 1945, which were said to be 'based on Colonel Valerio's report and other documents' in the hands of the Italian Communist Party; the third in another series of articles in *Unità* printed under his own name. I have made reference to these accounts in the text, but only where his evidence is corroborated by others and in particular by the evidence of Giuseppe Cantoní given to the journalist Ferruccio Lanfranchi have I made use of them. Signor Dino Rosselli and other residents of Musso, Dongo, Como, and Milan have provided me with several minor details from their own experiences and observations.

Bibliography

D'AGOSTINI, BRUNO, *Colloqui con Rachele Mussolini* (1946)

ALATRI, P., *Le origini del fascismo* (1956)

ALBERTINO, L., *In difesa della libertà* (1947)

ALFIERI, DINO, *Due dittatori di fronte* (1948) (translated as *Dictators Face to Face* by David Moore, Elek Books, 1954)

AME, C., *Guerra segreta in Italia 1940–1943* (1954)

AMICUCCI, ERMANNO, *I 600 giorni di Mussolini* (1948)

ANFUSO, FILIPPO, *Da Palazzo Venezia al Lago di Garda* (1957); *Roma-Berlino-Salò* (1950)

ANIANTE, ANTONIO, *Mussolini* (1932)

Archivio Società Romana di Storia Patria

Archivio Storico Italiano

L'Ariete (especially for '*L'Ultima intervista di Mussolini*', by Pia Reggidori Corti, 5 April 1952)

ARMELLINI, QUIRINO, *Diario di guerra* (1946); *La crisi dell'esercito* (1945)

D'AROMA, NINO, *Mussolini segreto* (1958)

ASHTON, E. B., *The Fascist* (1957)

Avanti! (especially written for '*Come Mussolini fu liberato da Campo Imperatore*', 19 July 1944, and for '*Parla il dottore che misurò il cadavere di Mussolini*', 18 May 1945)

BADOGLIO, PIETRO, *L'Italia nella seconda guerra mondiale* (1946)

BALABANOFF, ANGELICA, *My Life as a Rebel* (Hamish Hamilton, 1938)

BALBO, ITALO, *Diario 1922* (1932)

BARNES, J. S., *The Universal Aspects of Fascism* (Williams & Norgate, 1928)

BARTOLI, DOMENICO, *Victor Emmanuel* (1946)

BASKERVILLE, BEATRICE, *What next, O Duce?* (Longmans, 1937)

BATTAGLIA, R., *Storia della resistenza italiana* (1953)

BEDESCHI, EDOARDO, *La giovinezza del Duce* (1939)

DE BEGNAC, IVON, *Vita di Mussolini* (1936–40)

BELLOTTI, FELICE, *La repubblica di Mussolini* (1947)

BELTRAMELLI, ANTONIO, *L'uomo nuovo* (1923)

BENINI, ZENONE, *Vigilia a Verona* (1949)

BERIO, ALBERTO, *Missione segreta* (1946)

BISSOLATI, LEONIDA, *La politicia estera dell'Italia dal 1897 al 1920* (1923)

BITELLI, GIOVANNI, *Mussolini* (1938)

BOJANO, FILIPPO, *In the Wake of the Goose-Step* (Cassell, 1944)

BONAVITA, FRANCESCO, *Mussolini svelato* (1933)

DE BONO, EMILIO, *Anno XIII, The Conquest of an Empire* (1937)

BONOMI, IVANOE, *From Socialism to Fascism: A Study of Contemporary Italy* (1924)

BORGESE, G. A., *Goliath* (Viking Press, N.Y., 1938)

BOTTAI, GIUSEPPE, *Vent'anni e un giorno* (1949)

BULLOCK, ALAN, *Hitler* (Odhams Press, 1952)

CABELLA, G. G., *Testamento politico di Mussolini* (1948)

CADORNA, RAFFAELE, *La riscossa* (1948)
La caduta del fascismo e l'armistizio di Roma (1944)

CALAMANDREI, PIETRO, *La partecipazione dell'Italia alla guerra contro la Germania* (1955)

CAMPINI, DINO, *Strano gioco di Mussolini* (1952)

CANEVARI, EMILIO, *Graziani mi ha detto* (1947)

CARBONI, GIACOMO, *Memorie segrete 1935–1948* (1955)

CASSINELLI, GUIDO, *Appunti sul 25 luglio, 1943* (1944)

CAUDANA, MINO, *Il figlio del fabbro* (1960)

CAVALLERO, CARLO, *Il dramma del Maresciallo Cavallero* (1954)

CAVALLERO, UGO, *Comando supremo: Diario 1940–43 del capo di Stato Maggoire Generale* (1948)

CAVIGLIA, ENRICO, *Diario (1925–1945)* (1952)

CERRUTI, ELISABETTA, *Visti da vicino* (1951)

CHABOD, FEDERICO, *A History of Italian Fascism* (Weidenfeld & Nicolson, 1963)

CHIRUCO, G. A., *Storia della rivoluzione fascista 1919–1922* (1929)

CHURCHILL, WINSTON SPENCER, *The Second World War*, Vol. I 'The Gathering Storm' (Cassell, 1948); Vol. II 'Their Finest Hour' (Cassell, 1949); Vol. III 'The Grand Alliance' (Cassell, 1950)

CIANO, GALEAZZO, *Diario 1937–1938* (1948) (English translation by Andreas Mayor, Methuen, 1952); *Diario 1939–1943* (1946) (English translation edited by Malcolm Muggeridge, Heinemann, 1947); *Europa verso la catastrofe* (1948) (translated as *Ciano's Diplomatic Papers*, edited by Malcolm Muggeridge, Odhams Press, 1948)

CILIBRIZZI, SAVERIO, *Pietro Badoglio rispetto a Mussolini e di fronte alla storia* (1949)

CIONE, EDMONDO, *Storia della repubblica sociale italiana* (1948)
Come cadde Mussolini (1944)

COOPER, DUFF, *Old Men Forget* (Hart-Davis, 1953)

Corriere della Sera (especially for '*A colloquio col generale Ambrosio*', by Maner Lualdi, 11 March 1955; '*Rivelazioni di Dino Grandi sull'arresto di Mussolini*', by Indro Montanelli, 9 February 1955; and '*Gli archivi segreti di Mussolini*', 15 December 1946)

Corriere d'Informazione (especially for '*Ultimo colloquio a Gargnano*', by Gioacchino Nicoletti, 11 February 1948)

Corriere Lombardo (especially for '*Come finì Mussolini*', October 1945)

Critica fascista

CROCE, BENEDETTO, *Pagine politiche* (1945); *Pensiero politico e politico attuale* (1946); *Due anni di vita politica italiana 1946–1947* (1948); *Quando l'Italia era tagliata in due* (1949)

CUCCO, ALFREDO, *Non volevamo perdere* (1950)

DEAKIN, F. W., *The Brutal Friendship* (Weidenfeld & Nicolson, 1962)

DELACROIX, CARLO, *Un uomo e un popolo* (1928)

DELZELL, CHARLES F., *Mussolini's Enemies: The Italian Anti-Fascist Resistance* (Princeton and O.U.P., 1961)

DIES, LUIGI MARIA, *Istantanea mussoliniana a Ponza* (1949)

DINALE, OTTAVIO, *Quarant'anni di colloqui con lui* (1953)

Documents on British Foreign Policy (1946 onwards)

Documents on German Foreign Policy 1918–1945 (1948 onwards)

Documents on International Affairs (1928 onwards)

I Documenti Diplomatici Italiani (1952 onwards)

DOLFIN, GIOVANNI, *Con Mussolini nella tragedia* (1949)

DOLLMANN, EUGEN, *Roma nazista* (1949)

DOMBROWSKI, ROMAN, *Mussolini: Twilight and Fall* (Heinemann, 1956)

DONASTI, MARIO, *Mussolini e l'Europa* (1945)

DORSO, GUIDO, *Mussolini alla conquista del potere* (1949)

DULLES, ALLEN WELSH, *Germany's Underground* (Macmillan, N.Y., 1947)

Enciclopedia Italiana

Epoca (especially for '*Per la prima volta Umberto parla del 25 luglio*', February and March 1955; '*Documentario di piazzale Loreto*', by Paolo Monelli, 21 May 1945, and '*Le previsione segrete di Mussolini*', by Paolo Monelli, 27 March 1955)

Europeo

FARINACCI, ROBERTO, *Storia del fascismo* (1940)

FAVAGROSSA, CARLO, *Perchè perdemmo la guerra: Mussolini e la produzione bellica* (1946)

FEILING, KEITH, *Neville Chamberlain* (Macmillan, 1946)

FERMI, LAURA, *Mussolini* (University of Chicago Press, 1961)

FERRARIS, E., *La marcia su Roma veduta dal Viminale* (1946)

FERRI, ENRICO, *Il fascismo in Italia e l'opera di Benito Mussolini* (1927)

Le Figaro (especially for '*Ciano et les derniers mois de l'avant-guerre*' by André François-Poncet, 17 July 1945, and '*Le Premier Récit authentique de la mort de Mussolini*', 27 April 1946)

DE FIORI, VITTORIO, *Mussolini: The Man of Destiny* (translated by Mario A. Pei, Dent, 1928)

FOOT, MICHAEL ('CASSIUS'), *The Trial of Mussolini* (Gollancz, 1943)

FOSSANI, IVANOE, *Mussolini si confessa alle stelle* (1952)

FRANÇOIS-PONCET, ANDRÉ, *Souvenirs d'une ambassade à Berlin* (1946)

GALBIATI, ENZO, *Il 25 luglio e la M.V.S.N.* (1950)

GENOUD, FRANÇOIS, (ed.) *The Testament of Adolf Hitler: The Hitler–Bormann Documents* (Cassell, 1961)

Gerarchia

GERMINO, DANTE L., *The Italian Fascist Party in Power* (University of Minnesota Press, 1959)

GIOLITTI, GIOVANNI, *Memoirs of my Life* (1923)

Il Giornale del Mattino (especially for '*Rottami e spettri del passato*', by Jader Jacobelli, 21 September 1945)

Il Giornale d'Italia

Giorno

GISEVIUS, H. B., *Bis zum bittern Ende* (1946) (translation, Cape, 1948)

'G.M.' *Dal 25 luglio al 10 settembre* (1944)

GOBETTI, PIERO, *La rivoluzione liberale* (1948)

The Goebbels Diaries (translated and edited by Louis P. Lochner, Hamish Hamilton, 1948)

GORRESCO, VITTORIO, *L'esperienza di un dopoguerra* (1943)

GRAVELLI, ASVERO, *Mussolini Aneddotico* (1943)

GRAZIANI, RODOLFO, *Ho difeso la patria* (1947)

GUARIGLIA, RAFFAELE, *Ricordi 1922–1946* (1949)

GUTKIND, CURT, (ed.) *Mussolini e il suo fascismo* (1927)

The von Hassell Diaries 1938–1944 (Hamish Hamilton, 1948)

HENDERSON, SIR NEVILE, *Failure of a Mission* (Hodder & Stoughton, 1940)

HENTZE, MARGOT, *Pre-Fascist Italy* (Allen & Unwin, 1939)

Hitler e Mussolini: lettere e documenti (1946)

HOARE, SAMUEL, *Nine Troubled Years* (Collins, 1954)

L'Intransigeant

L'Italia libera (especially for '*Edda Mussolini a Lipari*', 21 September 1945 and '*Un impressionante documento di cinismo e d'irresponsabilità*', 9 January 1945)

Italia Nuova (especially for '*La fine del fascismo*', July 1944)

KEMECHEY, L., *Il Duce* (translated by Magda Vamos, Williams & Norgate, 1930)

KESSELRING, ALBERT, *The Memoirs of Field-Marshal Kesselring* (translated by Lynton Hudson, William Kimber, 1953)

KIRKPATRICK, IVONE, *The Inner Circle* (Collins, 1959)

KLIBANSKY, RAYMOND, (ed.) *Benito Mussolini: Memoirs 1942–1943* (translated by Frances Lobb, Weidenfeld and Nicolson, 1949)

LETO, GUIDO, *O.V.R.A. Fascismo e antifascismo* (1951)

Libera Stampa (for '*Le Memorie del Marchese Pucci*', September 1945)

Life (especially for 'Dino Grandi explains', 26 February 1945)

Look (especially for articles by Milton Bracker)

LUDWIG, EMIL, *Gespräche mit Mussolini* (1932) (translated by Eden and Cedar Paul as *Talks with Mussolini*, Allen & Unwin, 1933)

LUSSU, EMILIO, *Marcia su Roma e dintorni* (translated by Marion Rawson as *Enter Mussolini*, Methuen, 1936)

MACARTNEY, M. H. H., *One Man Alone* (Chatto & Windus, 1944)

MACARTNEY, M. H. H., and CREMONA, PAUL, *Italy's Foreign and Colonial Policy 1914–1937* (Oxford University Press, 1938)

MACGREGOR-HASTIE, ROY, *The Day of the Lion* (Macdonald, 1963)

MACK SMITH, DENIS, *Italy* (1960)

MAGISTRATI, M., *L'Italia a Berlino 1937–1939* (1956)

MANVELL, ROGER (with HEINRICH FRAENKEL) *Doctor Goebbels* (Heinemann, 1960)

MARVASI, ROBERTO, *Quartette: Le Roi, Mussolini, Le Pape, D'Annunzio* (1938)

MAUGERI, FRANCO, *Mussolini mi ha detto* (1944)

MAYER, DOMENICO, *La verità sul processo di Verona* (1945)

MECHERI, ENO, *Chi ha tradito* (1947)

MEGARO, GAUDENS, *Mussolini in the Making* (Allen & Unwin, 1938)

MELLINI PONCE DE LEON, ALBERTO, *Guerra diplomatica a Salò* (1950)

Mercurio

Meridiano d'Italia (especially for '*Un incontro segreto Mussolini-Hitler*', by Michele Campana, 14 October 1951, and '*Il re, Grandi, e Pietro Badoglio*', by Emilio Canevari, 12 October 1952)

Il Messaggero

MIRA, GIOVANNI (see SALVATORELLI)

MISSIROLI, MARIO, *Il colpo di stato* (1924); *L'Italia d'Oggi* (1932)

MÖLLHAUSEN, E. F., *La carta perdente* (1948)

MOLLIER, MADELEINE, *Pensieri e previsioni di Mussolini al tramonto* (1948)

Il Momento (especially for '*Memorie*', by Roberto Farinacci, January and February 1947)

Il Mondo (especially for '*Di un dibattito che non intendo proseguire*' by Benedetto Croce, 31 December 1949, and '*Mussolini e l'oro francese*', by Gaetano Salvemini, 7 January 1950)

MONELLI, PAOLO, *Mussolini: Piccolo Borghese* (English translation: *Mussolini: An Intimate Life*, by Brigid Maxwell, Thames & Hudson, 1953); *Roma 1943* (1945)

MONTAGNA, RENZO, *Mussolini e il processo di Verona* (1949)

MURATORE, G. (with C. PERSIA), *I dodici giorni di Mussolini a Ponza* (1944)

Mussolini as Revealed in his Political Speeches (edited and translated by Barone Bernardo Quaranta di San Severino, Dent, 1923)

MUSSOLINI, BENITO (*see also* SUSMEL); *Discorsi* (1922 onwards); *La mia vita* (1947); *My Autobiography* (translated by Richard Washburn Child, Hutchinson, 1928); *Il mio diario di guerra* (1931); *La nuova politicia dell'Italia* (1928); *Parli con Bruno* (1941); *Il trentino visto da un Socialista* (1911); *Storia di un anno* (1945) (*see also* KLIBANSKY); *Vita di Sandro e di Arnaldo* (1934)

MUSSOLINI, EDVIGE, *Mio fratello Benito* (1957)

MUSSOLINI, RACHELE (with Michael Chinigo), *La mia vita con Benito* (translated as *My Life with Mussolini*, Hale, 1959)

MUSSOLINI, VITTORIO, *Vita con mio padre* (1957)

NAPOLITANO, VITANTONIO, *25 luglio* (1944)

NAVARRA, QUINTO, *Memorie del cameriere di Mussolini* (1946)

Il Nazionale (especially for '*A Milano con Mussolini*', by Hans Otto Meissner, 5 August 1951)

La Nazione del Popolo (especially for '*Memorie politiche*', by Dino Grandi, 2 July 1945, and '*Così era Mussolini*', by Madeleine Mollier, August and September 1947)

NENNI, PIETRO, *Pagine di diario* (1947); *Storia di quattro anni 1919–1922* (1946)

Neue Zürcher Zeitung (for '*Enthüllungen über Mussolini*', 22 October 1945)

New York Times

NITTI, FRANCESCO, *Meditazioni dell'esilio* (1947)

Nuova Rivista Storica

Oggi (especially for '*Claretta Petacci al giudizio della storia*' by Ferruccio Lanfranchi, 19 December 1948–24 March 1949; '*In autoblindo col Duce sulla strada di Dongo*', by Elena Curti Cucciatti, 29 December 1949; '*Edda mi ha detto*', by Mino Caudana, June and July 1947; '*Un'amica di Mussolini racconta*', by Angela Curti, November and December 1949, and '*Tentai di riconciliare Edda Ciano e Mussolini*', by Giusto Pancino, September 1954)

ORANO, PAOLO, *Mussolini da vicino* (1928)

L'Osservatore Romano

PACKARD, REYNOLDS and ELEANOR, *Balcony Empire* (Chatto & Windus, 1943)

VON PAPEN, FRANZ, *Memoirs* (translated by Brian Connell, Deutsch, 1952)

PARRI, FERRUCCIO, *Il movimento di liberazione e gli alleati* (1955)

PASCAL, PIERRE, *Mussolini alla vigilia della sua morte e l'Europa* (1948)

PASTORE, LUIGI, *Crollo del fascimo e invasione tedesca* (1944)

PETACCI, CLARETTA, *Il mio diario* (1947)

PINI, GIORGIO, *Filo diretto con Palazzo Venezia* (1950); *Itinerario tragico* (1956); *Mussolini* (translated into English by Luigi Villari, Hutchinson, 1939); *Mussolini: l'uomo e l'opera*, with Duilio Susmel (1953–1955)

Il Popolo di Alessandria

Il Popolo d'Italia

Popolo e Libertà (especially for '*Le ultime giornate dell'ex-Duce Mussolini*', July 1945)

POZZI, ARNALDO, *Come li ho visti io* (1947)

RAHN, RUDOLF, *Ambasciatore di Hitler a Vichy e a Salò* (1948)

RE, EMILIO, *Storia di un archivio: Le carte di Mussolini* (1946)

Reader's Digest (especially for 'The Last Days of Dictator Benito Mussolini', by George Kent, November 1944)

Il Regime Fascista

Il Resto del Carlino

RHODES, ANTHONY, *The Poet as Superman* (Weidenfeld & Nicholson, 1959)

VON RINTELEN, ENNO, *Mussolini l'alleato* (1952) (a translation of *Mussolini als Bundesgenosse*)

Il Risorgimento Liberale (especially for '*Come si giunse al "25 luglio"*', August 1944, and '*Sono l'uomo più odiato d'Italia*', 2 August 1944; '*La giornata degli inganni*' by Lorenzo Barbaro, 25 July 1944; '*Dichiarazioni di Togliatti sull'esecuzione di Mussolini*', 14 March 1947, and '*Chi prese le carte di Mussolini?*', 3 April 1947)

Rivista Romana

Rivista Storica Italiana

ROATTA, MARIO, *Otto milioni di baionette* (1946)

ROSSI, A. (ANGELO TASCA), *La naissance du fascisme* (translated as *The Rise of Italian Fascism*, by Peter and Dorothy Wait, Methuen, 1938)

ROSSI, CESARE, *Mussolini com'era* (1947)

ROUX, GEORGES, *Mussolini* (1960)

SAINI, EZIO, *La notte di Dongo* (1950)

SALVATORELLI, LUIGI, *Casa Savoia nella storia d'Italia* (1945); *Il fascismo nella politica internationale* (1946); *Vent'anni fra due guerre* (1946); *Storia d'Italia nel periodo fascista*, with Giovanni Mira (1956)

SALVATORI, RENATO, *Nemesi* (1945)

SALVEMINI, GAETANO, *The Fascist Dictatorship in Italy* (Cape, 1928); *Mussolini diplomatico* (edition of 1952); *What to do with Italy* (1943), with George La Piana; *La terreur fasciste 1922–1926* (1930); *Under the Axe of Fascism* (Gollancz, 1936); *Prelude to World War II* (Gollancz, 1953)

SAPORITI, PIERO, *Empty Balcony* (Gollancz, 1947)

SARFATTI, MARGHERITA, *Dux* (translated as *The Life of Benito Mussolini* by Frederic Whyte, Thornton Butterworth, 1925)

SCHMIDT, PAUL, *Da Versaglia a Norimberga* (1951)

SCHNEIDER, HERBERT W., *The Fascist Government of Italy* (Van Nostrand, N.Y., 1936)

SCHUSCHNIGG, KURT VON, *Requiem in Rot-Weiss-Rot* (1946) (translated as *Austrian Requiem*, Gollancz, 1947)

SCHUSTER, IDELFONSO, *Gli ultimi tempi di un regime* (1946)

Il Secolo d'Italia (especially for 'La convulsa e vibrante vigilia che portò alla fondazione della R.S.I.', by Domenico Pellegrini-Giampietro, 24 November 1960)

SENISE, CARMINE, *Quando ero capo della polizia* (1946)

Settimana Incom (especially for '*Gli ultimi giorni di Mussolini*' by Aniceto Del Massa, April 1949)

SETTIMELLI, EMILIO, *Edda contro Benito* (1946)

SFORZA, CARLO, *L'Italia del 1914 al 1944 quale io la vidi* (1944); *Contemporary Italy* (translated by Drake and Denise DeKay, Dutton, N.Y., 1944)

SHIRER, WILLIAM, *A Berlin Diary* (Hamish Hamilton, 1941); *The Rise and Fall of the Third Reich* (Secker & Warburg, 1960)

SILONE, IGNAZIO, *The School for Dictators* (translated by Gwenda David and Eric Mosbacher, Cape, 1939)

SILVESTRI, CARLO, *Turati l'ha detto* (1946); *Matteotti, Mussolini e il dramma italiano* (1947); *Contro la vendetta* (1948); *Mussolini, Graziani e l'antifascismo* (1949)

SILVESTRI, GIUSEPPE, *Albergo agli Scalzi* (1946)

SIMONI, LEONARDO, *Berlino – Ambasciata d'Italia 1939–1943* (1946)

SKORZENY, OTTO, *Geheimkommando* (1950) (an abridged translation is Skorzeny's *Secret Missions*, Hale, 1957)

Le Soir (Brussels) (especially for '*De l'exécution de Mussolini au trésor de Dongo*', 7 May 1947; '*La correspondance de la Comtesse Ciano*', 10 January 1946, and for '*La vérité vraie sur la fin de Mussolini*', 5 July 1946)

SOLERI, MARCELLO, *Memorie* (1949)

SPAMPANATO, BRUNO, *Contromemoriale* (1951); *L'ultimo Mussolini* (1949)

SPRIGGE, CECIL J. S., *The Development of Modern Italy* (Duckworth, 1943); *Benedetto Croce* (Duckworth, 1952)

La Stampa

STARHEMBERG, PRINCE, ERNST RÜDIGER, *Between Hitler and Mussolini* (Hodder & Stoughton, 1942)

STORICUS, *Le ultime giornate di Mussolini e di Claretta Petacci* (n.d.)

STURZO, LUIGI, *Italy and Fascismo* (Faber, 1926); *The Survey of International Affairs* (1952 et seq.)

SUSMEL, EDOARDO, *Mussolini e il suo tempo* (1950)

SUSMEL, EDOARDO and DUILIO (eds.) (*see also* PINI), *Opera omnia di Benito Mussolini*, 23 vols (1951–7); *Scritti e discorsi di Benito Mussolini*, 12 vols (1934–9)

TAMARO, ATTILIO, *Due anni di storia 1943–1945* (1948); *Venti anni di storia 1922–1943* (1954–5)

TAYLOR, A. J. P., *The Origins of the Second World War* (Hamish Hamilton, 1961)

Tempo (especially for '*Vita sbagliata di Galeazzo Ciano*', by Duilio Susmel, October 1960; '*Ecco la verità*' by Karl Wolff, January and February 1951; '*Mussolini da Gargnano a Dongo*', by Antonio Bonino, March 1950; '*La Favorita*', by Paolo Monelli, November and December 1947 and January 1948; '*Dalla campagna d'Etiopia al colpo di stato*', September, October, and November 1952; '*Un pecoraio del Gran Sasso*', by Vincenzo Rovi, April 1954; '*La spia acustica*', November 1945, and '*Rivelazione su una tragicomica seduta di Palazzo Venezia*', 13 July 1944)

Time

The Times

TOSCANO, M., *Le origini diplomatiche del Patto di Acciaio* (1948)

TREVES, PAOLO, *Quello che ci ha fatto Mussolini* (1945)

TRIZZINO, ANTONIO, *Navi e poltroni* (1954)

TURCHI, FRANZ, *Prefetto con Mussolini* (1950)

Gli ultimi discorsi di Benito Mussolini (1950)

Gli ultimi giorni del fascismo (1944)

Unità (especially for '*L'esecuzione di Mussolini*', 30 April 1945; '*Come giustiziai Mussolini*', November and December 1945; and '*Edda ricatta Mussolini*', 23 June 1945)

VANSITTART, LORD, *The Mist Procession* (Hutchinson, 1958)

VEALE, F. J. P., *Crimes Discreetly Veiled* (Cooper Book Co., 1958)

VIANA, MARIO, *La monarchia e il fascismo* (1951)

VILLARI, LUIGI, *Affari Esteri* (1948); *Italian Foreign Policy under Mussolini* (Nelson Publishing Co., Appleton, Wisconsin, 1956);

The Liberation of Italy (Nelson Publishing Co., Appleton, Wisconsin, 1959)

La Voce

WARD PRICE, G., *I Know These Dictators* (Harrap, 1937)

WELLES, SUMNER, *A Time for Decision* (Harpers, N.Y., 1944)

WHEELER-BENNETT, JOHN, *Munich: Prologue to Tragedy* (Macmillan, 1948)

WICHTERING, RICHARD, *Benito Mussolini* (1952)

WISKEMANN, ELIZABETH, *The Rome–Berlin Axis* (Oxford University Press, 1949)

ZACHARIAE, GEORG, *Mussolini si confessa* (1948)

ZANUSSI, GIACOMO, *Guerra e catastrofe d'Italia* (1945)

Index